Integrating Neuropsychological and Psychological Evaluations

MW00850012

Integrating Neuropsychological and Psychological Evaluations is a resource for neuropsychologists, psychologists, teachers and parents who wish to address both the neurologically and emotionally based difficulties with which their children are presenting. In addition to a thorough description of neuropsychological and psychological assessment tools, this book also provides professionals with a unified approach to using the results from assessments to understand and integrate cognitive, behavioral, social and emotional functioning in school-age children. It posits that to educate and treat children who are struggling in school due to unique cognitive or emotional vulnerabilities, the whole child must be considered to decipher his or her needs and implement interventions. Cultivating a therapeutic relationship that integrates the emotional and relational functioning of children enhances both their learning and their ability to successfully navigate the world.

Daniel K. Reinstein, PhD, holds an adjunct faculty position in the Department of Psychiatry at the University of Massachusetts Medical School and the Massachusetts School of Professional Psychology. He is the Clinical Director and Director of Research at the Community Therapeutic Day School, a small private school for neurologically and emotionally troubled children.

Dawn E. Burau, LMHC and SpEd, is Adjunct Faculty at Lesley University in the Graduate School of Expressive Therapy and, over the last ten years, has worked as a therapeutic teacher at the Community Therapeutic Day School and has consulted to both public and private schools.

Integrating Neuropsychological and Psychological Evaluations
Assessing and Helping the Whole Child

Daniel K. Reinstein and Dawn E. Burau

Routledge
Taylor & Francis Group

NEW YORK AND LONDON

First published 2014
by Routledge
711 Third Avenue, New York, NY 10017

and by Routledge
27 Church Road, Hove, East Sussex BN3 2FA

Routledge is an imprint of the Taylor & Francis Group, an informa business

© 2014 Taylor & Francis

The right of Daniel K. Reinstein and Dawn E. Burau to be identified as authors of this work has been asserted by them in accordance with sections 77 and 78 of the Copyright, Designs and Patents Act 1988.

All rights reserved. No part of this book may be reprinted or reproduced or utilized in any form or by any electronic, mechanical, or other means, now known or hereafter invented, including photocopying and recording, or in any information storage or retrieval system, without permission in writing from the publishers.

Trademark notice: Product or corporate names may be trademarks or registered trademarks, and are used only for identification and explanation without intent to infringe.

Disclaimer: Every effort has been made to identify the owners of copyrights and to obtain permission to reproduce copyrighted material.

Library of Congress Cataloging-in-Publication Data
Reinstein, Daniel K.
Integrating neuropsychological and psychological evaluations : assessing and helping the whole child / by Daniel K. Reinstein and Dawn Burau.
    pages cm
    Includes bibliographical references and index.
    1. Psychological tests for children.   2. Pediatric neuropsychology.   I. Burau, Dawn.   II. Title.
    RJ486.6.R45   2014
    618.92'80475—dc23
    2013047737

ISBN: 978-0-415-70887-6 (hbk)
ISBN: 978-0-415-70888-3 (pbk)
ISBN: 978-1-315-88588-9 (ebk)

Typeset in Minion
by Apex CoVantage, LLC

Ring the bells that still can ring
Forget your perfect offering
There is a crack, a crack in everything
That's how the light gets in.
                    Anthem, Leonard Cohen

To my family, the children and families with whom I've been fortunate to work, my colleagues at CTDS and the memory of a dear friend, Margo Nason, PhD.—D. R.

To teachers and mental health professionals that dedicate their lives to improving the lives of others, and to my friends, colleagues and families that have touched my life. —D. B.

Contents

Foreword

This book is designed to bring to a wide audience of therapeutic, neuropsychological and educational professionals a means of understanding and making practical use of neuropsychological findings in order to improve their practice and develop interventions. We have entered an era where an understanding of brain functioning is beginning to have real meaning in the fields of psychiatry, psychology, neurology and education.

Traditional neuropsychological assessments, while not directly measuring physiologic change in the brain, measure functional levels and, over time, changes in functioning relative to discrete brain areas. They reveal the relationship between motor, sensory, executive, memory and language functions and their neural substrates. They have the potential to reveal the impact of brain function or dysfunction on academic, work, social, emotional and relationship environments. Traditionally, however, neuropsychological assessments have not included an evaluation of emotional functioning, an area of testing left to psychologists and the field of personality. Nevertheless, without a careful assessment of social, psychological and emotional functioning, the relationship between underlying neurology and these latter areas cannot be fully understood and integrated. This is the central point of the current volume: that neuropsychology and psychology, the brain and the "mind" must be integrated.

There is, of course, a protracted history of attempts to integrate neurology and psychological functioning. Sigmund Freud (1978) tried to create this integration, in 1895, in his *Project for a Scientific Psychology: "A Psychology for Neurologists."* Freud wrote: "It is in fact impossible to form a satisfactory general view of neuro-psychotic disorders unless they can be linked to clear hypothesis upon normal psychical processes" (p. 283). This early attempt to link up the theory of neurons (i.e., discrete brain cells) with "psychical processes" was an ambitious, and yet failed, attempt to merge psychiatry and psychology with neurology. It did, however, lead to Freud's development of the powerful tool of psychoanalysis, which initiated a field of study of normal and abnormal processes of the mind. Processes of the mind, but not yet the brain.

Ramón y Cajal, who worked in the same era as Freud, was a Spanish physician as well as an artist and scientist. He spent decades, starting in the late 1800s, studying the microanatomy of the nervous system, drawing exquisite pictures of neurons that still inhabit our contemporary neurology textbooks. He won a Nobel Prize in1906 in medicine or physiology in recognition of his work on the structure of the nervous system, demonstrating that the nervous system was made up of individual cells (neurons). He is considered the founder of modern neuroscience. He demonstrated that neurons process information, and are organized in networks, or groups, which accomplished a variety of functions. He established the concept of cerebral localization; occipital, olfactory, auditory and motor areas; and even considered localization of memory. This was the start of a scientific understanding of the brain and nervous system, but not the mind.

I was directly impacted by the then extant dichotomy in the field when I was studying in the early 1970s, in London. I was privileged to study with John Bowlby, Donald Winnicott and attend clinical seminars with Anna Freud as well as W. R. Bion. I was impressed then with fascinating clinical advances in the psychoanalytic field as well as with the medical research domain. Each of these gifted clinicians and researchers were struggling to find ways to understand the complexities evident in the human condition in health and disease. I was personally left with profound and useful insights from each of them. My experience with them left me with a rich understanding of human development and developmental psychopathology. The gifted electroencephalographers, Frederic and Erna Gibbs, during my time in their laboratory, in Chicago, in the late 1960s, showed me the beginnings of linking observable brain dysfunction seen in the EEG to certain clinical psychiatric and mental conditions. Through these experiences, I acquired the capacity to begin to integrate the new science of the brain with the depth of insight from an enriched clinical experience. This integration is an essential one.

One hundred years after Freud and Ramón y Cajal, the seminal work of these and many other men and women is finally being brought together. We can look at the developing brain scientifically, link up areas of brain function and dysfunction, and increasingly provide a robust analysis of the developing individual's intellectual, educational, linguistic, emotional and social life. Freud lacked these tools and abandoned neurology for psychoanalysis, where he could at least systematically study the developing personality and mind. Ramón y Cajal created his own tools and set to work methodically studying, cell by cell and brain unit by brain unit, to begin to explain brain system functionality.

A recent *New York Times* article bears witness to this evolutionary feat of science. Nobel laureate, Eric Kandel, MD, in an article dated September 6, 2013, wrote a commentary on "The New Science of the Mind." He describes the changes, citing several areas of the brain, involved in depression. In the biology of depression, he reviews techniques to identify several circuits in the brain of particular importance in depression. He notes specific linkages of brain regions that correlate with clinical psychiatric findings in two types of depression. He showed that researchers could pinpoint which patient would respond to antidepressant medication and which would respond to psychotherapy. In this demonstration he considers psychotherapy a biologic treatment—"a brain therapy." It produced lasting, detectable physical changes in the brain. Medication, in the other type of depression, also showed brain changes. This was a direct link between brain localization, and both medication treatment or psychotherapeutic treatment, and brain response to treatment.

A second reference is John Gabrieli's work on dyslexia. Using a functional magnetic resonance imaging (fMRI) machine, he demonstrated decreased blood flow in the brain area of dyslexic children, in the region of the brain where reading function is known to reside. Intensive reading programs for dyslexic children utilized between five and ten years of age show a correlation between improved reading skill levels and increased blood flow to these areas of the brain. This provides another direct link between scientifically demonstrated brain change, neuropsychological diagnosis of dyslexia and educational remediation.

These articles demonstrate a wide and exciting connection between brain development and the development of the human mind, as viewed from varied lenses. Gabrieli and Kandel, among many others, have methodically carried the work further, to be able to actually visualize the brain and changes wrought by medication, psychotherapy and education. However, they are not fully able to assess the psychological and emotional dynamics that would enable one to proscribe and integrate behavioral, psychological and emotional interventions within the domain of education.

What Daniel K. Reinstein and Dawn E. Burau have accomplished in this important volume is to provide an approach in respect to neuropsychological assessment that lets us make the link. Neurology, psychology, psychiatry and education are joined. The book analyzes the functional mind as it coalesces the complex, described areas of brain function and their interplay through the developmental process. It describes assessments covering cognitive, educational, social and emotional areas of the brain to help guide us as neuropsychologists, psychologists, psychotherapists and educators to understand the specific educational and therapeutic needs of our children in distress. Often, the recognition of which brain functional areas are impaired presents us with a map to remediating conditions that, if not treated, increasingly compromise the children, into their extended lives. It creates stress, anxiety and depression, leading to psychiatric illness. It creates school failure, leading to limited educational and vocational opportunity, impacting their future lives. We are at the beginning of a new era, a very exciting one, with opportunity for increasingly scientific study of brain function and expanding opportunities for remediation, both educationally and therapeutically.

Bruce Hauptman, MD
September 22, 2013

References

Freud, S. (1978). Project for a scientific psychology: A psychology for neurologists (pp. 283–396). In S. Freud (1978). *The standard edition of the complete psychological works* (Vol. 1). London, UK: Hogarth Press.

Gabrieli, J. D. E. (2009). Dyslexia: A new synergy between education and cognitive neuroscience. *Science, 325,* 280–283.

Kandel, E. R. (2013, September 6). The new science of mind. *The New York Times.* Retrieved from www.nytimes.com

Ramón y Cajal, S. (1989). *Recollections of my life.* Cambridge, MA: MIT Press.

Preface

In the fall of 2002, I began a neuropsychology postdoc at the Learning Evaluation Clinic (LEC) at McLean Hospital, an affiliate of Harvard Medical School, located in Belmont, Massachusetts. As such, this represented a return to a field I had left twenty years before, when I finished up a postdoc in the Department of Brain & Cognitive Sciences at MIT and began working at the Community Therapeutic Day School (CTDS), in Lexington, Massachusetts. The impetus to leave the field of neurosciences was partly a result of a severe allergy to mice and rats but mostly a wish to work with children and to better understand the relationship between neural, behavioral and emotional functioning in the developing child. Planning to do a two- or three-year internship at CTDS, I have found it very difficult to leave after these nearly thirty-two years.

The CTDS is a small, private school that serves the needs of thirty-one children who demonstrate significant behavioral and emotional needs that nearly always have a neurological underpinning but that are also a consequence of a very challenging match between their neurology or temperament and their environment. The latter may include either the home or, more often, their experience in the schools they have attended. Over the more than thirty years I have spent at CTDS, because of both the increased incidence of children with neurological, behavioral and emotional challenges as well as the increasingly limited resources available to public schools, we have seen a significant spike in children who are suffering a form of posttraumatic stress. Often, this is due to the steady accretion of stress due to poor matches between a child's very significant and complex needs and the limited ability on the part of the school system to not only meet those needs but to even understand what those needs are.

At CTDS, I was fortunate to have the opportunity to work directly with children and their families as well as with a community of extremely talented and dedicated teachers and clinical staff. It was here that I developed clinical therapeutic skills, and did so without developing any allergies to humans. Nevertheless, it became increasingly apparent that there was a progressively larger population of children whose difficulties warranted a very close examination of the underlying neurological issues that were impacting their psychological, behavioral and emotional development. In addition, after directing a series of therapeutic programs that, through CTDS, supported hundreds of children in public schools over a twenty-year period, it also seemed more and more important to comprehend why it was so difficult to understand and meet their neuropsychologically based needs within the public school domain. I felt strongly that the information from evaluations being provided to school systems about children who were struggling was inadequate and did not provide a picture of the whole child. With that in mind, I learned of the program at Harvard and the LEC and was accepted there as a postdoctoral fellow. The founders of CTDS, Bruce Hauptman, MD, our consulting psychiatrist, and Nancy Fuller, LISCW, the executive director, generously afforded me time to undertake the postdoc while continuing a less arduous schedule at the school.

At the LEC, I was again very fortunate to be trained by extremely talented neuropsychologists and psychologists, including the director, Jennifer White, PhD, as well as Jeff Pickar, PhD, Lee Reich, PhD, and Margo Nason, PhD. At the LEC, I was introduced to the belief that a full neuropsychological evaluation should include not only the traditional neuropsychological battery but also a thorough look at academic and emotional functioning. It was with Margo Nason that I worked most closely, and it was with her that we began discussing the need to assess the "whole child," the seed that was planted and which ultimately grew into the present volume. The seed lay dormant for some time, however, due to her very sad and untimely death.

The approach taken at the LEC was an unusual one within the context of the traditional neuropsychological evaluation. In that respect, the traditional assessment attempts, through a battery of tests, to locate the neurologically based correlate of some disturbance in cognitive functioning. It rarely includes an assessment of emotional functioning, as these tests are typically left to clinical psychologists to perform and are even more rarely integrated into the results from a neuropsychological battery. Thus, the perspective of the professionals at the LEC, one that included the necessity of thoroughly evaluating emotional functioning, was not typical.

Typically, individuals are referred for a neuropsychological evaluation by pediatricians, school systems or parents when there appears to be some deviation from the norm in cognitive functioning. I also tend to see children who are behaviorally out of control in either school or home, or who are evidencing any significant signs of emotional disturbance that are compromising their functionality. In my practice, parents pay for their child's evaluation, either privately or through insurance. If the school system supports the assessment, the school will defray the costs. The school may insist on conducting its own evaluation. However, a parent has the right to request an outside evaluation if he or she feels that the school's assessment was inaccurate or inadequate. In that case, the school may be responsible for payment. A complete neuropsychological evaluation is very time-consuming, requires considerable intensive effort and, therefore, is not inexpensive. An evaluation of this sort typically extends over the course of two days and frequently involves direct testing over seven hours. Scoring tests, analyzing and integrating the results, meeting with parents before and after the testing and report writing can take up to twenty-five hours or more for each evaluation. While this process is lengthy and intensive, it is necessary to understand the complex interaction between neurology, behavior and emotion and, as such, gives one the best chance of creating a picture or narrative of the whole child. Without this level of understanding, the ability of parents and teachers to affect real change for a struggling child is severely limited.

Working at CTDS afforded me not only an opportunity to experience, firsthand, the kinds of therapeutic interventions that were necessary to mitigate the traumas that children were suffering, but also the kind of environment that allowed children to bloom and reach their potential. The integration of information about a child's neurological, behavioral and emotional status was essential in order to plan and implement the necessary modifications and accommodations that were part of the "holding environment" created in the classrooms at the school. This concept of the holding environment formed one of the pillars of the school's philosophy and was based on the teachings of Donald Winnicott, a pediatrician and psychiatrist who practiced in England in the twentieth century (see Chapter 10). Fortunately, working at CTDS also brought me into contact with some very talented teachers and therapists, including Dawn E. Burau, LMHC, who shared a passion for understanding the brain in the context of children's educational and emotional development. Consequently, the resulting collaboration on this project not only broadened it's scope, but the end result was greatly enhanced by her insight, enthusiasm and ability to draw on her extensive experience of masterfully working with children in the classroom.

Daniel K. Reinstein

My relationship toward working with unique children and their families began in 2003, as a graduate intern at the CTDS. At the time, I was a student at Lesley University, studying expressive arts therapy and mental health counseling. As an intern, I was exposed to a group of children who presented with unique learning and therapeutic needs. Their teachers, my supervisors, engaged the children through play and laughter, developing relationships that sustained the children through profoundly difficult situations in the classroom and at home. Fortunately, at the end of the internship, I was hired and eventually held various positions within the school environment.

During those initial years, the children and their families taught me. I learned to recognize strengths and vulnerabilities of the individual children and how to help the children relate to one another as a group. Upon numerous occasions, students struggled with learning, regulation, their thinking, safety and in developing relationships. It became evident that the relationship built between myself, as a teacher, and the child was the vehicle for intervention. Working closely with their parents furthered the relationship and allowed for a home/school connection that supported the children. In addition, it was increasingly evident that a neurological contribution impacted their emotional state as it related to learning, socializing and in their, at times, highly erratic behavior. With the support of the CTDS, I attended coursework, attaining a certification as a special education teacher. I also completed coursework in biology, neurobiology and neuropsychology in an attempt to further understand the development, behaviors and experiences of the children and their families in our school. In addition to teaching in a therapeutic classroom, through the inclusion program I worked with individual children, provided support for their parents and consulted in various school settings. This afforded the opportunity to work in different school settings and see the difficulties faced by hardworking teachers and, also, the struggles of families overwhelmed by an environment that is unequipped to meet the needs of their children.

All the while, at CTDS, I was working with talented individuals, fellow teachers, supervisors and specialists. In this environment, communication, teamwork and, above all, compassion towards self and others supported my academic pursuits, providing the opportunity to integrate creativity, education, therapeutic principles and my developing understanding of neuropsychology. Daniel K. Reinstein was one of those individuals. During team meetings, his understanding of neuropsychological functioning and therapeutic understanding of family dynamics, child development and the emotional status of the child provided a framework for conceptualizing the child's, and the family's, needs that informed treatment planning and the delivery of curriculum material in the classroom.

During my years as a teacher at the CTDS, I was privy to various types of assessments, including speech and language, occupational therapy, academic and neuropsychological evaluations completed by outside psychologists. As a teacher, these reports were informative and could guide the development and integration of academic and therapeutic interventions in the classroom and during individual therapy. However, not all reports that crossed my desk were "complete." In reading numerous neuropsychological evaluations, some clearly described the child I was working with, and others only captured some aspects of the child's functioning. Parents expressed concern that the reports did not fully describe the child that they lived with, especially the child's emotional and behavioral states. It became clear to me that a neuropsychological evaluation could not only provide an opportunity to clearly describe a child, but it was potentially a tool for building an interdisciplinary bridge between psychological, therapeutic and educational settings. In working alongside Daniel and in the environment of CTDS, I developed a deep appreciation for the perspective put forth by this book: that the integration of neurological, psychological, relational and educational paradigms is necessary to understand the "the whole child" and for meaningful intervention to occur, tailored to the unique needs of each individual. As a result, I am honored to be part of this collaboration, the opportunity to share the philosophy of CTDS and to work alongside a talented and thoughtful neuropsychologist.

Dawn E. Burau

1 Introducing the Whole Child
Cognition, Behavior and Emotion

In this chapter, we describe what we mean by "the whole child" within the framework of the neuropsychological evaluation process. Within this context, we argue that a neuropsychological evaluation must consider a broad approach that includes not just an analysis of cognition as it relates to neural functioning, but also a careful examination of behavioral, social and, most importantly, emotional functioning as assessed by a battery of psychological tests. By taking a narrow perspective that serves to link only neural structure and cognitive functioning, one fails to appreciate the complex relationship between the behavioral, social and emotional factors that impact neurology as well as the neurological factors that contribute to the behavioral, social and emotional functioning of the child. It is the relationship between these factors that, ultimately, determines a child's ability to negotiate his or her educational and home environments. In the following pages, we will argue that, contrary to current usual practice, a full neuropsychological evaluation not only must include tests of cognitive and academic functioning but also must carefully assess a child's behavioral, social and emotional functioning as a means to understand the "whole child."

Without doing so, one is faced with a challenge not unlike that of the characters in the parable of the Blind Men and the Elephant in which a number of blind men are invited by their king to explore different parts of an elephant. Each describes their separate part; one feels the trunk and claims an elephant is like a snake, another feels an ear and describes the elephant as a winnowing basket, yet another feels a leg and describes an elephant as a tree trunk and so forth. They set to arguing, failing to consider that each is correct in describing their one part. Because they have not consulted with one another to integrate their perceptions, however, they are left blind to the bigger picture. Without a comprehensive assessment of a child's functioning, like the blind men, one is left with only a partial picture of the child.

The Need for Integration

Traditionally, the disciplines of neuropsychological and clinical psychological assessment have occupied separate domains. For decades, the purview of neuropsychology has been limited to understanding the relationship between structure and function, specifically, how behavior is impacted by a lesion in a localized neural structure. As described by Baron, "this concern with the linkage between behavior, or neurocognitive function, and

Figure 1.1 A child's drawing of an elephant.

the brain substrate defines the field of neuropsychology" (Baron, 2004, p. 5). Baron has gone on to explain that "a distinction between clinical psychology and neuropsychology can be made" (p. 5). However, it is becoming clear that this definition of neuropsychology is limited and limiting. Therefore, maintaining the boundary between these fields is a position that is increasingly difficult to defend. A failure to integrate them represents a profound disservice to those who are experiencing behavioral, social, psychological and/or emotional fallout from underlying neurologically based conditions. This is particularly true for children who are emotionally and behaviorally disturbed.

While there is substantial evidence that genetic and in utero factors can alter the structure of the brain (Becker, 2007), there is mounting evidence that postnatal environmental factors can have just as profound an effect. Traumatic stressors of both a physical or emotional nature, exposure to toxic substances, even addictive or repetitive behaviors can constitute triggers that alter neural development (Teeter et al., 2011). Data suggest that, as a result, there is not only a significant alteration in both neurological structure and function but a profound impact on emotional functioning as well. As Teeter et al. (2011) have argued, "Children with internalizing and externalizing psychiatric disorders appear to present with both functional-behavioral and neuropsychological-organic markers. These domains are intertwined and difficult to separate out" (p. 366). Neuropsychology and the practice of neuropsychological evaluation can no longer ignore the fact that these neurological changes are inextricably linked to emotional functioning and, conversely, that emotional factors can significantly impact neurological functioning. It is therefore imperative to consider both when evaluating the whole child and considering the best intervention strategies.

Over the last fifteen years, the need for the integration of psychological and neuropsychological assessments has been argued by a number of authors (Miller, 2010; Smith, 2007; Tramontana & Hooper, 1997; Winnicott, 1965). However, there has been no concerted or detailed effort to both make the case for integration and outline how one should go about doing so. In the subsequent chapters, we will make that case and provide a detailed explanation of how integration can be carried out. We further contend that, without an appreciation of the complex interplay between neurological, cognitive, behavioral, social and emotional factors, one cannot devise an intervention strategy that addresses the whole child and increases the chance that those strategies will create a "holding environment" (Reinstein, 2006; Winnicott, 1965) in which the child can feel supported and, ultimately, succeed.

Neurology, Development and Learning

To *succeed* can be defined as "Have the desired outcome, have a favourable result" (The New Shorter Oxford English Dictionary, 1993, p. 3127) Within this context, then, neuropsychological evaluations are intended to help uncover individuals' unique profile of vulnerabilities and strengths as a means to help them use those strengths and accommodate their vulnerabilities in order to succeed. In *Integrating Neuropsychological and Psychological Evaluations*, we are concerned with how neuropsychological evaluations are used to assess children with specific needs and how those results are applied to help the child succeed in the multiple areas of cognition, behavior, socialization and emotional functioning. When discussing children, this includes a consideration of both their development and their learning process.

Many developmental theorists assert that children develop new skills based upon both their genetic and neurological makeup and interactions with the environment (Chomsky, 1972; Erikson, 1963; Gesell & Ilg, 1945; Luria, as cited in Crain, 2000; Vygotsky, 1931). Genetics provides a general blueprint for development, while neurology defines the specific substrate for the development of various skill sets. Critically, a supportive environment fosters the potential of both genes and neurology. Take, for example, the development of skills necessary for written expression. Most people have the genetic potential to learn this skill, at least at a basic level. However, some are innately gifted with the ability to combine words and concepts at a much higher level to develop poetry, novels or essays. Some individuals will find their way to this end without much environmental support. However, all people require environmental exposure to some form of an alphabet, various reading materials, the mechanics of writing and the skills to socially navigate their world. If people who have the genetic potential to develop tremendous writing ability are left unexposed to these experiences, they will not reach their potential.

Furthermore, individuals' exposure to certain activities within their environment must be carefully timed in order for many of their skills to develop. This is related to the rate and sequence in which the nervous system develops. For example, in infancy, children are developing their regulatory and somatosensory systems. They are learning how their internal and external environment works and are then learning how to operate on and within it. During this time, the brain is learning how to regulate sleep, digestion, elimination, etc. It is also developing a more complex sensory system: learning to see, recognize faces and voices, interpret tastes and smells, organize tactile experience and so on. As the child ages and moves into toddlerhood, gross and fine motor skills develop, expressive and perceptual language skills emerge and play skills grow. This is mediated by the growth of the cerebral cortex. It isn't until a child is nine that sensory and regulatory systems fully develop. During this period of time, growth is immense, following a genetic blueprint, with neurological tracks that are dependent on exposure to key learning tools within the environment.

Returning to the example of writing, one would not expect a five-year-old child to write a novel. However, we could expose children to various types of literature, give them pencils and crayons to develop fine motor skills, and through play develop stories, plots and the use of their imagination. Over the course of children's development, exposure to these tools and experiences could lay the foundation for their eventual emergence as a novelist. Thus, exposure to critical environmental experiences and their successful integration into the child's repertoire depends on the child's ability to make use of such experiences—an ability that is determined by the child's stage within the process of his or her neurological development.

For children with specials needs, the ability to match the environment with their unique development and learning style is especially difficult. If, for example, their sensory system has not developed the kinesthetic and proprioceptive networks necessary for them to be able to discriminate bodily position in space or maintain adequate posture, sitting and listening to a book could be extremely difficult. If regulatory systems have yet to develop to support their ability to maintain their attention for the same period of time as their peers, cognitive skills may appear lower than they actually are. Neuropsychological evaluations can help clarify which neurological systems are operative or require intervention within a specific environment, or, alternatively, how to accommodate the environment by modifying a curriculum or teach new skills in a more appropriate manner. As Holmes-Bernstein and Weiler have argued,

> A comprehensive assessment of the child must take advantage of the knowledge and techniques of both the child psychology and developmental psychology traditions, as well as that of neuropsychology and of the neurosciences. It cannot restrict itself to discrete cognitive skills, or brain systems, as its primary focus, but must take the child as the "unit of analysis" in order to address (1) the whole of the behavioral repertoire that the child's brain makes possible, and (2) the full range of contextual transactions (social and environmental) in the course of a child's life that elicit, facilitate, maintain, and/or modify the way in which the workings of neural mechanisms are manifest in behavior.
>
> (Holmes-Bernstein & Weiler, 2000, p. 267)

Creating a more appropriate match between children and their environment can help them reach "a favorable or desired outcome" that best matches their true potential.

Book Overview

Learning and development is not a simple process requiring the usage of one or two parts of the brain. Instead, it is dynamic, interconnected, context dependent, and reliant on environmental supports and a uniquely individualized process, even for typically developing people. In *Integrating Neuropsychological and Psychological Evaluations*, the importance of using both neuropsychological and psychological evaluations to assess the unique learning style of individual children with special needs is stressed. Neuropsychological and psychological evaluations do this by measuring various neurological functional domains related to cognition, behavior and emotional functioning. These functional domains are the seat for various activities we perform throughout the day, the root of goal-directed behavior, the channel for information from the environment and our way of making meaning of the world around us. Aspects of our thinking, like memories and developing plans, or making sense of auditory or visual information are a just a few examples.

Reference Box 1.1 Functional Domains

1. Cognitive skills
2. Executive functions
3. Memory
4. Visual motor
5. Academic skills/achievement
6. Emotional and behavioral functioning

To make sense of these functional domains, as outlined in Reference Box 1.1, neuropsychological evaluations carefully measure various cognitive processes using myriad assessment tools. In this book, each functional domain is carefully described and related to the learning process. Chapter 2 outlines a complete neuropsychological evaluation, defines the various functional domains and provides examples of assessments used to measure these domains. The following chapters describe the functional domains in greater detail, including relevant neuroanatomy, various assessment tools, the ways in which different domains impact each other and how the domain influences functioning in the daily life of a child at home and at school. To make use of the information to develop treatment planning and effective intervention, these parts must be reassembled into a whole.

Chapters 9 and 10 approach the issue of the whole child. The final evaluation report is often a large and, at times, overwhelming document. Parents and educators often have various levels of understanding of the final results of an evaluation. Chapter 9 discusses the results and summary sections of an evaluation and relates the importance of using a feedback session with parents therapeutically. Chapter 10 then builds upon information presented in the final report on developing an integrated treatment plan. A list of suggested curriculum modifications and interventions for use in the home and school to assist the child and family with a challenge area is provided. Aside from being useful in treatment planning, a whole neuropsychological evaluation can also have legal ramifications. Chapter 11 explores the legal background of how children with special needs receive services and how neuropsychological evaluations directly impact this process.

Throughout the book, functional domains and other related topics are brought to life with two different types of vignettes. Short vignettes that illustrate specific topics or functional arenas are used to connect assessment scores or neurological concepts to real life. In order to provide the whole picture, the story of Charles, a young, homebound boy, is threaded throughout the entire book as an example of how each functional domain relates to the big picture. Charles's story is unique and special, providing a good example of how careful assessment and thoughtful intervention can impact an entire family. Chapter 12 concludes the book and the story of Charles.

Charles

The following section describes the history and referral process for Charles, the young boy who represents the continuous case study that will be followed throughout the subsequent chapters. It is extracted from the report that was written to document the results of his combined neuropsychological and psychological evaluation. As such, it integrates the findings to present a picture of Charles and the complex factors that were impacting his ability to function, not only within an academic environment but within relationships in the home environment as well. Previous testing, while documenting his cognitive abilities, had not fully considered the impact of his emotional status on his ability to manage school. As will be described in the following chapters, the information from a complete neuropsychological evaluation was used to generate a profile of his cognitive, social and emotional strengths and vulnerabilities. It was then used to create a program that supported his needs in each of these areas.

Charles A. was an eleven-year-old, right-handed boy who recently completed the fifth grade and who was homeschooled at the time of testing. Charles lived at home with his mother, J., an attorney, who was not currently practicing due to her commitment to matters at home; his father, D., a physician, who was no longer practicing due to a medical disability; and his twin brother, P., was thriving as a middle school student in the B. Public Schools; and his twenty-one-year-old fraternal twins, C. and D. who were both college students. His parents were both of Chinese descent. His mother was born in Shanghai and raised in the Boston area, while his father was born and raised in Guam. While his mother also spoke Chinese, English was the primary language in the home.

Charles (and P.) was the second pregnancy for his mother. His parents had difficulty conceiving, yet it was not a planned pregnancy. The twins were carried to full term, with his mother placed on bed rest for the last two months due to preeclampsia. An emergency C-section was performed due to problems with one of the umbilical cords. Charles weighed six pounds, had an APGAR score of 9, was slightly jaundiced and received light therapy for one day. The hospital stay for the twins and mother lasted five days. There were no postnatal complications, and Charles was successfully breast fed over the next two years. Developmental milestones were all within normal limits. Charles had no significant medical issues over the course of his development. He had an allergy to ground nuts. He was medicated a short time for anxiety with Prozac and then Ativan approximately three years prior to this evaluation, as prescribed by B., MD. An attempt to medicate again was made in fourth grade, but Charles quickly became resistant. He was not taking any medications at the time of testing.

Charles and his brother were cared for at home by a babysitter until the age of five. At two years of age, Charles's father became ill with nasopharyngeal cancer, which was treated and which was then in remission. However, his father subsequently became severely depressed and had significant, ongoing medical complications arising from his cancer, which required frequent medical interventions and hospitalizations. Charles began kindergarten at the T. School and had a good year. His father returned to the hospital for a protracted period the following summer, and Charles was unable to separate from his parents in the fall when he began first grade, tantruming and threatening to kill himself. He was inconsistently able to attend school and did so only when a parent was present in the classroom for some part of the day. By spring of that year, there was some improvement in his independent attendance. One day that summer, however, Charles discovered his father in a coma at home. He became very frightened, screamed for help and was clearly traumatized by this incident. His father was then hospitalized again for an extended amount of time. That fall, Charles had great difficulty returning to school for second grade, attending only if his mother was present throughout the day. By November, he was attending only half days with his mother, finding it too difficult to remain in school throughout the day. A tutor supplemented his education at home in the afternoons. By the last month of the year, however, he was able to attend school in the morning without his mother. Third grade was much better, and he attended school without difficulty because he made a strong alliance with his teacher, who provided considerable emotional support. Fourth grade provided less emotional support, and it became increasingly difficult, in spite of considerable effort on the part of school personnel. By the middle of the year, Charles was exclusively homeschooled by his mother. The school system in his town eventually recommended a private, therapeutic school placement. His parents declined to place him in one, finding it difficult to reconcile the fact that Charles's emotional needs were so acute. Therefore, Charles continued to be homeschooled through fifth grade. His father continued to be hospitalized on a regular basis and remained significantly depressed, while his mother took on the role of educating Charles.

Charles received neuropsychological testing through the town when he was in second grade. He required his mother's presence for the evaluation. On the *Wechsler Intelligence Scale for Children–Fourth Edition* (WISC-IV), he received a Verbal Comprehension Index of 124, a Perceptual Reasoning Index of 127, a Working Memory Index of 94 and a Processing Speed Index of 97. On the *Behavior Assessment System for Children Second Edition* (BASC2), his teacher expressed concerns about anxiety, adaptability, depression and withdrawal. His parents endorsed concerns about anxiety and withdrawal. Academic testing conducted at that time found all domains "well within grade and age expectations," with scores ranging from Average to Superior.

Parents reported that in addition to his fears, Charles had increasing difficulty with academics at home, including the introduction of new topics, extensive writing, accepting corrections and meeting anyone attached to school. Parents noted that Charles had friends in the neighborhood, but he was more of a follower. He did not participate in organized sports but collected cards and played video games. Family history was significant for anxiety and depression.

The current evaluation was sought by Charles's parents and B. Public Schools, and at the recommendation of Charles's therapist, Ms. G., LMHC, to address the concerns they continued to have regarding Charles's severe school phobia, separation and general anxiety and possible learning issues. Ms. G. had been meeting in the family's home for three hours a week, since the fall of his fifth-grade year, and continued to consult with his parents while making a relationship with Charles. She felt that the work over the year with both Charles and the family was no longer moving forward and that it was unclear what factors were contributing to the lack of progress. Charles was still extremely withdrawn and anxious, and his increasing resistance to the academic materials taught by his mother was preventing him from making adequate educational progress. Furthermore, his parents were increasingly concerned about his deteriorating behavior and frustrated with their inability to change it. While the support they were receiving from his therapist was extremely helpful, the family, school and therapeutic systems all felt that they were missing important information.

Because of his school phobia and resistance to anything and anyone related to the school system, it was felt that Charles could not be tested by a psychologist from his school. Furthermore, his therapist felt that his very significant emotional issues needed to be evaluated and understood within the context of his increasing academic difficulties—difficulties that could not be easily explained in light of his superior cognitive skills. Therefore, his therapist recommended a neuropsychological evaluation that included an extensive psychological workup, and which could integrate the findings from each to derive a picture of the whole child.

References

Baron, I. S. (2004). *Neuropsychological evaluation of the child.* New York, NY: Oxford University Press.

Becker, K.G. (2007). Autism, asthma, inflammation, and the hygiene hypothesis. *Medical Hypotheses, 69*, 731–740.

Chomsky, N. (1972). *Language and mind.* New York, NY: Harcourt Brace Jovanovich.

Crain, W. (2000). *Theories of development: Concepts and applications* (4th ed.). Upper Saddle River, NJ: Prentice Hall.

Erikson, E.H. (1963). *Childhood and society* (2nd ed.). New York, NY: W.W. Norton & Co.

Gessell, A., & Ilg, F.L. (1943). *Infant and child in the culture of today: The guidance of development in home and nursery school.* New York, NY: Harper & Brothers.

Holmes-Bernstein, J., & Weiler, M. D. (2000). Pediatric neuropsychological assessment examined. In G. Goldstein & M. Hersen (Eds.), *Handbook of psychological assessment* (3rd, ed., pp. 263–300). Pergamon Press.

Miller, J.A. (2010). Assessing and intervening with children and internalizing disorders. In D. C. Miller (Ed.), *Best practices in school neuropsychology: Guidelines for effective practice, assessment, and evidence-based intervention* (pp. 387–417). Hoboken, NJ: John Wiley and Sons.

New Shorter Oxford English Dictionary. (1993). Oxford: Oxford University Press.

Reinstein, D.K. (2006). *To hold and be held: The therapeutic school as a holding environment.* New York, NY: Routledge.

Smith, S.R. (2007). Integrating neuropsychology and personality assessment with children and adolescents. In S. R. Smith & L. Handler (Eds.), *The clinical assessment of children and adolescents: A practitioner's handbook* (pp. 37–52). New York, NY: John Wiley and Sons.

Teeter, P. A., Eckert, L., Nelson, A., Platten, P., Semrud-Clikeman, M., & Kamphaus, R. (2011). Assessment of behavior and personality in the neuropsychological diagnosis of children. In C. Reynolds & E. Fletcher-Janzen (Eds.), *Handbook of clinical child neuropsychology* (3rd ed., pp. 349–381). New York, NY: Springer.

Tramontana, M.G., & Hooper, S.R. (1997). Neuropsychology of child psychopathology. In C.R. Reynolds & E. Fletcher-Janzen (Eds.), *Handbook of clinical child neuropsychology* (2nd ed., pp. 117–146). New York, NY: Plenum Press.

Vygotsky, L.S. (1978). *Mind in society: the development of higher psychological process.* Cambridge, MA: Harvard University Press.

Winnicott, D.W. (1965). *The maturational process and the facilitating environment.* London, UK: Hogarth Press.

2 Understanding and Assessing the Whole Child

The Complete Neuropsychological Evaluation

How This Chapter Is Organized

Measuring discrete functional domains and then reintegrating each is a time-intensive and challenging endeavor, but it is necessary to better understand the needs of the whole child. In this chapter, we describe the components of functioning measured by a complete neuropsychological evaluation. This is done by outlining an evaluation administered to Charles, the student introduced in Chapter 1, describing what characteristics of cognition, behavior and emotion are measured, and briefly cataloging those common assessments.

The functional domains, and the assessments used to measure them, have been carefully researched and implemented. Clinicians, family members and teachers must have a broad understanding of how the assessments are developed, normed and implemented in order to construct a big-picture understanding of the child being assessed. Therefore, this chapter also includes information on the testing process, the employment of data collection methods, and current usage of neuropsychological and psychological evaluations. It does so by focusing on the neuropsychological battery administered to Charles as a means to walk the reader through the evaluation process. Vignettes describing how these domains impact a child's functioning are presented at the beginning of each section and are drawn from our experiences in working with children over the last thirty years.

Current Usage of Neuropsychological and Psychological Evaluations

Public schools are at a disadvantage in the way in which children are evaluated, due to their increasingly limited resources. In our more than twenty years of experience in working with public school systems, we have found that while it is unusual for most schools to conduct a comprehensive neuropsychological evaluation, it is even more rare for a neuropsychological assessment to include tests of emotional functioning. Even if the latter is done separately by a school psychologist, the testing usually includes a series of forms completed by teachers, parents and, sometimes, the child. There is a tendency to avoid tests that require a significant degree of interpretation. School systems are increasingly anxious about drawing conclusions or extrapolating beyond strictly quantitative data about a child's emotional functioning. This is largely because they are not equipped to deal with the complex consequences of doing so, in respect to meeting not only the child's emotional needs but also the needs of the overall family dynamic. Furthermore, there is little effort to integrate findings across domains and, in so doing, create a narrative that describes the whole child. There is more often a tendency for each specialist to weigh in with his or her findings and to create an Individualized Education Program that separately delineates specific strategies for each area of functioning.

Thus, in the context of curriculum planning, not only is there little attempt to describe how each specialist's finding interrelates, but there is also little appreciation of how the findings impact learning, socialization, behavior and the child's emotional reactivity to the demands placed on him or her within the school environment. Usually, a functional behavioral analysis is completed by a behavior specialist, and an attempt is made to shape the child's behavior through a program of reinforcement and punishment. In some cases, a child will be placed in a social skills group that uses a curriculum to teach a child social pragmatics without addressing the deeper issues of relationship or emotional connection. At best, twenty to thirty minutes a week of counseling is provided, in which a child will play a game or review his or her behavior chart with the school's social worker or school counselor. Because there are no findings from an evaluation that has assessed the whole child, there has been no integration of findings and, therefore, there has been no integration of services that would address the needs of the child on a moment-to-moment basis. This is particularly true for the child's emotional needs, which must be understood in order to understand the child's behavior and to understand how his or her emotional reactivity and behavior are a reaction to a struggle with underlying neurological issues. There is mounting evidence that documents this relationship between neurological insult and emotional pathology (Martinez & Semrud-Clikeman, 2004; Tramontana & Hooper, 1997). Without this level of understanding and integration of emotional supports into every facet of a child's learning and social environment, very troubled children, or even those who are less impaired neurologically and emotionally, are bound to fail.

The Complete Neuropsychological Evaluation

A complete neuropsychological evaluation attempts to clearly describe all aspects of the child. To do this, various domains of functioning are individually assessed, then are later reassembled, developing a comprehensive picture. Testing must consider not only the performance of the child on individual tests, designed to measure specific functionality, but also the overlap and interaction of a variety of functional behaviors measured by those tests. This must be done while also taking into account the child's behavior in a variety of contexts. In order to do so, it is critical that the evaluator conducts an extensive interview with the parents, consults with or receives reports from the child's teacher, employs a targeted battery of evaluations and undertakes a careful observation of the child. The child's history, reports, test scores and observations are used to create a narrative that delineates, integrates and summarizes all these findings and provides a comprehensive set of recommendations. Therefore, a complete neuropsychological evaluation includes and assesses the following:

1. Referral information and case history
2. Behavioral observations and mental status exam
3. Cognitive skills

4. Executive functions
5. Memory—Working memory, long-term memory and short-term memory
6. Visual motor skills
7. Academic skills or Achievement
8. Emotional and behavioral functioning
9. Summary
10. Recommendations
11. Feedback session with parents (and child, when appropriate).

1.   Referral Information and Case History

As introduced for the case of Charles in Chapter 1, referral information and the child's and family's history is a vital part of the evaluation process. To construct a picture of the various influences contributing to a child's profile, multiple sources of information are solicited and integrated. Of primary importance is the information gathered from not only the developmental history and behavior assessment scales that parents complete but also, even more importantly, the parent interview.

The developmental history covers information about whether or not the pregnancy was planned and if any complications around conception or the pregnancy itself were encountered. Information about length of pregnancy, delivery and postnatal status, including birth weight, condition at birth and whether or not any extraordinary measures were taken, such as time in the neonatal intensive care unit, is obtained. Developmental milestones, feeding and sleeping habits as they relate to self-regulation, any medical issues such as hospitalizations, broken bones or concussions, serious illnesses, results from genetic testing or significant changes or difficulties in early relationships are all explored. Questions about a child's ability to manage his or her emotional regulation, and his or her relationships with parents, siblings, extended family members, peers, teachers, others in the community are answered. Educational history and academic success or failure at a particular developmental stage or in a specific academic subject are noted. Current treatments and any previous evaluations are reviewed, and parents are asked to describe their child-rearing methods and any difficulties they have had or are having in managing their child. An extended family history is acquired, including whether or not there have been any psychiatric or learning issues in parents, siblings, grandparents, aunts, uncles or cousins. Parents are asked to describe what they feel are their child's vulnerabilities, strengths, interests and passions. Parents are often asked to sign a release if other modes of treatment are currently being utilized so that the evaluator can contact, for example, a psychiatrist, psychologist, speech and language therapist, occupational therapist, social worker, etc. A teacher form is also completed by the child's teachers, and a conversation with the teacher and/or an observation of the child in the classroom may be part of the evaluation.

Through all of these methods, a picture of the child's functioning in different environments is gradually constructed and used to round out the assessment when combined with the data from testing, as well as the observations of the child throughout the evaluation process.

2. Behavioral Observations and Mental Status

Margo presented as a very lively and appealing seven-year-old girl, who provided an enthusiastic greeting and introduced her stuffed dog, Ruff Ruff, who had also been her mother's when she was young. Margo was very neatly groomed and dressed and had been well prepared by her parents. She chatted comfortably with her parents and me, and had no difficulty separating to proceed to my office with Ruff Ruff and a snack, giving each parent an affectionate good-bye.

Once in the office, Margo appeared quite distractible, both by items in the environment as well as internal thoughts. She initially provided fleeting eye contact that improved over time, and gravitated to the toys and examined a number of them. She preferred ones she could manipulate with her hands and used them as "fidget toys" as a means to provide sensory input. She tended to play with them as she paced about the room, finding it difficult to remain seated for any protracted length of time. In this manner, she evidenced some significant sensory processing vulnerabilities. She was able to chat about Ruff Ruff, school and friends.

Margo transitioned easily to the first test and readily engaged with the task of assembling blocks into patterns. She was observed to provide an ongoing narrative as she attempted the task, a strategy that she employed for virtually all of the tasks throughout the evaluation. On the easier endeavors, she provided encouragement to herself. However, as any task became more challenging, she became quite anxious and immediately asked for help, exclaimed that she could not do it and began to panic and break down. She came to tears approximately five or six times during the three-hour session on the first day of testing, at times declaring, "I don't feel like I'm good at anything" or "I'm not good at enough stuff." This was particularly true for items that were timed. She required a considerable amount of reassurance, support and scaffolding to work through these moments and continue on with the tasks. It was possible to help her calm down, and it became somewhat easier as she gained trust in my ability to help her get through these upsets and she accrued successes with tasks she initially found daunting. For example, while initially unable to guess at an answer, over time she became more willing to do so and not panic at the idea that she may not get an answer right. When successful, she appeared quite pleased and often declared that she was having fun. Her despair at her perceived sense of failure often contrasted with her buoyancy when she was successful and was encapsulated in her respective comments of "I don't want to come back tomorrow" and "I'm so happy to see you tomorrow." On the second day of testing, there were far fewer moments of panic and breakdown and, by the third day, she started to unravel only once when faced with a task that inherently contained a degree of ambiguity, but she recovered once she understood that there was no "right" answer.

Despite Margo's emotionally labile presentation, when calm, she could process material quite logically and benefitted from an unlimited amount of time to do so. She employed a number of effective strategies to support her performance, using fidget toys, talking herself through tasks, humming, referencing Ruff Ruff, asking me questions, such as, "Why are we doing all these things? To get to know me?" and in this manner, demonstrating an ability to step back and reflect on matters. Nevertheless, even when calm, her perfectionism was evident and her anxiety just below the surface.

Overall, Margo was very cooperative, polite, pleasant and charming throughout the three days of testing and was a delight to get to know. Despite her considerable anxiety and perfectionism, and the caveats delineated above, she appeared to make her best effort on the tasks presented. Consequently, results from the testing were felt to be an accurate picture of her cognitive and emotional functioning at this time but, because of her varying level of anxiety, may have underestimated her potential in some areas.

As described in more detail in a following section, the term *process approach,* or the *Boston process approach* (Kaplan, 1988), refers to the emphasis on a qualitative analysis of a person's behavior and cognitive style during the testing procedure. As such, it is an invaluable source of information and allows one a framework in which to go beyond the nomothetic to the ideographic, providing information not only about how a child performs relative to other children his or her age but also how a child employs particular strategies to solve a problem. Thus, the evaluator is provided with both quantitative and qualitative frameworks in which to assess and interpret his or her findings. This is particularly important for an assessment that includes both tests of cognition and emotional functioning. For our purposes, much of the information about a child's approach to testing is typically included under the category of mental status and behavioral observation. It is also described in relationship to specific tasks presented during the evaluation and, along with the quantitative results, is included in the narrative about each area of functioning.

Purely observational data also provide an invaluable window into the way in which a child manages relationships, uses language, navigates the spatial world, responds to challenges and regulates mood, frustration and activity level as well as how he or she deploys and sustains effort and attention. In my (D. Reinstein) neuropsychological evaluation practice, observation of a child usually begins as I watch from my window as one or both parents walk with their child across the parking lot and up the walk to the farmhouse in which I have my office. I observe whether or not they walk together, hold hands or have their arms around each other. When I meet the family in the waiting room, how does the child greet me? Is there eye contact, a handshake, any comments, or is the child engrossed in some video game, book or toy and having difficulty shifting focus? How does the child interact with his or her parent? Does the child appear anxious, tend to cling to his or her mother or father or is the child oblivious and fail to acknowledge the parents? Has the parent brought a snack for their child, and what was the process involved? Did the child select the food, resist any nourishment or was he or she flexible, very rigid or not invested about what has been provided? As the time approaches to transition to my office for testing, does the child become more anxious, or has he or she become more comfortable after chatting a while? How does the child manage the separation? Depending on age, is a young child appropriately apprehensive, or is the child either too willing to go with a stranger or too anxious to part from his or her parent? For some children, it is appropriate for their parent to come to the office and spend time there until the child is comfortable. Some parents remain across the room for the entire evaluation, others sit by their child while others have the child in their lap for some of the time. Other children are quite at ease being in the office.

The environment of an office differs significantly from that of a home or a classroom. In an office used for an evaluation, a child may act differently, and skill sets may appear and be measured differently. Because testing occurs within the context of a one-to-one relationship in which attention is focused solely on the child, and because there is less sensory stimulation than in the classroom and therefore fewer distractions, the testing room is considered an "artificial environment." Despite this, careful observation can allow for an understanding of how the child's behavior may translate into real-time behavior elsewhere. My office, for example, is equipped with a wall of shelves that contain some books, but mostly an array of toys. It is always very diagnostic to observe a child's reaction to the presence of so many desirable objects. Some immediately gravitate to all or some very specific toys, while others merely comment about them, positively or negatively. Some children will readily comply with my direction to take a seat at the testing table, while others will resist, pretend they did not hear or will attempt to engage in a more protracted negotiation, resulting in either an informal or, in some cases, a more formal contract in which work time and play time are decided upon. Furthermore, is the initial time in the office spent negotiating, or is it spent chatting about topics that they prefer or that I introduce? Does the child offer information easily or with difficulty? Does the child ask questions about me or my family, based on whether or not he or she has noticed photos in my office? Is the child aware of where he or she is, or what time, day, month or year it is?

The next step involves the observation of how the child transitions to the testing materials. Has the child preferred to get down to work rather than chat, or is there an effort to prolong the conversation? Is there any apparent increase in any signs of anxiety, or does the child, in fact, become more comfortable with the provision of some structure? How does the child approach a task? Is there a tendency to narrate his or her actions, think out loud, ask for more information about a task or request information about what is next or how long a task will take? Is the child more willing to undertake nonverbal or verbal tasks? Does the child employ useful strategies, such as counting on his or her fingers, visualizing or subvocalizing information he or she needs to recall? How does the child respond to being timed? Does the child become more anxious or increase his or her motivation to beat the clock? Some kids will even ask if other kids have done a task faster and display an awareness that they are not alone in this experience.

How does the child hold his or her body—is there upper trunk hypotonia, or does the child maintain good posture, a factor that can impact his or her ability to sustain effort and organize fine motor output? How does the child react to a request to use paper and a pencil? What kind of grip does he or she use—is it mature for his or her age, or delayed; right or left handed? Does the child stabilize the paper with his or her other hand? Is there any additional motor overflow, such as tongue protrusion or vocalization while writing? Is the child able to see clearly, or does the child squint, placing his or her face close to the materials? Does the child have difficulty processing verbal instructions because he or she isn't hearing well or the information becomes too lengthy, complex or abstract? Is there motor overflow in the form of fidgeting? Can the child sit still for a protracted period, or does he or she tend to get up and walk about? Is the child distracted by external stimuli, such as the toys in the office or sounds from the outside traffic? Or, is the child distracted by internal sensations, thoughts or feelings?

How does the child use the developing relationship with me to respond to difficult challenges? Is the child compliant and cooperative, and can he or she take direction, or is the child resistant? Can the child use reassurance, redirection, limits or encouragement or, when overwhelmed with a task, does he or she shut down and refuse to continue? Is the child able to use humor to manage frustration, or does he or she use humor as an opportunity to become silly and dysregulated? Does the child become angry when frustrated, blame him- or herself or blame me? Is the child aware of how he or she is doing or lack an awareness of his or her performance? Is the child satisfied with his or her performance, doesn't care how he or she does or take a perfectionistic approach? Is the child able to reflect on his or her performance and bring his or her own observations into the process? Does the child's effort sustain or flag over time or with success or failure? How does the child manage his or her mood over time? How much does the child's emotional response to specific materials alter his or her ability to perform?

These are just some of the most important questions to consider as one observes a child and the process he or she employs to address the materials within the context of the testing situation. These observations are rooted in the child's experience within a relationship with the evaluator and further reflects how the child relates to him or her. As such, it can often provide a considerable amount of information about how a child can or cannot manage the structure or lack of structure in the classroom environment, access the relationship with the teacher, manage specific modalities of the curriculum's presentation or the demands for participation, engage in relationships with his or her peers, handle transitions, tolerate frustration and rise to challenges. We now return to the story of Charles, as an example of the importance of observation and a mental status assessment.

Mental Status and Behavioral Observation: Charles

Testing with eleven-year-old Charles was conducted in his home, as his parents were certain that he would refuse to come to my office. In addition, a number of significant modifications were necessary in order to persuade him to cooperate. The aid of his sister, C., was procured in order for Charles to feel comfortable meeting me and allowing the testing to take place. He was told that his sister was interested in learning about the evaluation process, that she could use his help in trying out the materials and that she would conduct the testing with my supervision. Consequently, it was necessary to tutor C. in the administration of the tests, primarily the tests of cognitive functioning that were to be conducted on the first day. The hope was that Charles would feel comfortable enough with me to allow me to administer the projective tests, the bulk of which would be presented on the second day of testing. In addition, Charles was given the choice of conducting the testing over a two- or three-day period, as a means to allow him some control. He was also offered a significant reward by his parents to cooperate. Lastly, parents arranged for his brother and themselves to be out of the house and for testing to be conducted in the family basement in order to minimize distractions. Consequently, the evaluation was conducted under extremely unusual circumstances.

Charles presented as a neatly groomed and dressed young boy who was well oriented to time and place. While initially waving from a distance as he greeted me in the home, he did display appropriate eye contact and verbalized a greeting. He easily accompanied his sister and me to the space that had been prepared in the basement, insisting on sitting in a particular chair so as to avoid looking at a distracting papier-mâché elephant mask. He was able to answer a few of my questions without any significant, apparent anxiety but seemed to prefer to begin testing rather than chat. He displayed no additional anxiety when his sister briefly left the room to retrieve her watch.

Charles was immediately cooperative as his sister began to administer the first subtest of the *Wechsler Intelligence Scale for Children–Fourth Edition* (WISC-IV; Wechsler, 2003) and was clearly motivated to do well. He took a very perfectionistic approach to all of the materials, making a considerable effort to correctly answer questions, even when he did not know or was unsure of an answer. This approach was also apparent on pencil-and-paper tasks. For these, he gripped the pencil tightly at the point, using a thumb wrap rather than a more mature three point grip. He also exerted considerable pressure, tended to rotate the paper and attempted to erase or correct his mistakes frequently. On most fine motor tasks, he preferred to use only his right hand, leaving his left in his lap. Eventually, as tasks became more difficult, he would bring his left hand into play to stabilize the paper or to assemble more complex block designs. Of additional note was his tendency to proceed with most tasks in a right-to-left direction, an unusual means of orienting for a child his age and for one who reads and writes in English.

Charles tended to sit in a hunched position, demonstrating some upper trunk hypotonia, and, as he tired, would lay his head on his arm at the table. He preferred not to take breaks but did exhibit some motor overflow in the form of leg movements and fidgeting. This increased activity also appeared to be correlated with an increased level of anxiety in response to more challenging materials. Furthermore, at one point in the testing, he used a blanket to wrap himself up, nominally because he was chilly, but it also appeared to be a source of comfort. On the second day, he wore a sweatshirt with his hood up for much of the time, a behavior characteristic of children with sensory processing issues.

Charles was clearly close to and very engaged with his sister, demonstrating a nice sense of humor and playfulness. He was able to tolerate my presence over the course of the two days, becoming more comfortable with me as we proceeded and as he witnessed C's comfort with me. He had no difficulty as I tutored C. and allowed me to intervene directly with him when the testing required further inquiry or instructions. By the second day, it was possible to test him directly on the projective tests, with his sister sitting at a little distance by his side. At one point, he was comfortable with his sister leaving the room for about twenty minutes. While he could answer my questions about responses he made on certain projectives, he had more difficulty when the questions related directly to his emotional functioning. He was very resistant to any self-reflection and commented, "I don't think about that stuff." He did so in a very matter-of-fact manner, without belligerence, but clearly indicating that he was well defended against such a discussion. Nevertheless, throughout the testing, Charles was extremely cooperative and capable of focusing on the tasks at hand. Within the context of the previous discussion, it was clear that he was quite motivated to do well and made a great effort to do so. Overall, he was engaged with his sister and the materials, and became more comfortable with my presence. Therefore, the results from the current testing, with the previous caveats, were felt to be an accurate picture of his cognitive and emotional functioning.

Tests Typically Used in Neuropsychological Evaluations: The Case of Charles

This section briefly defines functional domains and provides a description of tests typically used in most neuropsychological evaluations and, specifically, those that were given to Charles. It is not meant to be comprehensive. That would be beyond the scope of this book. Rather, it is an attempt to introduce instruments that can be employed to begin to construct a picture of the whole child. For a thorough and in-depth review of the range of instruments used in neuropsychological assessment, the reader is referred to Muriel Lezak's (Lezak, Howieson, Bigler & Tranel, 2012) excellent volume, *Neuropsychological Assessment, Fifth Edition,* published by Oxford University Press. As presented in Lezak, there is a multitude of assessments that, as neuropsychologists, we have at our disposal. Depending on the referral question and other considerations, we must carefully select those instruments that best lend themselves to answering not only as many as possible of the questions initially posed, but also those that arise throughout the testing. In this manner, we can depart from a "fixed battery" approach to one of a "flexible battery" that is tailored to the needs of the client (Baron, 2004).

In this section, we will focus on those assessments administered to Charles. We will also provide a more in-depth discussion of these and other typically used instruments in the chapters that follow as they relate to specific domains of functioning. First, it is necessary to describe what tests attempt to measure and how these measures relate to not only an individual's strengths and vulnerabilities but also to how that individual's profile compares to same-age peers.

Quantitative Versus Qualitative Measurements

Over the course of the history of neuropsychological and psychological evaluations, neuropsychologists and psychologists have relied on a quantitative analysis of functionality and have used a nomothetic or norm-based approach to understanding an individual's abilities and disabilities. The application of statistical methods to assessment has been necessary to ground these fields in the scientific method and evaluate them with scientific rigor. However, it has been argued convincingly that using a quantitative approach alone results in a loss of ideographic data, an essential body of information about an individual's cognitive and emotional process (D'Amato, Rothlesberg, & Rhodes, 1997; Fennell & Bauer, 1997; Hale & Fiorello, 2004; Miller, 2010).

In addition to losing important ideographic information, a strictly quantitative approach to measuring an individual's functioning can be misused. This is particularly critical within the context of academic settings where performance on tests such as the WISC-IV often determine whether or not children with special needs will receive services. This problem is twofold. First, relying solely on one source of data within the context of quantitative norms, such as scores on the WISC-IV, does not give one a comprehensive picture of a child's relative strengths and vulnerabilities, let alone take into account the interplay between cognitive and affective domains. For example, there are often very significant discrepancies between areas of functioning on the WISC-IV with a child receiving a Verbal Comprehension Index in the Very Superior range while scoring at the lower end of the Average range on the Processing Speed Index. Because the latter score falls in the Average range, schools will often contend that there are no data to support the provision of services. What the school fundamentally fails to appreciate is the fact that such a discrepancy, in functioning between these domains, is symptomatic of a very significant problem—one in which a child's language skills are operating, to borrow an analogy, at approximately eighty miles an hour while their output is sputtering along at forty-five. In our experience, this disconnect between domains is extraordinarily frustrating to a child and nearly always results in emotional and behavioral difficulties as he or she attempts to manage the academic demands of school. Secondly, scores alone do not provide crucial information about the process the child engaged in to solve the relatively narrow range of problems presented by the testing instrument. Even with a battery of tests that attempts to address additional functional domains, numbers alone cannot describe a child and the way he or she functions in the real world. Nevertheless, quantitative data, without a careful and thoughtful description of a child's process or qualitative approach to problem solving, is used far too often to describe and determine a child's needs and the response to those needs. It is therefore crucial that one understands and appreciates the utility as well as the limitations of both quantitative and qualitative data.

Beginning approximately one-hundred years ago, with Terman's (1916) application of an "intelligence quotient" to the *Stanford-Binet,* an attempt was made to quantify and standardize a measure of intelligence according to developmental age. The two major conceptual models that inform current neuropsychological assessment both rely on a quantitative approach to understanding neuropsychological functioning. The first model, drawn from theories developed by the famous Russian neurologist A. R. Luria, provides the fundamental principles on which the *Kaufman Assessment Battery for Children–Second*

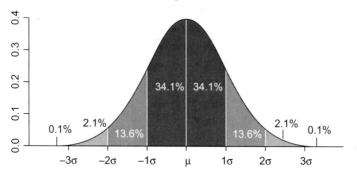

Figure 2.1 Standard deviations curve (Mwtoews).

Edition (K-ABC II; Kaufman & Kaufman, 2004) as well as *A Developmental Neuropsychological Assessment* (NEPSY II; Korkman, Kirk, & Kemp, 2007) are based. The second, the Carroll-Horn-Cattell (CHC) model (Carroll, 1993), uses a factor-analytic approach to provide a statistical basis for the *Woodcock-Johnson III Tests of Cognitive Abilities* (WJ III-COG; Woodcock, McGrew, & Mather, 2001), the *Stanford-Binet Intelligence Scales–Fifth Edition* (Roid, 2003) and the *Differential Abilities Scales (DAS; Elliot, 1990)*.

Quantitative scales are based on the assumption that, within a population, there is a normal, statistically derived distribution of characteristics or functioning. These include such measures as height, weight, intelligence and personality traits (Sattler, 2008). The normal curve is a symmetrically shaped bell curve that describes the frequency distribution of such measures (see Figure 2.1). The tests described previously all use this distribution to compare an individual's score on a particular test to those of same-age peers. Most people, approximately sixty-eight percent, will score somewhere in the Middle or Average range on these tests. That sixty-eight percent is considered to fall within one plus or minus *standard deviation* (a precise distance from the exact middle, or *mean*, of the curve). Approximately fourteen percent of people fall between either plus one and two or minus one and two standard deviations. Even fewer people, about two percent, fall between either plus two and three or minus two and three standard deviations, while only a tenth of one percent of people fall beyond either plus or minus three standard deviations,

Most intelligence tests—as well as tests of memory, executive functioning, visuospatial organization, fine motor functioning and achievement—all rely on comparisons across populations using the normal curve and standard scores derived from this statistical distribution. The standard score uses 100 as the mean, or middle, and fifteen points as one standard deviation. Thus, scores between 85 and 115 would be in the Average range, while those one standard deviation below would be considered to be Below Average and those one standard deviation above would be considered to be Above Average. Classification ratings for standardized tests are based on these scores and their distribution along the normal curve. Table 2.1 describes these classifications and percentiles for the WISC-IV (Sattler, 2008).

Standard scores on many tests are composites derived from scores on several subtests. These subtests are measured using the same normal curve but using a scale on which ten is average and plus or minus three is a standard deviation. These subtest scores are

Table 2.1 Classification ratings for the WISC-IV.

Standard Score	Classification	Percentiles
130 and Above	Very Superior	> 98%
120–129	Superior	91–97%
110–119	High Average	75–90%
90–109	Average	25–74%
80–89	Low Average	9–23%
70–79	Borderline	2–8%
69 and Below	Extremely Low	< 2%

Table 2.2 Scaled score classification ratings and percentiles for the WISC-IV.

Scaled Score	Classification	Percentiles
16–19	Superior	98–99%
13–15	Above Average	84–95%
8–12	Average	25–75%
5–7	Below Average	5–16%
1–4	Far Below Average	1–2%

called scaled scores, and Table 2.2 represents the scaled score classification ratings and percentiles for the WISC-IV.

Beginning in the early 1980s Edith Kaplan (Milberg, Hebben, & Kaplan, 2009) attempted to make a distinction between process and achievement within the context of neuropsychological development. She began to apply what would come to be known as the "Boston process approach" to neuropsychological assessment. This approach, also known as a "process approach," is "based on a desire to understand the qualitative nature of behavior assessed by clinical psychometric instruments, a desire to reconcile descriptive richness with reliability and quantitative evidence of validity, and a desire to relate the behavior assessed to the conceptual framework of experimental neuropsychology and cognitive neuroscience" (Milberg et al., 2009, p. 42). The focus on process resulted in significant changes to the way certain tests were administered and scored and led to the development of a number of tests as neuropsychological instruments. The Boston group also moved from the "fixed battery" approach, characteristic of the *Halstead-Reitan Battery*, in which a specific set of tests was rigidly administered, regardless of the referral question, to a "flexible battery" approach that, in addition to a core set of tests, "satellite" tests are administered to address specific questions about particular problems, based on the observations of the patient. Furthermore, Kaplan observed that individuals did not always perform consistently on a particular test, at times missing easy items and solving harder ones. Therefore, she introduced the idea that, beyond the standardized administration of a particular test, the evaluator should, at times, also administer items beyond the criteria for discontinuation of a subtest. This approach relates to the process of "testing the limits" and is increasingly being included in certain testing protocols, such as the WISC-IV Integrated. This allows an evaluator to systematically explore a child's learning style or potential by providing the child with additional cues or strategies to determine if he or she uses a more personalized approach to solving problems.

3.   Tests of Cognitive Functioning

When considering the cognitive domain, typical neuropsychological evaluations include some measure of language functioning or verbal reasoning, perceptual organizational skills or nonverbal reasoning, processing speed and working memory. In addition, tests of cognitive functioning will include assessments of executive functioning skills, memory and visual motor integration. Often, there will also be tests of academic functioning, including an assessment of reading, math and written expression. There may be some consideration of behavior or personality with the inclusion of results from questionnaires completed by parents, teachers and, depending on age, the child. However, this is where the typical neuropsychological assessment ends.

Cognition/IQ

Most neuropsychological evaluations include a measure of intelligence. There is considerable controversy over what passes as intelligence (Sattler, 2008), how intelligence is defined culturally and how many different kinds of intelligences there are (Gardner, Kornhaber, & Wake, 1996). For the purposes of this discussion, intelligence is defined as "the ability to adjust or adapt to the environment, the ability to learn, or the ability to perform abstract thinking (e.g., to use symbols and concepts)" (Sattler, 2008, p. 224). Within the context of a neuropsychological evaluation, this way of thinking about intelligence is measured psychometrically through a battery of tests assessing different aspects of cognitive functioning that are believed to underlie intellect.

The most widely used battery of tests used to measure cognition in children is the WISC-IV. The first version was developed by Dr. David Wechsler in 1949 (Sattler, 2008). Since then, several revisions have been made to accommodate new research and develop current norms. This battery is used for children ages six to sixteen and measures four cognitive domains: Verbal Comprehension, Perceptual Reasoning, Working Memory and Processing Speed. These domains can be used to develop a full scale IQ. Several subtests designed to capture specific skills required for each function measure the various aspects of these four domains. Tables 2.3 to 2.6 briefly define each index and the subtests administered to Charles that were used to develop the scores. Charles's scores and other cognition assessments will be discussed in Chapter 3.

Verbal Comprehension Index—This is an overall measure of the child's ability to verbally reason through to abstract concepts and is influenced by experience and exposure to information.

Perceptual Reasoning Index—This is an overall measure of the child's ability to utilize visual information to develop meaning, both abstract and concrete.

Working Memory Index—This is an overall measure of a child's ability to take information, hold it in his or her mind, manipulate the information and develop a response.

Processing Speed Index—This is an overall measure of a child's rate of ingesting information and developing a response.

Table 2.3 WISC-IV Verbal Comprehension Index subtests.

Subtest	Assessed Task
Vocabulary	Child is asked to define a word.
Comprehension	Child is asked questions about social situations or common concepts.
Similarities	Child is asked to state how two words are conceptually related.

Table 2.4 WISC-IV Perceptual Reasoning Index subtests.

Subtest	Assessed Task
Block Design	In a timed test, the child replicates red and white 3- and 2-dimensional patterns using blocks.
Picture Concepts	Given a series of pictures, the child is asked to determine which pictures are conceptually related.
Matrix Reasoning	The child is shown a matrix with 1 missing square, and selects the picture that fits the array from 5 options.
Picture Completion (Supplemental)	Given an image of common objects or scenes with missing parts, the child is asked to identify the missing part.

Table 2.5 WISC-IV Working Memory Index subtests.

Subtest	Assessed Function
Digit Span	The child hears a sequence of numbers and must repeat it back, either as presented or in reverse order.
Letter/Number Sequencing	The child is given a series of numbers and letters and repeats the numbers in ascending order and the letters in alphabetical order.
Arithmetic (Supplemental)	The child is given orally administered arithmetic questions.

Table 2.6 WISC-IV Processing Speed Index subtests.

Subtest	Assessed Task
Coding	The child between the ages 6 to 8 marks rows of shapes with different lines according to a visual code; the child over 8 transcribes a digit-symbol code. The task is time-limited with bonuses for speed.
Symbol Search	The child is presented with rows of symbols and a target symbol. The child is asked to scan the rows, marking the appearance of the target symbol.
Cancellation (Supplemental)	The child scans random and structured arrangements of pictures and marks specific target pictures within a limited amount of time.

4.   Tests of Executive Functions

Amelia bounded down the hallway. While attractive, with big blue eyes and dark brown hair, the girl was a mess. Her hair was disheveled, her socks mismatched and papers spilled out of her backpack. With a far-off look in her eye, she plunked down the bag and began digging for her homework. Out came a pencil box, erasers, markers, a tattered stuffed animal, notebooks and a yo-yo. A binder emerged from chaos, and leaving the mess behind, she slowly walked into the classroom. Pausing to give the teacher a shy smile, she stood momentarily then began walking toward the homework assignment bin. The binder had papers poking out from every direction. Later, when asked to show her math work, Amelia took several minutes to locate it within the binder. She was bright, completing advanced algebra despite being only eleven. However, pencil marks scattered across the page, and when asked what steps she took to complete an advanced problem, she could not describe, step-by-step, how she found the solution. This precocious child was well on her way to becoming an absentminded professor. Some would say she is a slob, messy or lazy, but Amelia struggles with executive functioning. This intellectually bright child struggles to organize, monitor her actions, regulate her behavior, and develop step-by-step plans to achieve a goal.

Executive functions (EF) have become an important topic in the fields of neuropsychology, psychology and education. Researchers and practitioners use a variety of terms to describe the range of behaviors described by the EF construct. Generally, these behaviors include the ability to use abstract and concrete thinking to initiate behavior and responses, make a plan and organize behavior to achieve a goal and monitor progress toward the goal. Many subdomains of behavior have been derived to more specifically describe how the EF construct impacts functioning. This includes but is not limited to abstract reasoning, attentional control, initiation/productivity, behavioral regulation, concept formation, goal setting, inhibition of impulses, mental flexibility, organization, problem solving, rule learning, self-monitoring, set formation and maintenance, set shifting and working memory (Miller, 2007). These subdomains have long been associated with the frontal and prefrontal cortex, which remains true. However, current research shows that connections with subcortical regions heavily influence this functional domain (Middleton & Strick, 2001). The breadth of functional behaviors and complex anatomical connectivity result in overlap between the EF construct and other cognitive domains (Baron, 2004).

Many assessments have been designed to measure the EF construct and, indeed, some tests of cognition also measure elements of EF. A more recently developed and very useful assessment includes the *Delis-Kaplan Executive Functions Systems* (D-KEFS). Table 2.7 displays the EF assessments given to Charles and the subdomains they measure. More information on the subdomains of EF and assessments are provided in Chapter 4.

Table 2.7 Executive Functioning subtests from the D-KEFS.

EF Test	Subdomain Measured
D-KEFS: Tower	Planning, inhibition, reasoning, problem solving
D-KEFS: Proverbs	Planning, abstract reasoning, problem solving
D-KEFS: Color Word Interface Test	Inhibition and shifting sets
D-KEFS: Design Fluency	Planning, reasoning, problem solving, nonverbal retrieval fluency, shifting sets
D-KEFS: Trail-Making	Visual scanning, sequencing, motor speed and shifting sets
D-KEFS: Verbal Fluency	Verbal retrieval fluency, shifting sets

Tests of working memory, considered a subdomain of EF, will be discussed in the following section on memory.

Attention

A burst of pumped-up, 8-year-old energy shot through the classroom door and took center stage announcing, "I went to an awesome flea market with my dad this weekend!" Jason hopped into the air then started pacing quickly around the room. The teacher called him over to the desk for a more private conversation. He followed the direction, all the while excitedly talking about the "treasures" he had found. As he approached the teacher, he was saying, "and there was this old camera from, like, the 1920s and like twenty electric guitars and . . . hey, I like that picture." He gestured over the teachers shoulder at a picture on the calendar of a palm tree on the beach. "My Pop gave me something like that when he came back from Hawaii. Hey, Sam!" Jason called out as a friend walked through the classroom door. He continued to ping around the room, starting to play with one toy, then another. Eventually, the teacher was able to settle him at a table with drawing materials. He excelled at drawing, and it was one of the few activities that could capture his attention for more than thirty seconds. If left alone, he could draw for hours. With almost any other activity, Jason's attention span was very brief. He was easily distracted by both internal and external events. Despite being bright and talented, it was difficult for him to access these strengths, resulting in a poor perception of himself as a student.

Attention, an important subdomain of EF, has historically received scrutiny by the media, education system and fields of psychology and neuropsychology. This is in part because attention, along with sensorimotor functions, is a baseline for other higher order processes. For example, relating two words to each other or repeating a word list is difficult if the child has difficulty attending to the task. Therefore, the test results purportedly

Table 2.8 Attention Assessments and subtests from the D-KEFS, WISC-IV and WRAML2.

Assessment and Subtest	Attentional Subdomain
D-KEFS: Color-Word Interference Test	Selective/Focused Attention
D-KEFS: Trail-Making, Verbal Fluency, Color-Word Interference Test, Design Fluency	Shifting Attention
WISC-IV: Coding, Symbol Search	Selective/Focused Attention
WISC-IV: Cancellation	Sustained Attention
WISC-IV: Digit Span	Attentional Capacity
WRAML2: Finger Windows, Number/Letter	Attentional Capacity

measuring memory can be impacted by the child's variable attention. The importance of attention has also been stressed because the incident rate of attentional difficulties in the United States is high. However, misdiagnosis of ADHD is also common, leading to difficulty understanding the root cause of attentional issues in individuals as well as the appropriate treatment plan (Miller, 2007).

The attentional process is an inherent function of almost every cognitive task, but not all tasks rely on the ability to employ it. This is reflected by the neuroanatomy of attention, which cannot be assigned to one region in the brain but rather by discrete anatomical networks, utilized by specific brain regions used for different processes (Fernandez-Duque & Posner, 2001; Posner & Peterson, 1990). As a result, several sub-domains of attention have been described and various terms used, including *attention, selective attention, sustained attention, switching* or *mental set shifting* and *divided attention* (Baron, 2004). These dimensions of attention will be discussed further in Chapter 4.

Assessing attention is an important aspect of the neuropsychological evaluation. This process naturally fluctuates as it relates to motivation, anxiety, self-esteem, mood, sleep deprivation, fatigue and overall health. During a testing session, attention will naturally waver, thus assessment of this domain must be done carefully, throughout the session. Several previously discussed assessment batteries include subtests that measure attention and its subdomains. Other assessment tools have also been developed to measure the various properties of attention, including the *Conners' Continuous Performance Test II Version 5* (CPT II V.5; Conners, 2004) and the *Test of Everyday Attention for Children* (TEA-Ch; Manley et al., 1999). Rating scales are also available, such as the *Conners Third Edition* (Conners 3; Conners, 2008). These will be discussed in depth in Chapter 4. Table 2.8 briefly lists assessments and subtests as well as targeted subdomains that were considered for Charles's evaluation.

5.   Tests of Memory

Memory is an important component of daily life, because it affects almost all levels of functioning. The word *memory* no longer refers to simply recalling facts learned in history class, but it is a more complex construct, with various subtypes. Memory is deeply connected to learning—learning to read, to brush teeth, to cook an egg or driving to work. All these tasks involve at least one subtype of memory. The subtypes work together to encode information, store it and make it readily available for conscious retrieval. The following list briefly describes each memory subtype:

- Episodic memory—Conscious memory of personal experiences of both facts and events (Tulving, 1972, 1983).
- Semantic memory—Conscious factual knowledge about words and concepts, and their meaning. It is part of long-term memory (Squire, 1982).
- Explicit/declarative memory—The umbrella term encompassing episodic and semantic memory (Baron, 2004).
- Implicit/procedural memory—Unconscious, often learned through repeated exposure or experience, but does not reference a previous learning episode. Accounts for the automaticity of certain behaviors.
- Short-term memory—The ability to hold information perceived from the environment (visual or auditory), keeping it in conscious awareness for a brief period of time (Loring, 1999).
- Long-term memory—The ability to encode and store information, allowing it to be readily available for retrieval when needed.
- Working memory—Temporarily holding information in a mental work space in order to manipulate or use the information. Information is generally held for thirty seconds or less (Baddeley, 1986). Working memory is also considered an aspect of executive functions.

All memory types can make use of various perceptual sensory information. These systems make use of various stimuli—visual, auditory, olfactory, tactile, kinetic and verbal—to acquire information from the environment and make that information available at a later time. There is also an affective component to recall that is considered emotional memory, and which is further discussed in Chapter 5.

Several neuropsychological tests are designed to measure the various types of memory and determine relative strengths and challenges of memory subtypes and sensory encoding. Often, the various memory subtypes are measured by subtests within a larger battery. There are also a few "stand alone" memory tests available. Common assessments include the *California Verbal Learning Test–Children's Version* (CVLT-C; Delis, Kramer, Kaplan, & Ober, 1994), subtests from the NEPSY II, the *Wide Range Assessment of Memory and Learning–Second Edition* (WRAML2; Adams & Sheslow, 2003) and the *Children's Memory Scale* (CMS; Cohen, 1997). Some subtests from the previously mentioned cognitive assessments also target memory. They will be included in the chapter on memory. Table 2.9 briefly supplies information on assessments administered to Charles and the memory types they measure.

Table 2.9 Memory Assessment subtests from the WRAML2 and CVLT-C.

Assessment and Subtests	Memory Type
WRAML2: Story Memory, Sentence Memory	Verbal memory
WRAML2: Design Memory, Picture Memory	Visual memory
CVLT-C	Verbal immediate and delayed recall

6.   Tests of Visual Motor Integration/Organization

Robert was nineteen and, despite his apparent intellect, he had a history of difficulty keeping up in public schools, including his relatively brief and disastrous stay at a public high school. As a senior at a small private high school for children with learning disabilities, he was still struggling and was repeating his senior year. In preparation for his application to college, he was given a neuropsychological evaluation. Results revealed Very Superior levels of functioning in Verbal Comprehension and Perceptual Organization but a Processing Speed Index at the bottom of the Low Average range, a Visual Motor Integration score in the twelfth percentile, a Motor Coordination score below the first percentile and a Writing Fluency score at the tenth percentile. Because he was so bright, he was taking a few courses at a local college but was having difficulty passing them as he was struggling with homework, taking tests and copying notes, problems he had had all his life. The results of the evaluation afforded him accommodations for his dysgraphia as he entered college. He was able to record lectures, obtain notes from professors, take tests on his computer with extra time, receive extended time for projects, and write papers with a voice to text program. With these supports in place, Robert not only finished a four-year program at a highly ranked college, but also he graduated summa cum laude. This was an outcome that would not have been possible without the implementation of accommodations derived from testing results—accommodations that circumvented his disability and allowed him to succeed.

We live in a world that prizes verbal communication. However, this is not the only means of communication, the only way to make sense of the environment or solve a problem. Long before children develop expressive and receptive language skills, they are assimilating information from their environment into their repertoire of experiences. This is done largely through the sensory systems: vision, hearing, touching/feeling, tasting, smelling and proprioception. The developing nervous system takes years to fully integrate visual, tactile, and proprioceptive information, achieving full integration around eight years of age (von Hofsten & Rosblad, 1988). Despite the inability to integrate complex amounts of perceptual information, infants can recognize faces and their expressions. Sounds take on meaning, for example, the tone of a voice or the revving of a car engine. The world of a child is composed of their sensory and perceptual experiences. These processes serve as a baseline for several higher order processes. Without a solid perceptual and sensory baseline, the development of higher order processes is disrupted. For example, if a child has difficulty distinguishing parts of an image from the whole picture, concepts such as fractions, ratios and percentages can be difficult to grasp. Visuoperceptual skills play a major role in developing handwriting, learning to blend individual sounds of letters and developing an understanding of the "big picture" when given details.

Table 2.10 Visual Motor Integration/Organization Assessment subtests from the *Rey-Osterrieth Complex Figure Test*, Beery-VMI, and WISC-IV.

Assessment and Subtests	Assessed Function	Method
Rey-Osterrieth Complex Figure Test	Visuospatial organization	The child is shown a stimulus card displaying a complex geometric figure and asked to copy it while looking at the stimulus card, draw it again immediately without the card, and draw a delayed recall.
Beery-VMI	Visual motor integration Graphomotor production	The child is presented with individual geometric designs in a test booklet and asked to reproduce them in a designated space below each design. Complexity and difficulty increase.
WISC-IV: Block Design	Visuoperceptual reasoning	In a timed test, the child replicates red and white patterns using blocks.
WISC-IV: Matrix Reasoning	Visuoperceptual reasoning	The child is shown a matrix with one missing square, and selects the picture that best fits the array from five options.
WISC-IV: Picture Concepts	Visuoperceptual reasoning	Given a series of pictures, the child is asked to determine which pictures relate.
WISC-IV: Coding	Visual scanning	The child ages 6 to 8 marks rows of shapes with different lines according to a visual code, the child 8 and older transcribes a digit-symbol code. The task is time-limited with bonuses for speed.

Assessing nonverbal abilities is not simple or easy. To assess a child's perception, the stimulus used often employs cognitive skills and executive functions and circumvents language and verbal processing. For this reason, several test batteries previously discussed also assess visuoperceptual and visuospatial processes. Both the WISC-IV and NEPSY II have subtests that incorporate visual motor integration and organization. Other assessments have been developed that also measure visuospatial and visuoperceptual processes. This includes the *Rey-Osterrieth Complex Figure Test* (Rey; Meyers & Meyers, 1995), *Beery-Buktenica Developmental Test of Visual-Motor Integration* (Beery VMI; Beery, Buktenica, & Beery, 2010), the *Bender Visual-Motor Gestalt Test–Second Edition* (Bender-Gestalt II; Brannigan & Decker, 2003). Table 2.10 describes assessments given to Charles and Chapter 6 will further explore the inclusion of assessing visual motor skills in larger batteries.

7.   Tests of Achievement

The academic achievement portion of a neuropsychological evaluation attempts to draw correlations between previously measured cognitive functioning and the ability to apply these skills to academic work. These evaluations are generally used to determine academic readiness. This portion of an evaluation has been important in school settings, often used to identify learning disabilities or qualify a child for special education services. In the past the emphasis on cognitive and achievement testing scores has not valued an understanding of a child's individual strengths and weaknesses and learning potential. Achievement assessments investigate various components of abilities required for the acquisition of skills in major academic areas: reading, writing, arithmetic, social studies and sciences as well as specific reading or language skills, such as phonological processing, auditory processing, expressive and receptive language and naming. A more detailed discussion of academic skills takes place in Chapter 7.

Several assessment batteries and stand-alone tests have been developed to assess a child's ability to apply cognitive skills to academic work. There is an inherent overlap between achievement tests and previously discussed cognitive, executive functioning, visuospatial processing and memory assessments. Historically, an emphasis has been placed on IQ tests as a predictor for school success. More recently, achievement assessments have followed a trend in measuring more domains of functionality as well as acquiring qualitative information (Miller, 2007). The following table provides a description of those achievement tests given to Charles. Additional batteries will be discussed in Chapter 7.

The *Woodcock-Johnson III Tests of Achievement* (WJ III-ACH; Woodcock, McGrew, & Mather, 2001b) is an individually administered, norm- referenced (ages two years to over ninety years) test of academic achievement in the areas of Reading, Oral Language, Mathematics, Written Language, Academic Knowledge and Phonological Processing. The relevant achievement subtests are described in Table 2.11.

Table 2.11 Subtests from the WJ III.

Subtest	Assessed Ability
Letter/Word Identification	Measures an individual's word identification skills.
Reading Fluency	Measures an individual's ability to quickly read simple sentences and decide if the statement is true by circling a Yes or No response.
Passage Comprehension	Measures, in developmental stages, a person's ability to either match symbols with pictures, pictures with phrases or identify a missing key word that makes sense from the context of a short passage.
Calculation	Measures an individual's ability to perform increasingly difficult mathematical calculations.
Math Fluency	Measures a person's ability to solve simple addition, subtraction and multiplication facts quickly.
Applied Problems	Measures a person's ability to analyze and solve increasingly difficult orally presented math problems.
Spelling	Measures one's ability to write increasingly difficult, orally presented letters and words correctly.
Writing Fluency	Measures one's ability to formulate and write simple sentences quickly from a visual prompt and the provision of three words that must be included.
Writing Samples	Measures one's skill in writing responses to a variety of increasingly difficult demands.

Interacting Functional Domains

Kindergarten did not go well for Nathan, despite being bright, funny and meeting most of his developmental milestones. He had run from the room, attacked peers, knocked over furniture and been restrained several times by school staff for safety purposes. His mother struggled with him every morning just to get him out the front door. In first grade, the amount of services he received had increased. He began to receive pull-out reading remediation because he was not reading in the classroom. Could Nathan read? Did he know his letters? Perhaps a reading disability was at the root of his behavioral problems. However, in the smaller reading group, he continued to manifest behavioral difficulties such as jumping on his chair, spitting at the teacher and crumpling his work. He was referred to have his reading skills assessed. The test administrator focused heavily on developing a relationship with Nathan, first playing with him and giving him a snack. The test scores surprised both parents and school staff. His reading scores were average to high average. Further assessment confirmed that emotional dysregulation was leading to the behavioral problems experienced at school. This bright boy, with many strengths, could not access these skills while emotionally overwhelmed. The treatment team began to address his emotional needs, and slowly, over time, the behaviors decreased and he was more able to access his cognitive strengths. In actuality, he was an excellent reader.

Attempting to measure any functional domain in isolation is difficult and nearly impossible due to the interconnected nature of the brain. For many years, neuropsychology has focused on relating neuroanatomy to functionality. However, as knowledge about neural functioning has accumulated, it has become increasingly clear that while some functions directly correlate to specific brain regions, these regions are also highly connected through complex circuitry, allowing for multiple regions of the brain to be used simultaneously. This reflects the argument that a neuropsychological evaluation cannot be considered complete without including psychological tests that assess emotions, affect and character development.

Keeping this in mind, when assessing or evaluating one function, for example, achievement in reading, the very nature of the assessment demands that the child employ attentional skills. While completing a task on the Woodcock-Johnson III for example, the child must be able to pay attention to the task at hand, filtering out both external and internal distractions. The intent is to capture the child's ability to read and develop reading skills, but the evaluator may also observe the child's ability to attend. The nature of the connectedness of the brain makes it virtually impossible to assess one skill or domain at a time. While this is frustrating, it is in this area of overlap that the child's strengths and struggles are revealed.

Another example of the interplay between functional domains highlights the impact emotions can have on general functioning, particularly when a child is asked to utilize a functional skill set he or she finds challenging. While evaluating a child's working memory using the WISC-IV, for example, an additional cognitive vulnerability could be revealed as an isolated domain. The child's awareness of this vulnerability could result in considerable frustration and their emotional response could negatively impact their capacity to perform the required task. Or while assessing visual processing skills using the *Rey-Osterrieth Complex Figure,* the child's frustration may cause him or her to give up, thus leaving the figure incomplete. Here, the level of frustration tolerance is measured, not only the child's ability to process complex visual information.

Through the use of a complete battery, including psychological evaluations, snapshots of functionality are attained as is their interaction. This interaction is just as important as isolated domain. Using both the snapshots and the gray areas of interacting domains, a complete image of the whole child emerges. With this information, interventions accounting for discrete strengths and challenges and their interactions can be made.

The Complete Neuropsychological Evaluation: The Need for Integration

When we talk about a "complete neuropsychological evaluation," we are referring to an assessment that includes testing of the multiple domains of cognitive functioning described previously but also a battery of tests designed to evaluate emotional functioning. There must then be an attempt to interrelate these domains to better understand how the underlying neurologically based issues are affecting the child's behavior, emotional experience and relationships and vice versa. In respect to how this plays out in the assessment process, it is critical to understand how personality assessment data and interpretation are dependent upon an individual's cognitive functioning as well as how personality or a child's internal state can impact the way in which he or she engages test materials (Smith, 2007).

The case for integration has been convincingly argued for some time but, for the most part, it has not been put into practice. As Smith (2007) has documented, there continues to be a significant division between neuropsychology and personality assessment. (For the purposes of this volume, personality assessment, psychological assessment and tests of emotional functioning will be used interchangeably). Smith contends that despite areas of overlap between these two domains:

> little has been done to examine how different forms of assessment can help inform the interpretation of tests. For example, how might a particular personality assessment test score modify how we interpret a neuropsychological test score? Similarly, how does a particular profile of neuropsychological deficit change our interpretation of personality assessment scores? In most of the literature it appears as though the meaning of all test scores is held constant, despite the pattern of test findings. . . . In clinical practice, test scores would give us a much more complete understanding of the patient if they were interpreted and understood by the integration of several different forms of measurement, both neuropsychological and personality.
>
> (Smith, 2007, pp. 39–40)

An increasing number of clinicians and researchers have also argued for the use of a multidimensional approach to testing. For example, Baron (2004) describes what she calls a Convergence Profile Analysis, "an expanded analysis of the entire spectrum of information about the child. It demands that suppositions based on one data point be matched or correlated sensibly with others before their import is overstated. Heavy emphasis is therefore placed on the neuropsychologist's clinical judgment" (p. 13). Dr. Baron also argues that normative data, or data gleaned from standardized tests, needs to be integrated with qualitative observations about the child's style and temperament. However, she does not make the case for the inclusion of tests of emotional functioning but instead tends to rely on parent or teacher report scales rather than personality assessment instruments, such as projective techniques.

The idea of using multiple instruments to converge on a particular strength or vulnerability as well as the need for the integration of qualitative observation is one shared by Smith (2007), who emphasizes the need for both a nomothetic (normative data base) and ideographic (characteristics unique to the individual) collection of information. Unlike Baron, he also makes the case for the inclusion of a personality assessment. As he notes, "the integration of these measurement techniques occurs at the level of interpretation (the effect of personality on neuropsychological measurement) and the deeper level of meaning (the effect of neuropsychology on personality assessment). When done well, integration of neuropsychological and personality assessment results yields a more complex and comprehensive picture of patient functioning that can significantly alter how we understand our patients" (p. 49).

8.   Tests of Emotional and Behavioral Functioning

So, what do we mean by tests of "emotional functioning"? There are a number of questionnaire type report scales, including self, parent and teacher, that are frequently used if any measure of behavior or affective functioning is considered in a battery. The following questionnaire, as described in Table 2.12, is typically used and was given to Charles and his parents, with his mother completing the teacher form as well. A more detailed description of additional assessments and analysis will be presented in Chapter 8.

These tests rely on the observations of parents and teachers as well as the self reports of the child. As such, they are very useful supplements to an in-depth assessment of a child's emotional status but are limited by a variety of factors. For example, a child may not accurately report his or her experience due to a lack of self-awareness, a wish to cover up their problems or an intentional effort to mislead. Both parent and teacher reports

Table 2.12 BASC-2 checklist.

Questionnaire	Description
The Behavior Assessment System for Children–2 (BASC2)	This checklist is a measure of emotional behavioral problems and adjustment to home, school and community environments. It can be completed by the teacher, parents/caregivers, and has a self-report when appropriate. It is normed for children/adolescents ages 2–21. It is available in Spanish. It develops five score sets. The Externalizing Problems Composite is based on scores for hyperactivity, aggression, and conduct problems. An Internalizing Problems Composite is based on scores for anxiety, depression and somatization. It also derives composite scores for Adaptive Skills, Behavioral Symptoms and School Problems.

are also subject to limitations due to the relatively restricted perspectives provided by the different home and school environments, the bias (positive or negative) of either the parent or teacher and so forth. As part of a multifaceted battery of tests looking at a child's emotional experience, however, these are useful instruments. Often the discrepancies between home and school are very informative, as are any differences between a child's reported behavior and affective style and the information gleaned from the child himself or herself. Nevertheless, these instruments alone are not sufficient to provide the more "complex and comprehensive" picture of the interrelationship between underlying neurological issues, behavior and emotional functioning.

Because the instruments described previously do not provide a comprehensive picture of the whole child, it is important to assess the emotional functioning of the child using a range of tests that get at the deeper affective processes and can better describe areas of emotional strength and vulnerability. The tests that are most often employed in clinical settings and which were administered to Charles include those detailed in Table 2.13.

Table 2.13 Projects Assessment examples.

Assessment	Description
Rorschach Inkblot Test	The intent of the Rorschach is to gather information regarding the motivation, personal/interpersonal perceptions and affective response of individuals to visual stimuli. Originally developed by Herman Rorschach in 1921, the Rorschach utilizes 10 cards with bilaterally, roughly symmetrical inkblots. Five cards use black ink, 2 use red and black and the final cards are multicolored. The child looks at each card while the examiner records their verbal responses to what each "might be." In the 1960s, the Exner Scoring System was developed to provide validity and interrater bias controls.
Roberts Apperception Test for Children– Second Edition	The Roberts-2 was developed to assess adaptive social perception and the presence of maladaptive or atypical social perceptions in children ages 6 to 18. It is a picture interpretation technique, asking an individual to view 16 pictures depicting white, black and Hispanic children and adolescents in everyday experiences. Developed by Glen E. Roberts.
The Conger or Sacks Sentence Completion Test	The child is given the stem of a sentence and asked to complete it with their own ideas.
House Tree Person (H-T-P)	The H-T-P was originally developed by John Buck as an ancillary to intelligence tests but also proved as a useful technique for gathering information regarding an individual's personality integration, maturity and efficiency. The individual is asked to draw a house, then a tree, then a person. These objects were chosen for their familiarity and requested in this order because each item is intended to produce more personal responses. Once the drawing is complete, the individual is asked to describe and tell a story about what they created.
Kinetic Family Drawing (KFD)	The KFD was developed in 1970 by Burns and Kaufman, requiring an individual to draw their entire family. The image is intended to elicit their attitude toward their family and illustrate the overall family dynamics. The instructions ask the child to "draw a picture of yourself and your family doing something." When the drawing is completed, the child is asked to describe what they created.

Of these tests, the Rorschach, the most commonly used instrument to assess psychopathology and personality (Archer & Newsom, 2000) has been rigorously standardized (Exner, 2003) but also lends itself to a clinician's skill in interpretation. It allows for an analysis of a child's coping style, psychological resources, self-image, affective style, interpersonal resources as well as a number of other pertinent factors (Exner, 2003).

When used in combination with several of the other projective techniques listed previously, data from the Rorschach enables the convergence of common threads that run throughout the tests and interpret them to arrive at a picture of a child's emotional experience. It is then most important to analyze how the information gleaned from tests of neuropsychological functioning relate to tests of emotional functioning and how each domain impacts the other.

9. The Summary

Alexandra (Ally) was a twelve-year-old girl who has been evaluated at the request of her mother, a physician, to determine her current pattern of cognitive strengths and weaknesses and to better understand her current emotional profile, particularly as it related to her issues with weight control. Over the last six years, she had been participating in a program at Children's Hospital but was not making progress. Ally was a bright and appealing young adolescent girl who demonstrated a relative vulnerability in right hemisphere functioning, working memory, processing and executive functioning and a relative strength in language processing and auditory memory skills. She demonstrated a logical and coherent thought process, good reality testing skills and judgment and an interest in making relationships. Her strong achievement orientation had evolved into a perfectionism that was likely exacerbated by her struggle and preoccupation with her weight and body image. There was, however, a level of denial regarding the full impact her obesity was having on her self-esteem, and her reluctance to acknowledge this appeared to be contributing to a sense of hopelessness about the possibility of change. Consequently, she tended to rely heavily on fantasy as an escape from these concerns, a strategy that, combined with her difficulty switching cognitive set and changing her habits, prevented her from effectively dealing with this issue. While her interest in relationships was an asset, evidence suggested that she was having difficulty establishing a clear sense of self and was depending to an inordinate degree on others to define who she was. Furthermore, this difficulty in establishing an independent identity appeared to be contributing to her failure to manage her weight, thus perpetuating a situation in the way she was cared for and focused upon within her family. While Ally was clearly close to her mother, her weight issue also may have been a means of being even closer and sharing in some medical experience. Thus, in therapy, it would be important to explore her feelings about her current developmental stage and self-image as well as any ambivalence she may have been experiencing about the process of separation and individuation as it related to her struggle with her weight.

Figure 2.2 Drawing of mother and child.

The summary section of a report should review the most salient results from all of the tested domains, including the findings from tests of emotional functioning, and integrate those findings to create a narrative that describes the whole child. There should be an effort to highlight both strengths and vulnerabilities and discuss how each is contributing to the total picture. It should address the referral question in a direct and succinct manner and give some indication of an overall recommendation, the details of which should be further explicated in the Recommendations section.

10. Recommendations

This section provides an opportunity to address specific recommendations for accommodations within the academic environment that target the specific strengths and vulnerabilities detailed in the body of the report. It should describe the ideal academic program, including an approach to learning that is based on the child's strengths and which accommodates their weaknesses. It must clearly outline all aspects of the program and a way in which specific strategies can be implemented. Parents are, therefore, encouraged to share all of the details of the report with the child's school so that teachers and staff appreciate the whole child and can determine the best way to meet the child's learning needs as well as the child's emotional, behavioral and social requirements.

It is also very useful to encourage parents to share some details of the report with the child, in an age-appropriate manner. Doing so can help children understand both their strengths and vulnerabilities and how to best draw on their resources. If appropriate, parents are also encouraged to bring the findings to the child's therapist as a means to weave this discussion into their work together. If there is no therapist, it is frequently important to recommend that a child begin a particular form of therapy. It is often the case that children who have a significant vulnerability within one domain will tend to generalize that weakness into a more global sense that they are somehow damaged. Giving children a context for their struggle and a place to learn about the resources that they do have helps them balance these relative strengths and vulnerabilities. It further helps them not only feel better about themselves but supports the development of a level of self-awareness that will enable them to become increasingly independent and able to advocate for themselves and their needs. Recommendations will be discussed in greater detail in Chapter 10.

11. The Feedback Session

Meeting with parents and caregivers to review the findings of the testing in detail is one of the most important steps in the evaluation process. It is an opportunity to create a context and narrative for them as a means to integrate all of the findings from the testing. It is crucial to be sensitive to the perspective about their child they bring to the evaluation process and to incorporate their experience into the narrative being created. Very often, it is also important to reframe their experience with their child to create a deeper level of understanding about the child's struggle and the resources available to them. It is not unusual for parents to be mystified about their child's reluctance to do homework, for example, and for them to interpret their child's resistance as mere oppositionality or stubbornness. Helping them understand that their child's poor graphomotor skills combined with their difficulties with organization make the task of writing an essay seem insurmountable. Refusing to do homework and spending time engaged in a struggle with a parent is, in fact, for the child, a much more satisfying alternative to experiencing the frustration and failure that he or she is sure lies ahead. These issues are considered further in Chapter 9.

Thus, the feedback session provides an opportunity for a therapeutic intervention that can impact not only the child, but the parents and the family system as a whole. It must be conducted with sensitivity and care, providing the parents and the child with a realistic understanding of not only the child's neurological and learning profile but also the equally important dimensions of his or her behavioral, social and emotional development. It must also provide the parents with a direction to pursue and to do so with hope.

References

Adams, W., & Sheslow, D. (2003). *WRAML2: Wide Range Assessment of Memory and Learning* (2nd ed.). Wilmington, DE: Wide Range.

Archer, R.P., & Newsome, C.R. (2000). Psychological test usage with adolescent clients: Survey update. *Assessment, 67,* 227–235.

Baddeley, A. D. (1986). *Working memory.* New York, NY: Oxford University Press.

Baron, I. S. (2004). *Neuropsychological evaluation of the child.* New York, NY: Oxford University Press.

Beery, K. E., Buktenica, N. A., & Beery, N. A. (2010). *Beery-Buktenica Developmental Test of Visual-Motor Integration* (6th ed.). San Antonio, TX: Pearson Assessments.

Brannigan, G. G., & Decker, S. L. (2003). *Bender Visual-Motor Gestalt Test* (2nd ed.). Itasca, IL: Riverside Publishing.

Carroll, J. B. (1993). *Human cognitive abilities: A survey of factor-analytic studies.* New York, NY: Cambridge University Press.

Cohen, M. J. (1997). *Children's Memory Scale.* San Antonio, TX: Harcourt Assessment.

Conners, C. K. (2004). *Conners Continuous Performance Test* (2nd ed.). Toronto, Canada: Multi-Health Systems.

Conners, C. K. (2008). *Conners 3rd edition manual.* Toronto: Multi-Health Systems Inc.

D'Amato, R. C., Rothlesberg, B. A., & Rhodes, R. L. (1997). Utilizing a neuropsychological paradigm for understanding common education and psychological tests. In C. R. Reynolds & E. Fletcher-Janzen (Eds.), *Handbook of clinical child neuropsychology* (2nd ed.). New York, NY: Plenum Press.

Delis, D., Kramer, J. H., Kaplan, E., & Ober, B. A. (1994). *California Verbal Learning Tests: Children's Version.* San Antonio, TX: Harcourt Assessment.

Elliott, C. D. (1990). *DAS Administration and Scoring Manual.* San Antonio TX: The Psychological Corporation

Exner, J. E. (2003). *The Rorschach: A comprehensive system. Volume 1: Basic foundations* (4th ed.). Hoboken, NJ: John Wiley and Sons.

Fennell, E. B., & Baurer, R. M. (1997). Models of inference in evaluating brain-behavior relationships in children. In C. R. Reynolds & E. Fletcher-Janzen (Eds.), *Handbook of clinical child neuropsychology* (2nd ed.). New York, NY: Plenum Press.

Fernandez-Duque, D., & Posner, M. I. (2001). Brain imaging of attentional networks in normal and pathological states. *Journal of Clinical and Experimental Neuropsychology, 23,* 35–48.

Gardner, H., Kornhaber, M. L., & Wake, W. K. (1996). *Intelligence: Multiple perspectives.* Ft. Worth, TX: Harcourt Brace College.

Hale, J. B., & Fiorello, C. A. (2004). *School neuropsychology: A practitioner's handbook.* New York, NY: Guilford Press.

Kaplan, E. (1988). A process approach to neuropsychological assessment. In T. Boll & B. K. Bryant (Eds.), *Clinical neuropsychology and brain function: Research, measurement, and practice* (pp. 143–155). Washington, DC: American Psychological Association.

Kaufman, A. S., & Kaufman, N. L. (2004). *Kaufman Assessment Battery for Children* (2nd ed. examiners manual). Circle Pines, MN: American Guidance Service.

Korkman, M., Kirk, U., & Kemp, S. (2007). *NEPSY-II: A developmental neuropsychological assessment.* San Antonio, TX: The Psychological Corporation.

Lezak, M. D., Howieson, D. B., Bigler, E. D., & Tranel, D. (2012). *Neuropsychological assessment* (5th ed.). New York,, NY: Oxford University Press.

Loring, D. (Ed.). (1999). *INS dictionary of neuropsychology.* New York, NY: Oxford University Press.

Manly, T., Robertson, I. H., Anderson, V., & Nimmo-Smith, I. (1999). *The Test of Everyday Attention for Children* (TEA-CH). Bury, St. Edmonds, UK: Thames Valley Test Company.

Martinez, E. S., & Semrud-Clikeman, M. (2004). Emotional adjustment and school functioning of young adolescents with multiple versus single learning disabilities. *Journal of Learning Disabilities, 23,* 411–420.

Meyers, J. E., & Meyers, K. R. (1995). *Rey Complex Figure Test and Recognition Trial: Professional Manual.* Lutz, FL: Psychological Assessment Resources, Inc.

Middleton, F. A., & Strick, P. I. (2001). A revised neuroanatomy of frontal-subcortical circuits. In D. G. Lichter & J. I. Cummings (Eds.), *Frontal-subcortical circuits in psychiatric and neurological disorders* (pp. 44–58). New York, NY: Guilford Press.

Milberg, W., Hebben, N., & Kaplan, E. (2009). The Boston process approach to neuropsychological assessment. In I. Grant & K. Adams (Eds.), *The neuropsychological assessment of neuropsychiatric and neuromedical disorders* (3rd ed., pp. 42–65). New York, NY: Oxford University Press.

Miller, D. C. (2007). *Essentials of school neuropsychological assessment* (pp. 234–260). Hoboken, NJ: John Wiley and Sons.

Miller, J.A. (2010). Assessing and intervening with children and internalizing disorders. In D. C. Miller (Ed.), *Best practices in school neuropsychology: Guidelines for effective practice, assessment, and evidence-based intervention*. Hoboken, NJ: John Wiley and Sons.

Mwtoews, based (in concept) on figure by Jeremy Kemp, on 2005–02–09 licensed by Creative Commons Attribution 2.5 Generic via Wikimedia Commons Retrieved 10/11/2013 from http://commons.wikimedia.org/wiki/File:Standard_deviation_diagram.svg

Posner, M.I., & Peterson, S. E. (1990). The attention system of the human brain. *Annual Review of Neuroscience, 13,* 25–42.

Roid, G. H. (2003). *Stanford-Binet intelligence scales* (5th ed.). Austin, TX: PRO-ED.

Sattler, J. M. (2008). *Assessment of children: Cognitive foundations* (5th ed.). Le Mesa, CA: Jerome M. Sattler.

Semrud-Clikeman, M., Kamphaus, R. W., Teeter, P.A., & Vaughn, M. (1997). Assessment of behavior and personality in the neuropsychological diagnosis of children. In *Handbook of Clinical Child Neuropsychology: Second Edition*. New York, NY: Plenum Press.

Smith, S.R. (2007). Integrating neuropsychology and personality assessment with children and adolescents. In S. R. Smith & L. Handler (Eds.), *The clinical assessment of children and adolescents: A practitioner's handbook*. New York, NY: John Wiley and Sons.

Squire, L. R. (1982). The neuropsychology of human memory. *Annual Review of Neuroscience, 5,* 241–273.

Terman, L. M. (1916). *The measurement of intelligence*. Boston, MA: Houghton Mifflin.

Tramontana, M.G., & Hooper, S.R. (1997). Neuropsychology of child psychopathology. In C.R. Reynolds & E. Fletcher-Janzen (Eds.), *Handbook of clinical child neuropsychology* (2nd ed.). New York, NY: Plenum Press.

Tulving, E. (1972). Episodic and semantic memory. In E. Tulving & W. Donaldson (Eds.), *Organization of memory* (pp. 381–403). New York, NY: Academic Press.

Tulving, E. (1983). *Elements of episodic memory*. New York, NY: Oxford University Press.

von Hofsten, C., & Rosblad, B. (1988). The integration of sensory information in the development of precise manual point. *Neuropsychologia, 26,* 805–821.

Wechsler, D. (2003). *Wechsler Intelligence Scale for Children, Fourth Edition*. San Antonio, TX: The Psychological Corporation.

Woodcock, R. W., McGrew, K. S., & Mather, N. (2001). *Woodcock-Johnson III Test of Cognitive Abilities*. Itasca, IL: Riverside Publishing.

Woodcock, R. W., McGrew, K. S., & Mather, N. (2001b). *Woodcock-Johnson III Tests of Achievement*. Itasca, IL: Riverside Publishing.

3 Understanding and Assessing Cognition

For our purposes, cognition is defined as a collection of mental processes that supports the processing of information. Using a computer analogy, Lezak has described four main categories of cognitive functions that correspond to:

> input, storage, processing (e.g., sorting, combining, relating data in various ways) and output. Thus, (1) receptive functions involve the ability to select, acquire, classify and integrate information; (2) memory and learning refer to information storage and retrieval; (3) thinking concerns the mental organization and reorganization of information; and (4) expressive functions are the means through which information is communicated and acted upon.
>
> (Lezak et al., 2012, p. 21)

While each of these areas of functioning can be classified separately, they are actually inseparable and work together across all functional domains to process the information we receive from both our external and internal environments. Over the course of this and the following five chapters, we will somewhat artificially break down domains of functioning as defined by the instruments designed and employed to test those domains when undertaking a neuropsychological evaluation. As discussed in the previous chapter, these domains include language and perceptual reasoning, executive functioning, memory, visual motor skills, academic skills, and behavioral and emotional functioning. We will be examining each of these parts of the hypothetical elephant prior to integrating those parts, while acknowledging that they are inextricably woven together, as we attempt to construct a picture of the whole child (or elephant, for that matter).

Theories of Cognition and Intelligence

As mentioned in Chapter 2, the concept of intelligence and its definition is complex. For the purposes of this discussion, intelligence is defined as "the ability to adjust or adapt to the environment, the ability to learn, or the ability to perform abstract thinking (e.g., to use symbols and concepts)" (Sattler, 2008). Assessment of cognition and intelligence has a protracted history. The instruments used to evaluate both have relied on theories of intelligence that have undergone many revisions over the last century. Historically, intelligence tests were developed to determine an individual's general intelligence, or g, a score that could predict an individual's success within a particular setting. Through both the development of cognitive and neuropsychological theories, we have learned that intelligence does not boil down to one, single predictable factor but rather to multiple factors contributing to an individual's overall functioning (Miller, 2007). The end result is a reduced emphasis within educational systems on assigning one number to a measure of a child's intellectual abilities but rather a focus on assessing and describing different cognitive functions that contribute to an individual's overall ability to adjust to the environment, learn and think abstractly.

The notion that one can assess an individual to determine a single predictive *g* has been highly influenced and changed by a combination of neuropsychological theories based on the work of the Russian neurologist A. R. Luria, and his theory of brain functioning, and the Cattell-Horn-Carroll (CHC) theory of cognitive abilities. First, Luria posits that classroom learning develops from the integration and application of some of the brain's most basic systems. Luria used the image of three building blocks (Reference Box 3.1) as foundations for learning (Hale & Fiorello, 2004). These three blocks must work together to foster learning, and even discrete imbalances in these systems can affect the acquisition of academic skills.

Reference Box 3.1 Luria's Three Blocks

Block 1—Reticular structures responsible for regulating cortical tone and arousal.
Block 2—Posterior occipital, parietal and temporal lobes (visual, somatosensory and auditory functioning) used for analyzing, coding and storing information.
Block 3—Anterior frontal cortex used for formulating plans, monitoring higher level thinking and reasoning skills.

Separately, since the 1940s, revisions of Cattell's Fluid-Crystallized theory of cognition clarified various cognitive abilities that contribute to an individual's cognitive functioning. Horn (1988), Carroll (1993) and McGrew (1997) all contributed to revisions of the original theory, resulting in today's CHC theory, which has influenced the revisions of eight important cognitive assessments within the last eight years (Flanagan, Alfonso, Ortiz, & Dynda, 2010). This integrated theory is composed of ten broad cognitive abilities (see Reference Box 3.2), with several narrow abilities contributing to functionality. Each of these broad abilities are assessed during neuropsychological evaluations.

Reference Box 3.2 CHC Broad Abilities

- Fluid intelligence (Gf)
- Quantitative knowledge (Gq)
- Crystallized intelligence (Gc)
- Reading and writing (Grw)
- Short-term memory (Gsm)
- Visual processing (Gv)
- Auditory processing
- Long-term storage and retrieval
- Processing speed
- Decision reaction time/speed

Assessing Cognition in Children

Many assessments have been developed to measure cognition. The complexities of assessing a child's intelligence are further complicated by a number of factors. The clinician and assessment tool must take into consideration the child's age-related characteristics, developmental level, background experiences, mental status and behavioral regulation (Wechsler, 2012). For these reasons, several tests of cognition have been specifically designed and normed for use with school-age children, matching language and motor development to age-appropriate levels of cognitive development.

Each of the following assessments measures various aspects of intelligence and cognitive functioning. A standard format is frequently used to capture different aspects of thinking. Each test has numerous subtests which are then compiled and used to generate composite scores. These composite scores are intended to reflect overall cognitive functioning. Each assessment tool, through various subtests, measures discrete areas of functioning, many of which are discussed in following chapters. In Chapter 2 a brief discussion introduced a number of assessment tools, including the WISC-IV. The following sections and tables review the WISC-IV and other assessment tools that focus on the measurement of language processing or verbal skills and visuospatial or nonverbal skills. Before doing so, we return to the story of Charles to provide an example of how cognitive functions are captured during assessment.

General Cognitive Functioning: Charles

Charles's current level of cognitive functioning was assessed with the WISC-IV, the most widely used measure of cognition for children. Because of the considerable variability in the subtest scores contributing to the Full Scale score, the Full Scale IQ should not be considered an accurate measure of Charles' overall intelligence and is not reported here. In addition, for his age group, Charles's verbal abilities fell in the Superior range (VCI = 124; 95th percentile) and his perceptual organizational abilities fell at the upper end of the High Average range (PRI = 117; 87th percentile). His working memory was in the Average range (WMI = 102; 55th percentile) while his processing speed was at the low end of the Average range (PSI = 94; 34th percentile).

There was no significant difference between the Verbal Comprehension Index and the Perceptual Reasoning Index, suggesting that Charles's verbal and perceptual skills, as measured by the WISC-IV, are commensurate. Both his Verbal Comprehension and Perceptual Reasoning Indices were significantly higher than his Working Memory and Processing Speed Indices, however, suggesting that both his verbal and nonverbal skills are strengths relative to both his ability to hold auditory information in his head when required to perform some operation as well as his ability to execute graphomotor tasks and sustain visual attention in a timely manner.

IQ and Index Scores have a mean of one hundred and a standard deviation of fifteen; scores at ninety, one hundred and one hundred and ten represent levels of performance at the twenty-fifth, fiftieth and seventy-fifth percentile for age, respectively. Subtest Scores have a mean of ten and a standard deviation of three; scores at eight, ten and twelve represent levels of performance at the twenty-fifth, fiftieth and seventy-fifth percentile for age, respectively. The findings are summarized in Table 3.1:

Table 3.1 Charles's WISC-IV Index and subtest scores.

	Score	*Percentile*
Verbal Comprehension	124	95
Perceptual Reasoning	117	87
Working Memory	102	55
Processing Speed	94	34

Subtest Scores Summary			
Verbal Comprehension Scales		*Perceptual Reasoning Scales*	
Similarities	16	Block Design	15
Vocabulary	14	Picture Concepts	12
Comprehension	12	Matrix Reasoning	11
		Picture Completion	(14)
Working Memory Scales		*Processing Speed Scales*	
Digit Span	9	Coding	10
L-N Sequence	12	Symbol Search	8
		Cancellation	(13)

Charles's scores on the WISC-IV reflect measures of his functioning in the four domains that were discussed in Chapter 2: Verbal Comprehension, Perceptual Reasoning, Working Memory and Processing Speed. In the following sections, we will consider two of those domains—Verbal Comprehension as it relates to language processing and Perceptual Reasoning as it relates to the organization of visuospatial information. In the first few sections, we will first examine language functioning and briefly discuss the underlying neuroanatomical correlates of language. Following that, we review the different assessment tools that relate to language functioning. We then return to Charles and an analysis of his Verbal Comprehension score on the WISC-IV.

Language Processing: Left Hemisphere Verbal Skills

Language is "a system of human communication using words, written and spoken, and particular ways of combining them; any such system employed by a community, a nation, etc." (The New Shorter Oxford English Dictionary, 1993, p. 1528).

A description of the neurological substrate for language processing is extremely complex and far too complicated to do it justice within the context of our current discussion. However, as mentioned previously, the left hemisphere of the human brain is dominant for certain aspects of language functioning. While the right hemisphere does mediate some of the gestural and prosodic dimensions of language, most of the semantic and almost all of the syntactic functions of language are performed by the left hemisphere (Benson, 1993). The left hemisphere dominance for these functions is supported by a history of studies examining neural lesions. These involve areas known as Broca's area, a localized portion of the left frontal lobe that mediates expressive language, and Wernicke's area, an area on the temporal lobe that subserves receptive language. More recently, research using imaging techniques such as positron-emission tomography (PET) scans or functional magnetic resonance imaging (fMRI) has further refined our understanding of the neuroanatomical correlates of different aspects of language. In a 2012 article reviewing imaging studies of speech, spoken language and reading, left temporal, left inferior frontal and temporoparietal, and left planum temporale regions were all involved in higher level speech processing. In addition, a number of left lateralized areas were involved in analyzing semantics (anterior and posterior temporal areas, ventral inferior frontal areas, dorsal superior frontal gyrus and the angular gyri). Word retrieval from semantics was associated with activation in the left-middle frontal gyrus and the left-middle and inferior temporal cortices (Price, 2012). Needless to say, these areas are highly interconnected and receive input and send output to a myriad of other cortical and subcortical regions and nuclei.

Specific aspects of language, such as reading and writing, and the means to evaluate them will be discussed in a later chapter. For our purposes, we will consider aspects of language functioning that are evaluated using a few of the more popular tests of verbal intelligence. These include, but are not necessarily limited to, the WISC-IV, the WPPSI-IV, the *Stanford Binet, Fifth Edition* (SB5), the *Kaufmann Assessment Battery for Children* (2nd Edition) and the *Woodcock-Johnson III Tests of Cognitive Abilities* (Woodcock et al., 2001). The following section describes subtests of these instruments, beginning with the Verbal Comprehension scales on the WISC-IV.

The Wechsler Intelligence Scale for Children, Fourth Edition (WISC-IV)

Verbal Comprehension Index–This is an overall measure of the child's ability to verbally reason through to abstract concepts and is influenced by experience and exposure to information.

The **Vocabulary** subtest of the WISC-IV is a test of word knowledge and, as such, measures a child's ability to define words that are arranged in order of increasing difficulty. It "assesses several cognitive factors—the child's learning ability, fund of information, richness of ideas, memory, concept formation and language development" (Sattler, 2008). Children's ability to define words depends on their exposure to vocabulary through their environment and their educational experiences. It is considered to correlate highly with overall intelligence. Scores on the Vocabulary subtest relate to word knowledge, verbal comprehension, verbal skills, language development, ability to conceptualize, intellectual striving, background, education, verbal communication at home (Sattler, 2008). In respect to neuroanatomical functioning, Lee et al. (2007) proposed that the posterior supramarginal gyrus (pSMG) is a crucial site for linking phonological and semantic information, which is central to vocabulary acquisition. Consistent with the findings of Lee et al. (2007), Richardson et al. (2010) found that vocabulary knowledge correlated with gray matter density in the pSMG for teenagers. They also found a significant correlation between vocabulary and gray matter density in the left posterior superior temporal sulcus (pSTS; Wernicke's area) and the left posterior temporoparietal cortex (pT-P) that was consistent across the lifespan.

The **Comprehension** subtest of the WISC-IV is a measure of a child's ability to understand social expectations and social behavior and requires that the child answer questions about specific problems that become increasingly abstract. A strong performance on this task "suggests that the child has common sense, social judgment, and a grasp of social conventionality. These characteristics imply an ability to use facts in a pertinent, meaningful and emotionally appropriate manner. Success is also based on the child's ability to verbalize acceptable actions" (Sattler, 2008).

The **Similarities** subtest of the WISC-IV measures verbal concept formation by requiring that the child explain the similarity between two conceptually related words. As the questions progress, the underlying concepts become increasingly abstract. It requires the child to perceive and combine common elements into a meaningful concept that may not be immediately obvious, which is a process of abstraction. Performance depends on verbal comprehension, conceptual thinking, ability to see relationships, ability to use logic and abstraction, ability to distinguish fundamental from superficial relationships, ability to conceptualize and verbalize appropriate relationships and cognitive flexibility (Sattler, 2008). Anatomically, poor Similarities scores are associated with left temporal and frontal involvement and these areas show increased glucose metabolism in normal subjects taking the Similarities subtest (Lezak et al., 2004).

The **Information** subtest of the WISC-IV is a measure of a child's acquired knowledge and requires that the child answer questions related to quantitative and calendar facts, as well as science, geography and history. It assesses crystallized knowledge, general verbal information, verbal comprehension, range of factual knowledge and receptive and expressive language. It is also influenced by cultural knowledge, long-term memory, background, alertness and interest in surroundings, intellectual ambition and curiosity and urge to collect knowledge (Sattler, 2008). Neuroanatomically, glucose metabolism increases in the left temporal lobe and surrounding areas during administration of the Information subtest (Chase et al., 1984).

The **Word Reasoning** subtest of the WISC-IV is a measure of a child's ability to reason through analogies, integrate and synthesize different kinds of information, and understand abstract concepts. The child has to guess a word or common concept being described in a series of clues. Over the course of twenty-four items, the series of clues describe increasingly abstract concepts.

The Wechsler Preschool and Primary Scale of Intelligence, Fourth Edition (WPPSI-IV)

While the WISC-IV is a comprehensive instrument for assessing various cognitive processes in children, it is not appropriate to use with younger children. The tasks included in the assessment of a preschool age group must consider the relationship between developing motor and language skills with cognitive abilities. When assessing children this young, special considerations for age must be taken into account. Perhaps they haven't been exposed to test-taking materials or the expected behavior. Attention span and focus are not as well developed for this age group and they may require more breaks (Brassard & Boehm, 2007). The *Wechsler Preschool and Primary Scale of Intelligence–Fourth Edition* (WPPSI-IV; Wechsler, 2012) was developed as a measure of intelligence for children aged 2 years 6 months to 7 years 7 months. Some subtests are used for different age groups in order to appropriately measure different developmental tasks.

The **Information, Similarities, Vocabulary** and **Comprehension** subtests of the WPPSI-IV are essentially the same as those described on the WISC-IV. The questions on each are different, however, and are tailored for children within the designated age ranges.

The **Receptive Vocabulary** subtest of the WPPSI-IV measures receptive language ability and language development. It requires that the child associate a picture that most accurately represents a word read aloud. As noted previously, receptive language is mediated by a variety of neuronal structures primarily located in the left hemisphere.

The **Picture Naming** subtest of the WPPSI-IV measures a child's expressive language ability, word retrieval and the ability to associate a visual stimulus with language. Again, as noted previously, the left hemisphere supports a number of expressive language functions. For a comprehensive review and detailed discussion of fMRI studies related to expressive vocabulary, including word retrieval and associating visual stimuli with language, see Price (2012).

The Stanford-Binet Intelligence Scale, Fifth Edition

The *Stanford-Binet Intelligence Scales, Fifth Edition* (SB5) has a long, venerable history dating back to the early 1900s, when the French government commissioned its development in order to place children into special education programs. Since its inception it has undergone several rigorous revisions, resulting in the most recent form, which has been normed for ages two to eighty-five. It identifies and measures five factors: fluid reasoning, knowledge, working memory, visuospatial processing and quantitative reasoning (Baron, 2004; Rhodes, D'Amato, & Rothlisberg, 2009). Table 3.2 displays subtests related to language processing.

The Kaufman Assessment Battery for Children, Second Edition

The first edition of the *Kaufman Assessment Battery for Children* was the first major assessment tool to use a specific theoretical approach, both the Lurian model and the CHC model, to develop its structure. The *Kaufman Assessment Battery for Children, Second Edition* (KABC-II) allows for interpretation under both models and is intended to

Table 3.2 SB5—Subtests of Verbal Processing.

Subtest	Cognitive Domain	Assessed Task
Early Reasoning	Verbal Fluid Reasoning	The individual is asked to look at three pictures and tell what is happening. The individual is also asked to sort pictures into logical groups.
Verbal Absurdities	Verbal Fluid Reasoning	The individual is asked to tell what is silly about statements presented orally.
Verbal Analogies	Verbal Fluid Reasoning	The individual is asked to complete a four-word analogy by supplying both the first and last word.
Vocabulary	Verbal Knowledge	The individual is asked to display knowledge regarding body parts, toys, actions in images and defining real words aloud.
Quantitative Reasoning	Verbal Quantitative Reasoning	The individual is required to apply basic mathematical knowledge to solve problems in increasingly difficult problems and concepts.
Position and Direction	Verbal Visuospatial Reasoning	The individual is asked to move objects into appropriate positions, gives and follows spatial directions.
Memory for Sentences	Verbal Working Memory	The individual is asked to repeat brief phrases or sentences.
Last Word	Verbal Working Memory	The individual is asked to remember the last word in each question out of a set of questions.

Table 3.3 K-ABC-II Planning Ability/Fluid Reasoning/*Gf* Scale.

Subtest	Assessed Task
Pattern Reasoning	The child is asked to select one missing stimulus that will complete a logical pattern.
Story Completion	The child is asked to select one or more pictures that best complete a pictorial story.

better match diagnosis to intervention. Developed in 2004, it uses four scales, plus one optional scale: Stimulus, Sequential, Planning, Learning and Knowledge (CHC model only; Rhodes et al., 2009). Table 3.3 details subtests geared toward verbal processing.

The Woodcock-Johnson, Third Edition, Cognitive

The *Woodcock-Johnson III Tests of Cognitive Abilities* (WJ III-COG; Woodcock et al., 2001) is a battery of cognitive tests designed for individuals ages two to ninety plus years. Not all of the tests are used at the youngest age levels. The CHC theory of intelligence

Table 3.4 WJ III-COG—Tests of Verbal Processing.

Subtest	Measured Domain	Assessed Task
Picture Vocabulary	Verbal Comprehension	Requires the child to identify pictures of familiar and unfamiliar objects, first by pointing at a picture, then by naming the picture orally.
Synonyms	Verbal Comprehension	Requires the child to hear a word and provide a synonym.
Antonyms	Verbal Comprehension	Requires the child to hear a word and provide an antonym.
Verbal Analogies	Verbal Comprehension	Requires the child to hear 3 words and complete the analogy by providing the fourth.
General Information	General Verbal Knowledge	Divided into two subtests. The child is asked "Where would you find . . . (an object)?" and "What would you do with . . . (an object)"

provides the theoretical basis for this assessment and the subtests are divided into seven clusters intended to capture Comprehension-Knowledge, Long-Term Retrieval, Visual-Spatial Thinking, Auditory Processing, Fluid Reasoning, Processing Speed and Short-Term Memory. Table 3.4 outlines which subtest focuses on verbal processing.

Verbal Functioning: Charles

We return to eleven-year-old Charles who, being schooled at home by his mother, was increasingly resistant to certain academic tasks, despite his apparent ability and intelligence.

Charles's Verbal Comprehension Index of 124 on the WISC-IV placed him in the Superior range for verbal functioning. His performance on the three subtests administered in this area demonstrated some significant variability.

Charles's strongest performance in the verbal area was on Similarities, a subtest measuring his ability to reason through and articulate how two words were alike. This is usually considered a good measure of abstract reasoning and he was able to concisely and precisely provide good abstract responses. He made considerable effort, offering responses even when unsure and making further effort when queried to provide more information. He also performed above average on Vocabulary, a test of his knowledge of word meaning. On this subtest, he was able to provide answers that were both concise and precise. When unsure of a response, he initially attempted to make up definitions, using a root of the target word. For example, he offered "someone who is stren" as a definition of the word *strenuous*. As the words became increasingly difficult, however, he was able eventually to clearly indicate whether or not he knew their meaning. His relatively weaker performance in the verbal area was on Comprehension, a test of his ability to learn social expectations and reasons for behaviors. The less structured format of this subtest lent itself to a more exhaustive mode of responding that was less precise. Charles also tended to occasionally personalize a question and impose his experience on an answer in a manner that sometimes distorted the original meaning of the question.

Thus, on tasks of verbal functioning, Charles displayed a strong ability to reason abstractly when familiar with the material, but when unsure of an answer, tended to fall back on a more experientially based and exhaustive approach to answering questions. When provided with a more structured format, he was able to be both concise and precise in his responding. When questions were more open ended, he tended to become more experiential and idiosyncratic in a way that sometimes altered the meaning of the question and reflected the intrusion of emotional material related to his anxiety about not knowing or not being able to draw inferences.

Visuospatial Organization: Right Hemisphere Nonverbal Abilities

Along with assessing verbal abilities, a complete neuropsychological evaluation measures nonverbal functioning, also referred to as perceptual reasoning or visuospatial organization. As described by Lezak et al. (2004), the right hemisphere "is superior for 'configurational' processing required by material that cannot be described adequately in words or strings of symbols, such as the appearance of a face, or three-dimensional spatial relationships" (p. 61). Lezak goes on to note that:

> the right hemisphere dominates the processing of information that does not readily lend itself to verbalization. This includes the reception and storage of visual data, tactile and visual recognition of shapes and forms, perception of spatial orientation and perspective, and copying and drawing geometric and representational designs and pictures. Arithmetic calculations (involving spatial organization of the problem elements as distinct from left hemisphere-mediated linear arithmetic problems involving, for instance, stories or equations with and a + b = c form) have a significant right hemisphere component. Some aspects of musical ability are also localized on the right, as are abilities to recognize and discriminate nonverbal sounds.
>
> (2004, p. 61)

Visuospatial organization skills allow us to navigate the nonverbal world. We use these skills when we remember where we parked the car in a large parking lot, while reading maps and navigating new environments or when grocery shopping and scanning the shelf for the preferred can of soup. This skill set also contributes to the development of academic skills such as reading graphs, recognizing shapes and their relationship to each other, understanding concepts such as ratios and the ability to develop reading skills. Interpersonally, visuospatial skills allow individuals to recognize facial expression and the attached emotion. They also allow for an integrated understanding of gestures and body posture. While verbal skills are prized for communication, difficulties with perceptual abilities can also impact the functioning of an individual in many aspects of daily living.

As with verbal abilities, the underlying neuroanatomy of perceptual abilities and visuospatial organization is complex and beyond the scope of this discussion. This brief overview highlights the complexity and interconnectedness of the brain. Through lesion studies, CAT scans and fMRIs, the right hemisphere has been implicated in certain pragmatic communication skills. This includes eye contact, turn taking, and generating inferences. Adults with right hemisphere lesions display difficulty interpreting abstract concepts and nonliteral or ambiguous information. They can appear egocentric, have difficulty understanding the perspective of others and appear disorganized and impulsive (Lehman Blake, 2007). The right hemisphere is responsible for integrating visual information received from the occipital lobe to make meaning, including the interpretation of facial expressions and emotional processing, especially for negative affect (Asthana & Mandal, 2001). Lesions in the right parietal lobe can cause difficulties in processing visual information. For example, the condition Contralateral Neglect, is an example of the importance of right parietal lobe functioning. When asked to draw an image, such as the face of a clock, the individual might crowd all the numbers to the right side of the image. Tactile sensation on the left side of the body may be ignored. When reading compound words, such as *football,* they may only read *ball.* This indicates that the right parietal hemisphere is involved in the integration of information from the visual field. As a result, the "gestalt" of images, and even concepts and sensation, is obstructed (Kolb & Whishaw, 2009). In fact, using a neuropsychological assessment to identify discrete areas of functioning in order to understand the whole child (or elephant) relies on the ability of the right hemisphere to integrate the part to whole relationship of the child's functioning in specific functional domains, to their overall presentation and experience.

Both the right and left hemisphere process sensory information gathered from internal and external environments. Integration and development of a response to sensory information are key features of both hemispheres. When assessing right hemisphere functioning, visual acuity is particularly important and must be considered.

Many assessment batteries discussed in the previous section test multiple aspects of cognitive functioning. Several subtests have been developed to capture perceptual reasoning, and some assessment tools have been developed as stand-alone tests, intended to capture nonverbal functioning. Tables 3.5 to 3.7 display subtests from the WISC-IV, WPPSI-IV, SB5, KABC-II and the WCJ-III COG, as well as the *Test of Nonverbal Intelligence* (TONI).

The Wechsler Intelligence Scale for Children, Fourth Edition

Perceptual Reasoning Index—This is an overall measure of the child's ability to utilize visual information to develop meaning, both abstract and concrete.

The **Block Design** subtest assesses a child's ability to consider an image's whole, and recognize its parts. This is achieved by asking the child to recreate a geometric design using blocks displaying elements of the design. The child must rotate the blocks and assemble them to represent the original design. To complete this task, the child must develop an approach and strategy. This is called "analysis and synthesis." This requires perceptual organization, spatial visualization and abstract conceptualization. A time-dependent test, it relies on motor abilities and vision (Sattler, 2008). As reported by Chase et al. (1984), tests of perceptual reasoning, such as Block Design, resulted in increased glucose metabolism in the right postereoparietal cortical regions, a result consistent with lesion studies (Wilde, Boake, & Sherer, 2000).

The **Picture Concepts** subtest evaluates abstract and categorical reasoning on a task requiring the child to select items from two or three rows that go together to form a concept. Among other things, it assesses fluid reasoning, visual perceptual reasoning, conceptual thinking, nonverbal reasoning and visual processing (Sattler, 2008).

The **Matrix Reasoning** subtest measures a child's visuoperceptual analogic reasoning without a time constraint. It assesses a variety of cognitive factors, such as nonverbal fluid reasoning, visual processing, visuoperceptual organization, reasoning ability, attention to detail, spatial ability and visual discrimination (Sattler, 2008).

The **Picture Completion** subtest is a test of visual discrimination that requires the individual to distinguish essential and nonessential details. Some of the factors that it measures include crystallized knowledge, visual processing, nonverbal reasoning, visuoperceptual organization and discrimination, scanning ability, spatial perception and visual long-term memory (Sattler, 2008). Data from PET scans suggests the involvement of the right posterior hemisphere in completing this task (Chase et al., 1984).

The Wechsler Preschool and Primary Scale of Intelligence, Third Edition

Introduced earlier in the chapter, the *Wechsler Preschool and Primary Scale of Intelligence–Fourth Edition* (WPPSI-IV) was developed as a measure of intelligence for children aged 2 years 6 months to 7 years 7 months. Some subtests are used for different age groups in order to appropriately measure different developmental tasks. The Block Design, Matrix Reasoning and Picture Concepts subtests are similar to the WISC-IV subtests but are age adjusted for the WPPSI. The Object Assembly subtest is unique to the WPPSI.

The **Object Assembly** subtest measures visuoperceptual organization and assesses a number of cognitive factors, such as visual processing, spatial relations, visuoperceptual discrimination, visual motor coordination, part to whole relationships and nonverbal reasoning. It is a timed test.

The Stanford-Binet, Fifth Edition

The SB5 has been normed for use with individuals ages two to eighty-five. It identifies and measures five factors: fluid reasoning, knowledge, working memory, visuospatial processing and quantitative reasoning (Baron, 2004; Rhodes et al., 2009). Table 3.5 describes the subtests used to assess nonverbal functioning.

Table 3.5 SB5—Nonverbal processing.

Subtest	Cognitive Domain	Assessed Task
Procedural Knowledge	Nonverbal Knowledge	The individual is asked to complete common activities and demonstrate knowledge of common objects.
Picture Absurdities	Nonverbal Knowledge	The individual is asked to identify absurd or missing details in an image.
Quantitative Reasoning	Nonverbal Quantitative Reasoning	The individual is required to apply basic mathematical knowledge to solve problems in increasingly difficult problems and concepts.
Form Board	Nonverbal Visuospatial Reasoning	The individual is first asked to match various shapes with increasing difficulty eventually constructing a whole image from parts. No time limit.
Delayed Response	Nonverbal Working Memory	The individual is asked to find an object hidden under a cup after a 3-second delay.
Block Span	Nonverbal Working Memory	The individual is asked to tap blocks in the same sequences as the examiner.

The Kaufman Assessment Battery for Children, Second Edition

The K-ABC-II is a comprehensive measurement of cognitive functioning, introduced earlier in this chapter. Recall, it uses four scales, plus one optional scale: Stimulus, Sequential, Planning, Learning and Knowledge (CHC model only; Rhodes et al., 2009). Based on the Lurian and CHC model of intelligence, it contains several subtests intended to measure nonverbal processing. Table 3.6 highlights these subtests.

Table 3.6 K-ABC-II—Tests of Nonverbal Processing Simultaneous Processing/Visual Processing/ Gv Scale.

Subtest	Assessed Task
Block Counting	The child is asked to count blocks that are shown in a design, some of which are partially or completely hidden.
Conceptual Thinking	The child is asked to select one picture that does not belong with other pictures.
Face Recognition	The child is asked to recall pictures of faces from memory.
Rover	The child is asked to find the quickest path through a grid containing obstacles.
Triangles	Using puzzle-like pieces, the child is asked to construct simple and abstract designs.
Gestalt Closure	The child is asked to identify incompletely drawn images.

Table 3.7 K-ABC-II Planning Ability/Fluid Reasoning/Gf Scale.

Subtest	Assessed Task
Pattern Reasoning	The child is asked to select one missing stimulus that will complete a logical pattern.
Story Completion	The child is asked to select on or more pictures that best complete a pictorial story.

The Test of Nonverbal Intelligence, Fourth Edition

The *Test of Nonverbal Intelligence, Fourth Edition* (TONI-4; Brown et al., 2010) is a relatively short, fifteen- to twenty-minute, evaluation proctored as a language-free evaluation. It is normed for ages six to eighty-nine and is applicable towards many profoundly impairing conditions. Instructions are pantomimed, making it useful for non–English-speaking children and adults. The TONI-4 presents forty-five abstract/figural problems solving items that increase in order of difficulty. Answers are multiple choice, and the child is asked to point to the best option. It should be considered when evaluating children who cannot comprehend language and is often used to assess early stages of traumatic brain injury.

The Rey-Osterrieth Complex Figure Test

The *Rey-Osterrieth Complex Figure Test* (ROCF; Osterrieth, 1944) has proved to be one of the best assessments of nonverbal functioning as well as nonverbal memory. A printed copy of a complex geometric figure is presented to the child and he or she is asked to copy the image as accurately possible. This figure is composed of one large rectangular box, divided into smaller sections with geometric details. On each side of the rectangle, additional external details are positioned (see Figure 3.1). The individual is asked, in an immediate recall assessment, to recreate the image, without looking at the sample image. The delayed recall assessment takes place twenty to twenty-five minutes later. The individual is asked one more time to redraw the image, without looking at the sample image. Through this process, visual organization and visual memory are assessed (Knight, 2003).

As the individual approaches the ROCF, they must develop a method or strategy for copying the figure. In doing so, their orientation to processing visuospatial information is revealed. Do they notice the details first or the overall composition? How do they grasp the part-to-whole relationship? In essence, do they see the forest or the trees? As the child makes his or her copy, it is observed how much the child relies on the greater structure of the rectangle to develop the end product, or if he or she focuses on one detail at a time. This can indicate if the individual is overwhelmed by visual information, requiring visual stimuli to be broken into smaller, simplified images. As the individual approaches this task, underlying organizational abilities surface. Does the child approach the copy with a developed strategy, or is he or she more likely to respond impulsively to a visual component without planning? To navigate this process, perhaps the child will develop a story or narrative related to the shape, using verbal skills to mediate a visuospatial difficulty.

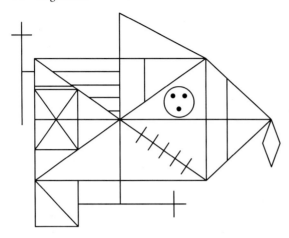

Figure 3.1 The Rey-Osterrieth Complex Figure (Bernstein & Waber, 1996).

Note: From "Filetest de copie d'une figure complex: Contribution a l'etude de la perception et de la memoire [The test of copying a complex figure: A contribution to the study of perception and memory]," by P. A. Osterrieth, 1944, *Archives de Psychologie 30*, pp. 286–356.

In the process of copying the figure, the examinee must have intact bodily systems functioning at levels that support higher cortical activity, including arousal and consciousness, postural stability, peripheral sensory functioning, peripheral motor strength and coordination. The individual must make decisions regarding execution, sequence a series of steps and make ongoing visuospatial analysis of his or her drawing. Thus, cognitive operations measured by the ROFC reflect a complex and coordinated sequence of whole-brain mediated activity (Knight, 2003). As a result, the use of some specific anatomical locations and structures are implicated and used. For example, unilateral lesions of the right hemisphere are implied in spatial processing errors. However, left-hemisphere damage is also associated with impaired ROFC performance (Bigler, 2003).

The ROFC has been proven useful for assessing several domains of functioning. The list includes: perceptual apprehension, attention and control, visual memory and perceptual organization, visual-constructive function, long-term memory, motor functioning and other aspects of memory. As a result, it is a useful diagnostic tool, targeting many aspects of nonverbal functioning. Thus, the ROFC will be discussed further in subsequent chapters as it relates to other functional domains.

Visuospatial/Organizational Functioning: Charles

Charles's performance on tasks of nonverbal reasoning on the WISC-IV gave him an overall score of one hundred and seventeen, at the upper end of the High Average range for perceptual organizational skills. There was a similar range of variability between these nonverbal subtests as there was on the verbal scores. His strongest performance in this area was on Block Design, a timed test in which one uses blocks to copy a pattern from both three dimensional and two-dimensional models. Charles assembled the blocks in a logical, stepwise and sequential fashion but tended to proceed from the right to the left, usually using only his right hand. In addition, he tended to assemble the blocks in pairs and then place them within the larger design, appearing to integrate the parts into the whole. Lastly, he made a few mistakes, but then corrected himself before the time was up.

He also performed strongly on Picture Completion, a task requiring him to identify what was missing from pictures of common objects. For the most part on this test, he saw the missing detail quickly, demonstrating an above-average ability to distinguish figure ground relationships. He did somewhat less well on Picture Concepts, a test on which he had to formulate a category by which various everyday objects were organized. He appeared to be supported by the use of language to organize categories, but when unsure tended to become more idiosyncratic in his responses, drawing more on his experience and becoming more concrete rather than reasoning through to more abstract answers. In addition, at one point he more impulsively associated objects within rows, forgetting that he had to relate objects across rows, thus losing the cognitive set. His weakest performance in the nonverbal area of the WISC-IV was on Matrix Reasoning, a test on which he had to fill in the missing visual portion of a grid with one of a number of options below the grid. Charles had relative difficulty on those tasks that required that he process more complex visual and spatial patterns and was unable to benefit from a hands-on approach.

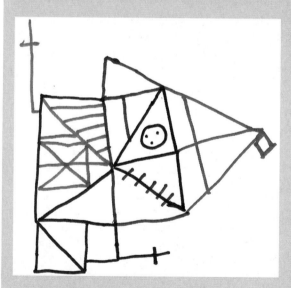

Figure 3.2 Charles' Rey—Copy.

Charles took an unusual approach in processing complex visual and spatial information on the *Rey-Osterrieth Complex Figure Test* (see Figure 3.2).

On this task, he was required to copy a complex geometric figure followed by immediate and delayed reproductions from memory. Both visual organization and visual memory abilities are assessed by this task. On the copy portion, Charles took a part-oriented approach and proceeded to draw the figure from right to left, starting with components of the internal structure. As he had on the Block Design subtest of the WISC-IV, he tended to organize his reproduction in chunks that he then integrated into the whole design.

He did so successfully, scoring strongly for organization (Basal Level V; Organization thirteen; one hundredth percentile). On the immediate recall portion, he again took a part-oriented approach and proceeded from right to left. He was able to reconstruct the external configuration but had difficulty integrating the internal underlying organizational structure and tended to perseverate on an internal detail, performing at the low end of the Average range (Basal Level II; Organization five; twenty-fifth percentile). He did somewhat better on his delayed recall reproduction (Basal Level III; Organization seven; fiftieth < seventy-fifth percentile) by more accurately consolidating and reproducing the configuration in spite of his part oriented, right to left approach. He again had difficulty with the internal underlying organizational structure but appeared to benefit from a motor memory consolidated from his previous attempts. Nonetheless, relative to his copy, he had some difficulty integrating and recalling complex visual information.

Thus, together, results from tests of visuospatial organization indicate that Charles demonstrates above-average skills in the processing of visuospatial information. He is able to integrate part to whole relationships when he can break down visual complexity into more manageable parts but has relative difficulty consolidating and recalling the underlying organizational structure of complex visual details. Therefore, he will benefit from clear structure and models that are able to be broken down into manageable chunks and analyzed in a step-by-step fashion.

Split Scores

During assessment, and when interpreting test results, it can become apparent that either verbal or perceptual abilities are a stronger skill set. This is a means for determining relative strengths and struggles but can also imply right- or left-hemisphere dysfunction. Carefully understanding scoring procedures and standard deviations allows clinicians to properly interpret disparities. The interrelated nature of neural functioning and the inherent reliance upon visual motor functioning during assessment of perceptual reasoning must be considered. While it may be easy to make assumptions based on split scores, this information is highly valuable and should be considered carefully during feedback sessions and during treatment planning. This information provides helpful clues that allow the child, and the treatment team, to take a strengths-based approach to circumventing neuropsychological difficulties, relying on the plasticity of the brain to allow the child optimal functioning and development.

References

Asthana, H.S., & Mandal, M.K. (2001). Visual-field bias in the judgment of facial expression of emotion. *The Journal of General Psychology, 128*(1), 21–29.

Baron, I. S. (2004). *Neuropsychological evaluation of the child.* New York, NY: Oxford University Press.

Benson, D. F. (1993). Aphasia. In K. Heilman, & E. Valenstein (Eds.), *Clinical neuropsychology* (3rd ed.). New York, NY: Oxford University Press.

Bernstein, J. H., & Waber, D. (1996). *Developmental scoring system for the Rey-Osterrieth Complex Figure.* Lutz, FL: Psychological Assessment Resources.

Bigler, E. D. (2003). Neuroimaging and the ROCF. In J.A. Knight & E. Kaplan (2003). *The handbook of Rey-Osterrieth complex figure usage: Clinical and research applications.* Lutz, FL: Psychological Assessment Resources.

Brassard, M.R., & Boehm, A.E. (2007). *Preschool assessment: Principles and practices.* New York, NY: Guilford Press.

Brown, L., Sherbenou, R.J., & Johnson, S.K. (2010). *Test of Nonverbal Intelligence* (4th ed.). Austin, TX: Pro-Ed, Inc.

Carroll, J.B. (1993). *Human cognitive abilities: A survey of factor-analytic studies.* Cambridge, UK: Cambridge University Press.

Chase, T. N., Fedio, P., Foster, N. L., et al. (1984). Wechsler Adult Intelligence Scale performance: Cortical localization by fluorodeoxyglucose F18-positron emission tomography. *Archives of Neurology, 41,* 1244–1247.

Flanagan, D.P., Alfonso, V.C., Ortiz, S.O., & Dynda, A. M. (2010). Integrating cognitive assessment in school neuropsychological evaluations. In C. Miller (Ed.), *Best practices in school neuropsychology: Guidelines for effective practice, assessment, and evidence-based intervention.* Hoboken, NJ: John Wiley and Sons.

Hale, J.B., & Fiorello, C.A. (2004). *School neuropsychology: A practitioner's handbook.* New York, NY: Guilford Press.

Horn, J.L. (1988). Think about human abilities. In J. R Nesselroade & R.B. Cattell (Eds.), *Handbook of multivariate experimental psychology* (2nd ed., pp. 645–685). New York, NY: Plenum Press.

Knight, J. A. (2003). The Rey-Osterrieth complex figure: Overview of the handbook, current uses and future directions. In J.A. Knight & E. Kaplan (2003). *The handbook of Rey-Osterrieth complex figure usage: Clinical and research applications.* Lutz, FL: Psychological Assessment Resources.

Kolb, B., & Whishaw, I.O. (2009). *Fundamentals of human neuropsychology* (6th ed.). New York, NY: Worth.

Lee, H. L., Devlin, J. T., Shakeshaft, C., Stewart, L. H., Brennan, A., Glensman, J., et al. (2007). Anatomical traces of vocabulary acquisition in the adolescent brain. *Journal of Neuroscience, 27,* 1184–1189.

Lehman Blake, M. (2007). Perspectives on treatment of communication deficits associated with right hemisphere brain damage. *American Journal of Speech-Language Pathology, 27,* 331–342.

Lezak, M. D., Howieson, D.B., & Loring, D.W. (2004). *Neuropsychological assessment* (4th ed.). New York, NY: Oxford University Press.

Lezak, M. D., Howieson, D. B., Bigler, E. D., & Tranel, D. (2012). *Neuropsychological assessment* (5th ed.). New York, NY: Oxford University Press.

McCarthy, D. (1972). *Manual for the McCarthy Scales of Children's Abilities.* New York: The Psychological Corporation.

McGrew, K.S. (1997). Analysis of the major intelligence batteries according to a proposed comprehensive Gf-Gc framework. In D.P. Flanagan, J.L. Genshaft, & P.L. Harrison (Eds.), *Contemporary intellectual assessment: Theories, tests and issues* (2nd ed., pp. 136–181). New York, NY: Guilford Press.

Miller, D. C. (2007). *Essentials of school neuropsychological assessment.* Hoboken, NJ: John Wiley and Sons.

New Shorter Oxford English Dictionary. (1993). Oxford: Oxford University Press.

Osterrieth, P. A. (1944). Filetest de copie d'une figure complex: Contribution a l'etude de la perception et de la memoire [The test of copying a complex figure: A contribution to the study of perception and memory]. *Archives de Psychologie, 30,* 286–356.

Price, C. (2012). A review and synthesis of the first 20 years of PET and fMRI studies of heard speech, spoken language and reading. *Neuroimage, 62*(2), 816–847.

Rhodes, R. L., D'Amato, R. C., & Rothlisberg, B. A. (2009). Utilizing a neuropsychological paradigm for understanding common educational and psychological tests. In C. R. Reynolds & Fletcher-Janzen (2009). *Handbook of clinical child neuropsychology.* New York, NY: Springer Science + Business Media, LLC.

Richardson, F. M., Thomas, M. S., Filippi, R., Harth, H., & Price, C. J. (2010, May). Contrasting effects of vocabulary knowledge on temporal and parietal brain structure across lifespan. *Journal of Cognitive Neuroscience, 22*(5), 943–954. doi:10.1162/jocn.2009.21238

Ruff, R. M. (1988). *Ruff Figural Fluency Test: Professional manual.* Odessa, FL: Psychological Assessment Resources, Inc.

Sattler, J. (2008). *Assessment of children: Cognitive foundations* (5th ed.). San Diego, CA: Jerome M. Sattler.

Wechsler, D. (2003). *Wechsler intelligence scale for children* (4th ed.). San Antonio, TX: The Psychological Corporation.

Wechsler, D. (2012). *Wechsler preschool and primary scale of intelligence* (4th ed.). San Antonio, TX: The Psychological Corporation.

Wilde, M. C., Boake, C., & Sherer, M. (2000). Wechsler Adult Intelligence Scale–Revised Block Design broken configuration errors in nonpenetrating traumatic brain injury. *Applied Neuropsychology, 7*(4), 208–214.

Woodcock, R. W., McGrew, K. S., & Mather, N. (2001). *Woodcock-Johnson III Test of Cognitive Abilities.* Itasca, IL: Riverside Publishing.

4 Understanding and Assessing Executive Functioning

The concept of executive function (EF) is a relatively recent one and, despite the efforts of many, remains somewhat difficult to define. While it is not our goal here to consider the controversies surrounding the concept of EF, one is referred to in Meltzer (2007). In general, most psychologists and neuropsychologists agree that "executive function is an umbrella term for the complex cognitive processes that serve ongoing, goal-directed behaviors" (Meltzer, 2007). As described by Meltzer, "most of the definitions of executive function include many, but not all, of the following elements:

- Goal setting and planning
- Organization of behaviors over time
- Flexibility
- Attention and memory systems that guide these processes (e.g., working memory)
- Self-regulatory processes such as self monitoring." (pp. 1–2)

The roots of our understanding of EF extend back into adult behavioral neurology, particularly as they related to dementias (Denckla, 2007). As far back as the 1970s, A. R. Luria broadly described EF as a skill that enabled one to set a goal and maintain behavior to achieve it (1973). This understanding of EF was based on adult studies of lesions and brain injuries, a focus that excluded a consideration of EF in children over the course of development. This was largely due to three factors. First, the prefrontal cortex, considered to be the neural correlate of EF, was believed to mature only around adolescence. Second, symptoms of prefrontal injuries were believed to appear only in adulthood, and third, early EF tests were designed for adults and were not transferrable to children (Hughes, 2011). As a consequence, our understanding of EF within the context of development was sorely limited.

Although attention-deficit/hyperactivity disorder (ADHD), as we currently understand it, is a relatively recent diagnosis, hyperactivity, impulsivity and inattention in children has been well documented since the early nineteenth century and has been treated with stimulant medications since the nineteen thirties (Lange, Reichl, Lange, Tucha, & Tucha, 2010). In the 1990s, Barkley (1997) began to posit that problems in executive functioning skills underlay attention-deficit/hyperactivity disorder. Both lesion and neuroimaging studies supported the idea that both executive dysfunction (EDF) and ADHD were related to frontal lobe injury. As Denckla (2005) theorized, there were three levels of description that could be integrated—ADHD at the level of syndrome, EDF at the intermediate cognitive analysis level and at the neurological level, frontal, as well as striatal and cerebellar localizations. This linkage between ADHD and EDF then served as the impetus to look further into EF over the course of development and the underlying neural substrate related to both.

An accumulation of research on the development of executive functioning indicates that a number of executive functioning skills, such as cognitive flexibility and volitional control, can be discerned in infants as young as five months (Hughes, 2011). In a comprehensive review of the developmental literature related to executive functions, Hughes concludes that, "from infancy through adolescence, poor EF appears to be associated with risk taking and sensation seeking; this association highlights a developmental continuity in the interplay between top-down systems of EF and bottom-up reward-oriented systems" (2011, p. 264). Hughes further notes that "improvements in some aspects of EF (such as inhibitory control) can be seen from a very early age, while other aspects (e.g. planning) do not show marked improvements until much later on in development" (2011, p. 265).

In respect to the neural substrates of EF over the course of development, research indicates that "age-related improvements in EF appear hand in hand with increased frontostriatal activation, such that development is characterized by a progression from diffuse to specific neural substrate. Several age-related functional changes in children's performance on EF tasks suggest that this progressive localization of neural substrate may reflect increases in how strategic children and adolescents are when completing EF tasks" (Hughes, 2011, p. 265). However, it is important to note, particularly within the context of a constellation of abilities that are difficult to clearly define under one rubric, and which are changing over time, that any attempt to localize a specific skill becomes extremely complex. As Bernstein and Waber have argued,

> developmental abilities and disabilities, therefore, are likely to reflect processes associated with the construction, integration, and establishment of functional networks, rather than the functions of specific brain regions. From this perspective, the developmental terrain is far more complex and forbidding than that of the adult. The dramatic changes in executive capacities that occur over developmental time may well reflect these processes of construction of functional networks. . . . Moreover, it follows from this more systemic view that behavioral manifestations of executive functions can reflect a multiplicity of underlying factors that can influence the effectiveness and integrity of the network on which task execution depends rather than the integrity of a specific region or regions, as a more modular approach would suggest.
>
> (2007, p. 45)

While there is clearly a strong genetic contribution to the development of executive functions, evidence is mounting that indicates that environmental influences are also very significant (see Bernstein & Waber, 2007). A number of studies have documented factors such as premature birth, pre- and postnatal exposure to a variety of environmental toxins, such as alcohol, adverse family environments, maltreatment or neglect and early brain injury to have a deleterious effect on the development of EF skills. Longitudinal studies emphasize the importance of parenting skills and early intervention in terms of improving children's behavior and theory of mind skills (Hughes, 2011). Thus, while there is a genetic predisposition towards either intact or compromised EF skills, the neural substrate for the development of executive functions is also vulnerable to the influences of negative environmental factors. Fortunately, in some cases, the negative impact of these factors can be mitigated to some degree by early intervention and a sustained effort to teach EF skills (see Meltzer, 2007).

Neuroanatomy of Executive Functions

As suggested above, the frontal lobes have historically been considered to be the neural substrate for executive functions. This assumption has its historical roots in clinical observations, including the classic story of Phineas Gage, whose dynamiting accident resulted in a tamping iron penetrating his skull and creating a lesion in his left frontal lobe. His accident and subsequent radical change in personality were carefully documented in the nineteenth century. Subsequent research and observations in the clinic have generally supported the contention that the frontal lobes play a role in regulating executive functions. Nevertheless, as many have contended, the frontal regions may constitute a necessary but not sufficient neural substrate for carrying out the constellation of abilities subsumed under the category of executive functions.

The frontal lobes can be divided into the primary motor cortex located on the precentral gyrus and the premotor areas. On the lateral and medial surfaces are the prefrontal association areas. These include the dorsolateral prefrontal cortex (dlPFC) (see Figure 4.1), the ventromedial prefrontal cortex (vmPFC) and the medial prefrontal cortex (mPFC) (see Figure 4.2).

Functional neuroimaging studies have linked the dlPFC to working memory, "fluid" intelligence and verbal fluency (Lezak, Howieson, Bigler, & Tranel, 2012). Results from lesion studies indicate in the vmPFC regulation and maintenance of set, and regulation

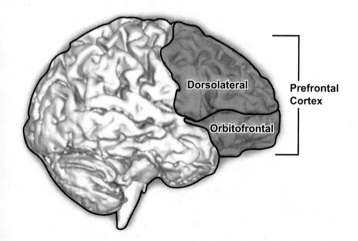

Figure 4.1 The dorsolateral prefrontal cortex (Zahr & Sullivan, 2008).

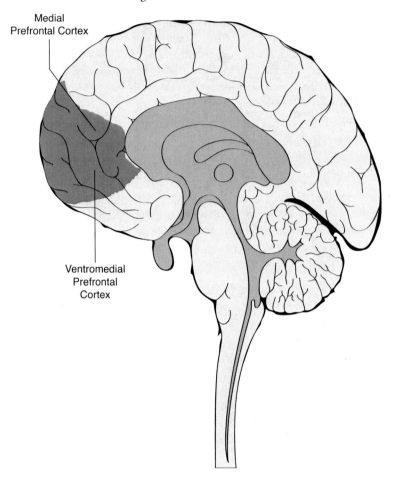

Figure 4.2 Ventromedial and medial prefrontal cortex (adapted from Patrick J. Lynch).

of ongoing behavior, including social conduct (Lezak et al., 2012). The mPFC is implicated in drive states, self-focused cognitive processes and the monitoring of ongoing
internal states (Lezak et al., 2012).

While these localized areas may be necessary pathways for the carrying out of a variety of executive functions, they are not solely sufficient. Each of these regions of the
prefrontal cortex is highly interconnected with both cortical and subcortical regions. As
Alvarez and Emory (2006) have contended, "the frontal lobes have multiple connections
to cortical, subcortical and brain stem sites. . . . The basis of 'higher-level' cognitive functions such as inhibition, flexibility of thinking, problem solving, planning, impulse control, concept formation, abstract thinking, and creativity often arise from much simpler,
'lower-level' forms of cognition and behavior. Thus, the concept of executive function
must be broad enough to include anatomical structures that represent a diverse and diffuse
portion of the central nervous system." (pp. 18–19).

In considering the neuroanatomy of executive functions in children, it is important to be mindful of the differences between the adult brain and that of the developing child. As Bernstein and Waber have noted,

> in development, executive processes are best understood in the context of functional networks constructed over the course of development. Whereas in the adult, disorders of executive processes are regularly associated with discrete lesions to regions of frontal cortex, executive functions in the child can be adversely affected by any influences that affect not only components of the network but also, its construction. Importantly, this may include experiential influences or context, which are intimately involved in the construction of these more differentiated networks. Understanding of executive functions requires scrutiny of contextual variables as well a neural correlates of behavior.
>
> (2007, p. 50)

In the following sections, we discuss various executive function subdomains and relate them to assessments that purport to measure them.

Subdomains of Executive Functions

As described above, a variety of definitions of EF have been proposed, and these definitions frequently overlap. Over fifty years ago, the neuropsychologist, A. R. Luria (1973) submitted that EF encompasses the ability to set and maintain behavior to achieve a future goal, a general definition that continues to pertain today. Doing so requires the simultaneous use of many cognitive processes, such as strategic planning, organization, flexibility and inhibition. In this manner, executive functions involve the engagement of higher order cognitive processes as a means to integrate other, more basic processes, such as perception, attention and memory. As a result, EF is a collection of subdomains, that guide, direct and manage cognitive, emotional and behavioral functions (Baron, 2004).

Many terms have been applied to EF, and some are considered subdomains. These specific skill sets work in harmony to reach a specific goal. It is no surprise then, that some of these skill sets overlap with other cognitive processes, as measured by separate portions of a neuropsychological assessment. As a result, many assessment batteries and tests have been developed in an attempt to isolate specific strengths and vulnerabilities within a child's set of skills. The following section further describes specific subdomains, what is known about each subdomain's neuroanatomy and commonly used assessments. Brief vignettes of individual children are used to highlight how each subdomain is relevant to cognitive, emotional and behavioral functioning.

Executive Functions and Intelligence

Are EF skills and intelligence related? In the previous chapter, cognition and intelligence were considered and assessment strategies discussed. Intelligence was defined as "the ability to adjust or adapt to the environment, the ability to learn or the ability to perform abstract thinking" (Sattler, 2008, p. 224). In contrast, the executive functions can be loosely defined as an "umbrella term for the complex cognitive processes that serve ongoing, goal-directed behaviors" (Meltzer, 2007, p. 1). While intelligence may deal with abstract reasoning, manipulating information and generating output, EF skills further contribute to daily activities, such as the morning routine required to get out of the house or acquiring groceries. Consider that an eleven-year-old girl may be able to successfully complete complex abstract mathematical problems but displays rigid and inflexible thinking or lacks good common sense. Likewise, a child who displays an average to low average IQ score may develop well-adapted compensatory study skills, relying on organization in order to become an overachiever. Helping parents understand the difference between EF and intelligence is important, as many children may display average or above average intellectual abilities but have difficulty completing basic tasks, such as packing a backpack.

Some moderate-to-strong correlation might exist between EF and intelligence (Baron, 2004). It is possible that the lower the IQ range, the greater the relationship may be between EF and IQ (Duncan, 1995). When assessing both EF and intelligence, it is important to be sure the tools are measuring the targeted construct. While more research is warranted, a small statistical study in adults found that EF skills and higher order cognitive processing, as measured by the D-KEFS (Delis, Kaplan, & Kramer, 2001) and the Wechsler Adult Intelligence Scale—Third Edition (WAIS-III), reveal some overlap (Davis, Peirson, & Finch, 2011). This study indicated that each assessment tool was indeed measuring a different construct but that a relationship exists between EF and general intelligence. This supports the practice assessing both general intelligence and EF.

Assessing Executive Functioning

Several types of executive functioning assessments have been developed. As a result of overlapping functionality in behavioral presentation, four different types of assessments capture various subdomains of EF:

1. Test batteries specifically designed to measure executive functioning. The *Delis-Kaplan Executive Function System* (D-KEFS; Delis, Kaplan, & Kramer, 2001) is one example and will be discussed at length in the following section.
2. Comprehensive test batteries, such as the *Wechsler Intelligence Scale for Children–Fourth Edition* (WISC-IV, 2003), that were designed to capture all neuropsychological functions. Certain subtests of these batteries assess EF abilities. As a result, certain subtests that were discussed related to cognitive assessments will also be discussed in this chapter.
3. Certain tests of cognitive function, such as the *Woodcock-Johnson III Tests of Cognitive Abilities* (WJ III, 2001) or the *Stanford-Binet Intelligence Scales: Fifth Edition* (SB5, 2003) also assess EF skills as they relate to cognitive functioning and intelligence.
4. Stand-alone tests were designed to measure EF, such as the *Wisconsin Card Sorting Test* (WCST, Heaton et al., 1993).

Many of these assessments and subtests were developed based on several core principles or tasks. As a result, there are similarities between subtests of many neuropsychological batteries. For example, both the NEPSY II (Korkman et al., 2007) and the

WISC-IV (Wechsler, 2003) utilize blocks to recreate geometric images. Go/no-go tests, category tests, tower tests, and trail-making tests encompass tasks frequently used in assessment batteries.

Go/no-go tests are a type of task often employed when assessing *inhibition.* These tests ask an individual to learn a response to a stimulus. For example, raise the left hand when one knock is heard, raise the right hand when two knocks are heard. After a pattern has been established, the rules change, requiring one to inhibit the previously learned pattern. For example, the individual is asked to keep the left hand still when one knock is heard, but the rule for the right hand remains unchanged (Miller, 2007). This type of task is required by subtests of several assessment batteries.

Category tests are designed to assess an individual's ability to accurately place items into given categories. For example, the Card Sorting Test on the D-KEFS (Delis et al., 2001) and the Wisconsin Card Sorting Test (WCST, Heaton et al., 1993) are tests that both use cards to assess an individual's ability to perceive and organize information into different categories. The ability to categorize items based on a known property is the foundation for other tests and subtests used to measure *concept generation, mental shifting or flexibility, rule learning and problem solving* (Baron, 2004).

Tower tests are a subset of tests that ask an individual to use manipulatives or computer images to build a specific structure. Depending on the test, the individual works from a visual model or is given explicit instructions to follow in order to create the structure. The different versions of this type of test are intended to measure EF including *working memory, planning, behavioral inhibition and rule application* (Baron, 2004).

Trail-making tests measure *alternating and sustained visual attention, sequencing, psychomotor speed, cognitive flexibility and inhibition/disinhibition.* These tasks ask individuals to scan a stimulus card containing randomized letters, numbers or letters and numbers. The individual is then asked to tap the letters or numbers in alphabetical or numerical order. They are then asked to tap out a number-letter sequence (1-A-2-B-3-C . . .). Trail-making tasks are widely utilized by practitioners because they are sensitive to overall brain dysfunction. However, they do not reliably localize the dysfunction. Poor performance may be due to slow processing speed, poor psychomotor speed, poor fine motor coordination, poor visual scanning or impairment in number or letter sequencing (Baron, 2004). The D-KEFS version of the trail-making test attempts to address these concerns.

While many neuropsychological batteries such as the NEPSY-II make use of elements of go/no-go, category, tower and trail-making tasks, the D-KEFS assessment battery was designed to comprehensively and specifically assess EF in both children and adults (Delis, Kaplan, & Kramer, 2001). Prior to the D-KEFS, psychometric instruments intended to measure EF skills utilized a single-score method for quantifying the broad range of skills encompassed in EF. The D-KEFS is composed of nine stand-alone tests that are intended to capture the various subdomains considered important to EF. While the WISC-IV and other neuropsychological batteries include subtests that may measure certain EF constructs; these serve more as a bench marker, signaling that more careful assessment of this EF skill may be warranted. Utilizing one of the D-KEFS stand-alone tests offers greater insight into areas of possible concern. The D-KEFS also offers an impressive normative sample and improved standardization procedures over previous EF assessment models (Davis et al., 2011). As a result, a direct comparison of subdomain abilities becomes possible, revealing EF strengths and vulnerabilities. The D-KEFS tests were designed and normed for use with individuals ranging in ages from 8–89, with the exception of the Proverbs Test which was designed for ages 16–89. Many of the tests are intended to be game-like and engaging for this wide age group. As a result, they address developmental concerns related to assessing EF in children.

Neuroanatomical studies have correlated EF with frontal lobe functioning, a portion of the brain that does not fully develop and mature until late adolescence or early adulthood (Kolb & Whishaw, 2009). Historically, it was thought that EF emerges during adolescence, but now evidence suggests that higher order processing skills are developing long before they are observable, functional and testable (Hughes & Graham, 2008). The prefrontal cortex, a nexus for EF, develops in growth spurts, thus, different elements of EF emerge irregularly. Organized, strategic, planned behavior is observable by age six. Organized speech, set maintenance and inhibition develop by age ten. By age twelve, complex planning and verbal fluency mature (Maricle, Johnson, & Avirett, 2010). Thus, assessing EF in children is a bit like assessing a moving target.

In the following section, various EF subdomains are further defined and a comprehensive table of assessment tools used to measure the subdomains is provided. The D-KEFS subtests are more elaborately discussed to demonstrate how each subdomain is assessed. Each section begins with a brief vignette relating the particular subdomain to a classroom environment.

Concept Generation/Formation

A fragile ten-year-old girl bounced through the door of a small therapeutic classroom aware that the day started with a play period. She was dressed brightly, had a large smile and enthusiastic presence. She didn't greet her well-known teachers, but proceeded to bounce to the center of the classroom. The shelves were filled with toys, stuffed animals, art materials and games. She had a variety of interests, primarily animals and weather patterns. In the middle of the lively and inviting room, she spun in a circle, smiling, and exclaimed, "I don't know what to do!" One of her teachers invited her to play with stuffed animals, but she simply shrugged her shoulders. She was then offered drawing materials, but again, a shy smile and shrug. For the next ten minutes, the teacher continued to offer activities that aligned with her interests, but she remained unable to decide how to spend the remainder of morning play. When it was announced it was time for morning snack, her petite body vibrated with frustration and she stomped to the classroom sink to wash her hands. Growling she stated, "I didn't even get to play."

Recalling that a core tenet of EF is "goal directed behavior," it seems implicit that a goal or intended behavior is either determined by an individual or assigned by another. This can be the first road block for an individual displaying EF difficulties. Developing goals or generating ideas requires a number of cognitive activities, such as determining relevant from irrelevant information, following general rules or guidelines and making use of existing knowledge in a new situation (Smidts, Jacobs, & Anderson, 2004). Difficulties with utilizing this type of information to develop goals leave individuals at a loss, such as the little girl in the brief vignette.

Measures of Concept Generation

D-KEFS Card Sorting Test: This test is composed of a series of cards with perceptual images and printed words. This allows the examinee to utilize both verbal and nonverbal approaches to this task. Two sorting conditions are required, Free Sorting and Sort Recognition. In the first approach, Free Sort, the individual is given six cards, asked to sort them into two groups, with as many category concepts or rules as possible, based on either the image or the word. For the second approach, Sort Recognition, the examiner separates six cards into two groups according to a concept or rule, then asks the examinee to describe the condition or rule (Delis et al., 2001). Neuroanatomical correlates of the Sorting Test have been identified through lesion and MRI studies. Patients with dorsolateral and ventromedial prefrontal lesions were impaired in their ability to correctly sort cards into categories (Keifer, 2010). Dimitrov, Grafman, Soares, and Clark (1999) found that patients with frontal lesions had difficulty with strategy planning, initiation, concept formation and flexibility. An MRI study found that the Sorting Test was significantly related to left frontal lobe functioning (Fine et al., 2009).

D-KEFS Twenty Questions: The individual is given a stimulus page with pictures of thirty common objects. The individual is then required to ask yes/no question to determine a target object. The fewer questions, the higher the score. The thirty common objects can be divided into different categories, such as living things versus nonliving. Asking the question, "Is the object living?" eliminates fifteen objects from the game versus asking specific concrete questions, such as, "Is it a goldfish?" (Delis et al., 2001). A study by Huey et al. (2009) found a significant correlation between left frontal atrophy and poor performance on this task. Patients with prefrontal lesions also asked more questions and used poorer strategies on Twenty Questions (Baldo, Delis, Wilkins, & Shimamura, 2004).

Wisconsin Card Sorting Test: The individual is given a stack of cards containing various stimuli of different numbers, shapes and colors. The individual is asked to sort them into the correct categories known only to the examiner, only being told when he or she is correct or incorrect. The correct solution changes in a prescribed manner known only to the examiner. This test is designed for ages 6.6 to 89.11.

Plan, Organize, Reason and Problem Solving

It was time to make art. The eleven-year-old boy always looked forward to the one time a week when teachers put out a few art materials and invited the students to make whatever they chose. Today was paper folding with tape and staples, his favorite. He sat for a brief period of time, eagerly waiting for an idea. Inspiration struck, and he simply began twisting paper into shapes, bending, folding and forming . . . something. When a teacher asked him what he was making he shrugged, saying, "It started as a building from Zelda, but it doesn't look like that." The teacher offered assistance, but it quickly became clear that the boy had an idea in mind, but no ability to sequence the steps necessary to achieve the outcome or consider the properties of the material. As the teachers asked what the tower building looked like, she tried to help him develop a plan to reach the desired outcome utilizing the material at hand. He balked at developing a sequence of steps, preferring to adjust his idea of what he was making, rather than attempt to make a plan. Soon, paper surrounded him, crumpled and twisted, on the table and floor. He was still happy and content, but produced nothing that met his description. When clean up time was announced, he gathered MOST of his papers, stuffed them into his backpack returning to clean up the missed papers only when the teacher pointed them out.

Once a goal or idea is selected or given, an intentional pathway towards achievement must be generated. This generally includes developing novel cognitive plans or strategies for solving problems (Kolb & Whishaw, 2009). To do so, individuals must utilize reasoning and decision-making skills (Goel, Makale, & Grafman, 2004; Goldberg, Podell, Bilder, & Jaeger, 2000). Inherent to these abilities, underlying cognitive skills, such as organizing material, sequencing steps, understanding the material or information, and adhering to rules or constraints, are necessary. The processes of reasoning and decision making are also crucial components of EF.

Reasoning is the process of forming conclusions or making inferences based on presented information that can lead to a decision. Several types of reasoning have been defined, such as deductive, inductive and abductive. In simple testing situations, most often, reasoning leads to a decision about selecting a single answer, known as a veridical decision (Goldberg & Podell, 2000). While this assesses cognitive abilities and often determines an overall level of intelligence, it does not replicate the complexities of daily life. Adaptive decision making involves objective information and weighing individual priorities and preferences in relationship to external parameters (Goldberg & Podell, 2000). In doing so, decisions are made that take into account the ambiguity of daily life. For example, imagine deciding on which route to take to the grocery store. There may be multiple routes and varying traffic patterns. A more direct route takes you through an industrial strip filled with stop lights, or you can take a slightly longer, more scenic route along the river. Your priorities, time, or scenery may factor into the decision you make. Here, in adaptive decision making, cognition and emotional expectations commingle to develop expected outcomes of decisions (Weller, Levin, & Bechara, 2010). When assessing reasoning abilities, it is important that the assessment tool captures both veridical and adaptive reasoning abilities (Goldberg & Podell, 2000). Part of this process also includes ongoing immediate feedback as well as learning from previous experiences. This information influences the decision-making process as it occurs.

Research shows that different types of reasoning and decision making utilize different regions of the brain. Reasoning with meaningful, familiar material engages the temporal lobe of the left hemisphere. A bilateral parietal system is involved when reasoning with meaningless, unfamiliar material. Both reasoning systems engage the bilateral basal ganglia nuclei, right cerebellum, fusiform gyri and left prefrontal cortex (Goel et al., 2004). The integration of emotional and cognitive information is strongly believed to have a foundation in the ventromedial prefrontal cortex (vmPFC; Bachara, Damasio, Damasio, & Anderson, 1994). Adults with damage to the vmPFC are unable to develop anticipatory emotional responses, impacting the ability to detect future punishment, a helpful skill when making decisions (Bachara, Damasio, Tranel, & Damasio, 1997). As a result, individuals with vmPFC damage have intact general cognitive abilities (IQ) but suffer socially at work and interpersonally tend to engage in risky behaviors and struggle making financial decisions (Damasio, 1994).

Measures of Planning, Reasoning and Problem Solving

Four D-KEFS subtests can be used to assess planning, reasoning and problem solving.

D-KEFS Twenty Questions: See above.

D-KEFS Tower: The task begins when the examiner places five disks of varying sizes in a predetermined pattern on three pegs. The individual is then shown a picture of the same materials, arranged differently, creating a tower. They are asked to move the disks across the pegs, using as few moves as possible, to achieve the end position. Two rules are outlined: 1) only one disk can be moved at a time and 2) never place a larger disk on a smaller disk (Delis et al., 2001). Focal lesions of the dorsolateral prefrontal cortex result in impaired performance on the tower test, particularly in respect to rule violations (Yochim, Baldo, Kane, & Delis, 2009).

D-KEFS Proverbs: This task presents proverbs under two conditions: 1) Free Inquiry and 2) Multiple Choice. Under the Free Inquiry condition, the examiner reads a proverb, then the examinee attempts to orally interpret the proverb without assistance. Answers are scored in terms of accuracy and level of abstraction. Under the Multiple Choice condition, the examiner reads a proverb to the examinee who is then given four possible explanations, and who then must select the best option. The set of multiple-choice answers include a correct abstract interpretation, a correct concrete interpretation and incorrect phonemically similar response and an unrelated saying (Delis et al., 2001). As a measure of concept formation, the Proverbs subtest of the D-KEFS was adapted from earlier Proverbs tests. Performance on this subtest is impaired to a greater degree in patients with frontal lobe epilepsy than it is in patients with temporal lobe epilepsy (McDonald et al., 2008).

D-KEFS Word Context: The main task is for the individual to discover the meaning of a made-up or mystery word utilizing context clues within a sentence. Each mystery word is embedded into five sentences from which the examinee must derive the word meaning. The individual must use as few sentences possible to determine the meaning. The first sentence revealed to the examinee is the most vague. Following sentences increase in specificity (Delis et al., 2001).Relative to healthy patients, patients with frontal lobe lesions were significantly impaired on this test with left frontal lobe lesion patients performing somewhat worse (Keil et al., 2005).

Table 4.1 briefly describes other assessments tools targeted towards assessing planning reasoning and problem solving.

Table 4.1 Planning, reasoning and problem solving.

Assessment	Description	Age Range
Category Tests	see text above	8.0–89.0
Tower Tests	see text above	8.0–89.0
Trail Making	see text above	
NEPSY II: Block Construction	This timed test requires the child to reproduce three-dimensional constructions from models or from two-dimensional drawings.	3–16
NEPSY II: Route Finding	The child is shown a schematic map with a target house, then asked to find the same house on a larger map with other houses and streets.	5–12
SB5: Fluid Reasoning Test, Nonverbal: Object Series	The individual is asked to hand the examiner an object that is the same shape as a target object.	2–85+
SB5: Fluid Reasoning Test, Non-Verbal: Matrices	The individual is asked to point to an image that best completes a series or matrix.	2–85+
SB5: Fluid Reasoning Test, Verbal: Early Reasoning	The individual looks at a series of pictures and relates what is happening or they are given a series of chips with images on them. They must then sort the chips into logical groups.	2–85+
SB5: Fluid Reasoning Test, Verbal: Verbal Absurdities	The individual listens to a statement, then tells what is silly or impossible about the statement.	2–85+
SB5: Fluid Reasoning Test, Verbal: Verbal Analogies	The individual must complete a four word analogy by supplying the first and last word.	2–85+
UNIT Reasoning Test: Analogic Reasoning (Symbolic)	The individual is presented with an incomplete conceptual or geometric analogy in matrix form and asked to complete it by pointing at one of four options.	5–17
UNIT Reasoning Test: Cube Design (Nonsymbolic)	Viewing a stimulus image, the individual is requested to replicate the image using green and white one inch cubes.	5–17
UNIT Reasoning Test: Mazes (Nonsymbolic)	In a time limited task, the individual is asked to draw a path from the center of a maze to the exit without mistakes.	5–17
WJ III-COG: Concept Formation	The individual is presented with a variety of shapes that are related conceptually. They are asked to determine the rule for each set of stimuli.	2–80+
WJ III-COG: Planning	The individual traces a pattern without removing the pencil from the paper or retracing any lines.	2–80+
WJ III-COG: Pair Cancellation	The individual is asked to locate and mark a repeated pattern in a 3 minute time period.	2–80+
WJ III-COG: Analysis-Synthesis	The individual is given instructions on how to perform an increasingly complex procedure. Involves a miniature system of mathematics, symbolic formulation and logic.	2–80+

Assessment	Description	Age Range
WISC-IV: Block Design	Using blocks that are colored red, white or diagonally divided into red and white, the child is asked to reproduce model designs with increasing complexity.	6–16.11
WISC-IV: Matrix Reasoning	The child is shown a matrix with one missing square, and is asked to select the picture that fits the array from five options.	6–16.11
WISC-IV: Picture Completion	Given an image of common objects or scenes with missing parts, the child is asked to identify the missing part.	6–16.11
WISC-IV Integrated: Elithorn Mazes	The child is asked to draw a path beginning at the bottom of a maze through a specified number of dots to an exit at the top of the maze.	6–16.11

Shift Set/Perseveration

Sam was a sweet, ten-year-old kid with a good sense of humor and loquacious nature. When discussing one of his many interests, ranging from 1980s TV shows to mythological creatures, Sam had difficulty stopping. Regardless of the classroom activity, math, science, art and during transitions, if a topic of discussion cued Sam to think about a preferred interest, he could NOT stop talking about it. During a reading lesson about a folktale, Sam associated an animal character to the Minotaur and began a monologue. Teachers and peers were able to help him quiet down so the lesson could continue, but Sam sat quietly slumped in his chair. When asked about the characters of the folktale, Sam looked at the teacher, blinking, and continued his monologue where he had stopped five minutes earlier.

Shifting sets is the ability to perform a task, then stop and begin another. When making a transition from one task to another, the individual must set aside one goal, its requirements and rules and begin a new activity with its own set of requirements and rules. Some evidence suggests that when allowed to focus on one task at a time, performance speed is faster than when asked to switch between two or more tasks (Hubner, Dreisbach, Haider, & Kluwe, 2003). For example, while at work, perhaps you are completing a report, but are constantly receiving e-mailed memos that distract you from your goal, writing the report. Shifting between reading memos and writing the report may slow your progress.

A related construct, perseveration, is the repetition of a behavior when it is inappropriate or unhelpful (Yerys & Munakata, 2006). Typically developing children have the tendency to rely on what appears to be perseverative behaviors as they integrate new, meaningful experiences into their behavioral repertoire (Moriguchi, Kanda, Ishiguro, & Itakura, 2010). The inability to recognize and stop perseveration of speech or behaviors can be an indication of learning or social disabilities. The classic example of a child diagnosed with autism, who doesn't play with toy cars, but prefers to line them up in rows, illustrates one end of the perseveration spectrum. On the other end, using one problem-solving strategy, despite its ineffectiveness, is another. Some studies suggest that perseveration on life events and thought processes are present in adolescent individuals suffering from depression (Lien, Yang, Kuo, & Chen, 2011).

Cognitive flexibility relies on the ability to move between tasks or shift set, avoiding perseveration, while integrating new information or stimuli. The ability to move between two task sets and make adjustments varies greatly among individuals. The following section outlines numerous assessments for shifting set and perseveration.

Measures of Set Shifting

Four D-KEFS subtests can be used to assess set shifting ability. Each of these subtests has various test conditions, with one geared towards set shifting and cognitive flexibility.

D-KEFS Color-Word Interference Test (Condition 4): The individual is presented with a page on which patches of color are printed in rows and is asked to name the colors as rapidly as possible. The individual is then asked to read rows of color words printed in black ink. On the third condition, the individual is asked to name the different colors of the ink that rows of words are printed in. Lastly, the individual is required to switch between naming the ink color of words or reading the word if it is enclosed in a rectangle. This requires that the examinee inhibit responding to certain stimuli and display cognitive flexibility by switching cognitive set. The individual is assessed in time, correct responses and uncorrected and self-correct measures (Delis et al., 2001). This test is a variation on the Stroop test (see Table 4.2) with the added subtest requiring the individual to switch cognitive set. Impaired performance on the Stroop was most often correlated with frontal lobe lesions (Demakis, 2004) while functional imaging studies have also implicated the anterior cingulate cortex (Ravnkilde et al., 2002).

D-KEFS Design Fluency (Condition 3): This subtest has three conditions, each utilizing a row of boxes containing an array of dots. The examinee must use four lines to connect the dots in as many combinations as possible, making unique designs in each box. Condition 1: Filled Dots, requests that within sixty seconds, the examinee connects five solid dots, using four lines, making as many patterns possible. In Condition 2: Empty Dots, the examinee is presented with rows of boxes filled with five filled dots and five empty dots. They are asked to connect only the empty dots using four lines, making as many patterns as possible in sixty seconds. In the final condition, Condition 3: Switching, the examinee is again presented with boxes containing filled and empty dots. They are requested to connect the dots, making unique patterns using four lines, alternating between filled and unfilled dots, again within sixty seconds (Delis et al., 2001). The third condition requires cognitive flexibility. Furthermore, responding to three sets of directions, each requiring different behavior, also requires set shifting. McDonald et al. (2005a) found that patients with frontal lobe epilepsy created fewer designs in the third, switching, condition than did those with temporal lobe epilepsy and healthy controls.

D-KEFS Trail-Making (Condition 4): This subtest of the D-KEFS has five separate conditions: Visual Scanning, Number Sequencing, Letter Sequencing, Number-Letter Switching and Motor Speed. Most relevant to shifting set abilities is the fourth condition, Number-Letter Switching. The other conditions rule out difficulties in fundamental functional components required for the Number-Letter Switching condition, including visual scanning, number sequencing, letter sequencing and motor speed in drawing lines. After determining these fundamental components are intact, the examinee is presented with the Number-Letter Switching condition. An array containing numbers and letters is shown. They are asked to draw a line, starting at 1 connecting it to *A,* then to 2, and from 2 connecting it to *B* and so on. The examinee is given two hundred and forty seconds to complete this alternating pattern of numbers and letters which ends at the letter *P.* The examiner stops the individual if they make a mistake, places an *X* on it with no explanation and asks them to continue the task (Delis et al., 2001). Yochim, Baldo, Nelson, and Delis (2007) found that patients with dorsolateral prefrontal cortical lesions were slower and made an elevated number of errors compared to controls on this task. McDonald et al. (2005b) reported that individuals with frontal lobe epilepsy had difficulty with the switching task.

D-KEFS Verbal Fluency (Condition 3): This subtest is composed of three conditions, the third targeting set shifting. Under the first condition, Letter Fluency, the examinee is asked to say words that begin with a specified letter as quickly as possible in three trials of sixty seconds each. The second condition, Category Fluency, the individual is asked in two trials of sixty seconds each to say words that belong to a determined semantic category as quickly as possible. In the third condition, related to set shifting, Category Switching, the examinee is again asked to say a list of words as quickly as possible during a sixty-second time limit. This time, they must alternate between two different semantic categories (Delis et al., 2001). In respect to the third condition that requires set shifting, Troyer et al. (1998) found that patients with left dorsolateral and superior medial frontal lobe lesions tended to switch clusters of categories on a verbal fluency test less frequently than those without lesions in these areas.

Table 4.2 briefly describes other assessment tools that are useful when measuring set-shifting abilities.

Table 4.2 Cognitive flexibility.

Assessment	Description	Age Range
NEPSY II: Auditory Attention and Response Set	The child listens to a series of words and touches the appropriate circle when the target word is heard.	5–16
Stroop Color Word Test	The child is asked to name patches of colors in rows as quickly as possible. The child then reads rows of color words as quickly as possible. Lastly, the child names the color of ink in which rows of color words are printed rather than read the word itself (e.g. the word red printed in green ink).	5–18
Wisconsin Card Sorting Test	The individual is given a stack of cards containing various stimuli of different numbers, shapes and colors. They are asked to sort them into the correct categories, only being told when they are correct. The correct solution can change unexpectedly.	6.6–89.11
Cognitive Assessment System: Expressive Attention	For children under 8 the child is asked to name the color of ink. For children 8 and older, they are asked to read color words printed in black ink. Next they are asked to name the color of a series of triangles. Finally, they are asked to read color words printed in dissonant ink colors.	5–17.11

Inhibition/Distractibility

A small group of eight- and nine-year-old students were playing a math game, rolling a set of dice, adding the digits together and moving their pawn along a colorful board game. Each player was responsible for adding their own roll. However, Casey could not stop herself from calling out the addend as other kids rolled. She sat restlessly in her chair. Her peers were growing increasingly frustrated as she called out answers during their turns. The teacher gently reminded her to allow others to add during their turns, but she continued to call out answers. The game halted, and the group had a brief discussion and it was explained that Casey was not trying to interfere, but had difficulty stopping herself. The other children were understanding, and Casey was relieved to know she wasn't in trouble. She was given a special cushion to sit on and a fidget toy to play with while other children took their turns. The understanding and use of a sensory diet helped, but Casey occasionally called out answers anyway.

The ability to inhibit both behavioral and cognitive responses is becoming a focus of greater investigation as it relates to attention. Disinhibition is a clinical feature of many frontal lobe disorders, including ADHD (Miller, 2007). Simply put, inhibition is the ability to filter various forms of information to allocate attention. While reading this section, you may be in a crowded café. The murmur of conversation, the sound of music and the smell of pastries are all around. You may be pondering your next activity, perhaps grocery shopping, or you are reflecting on a disagreement with a colleague. Yet, you inhibit the desire to purchase a pastry and put off thinking about your future plans to finish reading this section, while taking copious notes. You are inhibiting both behavioral and cognitive responses to external and internal stimuli, allowing yourself to achieve a goal.

Neuronal networks use neurotransmitters to coordinate and communicate functioning. The type of neuron, neurotransmitter and receptor determine if the next neuron in the line of communication will fire an action potential. GABA, a common neurotransmitter in the brain, most commonly causes an inhibitory response in neighboring neurons, alerting them not to fire. This inhibitory communication allows for specific communication between neurons and neural networks to occur. Without inhibitory responses, many neurons of all kinds would fire incessantly, making functional behavior impossible (Bear, Connors, & Paradiso, 2007). This process of fine tuning neuronal communication through inhibition is a bit like a red stop light. The stop light halts the flow of traffic, allowing cars from another direction to pass through a specifically determined pathway. Without the red light, the cars would mingle, eventually reaching their destination, but not without passing through a messy traffic jam.

The ability to selectively respond to cognitive and sensory information plays a role in planning and problem solving (Baron, 2004). Several forms of inhibition are currently being investigated, including cognitive inhibition, interference control, and oculomotor inhibition. One theoretical model of EF posits the following for behavioral inhibition: 1) developing a response to an event requires inhibition, 2) stopping an ongoing response or response pattern allows for the decision-making process of HOW to respond and 3) this protects the delay period and self-directed response, filtering competing events and possible responses (Barkley, 1994, 1997).

Research indicates that response inhibition is mediated by the frontal cerebral regions (Baron, 2004). Studies of orbitofrontal, inferior frontal and gyrus rectus lesions implicate these regions in inhibitory efficacy, regions of the brain that develop throughout childhood and adolescence. Thus, inhibition responses may look different at different ages. Adult levels of efficacy on EF tasks may be observed in early adolescence or in young adulthood. This indicates that EF impairment in childhood may not necessarily be related to disturbances in anterior frontal lobe development as it would in adulthood. Because of the variance in the timing of frontal lobe development, how well a child performs on an EF assessment of inhibition can be difficult to predict.

Measures of Inhibition

D-KEFS Color Word Interference Test: As described previously, this test is composed of four conditions, the first two of which establish baseline abilities before measuring inhibition. Condition 1 requires the individual to name color patches. Condition 2 asks the individual to read color words printed in black ink. Condition 3 measures inhibition by presenting the individual with a list of color words, each printed in an ink different from the word. The individual must name the color printed, not the written word. Condition 4 measures both inhibition and set shifting by asking the individual to name the color of the ink with which the word is printed unless the word is enclosed in a rectangle, in which case, the individual merely reads the word. In this manner, one must switch between naming the ink color and reading the word. As described above, impaired performance on the Stroop test, a test comparable to the first three conditions of the Color Word Interference Test, was most often correlated with frontal lobe lesions (Demakis, 2004), while functional imaging studies also implicated the anterior cingulate cortex (Ravnkilde et al., 2002).

The D-KEFS Design Fluency and Towers subtests as well as the Stroop and the Category test are also used as measures of Inhibition.

Table 4.3 outlines other helpful tests and subtest for measuring inhibition.

Table 4.3 Inhibition.

Assessment	Description	Age Range
Contingency Naming Test (CNT)	The individual is required to name the color or shape of various stimuli according to different rules.	7–15
Go-No-Go tests of reciprocal motor movements	See text above	
NEPSY II: Auditory Attention and Response Set	On the first section, the child listens to a series of words and touches the appropriate colored circle when the target word is heard. On the second section, the child touches a yellow circle when hearing red and a red circle when hearing yellow, thus inhibiting an automatic response.	5–16

(Continued)

Table 4.3 (Continued)

Assessment	Description	Age Range
NEPSY II: Statue	The child is asked to maintain a body position with eyes closed during a 75-second period and inhibit the impulse to respond to auditory distractors.	3–6
Trail Making	See text above	
WJ III-COG: Pair Cancellations	The child is asked to locate and mark a repeated pattern in a 3-minute time period.	2–80+

Fluency

Fluency is related to the ability to spontaneously respond to environmental cues or stimuli (Kolb & Whishaw, 2009). This includes the ability to generate new responses to the cues and stimuli (Henry, Messer, & Nash, 2012). In testing situations, both verbal and nonverbal fluency is assessed. Verbal fluency is measured through the ability to generate words in response to a set criteria, such as "list as many animals as you can." Damage in the left orbitofrontal region of the prefrontal cortex and perhaps the right orbitofrontal cortex have been implicated in difficulties with verbal fluency (Kolb & Whishaw, 2009). Because of the role played by frontal lobes regarding verbal fluency, it is likely that this skill will continue to develop into adolescence and is more sensitive to neurodevelopment. It is important to note that tests of verbal fluency are not independent of intelligence, vocabulary, attention and working memory (Baron, 2004).

Several terms have been used referring to tests of verbal fluency. This includes tests of word fluency, verbal word generation, word retrieval, phonemic fluency, rapid verbal naming, controlled oral word association (COWA), the FAS Test, and controlled word association (CWA). Tests of *semantic fluency* require individuals to list words in response to a category cue. Letter fluency tests require individuals to list words, verbally or written, that begin with the same letter.

A nonverbal analogue to verbal fluency has also been developed, sometimes called design fluency. Difficulty with drawing simple, spontaneous and unique images is also associated with frontal lobe deficits. In children, poor performance on verbal and design fluency tests has been associated with a variety of clinical conditions, including fetal alcohol syndrome, closed head injury and autism. In adults, diminished verbal and performance fluency has been associated with Alzheimer's disease, Parkinson's disease and traumatic brain injury (Van der Elst, Hurks, Wassenberg, Meijs, & Jolles, 2011).

There is evidence that both EF and emotional processing are mediated by the frontal circuits. In terms of fluency, some studies suggest that being in a positive affective state increases performance on verbal fluency tests. Interestingly, negative affect states do not have an impact on performance in either verbal or design fluency. While fluency and positive affect share some neuroanatomical regions, specific circuitry is unknown (Carvalho & Ready, 2010).

Measures of Fluency

D-KEFS Design Fluency (Condition 1): This subtest has three conditions, each utilizing a row of boxes containing an array of dots. The examinee must use four lines to connect the dots in as many combinations possible, making unique designs in each box. Condition 1: Filled Dots, requests that within sixty seconds, the examinee connects five solid dots, using four lines, making as many patterns possible (Delis et al., 2001). Keifer (2010) reported that composite scores on the Design Fluency subtest were lower in patients with dorsolateral prefrontal lesions compared to patients with ventromedial prefrontal lesions, and both were lower than nonfrontal patients.

D-KEFS Verbal Fluency (Condition 1 and 2): This subtest is composed of three conditions, the third targeting set shifting. Under the first condition, Letter Fluency, the examinee is asked to say words that begin with a specified letter as quickly as possible in three trials of sixty seconds each. In the second condition, Category Fluency, the individual is asked in two trials of sixty seconds each to say, as quickly as possible, words that belong to a determined semantic category (Delis et al., 2001). A number of structural and functional imaging studies have demonstrated that frontal damage impairs mostly letter fluency with the greatest effects due to left hemisphere lesions, while semantic or category fluency is most impacted by lesions in the temporal lobe (Lezak et al., 2012).

Table 4.4 further describes fluency assessments.

Table 4.4 Fluency.

Assessment: Letter Fluency	Description	Age
NEPSY II—Word Generation (Condition 3 and 4)	In two trials, the individual is given 60 seconds to list as many S and F words as possible, without using proper nouns.	7–16
FAS and C, P, B, R	Under a time limit, individuals are asked to say or write as many words beginning with the indicated letter as quickly as possible. Certain letters have been determined to fall within differing ranges from easy to difficult.	Varies, based on usage

Semantic Fluency	Description	Age
Animal Fluency	Within a time limit, individuals are asked to name as many animals as possible.	Varies, based on usage
McCarthy Scales of Children's Abilities: Category Verbal Fluency	The child is asked to name things to eat, animals, things to wear and things to ride.	2.6–8.6
NEPSY II—Word Generation (Condition 1 and 2)	In two trials of 60 seconds, the child is asked to first list as many animals as they can, then to list items you can eat and drink.	3–16

(*Continued*)

Table 4.4 (Continued)

Design Fluency	Description	Age
NEPSY—Design Fluency Modification	The child is given an array of structured dots, asked to connect them generating as many unique patterns as possible, using four lines, in 60 seconds. They are then asked to do the same in an array of unstructured dots.	5–12
Ruff Figural Fluency Test	A five part test, the individual is given an array of boxes. For each part, dots are arranged differently and some with other shapes. Individuals are asked to connect the dots, creating unique patterns in each box.	19–80

Behavioral and Emotional Regulation

A small group of eight- and nine-year-olds were lining up, transitioning to the computer lab. As children laughed, chatted and mingled into a group, they formed a semblance of a line. The happy atmosphere was disrupted when an angry voice rose above the rest: "You took my place in line!" Tears of rage streamed down Connor's face as he continued to rant, stepping forward, closing the space between himself and a peer. "You can't do that!!" he screamed. A teacher stepped between the two children, asking what had happened. Connor continued in an aggressive manner to relay that his peer, whom he'd been happily chatting with, stepped in front of him, placing Connor in the last position in line. "I hate being last! I don't have to be first, but I hate last!" In a series of mediations and negotiations, the two children agreed to walk alongside each other, so neither would be last. But the trio agreed Connor's reaction was too big for the situation. Also agreed was that, further conversations would take place, hopefully elucidating the underlying cause for the big reaction.

The ability to regulate emotional and behavioral responses to internal and external cues is an important element of executive functioning. Being mindful that the EF skills allow us to attain a certain goal, managing emotional and behavioral responses to the goal itself is crucial. Like fraternal twins, behavioral and emotional regulation are related and influenced by the same inner and outer factors, but distinctly different and separate. While separate, an inherent difficulty making conceptual distinctions between the two is common (Batum & Yagmurlu, 2007). The following discussion briefly defines these concepts as they relate to EF and provides a historical context for their development.

In the process of an event taking place, such as attaining a goal, an emotion registers the significance of the event or action as the individual perceives the event as noteworthy. The degree of determined significance influences the extent of the emotional response, as well as the urgency (Campos, Frankel, & Camras, 2004). Emotional stimuli span all nature of events, both physical and mental. Examples include perceived insult, threat to life, social and relational interactions, and avoidance or resolution of a problem.

Emotional regulation refers to the modification of this system as emotions develop and manifest in behavior (Campos et al., 2004). The regulation of emotional response refers to the ability to evaluate and modify the emotional reaction and employ strategies, such as self-soothing, delay of gratification and tolerance in accordance with intensity and temporal features (Degangi, Breinbauer, Roosevelt, Porges, & Greenspan, 2000; Fox, 1994). This applies to the modulation of both positive and negative emotions (Bridges, Denham, & Ganiban, 2004). Children are often in the process of learning how to regulate their own emotions. At a young age, regulation occurs from an external source (Eisenberg & Spinrad, 2004). For example, a young child or infant cries at the sound of thunder and receives comfort (soothing) from an adult. As the child grows, he or she is more able to self-soothe, perhaps by reaching for a blanket or stuffed animal. At times, this process of regulating emotions is referred to as affect regulation. While the word *emotion* connotes an internal experience, affect is associated with the observable expression of the emotion. A smile for happy, tears for sadness, a scowl for anger.

In contrast, behavioral regulation is often described in terms of attentional processes, inhibitory control and impulsivity (Posner & Rothbart, 2000). These mechanisms are thought to be responsible for an individual's ability to suppress an inappropriate behavioral response to internal or external cues or to maintain a desired response (Posner & Rothbart, 2000). Part of behavioral regulation is the awareness that certain social rules and standards exist and act as guidelines (Kalpidou, Power, Cherry, & Gottfried, 2004). In other words, this is the ability to modulate behavior utilizing inhibition and attention to maintain appropriate actions and reactions during an emotional response.

Reference Box 4.1 Thomas and Chess Nine Temperament Characteristics

- Activity level
- Regulation/Rhythmicity of biological functioning
- Approach/Withdrawal to novel situations
- Adaptability to environmental change
- Intensity of energy or emotional responses
- Mood—tendency toward positive or negative affect
- Distractibility
- Persistence and attention
- Sensory threshold

Effortful control is a concept that attempts to explain the connection between emotional and behavioral regulation, EF and temperament (Rothbart & Rueda, 2005). Even infants display different temperamental tendencies. These innate tendencies are biologically derived and influenced by environmental factors, even prior to birth (Shiner et al., 2012). In 1956, Thomas and Chess began studying temperament styles in children, including infants, and developed a list of nine observable characteristics Reference Box 4.1). More recent studies link these biologically determined mechanisms and their behavioral consequences. The term *effortful control* describes the link between temperamental style and EF constructs.

The ability to inhibit a dominant response, in order to perform the socially acceptable response, detect errors and engage in planning, has a biological basis (Rothbart & Rueda, 2005). An individual must have the ability to inhibit a response, shift attention and delay impulses. The link between temperament and EF was described in three studies measuring symptoms of sleep disturbances, hypersensitivity to sensory stimulation, irritability and poor self-calming to later issues of developing homeostasis, separation and sensory processing (Degangi et al., 2000). In the typically developing infant, attentional ability is stimulus driven, attending to interesting sensory information or as a distress regulator alerting caregivers. Within one year, infants develop the ability to selectively control their attention (Rueda, Posner, & Rothbart, 2005). At the age of two years, children increasingly develop executive attention skills. Thus, they are more able to suppress reactive responses, take in information and plan and utilize coping strategies. This ability continues to develop during the preschool period (ages three to five) with five-year-olds displaying greater compliance to social norms and rules, regulation of reactivity and improved social problem solving (Kalpidou et al., 2005).

Assessing self-regulation in children poses interesting challenges that do not diminish the necessity of its inclusion in an evaluation on EF. This brief discussion on emotional and behavioral regulation suggests something about the complexity of regulatory operations. Current assessment of effortful control relies on two methods, self-report and observation, utilizing questionnaires and performance-based measures. Inherent issues of rater bias and assuring individuals understand self-regulatory concepts impact the results of these assessment tools. While the link between effortful control, emotional regulation and behavioral regulation to externalizing problems in children has been made, continued research to develop reliable and valid assessment instruments is necessary (Muris, van der Pennen, Sigmond, & Mayer, 2008).

A child's difficulty with self-regulation poses particular difficulties during the evaluation process and, on a pragmatic level, the distinction between behavioral and emotional regulation becomes moot, as they often tend to overlap and create a synergy between each other.

Measures of Emotional and Behavioral Regulation

Table 4.5 outlines questionnaires that are useful for assessing emotional and behavioral regulation.

Table 4.5 Emotional and behavioral checklists.

Assessment	Description	Age
Millon Pre-Adolescent Clinical Inventory (M-PACI) and/or The Millon Adolescent Clinical Inventory (MACI)	Questionnaire assesses personality development and identifies current clinical concerns.	9–12 and 13–18

Assessment	Description	Age
Children's Behavior Questionnaire	Assess 15 elements of temperament.	3–7
Behavior Assessment System for Children, 2nd Edition (BASC2)	This checklist is a measure of social, emotional and behavioral problems, and adjustment to home, school and community environments. Different forms can be completed by the teacher as well as parents/caregivers. It also has a self-report form when appropriate. It develops, among others, both Internalizing and Externalizing composites based on a variety of separate scales.	2–21
Achenbach Child Behavior Checklist	Using a Likert scale, parents rate the behavior of their child across various domains.	6–18

Use of Feedback/Self-Monitoring

Part of problem solving and attaining a goal is monitoring the performance of one's actions. While working on a task, there is the possibility of making an error. Observing and correcting errors ensures greater success and is considered part of the EF system (Gehring & Knight, 2000). It is important for the individual to have awareness of both self-monitoring of performance (accuracy) and self-monitoring of attention for efficacy of learning (Harris, Frielander, Saddler, Frizzelle, & Graham, 2005). It is also important for the individual to monitor the environment and passage of time, understanding *when* to perform a task and *how much time* is required (Mantyla, Carelli, & Forman, 2007). Self-monitoring is related to self-regulation, impacting both behavior and academic performance. Response to feedback and self-monitoring also influences the process of maintaining a decision or adapting a course of action.

The lateral prefrontal cortex and interactions with the anterior cingulate cortex have been linked to self-monitoring activities by electrophysiological and neuro-imaging studies (Gehring & Knight, 2000). Furthermore, fMRI and event-related potential (ERP) studies indicate that the dorsolateral prefrontal cortex, including the supplementary eye fields, rostral cingulate motor area and dorsal anterior cingulate cortex are involved in functional monitoring (Sokhadze et al., 2012). Difficulty with self-monitoring is considered part of the clinical profile for several developmental disabilities including ADHD (Harris et al., 2005), emotional disturbance (Rafferty & Raimondi, 2009), behavioral disorders (Mooney, Ryan, Uhing, Reid, & Epstein, 2005) and autism (Sokhadze et al., 2012).

Measures of the Use of Feedback

D-KEFS Twenty Questions: See section above.

Working Memory

Joy was a ten-year-old girl who was still working on basic addition facts. During math instruction, she was learning to use manipulatives, small bars of blocks that represented each digit. To add 4 + 5, she would locate a pink block of four, line it up with green block of five, then count, "one, two, three, . . . ," eventually reaching nine. Without the blocks, Joy could not hold the numbers in her mind, start at four, and count up to five to reach nine. Subtraction posed an even greater challenge. The blocks essentially acted as a visual representation of Joy's working memory.

Working memory (WM) refers to the "temporary storage and manipulation of information necessary for cognition. The ability to keep representations in an active and accessible state is critical for adaptive, intelligent behavior" (Fougnie & Morois, 2011). Baddeley (1992) has proposed that working memory can be divided into a "central executive" attentional control system and lower level modality specific systems (phonological loop and visual sketch pad). Tasks that require working memory also involve an executive control function that enables one to filter out distractions and focus one's concentration (Conway, Kane, & Engle, 2003).

One employs working memory when solving a mathematical operation in one's head, such as adding a string of numbers or determining how many hours it will take to drive from Boston to New York, knowing the distance and given an average speed (disregarding traffic). The most commonly used assessments of WM for children are the Digit Span (composed of two parts, Digits Forward and Digits Backward) and Letter Number Sequencing subtests of WISC-IV. In respect to the Digit Span subtest, the Digits Backward segment places more of a load on working memory processing and is designed to determine how many bits of information (a sequence of numbers) an individual can hold on to and then repeat in reverse order. Tests that assess one's ability to reverse serial order are very sensitive to more diffuse brain damage, such as dementia (Lamar et al., 2007). Brain imaging studies have identified the involvement of both right and left hemispheres in verbal working memory (Philipose, Alpsh, Prabhakaran, & Hillis, 2007), however, individuals with left hemisphere damage and aphasia had shorter Digit Forwards and Digit Backwards spans than individuals with right hemisphere damage and no aphasia (Laures-Gore, Marshall, & Verner, 2011). An MRI study found a correlation between digit-backwards performance and dorsolateral prefrontal and inferior parietal volumes in patients with neurodegenerative diseases (Amici et al., 2007).

Measures of Working Memory

Recall from Chapter 2 that the WISC-IV measures four cognitive domains, used to develop a full scale IQ. This includes the assessment of WM through three subtests and is normed for ages 6 to 16.11.

WISC-IV: Digit Span (forward and backwards)—The child hears a series of numbers ranging from two to nine digits. The numbers are unrelated, having no logical relationship. On Digit Span Forward, they are asked to repeat the digits as given. This involves rote learning, auditory short-term memory and auditory sequential processing. On Digit Span Backwards, they are asked to repeat the digits in reverse order. This task involves the same processes as Digit Span Forward, and also planning ability and transforming the stimulus before responding (Sattler, 2008).

WISC-IV: Letter-Number Sequencing—Containing 10 items, this subtest consists of three trials. In each trial, the child hears a series of orally presented letters and numbers in a specified random order. They are then asked to order the letters and numbers sequentially. Children ages 6 and 7 must display the ability to count up to three and recite the alphabet up to C. This process assesses short-term auditory memory and auditory sequential processing (Sattler, 2008).

WISC-IV: Arithmetic (Supplemental)—This subtest consists of thirty-four arithmetic problems, five presented on picture cards and twenty-nine presented orally. They are similar to math encountered at school, but the child is not allowed to use paper and pencil. Skills range from counting, subtraction using objects, addition, automatized number facts, probability and relationships at a glance. This subtest measures quantitative knowledge, short-term memory, mental computation, concentration, attention, mental alertness and auditory sequential processing (Sattler, 2008).

Table 4.6 outlines other tests and subtests useful for measuring WM.

Table 4.6 Working memory.

Assessment	Description	Age
TEA-Ch: Code Transmission	The child listens to a monotone series of numbers with two 5s occasionally spoken in a row. They are asked to recall the number before the 5s.	6–16
WRAML2: Verbal Working Memory	The child listens to a list of words (some animals, some not) and is then asked to recall animal words first, then non-animal words in any order.	9-adult
WRAML2: Symbolic Working Memory	The examiner dictates a series of numbers and letters and then asks the child to point out the numbers or number-letters in a prescribed order.	9-adult
K-ABC-II: Word Order (with color interference)	The child touches a series of silhouettes of common objects in the same order as the examiner names them. Prior to completing the sequence of words, the child must name the colors, providing some interference.	3–18
SB5: Memory for Sentences	The child recalls sentences read by the examiner.	2–85+
SB5: Last Word	The examiner reads a list of words, then reads one word at a time in random order and asks the child to respond with yes or no as to whether the word was the last word in the sequence.	2–85+

(Continued)

Table 4.6 (Continued)

Assessment	Description	Age
SB5: Delayed Response	An object is hidden under a small shell or cup and the child must identify the location of the toy after a brief delay.	2–85+
SB5: Block Span	The examiner taps out a sequence on blocks then asks the child to tap out the same sequence in the same order or in reverse order.	2–85+
Children's Memory Scales (CMS): Numbers (backwards)	The child repeats a series of numbers in reverse order than presented.	5–16
WISC-IV Integrated: Arithmetic Process Approach	Items are presented in different modalities to test the limits of the child's arithmetic skills.	6–16.11
WISC-IV Integrated: Digit Span Backwards	The child is read a list sequence of numbers, and they are asked to recall the numbers in reverse order.	6–16.11
WISC-IV Integrated: Letter-Number Sequencing Process Approach	The examiner reads a sequence of letters and numbers, some of which contain an embedded word. The child is asked to recall the letters in alphabetical order and the numbers in ascending order.	6–16.11
WISC-IV Integrated: Spatial Span: Backwards	The child watches the examiner tap a sequence on blocks, then repeats the sequence in reverse order.	6–16.11
WJ III-COG: Numbers Reversed	The child hears a sequence of numbers and repeats it in reverse.	2–80 +
WJ III-COG: Auditory Working Memory	The individual hears a series of object words and numbers. The individual is then asked to reorder the information first listing words in order presented, then numbers.	2–80 +
Test of Memory and Learning (TOMAL): Digits Backwards	The child repeats a series of numbers in reverse order than presented.	5–19.11
TOMAL: Letters Backwards	The child repeats a series of letters in reverse order than presented.	5–19.11
Go-No-Go Tests	See above	
Consonant Trigram Test	The individual listens to a list of three consonants, then is asked to count backwards. The individual is then asked to remember the consonant trigram.	16–69

Attention

Attention can be understood as the "capacities or processes of how the organism becomes receptive to stimuli and how it may begin processing incoming or attended-to excitation (whether internal or external)" (Lezak et al., 2012, p. 36). Attentional systems have a limited capacity, and processing of one task requiring controlled attention can interfere with the processing of another task requiring a similar function. In addition, there are bottom-up processes that demand a focus on salient, attention-getting stimuli and top-down processes that are controlled by an individual's present goal. Lezak et al. (2012) goes on to distinguish four other aspects of attention:

- Focused or Selective Attention—"the capacity to highlight the one or two important stimuli or ideas being dealt with while suppressing awareness of competing distractions."
- Sustained Attention or Vigilance—"the capacity to maintain an attentional activity over a period of time."
- Divided Attention—"the ability to respond to more than one task at a time or to multiple elements or operations within a task, as in a complex mental task. It is thus very sensitive to any condition that reduces attentional capacity."
- Alternating Attention—"allows for shifts in focus and tasks" (Lezak et al., 2012, pp. 36–37).

The neuroanatomical correlates for attentional processes are complex and varied, given the number of different dimensions of attention. Generally, deficits in attention are the most common problems associated with brain damage, and while many or all other cognitive functions can remain unimpaired, overall cognitive output can be significantly compromised because of damage related to attentional processes (Lezak et al., 2012).

Functional MRI studies have delineated a complex network of neural substrates involved in different types of attention. For example, using combined fMRI and event-related potentials to map neural correlates of spatial attention, Martinez et al. (1999) identified a network involving extrastriate visual areas that serve to amplify visual inputs that are then directed through the occipitotemporal stream to the primary visual cortex.

Joint attention, the sharing of a common point of reference with a social partner, underlies social cognition. It requires the integrity of the early developing "posterior orienting and perceptual attention system" supported by the parietal and superior temporal cortices as well as the later developing "anterior attention system" that controls volitional, goal-directed attention. This latter network involves dorsal frontal areas related to intentional eye control, prefrontal association cortex, orbital frontal cortex and the anterior cingulate area (Mundy & Newell, 2007).

Much of the research into the neural substrate of attention has been driven by attempts to understand and describe attentional deficits related to the diagnosis of ADHD. Imaging studies reviewed by Cortese et al. (2012) found that in children, hypoactivation in ADHD relative to comparison subjects was observed mostly in systems involved in executive function (frontoparietal network) and attention (ventral attentional network). Significant hyperactivation in ADHD relative to comparison subjects was observed predominantly in the default, ventral attention, and somatomotor networks. ADHD-related dysfunction was related to multiple neuronal systems involved in higher level cognitive functions but also in sensorimotor processes, including the visual system, and in the default mode network (DMN—the network of neuronal activity in individuals in a baseline or resting state when measured by MRI). An MRI study by McAlonan et al. (2007) found that in children diagnosed with ADHD, significant regional deficits were observed within a frontal–pallidal–parietal gray matter network, predominantly on the right side, and white matter tracts bilaterally. Thus, the neural substrate of attention and deficits in attention are complex and involve networks throughout the brain but clearly involve systems related to executive functions.

Measures of Attention

The following WISC-IV subtests are included on the Processing Speed Index. While they both primarily assess the rate of processing information, they are also both good measures of attention and concentration.

WISC-IV: Coding—This subtest consists of two separate and distinct parts. Coding A, given to children ages six to seven, consists of five shapes with special marks drawn through them, such as a vertical line, two horizontal lines, etc. They are asked to mark empty test shapes to match the sample shapes. There are five practice shapes and fifty-nine test shapes. Coding B is given to children ages eight to sixteen. They are given a key, which indicates that numbers are matched with a special symbol. The test stimulus is made of stacked boxes; the lower box is empty, while the upper box contains a number. The child is asked to fill in the empty box with the corresponding symbol from the key. The child is given an opportunity to practice prior to starting the assessment. This is a timed test. This subtest is related to rate of motor activity, motivation, persistence, visual acuity, and working under pressure (Sattler, 2008).

WISC-IV: Symbol Search—This subtest consists of two tests, each requiring a stimulus page containing an array of symbols, with a target symbol. In Search A, given to six- to 7.11-year-olds, the child views an array containing the target symbol and three other symbols. They are asked to draw a slash through a yes box if the array contains the target and a slash through a no box if the target symbol is absent. For Search B, children ages eight to eleven view an array containing five distraction symbols and two possible target symbols. Again, the child makes a slash in a yes box if the target symbols are present and a slash in a no box if they are absent. Most of the symbols, for both tests, are meaningless. This test is timed (Sattler, 2008). While this test measures psychomotor speed, perceptual speed rate and fine motor coordination, it also assesses attention, concentration and short-term memory. The following section outlines different assessment tools used to measure various subtypes of attention.

Table 4.7 lists assessments designed to evaluate selective/focused attention.

In addition to the D-KEFS Trail-Making, Verbal Fluency, Color-Word and Design Fluency subtests discussed previously as well as the CAS: Expressive Attention and NEPSY II: Auditory Attention and Response Set discussed above, Table 4.8 describes additional tests evaluating the ability to shift attention.

In addition to the CAS Number Detection and Receptive Attention subtests as well as the Continuous Performance tests, the NEPSY Auditory Attention and Response Set and Ruff, Table 4.9 details assessments of sustained attention.

The WISC-IV Integrated Letter Number Sequencing and the WJIII-COG Auditory Working Memory subtests address divided attention as well as the subtest in Table 4.10. Table 4.11 displays measures of attentional capacity, and Table 4.12 catalogs useful behavior rating scales that are used to measure different aspects of attention.

We return to the case of eleven-year-old Charles, whose difficulty with behavioral and emotional regulation and resistance to certain types of work suggested that he might be struggling with some EF issues.

Table 4.7 Selective/focused attention.

Assessment	Description	Age
Das-Naglieri Cognitive Assessment System (CAS): Expressive Attention	Like the Stroop test, the individual must look at an array of color words printed in dissonant ink colors, naming the ink color.	5–17
CAS: Number Detection	The child looks at a page containing the numbers 1, 2 and 3. They are asked to circle digits printed in an open font and ignore those in another font.	5–17
CAS: Receptive Attention	Children 5 and older are asked to attend to letters that are identical. Children 8 and up complete a second page and are asked to attend to letters that are the same regardless of font.	5–17
D-KEFS: Color-Word Interference Test	See above	8–89
d2-Test of Attention	The child views an array of *p*s and *d*s marked with one to four dashes. They are asked to cross out *d*s with two dashes ignoring other stimuli.	9–60
NEPSY II: Auditory Attention and Response Set	See above	5–16
Ruff 2 & 7 Selective Attention Test	In 20 trial pages, individuals are asked to cross out the numbers *2* and *7* as quickly as possible. Each trial page contains various distractor stimuli.	16–70
TEA-CH: Map Mission	Searching a map, the child is asked to find as many target symbols as possible.	6–16
TEA-CH: Sky Search	Part 1 requires that the child locate as many target spaceships on a page filled with spaceships as possible. Part 2 asks the child to circle all target spaceships on a page containing no distractors. This attempts to remove influence of motor output aspects.	6–16
WJ III-COG: Auditory Attention	The individual listens to a tape recording of words while looking at a four picture array. They are asked to point to the image that matches the word. Difficulty increases in sound discrimination and as background noise of the recording grows.	2–80+

Table 4.8 Alternating/shifting attention.

Assessment	Description	Age
TEA-Ch: Creature Counting	The child is asked to count aliens hiding in burrows. Arrows indicate if the child should count up in ascending order or switch to counting down in descending order.	6–16
TEA-Ch: Opposite Words	The child views pictures of two worlds with pathways containing the digits 1 and 2. In the "Same" world, the say the correct name of the digit as they travel the path. In "Opposite" world they say "two" when encountering a 1 and "one" upon a 2.	6–16
Wisconsin Card Sorting	See above	

Table 4.9 Sustained attention.

Assessment	Description	Age
TEA-Ch: Code Transmission	The child listens to a monotone series of numbers with two 5s occasionally spoken in a row. They are asked to recall the number before the 5s.	6–16
TEA-Ch: Score!	The child listens to a recording and is asked to note a targeted sound.	6–16
TEA-Ch: Score DT	The child is asked to count a targeted sound, while being instructed to listen to a background newscast specifically to hear an animal's name.	6–16
TEA-Ch: Walk Don't Walk	The child is given a piece of paper with a path marked on it. He or she is instructed to trace the path with a pencil each time he or she hears a tone.	6–16

Table 4.10 Divided attention.

Assessment	Description	Age
TEA-Ch: Sky Search DT	Once the Sky Search and Score! subtests have been completed, the child is asked to combine the tasks, locating spaceships and tracking a target sound.	6–16

Table 4.11 Attentional capacity.

Assessment	Description	Age
Children's Memory Scale (CMS: Numbers (Forward))	The child hears a string of numbers and is asked to repeat the numbers in the same order.	5–16
K-ABC II: Word Order (without color interference)	The examiner says the name of common objects, then asks the child to touch silhouettes of the objects in the same order as spoken.	3–18
K-ABC II: Number Recall	The child hears a sequence of numbers, ranging from 2 to 9, and the child is asked to recall them in the same order.	3–18
K-ABCII: Hand Movements	The examiner shows the child a series of hand movements on the table and the child mimics them. Series of movements increases as task progresses.	4–18
Test of Memory and Learning (TOMAL): Digits Forward	The child repeats a list of digits in the order presented.	5–19.11
Test of Memory and Learning (TOMAL): Letters Forward	The child repeats a list of letters in the order presented.	5–19.11
Test of Memory and Learning (TOMAL): Manual Imitation	The child mimics a series of hand movements increasing in length as the test progresses.	5–19.11
WISC-IV: Digit Span	See above	6–16.11
WISC-IV Integrated: Letter Span	The child repeats a list of non-rhyming and rhyming words in the same order spoken by the examiner.	6–16.11

Assessment	Description	Age
WISC-IV Integrated: Letter-Number Sequencing	The child hears a list of letters and is asked to repeat them in the same order. The child hears a list of numbers and is asked to repeat them in the same order.	6–16.11
WISC-IV Integrated: Visual Digit Span	The child is shown a visual sequence of numbers, then asked to recall those numbers in the same order they were presented.	6–16.11
WISC-IV Integrated: Spatial Span	The child repeats a sequence of tapped blocks in the same order that was displayed by the examiner.	6–16.11
WRAML2: Finger Windows	The child is shown a rigid piece of plastic with random holes cut out. The examiner inserts a pencil into a series of holes. The child is required to copy the order of holes tapped using their finger. Sequence length increases with difficulty as task progresses.	5–90
WRAML2: Number/Letter	Mixing letters and numbers, the child is asked to repeat a sequence of both.	5–90

Table 4.12 Behavior rating scales.

Assessment	Description	Age
Attention Deficit Disorders Evaluation Scales–Third Edition (ADDES-3)	Teachers, parents, school personnel and guardians fill out this questionnaire which delineates ADHD subtypes: inattentive and attentive.	4–18
Attention Deficit Disorders Evaluation Scale: Secondary Age (ADDES-S)	Same as ADDES-3, but normed for a slightly older age group.	11.5–18
ADHD Symptoms Scale	Used at home or school for both clinical or research purposes. Two subscales: Hyperactive-Impulsive and Inattention.	5–18
Attention-Deficit/ Hyperactivity Disorder Test	Used by teachers, parents or others, this questionnaire assesses three subtypes of symptoms: hyperactivity, impulsivity and inattention.	3–23
Brown Attention-Deficit Disorder Scales	40-item questionnaire for teachers, parents or self, measures organization, focusing/shifting sets, alertness and processing speed, emotional modulation, working memory and self-monitoring.	3–7; 8–12; 12–18
Conners' Scales ADHD/*DSM-IV* Scales	Teacher, parent and self-reporting scale, assesses cognitive, behavioral problems, focusing on ADHD and comorbid disorders.	3–17

Charles

Charles's attentional and executive functioning skills were measured using the D-KEFS. For the purposes of this evaluation, Charles was administered five of the subtests. On the Trail-Making test, Charles scored in the Average range on scanning, letter sequencing and motor speed. His number sequencing was low average due to his difficulty finding one of the numbers in the array. His switching score was also low average, but significantly below average relative to his scanning and letter sequencing scores. On the Verbal Fluency subtest, Charles scored above average on measures of fluency and switching but tended to make a significant number of repetition errors, suggesting that he was having difficulty self-monitoring. On Design Fluency, he had a relative difficulty switching cognitive set, scoring significantly below average. On the Color Word subtest he demonstrated a vulnerability in his ability to inhibit automatic responding on both the inhibition and switching tasks as measured by his increased number of errors. Lastly on the Tower test, Charles's move accuracy ratio was significantly below average, suggesting that he had difficulty with planning and response inhibition. Together, these findings suggest that Charles has a vulnerability in executive functioning skills, particularly those related to organization, planning, distractibility, response inhibition, cognitive flexibility, self-monitoring and sustaining attention. These vulnerabilities have the potential to undercut his strengths in other areas.

Charles's Working Memory Index of 102 on the WISC-IV was in the middle of the Average range. He performed in the Average range on Digit Span, a subtest that is composed of two parts. On the first part of the Digit Span subtest, Digit Span Forward, he could inconsistently recall five digits of a random number sequence presented auditorially, a performance at the lower end of the Average range. When he had to reverse the order, he again inconsistently recalled five numbers, a performance slightly above average. On both these tasks, he evidenced a variable degree of attention. He did significantly better on Letter Number Sequencing, a test requiring him to listen to a sequence of letters and numbers and repeat them back in numerical and alphabetical order. He again could inconsistently recall five bits of information, also demonstrating some variable attention on this task.

Together, these findings suggest that Charles has a vulnerability in executive functioning skills related to organizing, planning, filtering distractions, inhibiting responses, switching set and consistently self-monitoring. While he also has difficulty sustaining attention, he does have the ability to rally and deploy his attention more effectively when he is challenged. On tasks of working memory, his ability to hold information on line while performing operations upon it is at least in the average range but is vulnerable to his variable attention. Furthermore, based on parent reports and data from the

BASC-2, Charles was having difficulty regulating his behavioral and emotional responsiveness. All of these are skills that form the bases for more complex cognitive functioning.

References

Alvarez, J.A., & Emory, E. (2006). Executive function and the frontal lobes: A meta-analytic review. *Neuropsychology Review, 16*(1), 17–42.

Amici, S., Ogar, J., Brambati, S. M., et al. (2007). Performance in specific language tasks correlates with regional volume changes in progressive aphasia. *Cognitive and Behavioral Neurology, 20,* 203–211.

Bachara, A., Damasio, A.R., Damasio, H., & Anderson, S. (1994). Insensitivity to future consequences following damage to the human prefrontal cortex. *Cognition, 50,* 7–15.

Bachara, A., Damasio, H., Tranel, D., & Damasio, A.R. (1997). Deciding advantageously before knowing the advantageous strategy. *Science, 275,* 1293–1294.

Baddeley, A. (1992). Working memory. *Science, 255,* 556–559.

Baldo, J. V., Delis, D. C., Wilkins, D. P. & Shimamura, A. P. (2004). Is it bigger than a breadbox? Performance of patients with prefrontal lesions on a new executive function test. *Archives of Clinical Neuropsychology, 19,* 407–419.

Barkley, R.A. (1994). Impaired delayed responding: A unified theory of attention deficit disorder. In D.K. Routh (Ed.), *Disruptive behavior disorders in childhood* (pp. 11–57). New York, NY: Plenum Press.

Barkley, R.A. (1997). Behavioral inhibition, sustained attention, and executive functions: Constructing a unifying theory of ADHD. *Psychological Bulletin, 121,* 65–94.

Baron, I.S. (2004). *Neuropsychological evaluation of the child.* New York, NY: Oxford University Press.

Batum, P., & Yagmurlu, B. (2007). What counts in externalizing behaviors? The contributions of emotion and behavioral regulation. *Current Psychology: Developmental, Learning, Personality, Social, 25*(4), 272–294.

Bear, M. F., Connors, B.W., and Paradiso, M.A. (2007). *Neuroscience: Exploring the brain* (3rd ed.). Baltimore, MD: Lippincott, Williams & Wilkins.

Bernstein, J. H., & Waber, D. (2007). Executive capacities from a developmental perspective. In L. Meltzer (Ed.), *Executive function in education: From theory to practice* (pp. 39–54). New York, NY: Guilford Press.

Bridges, L.J., Denham, S.A., & Ganiban, J.M. (2004). Definitional issues in emotion regulation research. *Child Development, 75*(2), 340–345.

Campos, J.J., Frankel, C.B., & Camras, L. (2004). On the nature of emotional regulation. *Child Development, 75*(2), 377–394.

Carvalho, J.O., & Ready, R.E. (2010). Emotion and executive functioning: The effects of mood states on fluency tasks. *Journal of Clinical and Experimental Neuropsychology, 23*(3), 225–230.

Chess, S., & Thomas, A. (1987). *Origins and evolution of behavior.* Cambridge, MA: Harvard University Press.

Conway, A. R., Kane, M. J., & Engle, R. W. (2003). Working memory capacity and its elation to general intelligence. *Trends in Cognitive Sciences, 7,* 547–552.

Cortese, S., Kelly, C., Chabernaud, C., Proal, E., Di Martino, A., Milham, M., et al. (2012). Toward systems neuroscience of ADHD: A meta-analysis of 55 fMRI studies. *American Journal of Psychiatry, 169,* 1038–1055.

Damasio, A. R. (1994). *Descartes' error: Emotion, reason and the human brain*. New York, NY: Avon.

Davis, A. S., Peirson, E. E., & Finch, W. H. (2011). A canonical correlation analysis of intelligence and executive functioning. *Applied Neuropsychology, 18*, 61–68.

Degangi, G. A., Breinbauer, C., Roosevelt, J. D., Porges, S., & Greenspan, S. (2000). Prediction of childhood problems at three years in children experiencing disorders of regulation during infancy. *Infant Mental Health Journal, 21*(3) 156–175.

Delis, D. C., Kaplan, E., & Kramer, J. H. (2001). *Delis-Kaplan executive function system: Examiner's manual*. San Antonio, TX: The Psychological Corporation.

Demakis, G. J. (2004). Frontal lobe damage and tests of executive processing: A meta-analysis of the Category Test, Stroop Test, and Trail-Making Test. *Journal of Clinical and Experimental Neuropsychology, 26*, 441–450.

Denckla, M. B. (2005). Executive function. In D. Gozal & D. Molfese (Eds.), *Attention deficit hyperactivity disorder: From genes to patients* (pp. 165–183). Totowa, NJ: Humana Press.

Denckla, M. B. (2007). Executive function: Binding together the definitions of attention-deficit/hyperactivity disorder and learning disabilities. In L. Meltzer (Ed.), *Executive function in education: From theory to practice*. New York, NY: Guilford Press.

Dimitrov, M., Grafman, J., Soares, A. H., & Clark, K. (1999). Concept formation and concept shifting in frontal lesion and Parkinson's disease patients assessed with the *California card sorting test*. *Neuropsychology, 13*, 135–143.

Duncan, J. (1995). Attention, intelligence, and the frontal lobes. In M. Gazzinga (Ed.), *The cognitive neurosciences* (pp. 721–733). Cambridge, MA: MIT Press.

Eisenberg, N., & Spinrad, T. (2004). Emotion-related regulation: Sharpening the definition. *Child Development, 75*(2) 334–339.

Fine, E. M., Delis, D. C., Dean, D., et al. (2009). Left frontal love contributions to concept formation; a quantitative MRI study of performance on the *Delis-Kaplan executive function sorting test*. *Journal of Clinical and Experimental Neuropsychology, 31*, 624–631.

Fougnie, D., & Marois, R. (2011). What limits working memory capacity? Evidence for modality-specific sources to the simultaneous storage of visual and auditory arrays. *Journal of Experimental Psychology: Learning, Memory & Cognition, 37*(6), 1329–1341.

Fox, N. (Eds.). (1994). The development of emotional regulation: Biological and behavioral considerations. *Monographs for the Society for Research in Child Development, 59*, 2–3.

Gehring, W. J., & Knight, R. T. (2000). Prefrontal-cingulate interactions in action monitoring. *Nature Neuroscience, 3*(5), 516–520.

Goel, V., Makale, M., & Grafman, J. (2004) Hippocampal system mediates logical reasoning about familiar spatial environments. *Journal of Cognitive Neuroscience, 16*(4), 654–664.

Goldberg, E., & Podell, K. (2000). Adaptive decision making, ecological validity, and the frontal lobes. *Journal of Clinical and Experimental Neuropsychology, 22*, 56–68.

Goldberg, E., Podell, K., Bilder, R. M., & Jaeger, J. (2000). *The executive control battery*. Melbourne, Australia: Psych Press.

Harris, K. R., Friedlander, B. D., Saddler, B., Frizzelle, R., & Graham, S. (2005). Self-monitoring of attention versus self-monitoring of academic performance: Effects among students with ADHD in the general education classroom. *The Journal of Special Education, 39*(3), 145–156.

Heaton, R. K., Chelune, G. J., Talley, J. L., Kay, G. G., & Curtiss, G. (1993). *Wisconsin Card Sorting Test Manual*. Lutz, FL: Psychological Assessment Resources, Inc.

Henry, L. A., Messer, D. J., & Nash, G. (2012). Executive functioning in children with specific language impairment. *Journal of Child Psychology and Psychiatry, 53*(1), 37–45.

Hubner, M., Dreisbach, G., Haider, H., & Kluwe , R. H. (2003). Backward inhibition as means for sequential task-set control: Evidence for reduction of task competition. *Journal of Experimental Psychology: Learning Memory and Cognition, 20*(2), 289–297.

Huey, E. D., Goveia, E. N., Paviol, S., et al. (2009). Executive dysfunction in frontotemporal dementia and corticobasal syndrome. *Neurology, 72,* 453–459.

Hughes, C. (2011). Changes and challenges in 20 years of research into the development of executive functions. *Infant & Child Development, 20*(3), 251–271. doi:10.1002/icd.736

Hughes, C., & Graham, A. (2008). Executive functions and developing. In J. Reed & J. Warner-Rogers (Eds.), *Child neuropsychology: Concepts, theory and practice.* New York, NY: Wiley-Blackwell.

Kalpidou, M. D., Power, T. G., Cherry, K. E., & Gottfried, N. W. (2004). Regulation of emotion and behavior among 3- and 5-year-olds. *The Journal of General Psychology, 131*(2), 159–178.

Keifer, E. (2010). Performance of patients with ventromedial prefrontal, dorsolateral prefrontal, and non-frontal lesions on the *Delis-Kaplan executive function system.* Unpublished doctoral dissertation, University of Iowa.

Keil, K., Baldo, J., Kaplan, E., et al. (2005). Role of frontal cortex in inferential reasoning: Evidence from the Word Context Test. *Journal of the International Neuropsychological Society, 11,* 426–433.

Kolb, B., & Whishaw, I. Q. (2009). *Fundamentals of human neuropsychology* (6th ed.). New York, NY: Worth.

Korkman, M., Kirk, U., & Kemp, S. (2007). *NEPSY-II: A developmental neuropsychological assessment.* San Antonio, TX: The Psychological Corporation.

Lamar, M., Price, C., Libon, D., et al. (2007). Alterations in working memory as a function of leukoaraiosis in dementia. *Neuropsychologia, 45,* 245–254.

Lange, K. W., Reichl, S., Lange, K. M., Tucha, L., & Tucha, O. (2010). The history of attention deficit hyperactivity disorder. *Attention Deficit Hyperactivity Disorder, 2*(4), 241–255.

Laures-Gore, J., Marshall, R., & Verner, E. (2011). Performance of individuals with left hemisphere stroke and aphasia and individuals with right brain damage on forward and backward digit span tasks. *Aphasiology, 25,* 43–56.

Lezak, M. D., Howieson, D., Bigler, E., & Tranel, D. (2012). *Neuropsychological assessment* (5th ed.). New York, NY: Oxford University Press.

Lien, Y., Yang, H., Kuo, P., & Chen W. J. (2011). Relation of perseverative tendency and life events to depressive symptoms: Findings from a prospective study in non-referred adolescents in Taiwan. *Behavioral Medicine, 37,* 1–7.

Luria, A. R. (1973). *The working brain: An introduction to neuropsychology.* Harmondsworth, UK: Penguin.

Lynch, P., & Jaffe, C. Carl, cardiologist. (1987–2000). Medical illustrations generated for multimedia teaching projects by the Yale University School of Medicine, Center for Advanced Instructional Media. Retrieved October 15, 2013 from http://commons.wikimedia.org/wiki/File:Brain_human_sagittal_section.svg

Mantyla, T., Carelli, M. G., & Forman, H. (2007). Time monitoring and executive functioning in children and adults. *Journal of Experimental Child Psychology, 96,* 1–19.

Maricle, D. E., Johnson, W., & Avirett, E. (2010). Assessing and intervening in children with executive function disorders. In D. C. Miller (Ed.), *Best practices in school neuropsychology: Guidelines for effective practice, assessment, and evidenced-based intervention.* Hoboken, NJ: John Wiley and Sons.

Martinez, A., Anilo-Vento, L., et al. (1999). Involvement of striate and extrastriate visual cortical areas in spatial attention. *Nature Neuroscience, 2*(4), 364–369.

McAlonan, G., Cheung, V., Cheung, C., et al. (2007). Mapping brain structure in attention deficit-hyperactivity disorder: A voxel-based MRI study of regional grey and white matter volume. *Psychiatry Research: Neuroimaging, 154,* 171–180.

McDonald, C. R., Delis, D. C., Kramer, J. H., et al. (2008). A componential analysis of proverb interpretation in patients with frontal lobe epilepsy and temporal lobe epilepsy: Relationships with disease-related factors. *The Clinical Neuropsychologist, 22,* 480–496.

McDonald, C. R., Delis, D. C., Norman, M. A., et al. (2005a). Discriminating patients with frontal lobe epilepsy and temporal lobe epilepsy: Utility of a multilevel design fluency test. *Neuropsychology, 19*, 806–813.

McDonald, C. R., Delis, D. C., Norman, M. A., et al. (2005b). Is impairment in set-shifting specific to frontal lobe dysfunction? Evidence from patients with frontal lobe or temporal lobe epilepsy. *Journal of the International Neuropsychological Society, 11*, 477–481.

Meltzer, L. (2007). Executive function: Theoretical and conceptual frameworks. In L. Meltzer (Ed.), *Executive function in education: From theory to practice*. New York, NY: Guilford Press.

Miller, D. C. (2007). *Essentials of school neuropsychological assessment*. Hoboken, NJ: John Wiley and Sons.

Mooney, P., Ryan, J. B., Uhing, B. M., Reid, R., & Epstein, M. H. (2005). A review of self-management interventions targeting academic outcomes for students with emotional and behavioral disorders. *Journal of Behavioral Education, 14*(3), 203–221.

Moriguchi, Y., Kanda, T., Ishiguro, H., & Itakura, S. (2010). Children's perseverate to a human's actions, but not to a robots actions. *Developmental Science, 13*(1), 62–68.

Mundy, P., & Newell, L. (2007). Attention, joint attention, and social cognition. *Association for Psychological Science, 16*(5), 269–274.

Muris, P., van der Pennen, E., Sigmond, R., & Mayer, B. (2008). Symptoms of anxiety, depression and aggression in non-clinical children: Relationships with self-report and performance based measures of attention and effortful control. *Child Psychiatry and Human Development, 39*, 455–467.

Philipose, L. E., Alpsh, A., Prabhakaran, V., & Hillis, A. E. (2007). Testing conclusions from functional imaging of working memory with data from acute stroke. *Behavioral Neurology, 18*, 37–43.

Posner, M. I., & Rothbart, M. K. (2000). Developing mechanisms of self-regulation. *Development and Psychopathology, 12*, 427–441.

Rafferty, L. A., & Raimondi, S. L. (2009). Self-monitoring of attention versus self-monitoring of performance: Examining the differential effects among students with emotional disturbance engaged in independent math practice. *Journal of Behavioral Education, 18*, 279–299.

Ravnkilde, B., Videbech, P., Rosenberg, R., et al. (2002). Putative tests of frontal lobe function: A PET-study of brain activation during Stroop's Test and verbal fluency. *Journal of Clinical and Experimental Neuropsychology, 4*, 223–238.

Roid, G. H. (2003). *Stanford-Binet intelligence scales* (5th ed.). Austin, TX: PRO-ED.

Rothbart, M. K., & Rueda, M. R. (2005). The development of effortful control. In U. Mayr, E. Awh, & S. W. Keele, (Eds.), *Developing individuality in the human brain: A tribute to Michael I. Posner* (pp. 167–188). Washington DC: American Psychological Association.

Rueda, M. R., Posner, M. I., & Rothbart, M. K. (2005). The development of executive attention: Contributions to the emergence of self-regulation. *Developmental Neuropsychology, 28*(2), 573–594.

Sattler, J. M. (2008). *Assessment of children: Cognitive foundations* (5th ed.). Le Mesa, CA: Jerome M. Sattler.

Shiner, R. L., Buss, K. A., McGlowry, Putnam, S. P., Saudino, K. J., & Zentner, M. (2012). What is temperament now? Assessing progress in temperament research on the twenty-fifth anniversary of Goldsmith et al. (1987). *Child Development Perspectives, 6*(4), 436–444.

Smidts, D. P., Jacobs, R., & Anderson, V. (2004). The object classification task for children (OCTC): A measure of concept generation and mental flexibility in early childhood. *Developmental Neuropsychology, 26*(1), 385–401.

Sokhadze, E. M., Baruth, J. M., Sears, L., Sokhadze, G. E., El-Baz, A. S., & Casanova, M. F. (2012). Prefrontal neuromodulation using rTMS improves monitoring and correction function in autism. *Applied Psychophysiological Biofeedback, 37*, 91–102.

Van der Elst, W., Hurks, P., Wassenberg, R., Meijs, C., & Jolles, J. (2011). Animal verbal fluency and design fluency in school-aged children: Effects of age, sex and mean level of parent education, and regression-based normative data. *Journal of Clinical and Experimental Neuropsychology, 22*(9), 1005–1015.

Weller, J. A., Levin, I. P., & Bechara, A. (2010). Do individual differences in Gambling Task performance predict adaptive decision making for risky gains and losses? *Journal of Clinical and Experimental Neuropsychology, 32*(2), 141–150.

Woodcock, R. W., McGrew, K. S., & Mather, N. (2001). *Woodcock-Johnson III Test of Cognitive Abilities*. Itasca, IL: Riverside Publishing.

Yerys, B. E., & Munakata, Y. (2006). When labels hurt but novelty helps: Children's perseveration and flexibility in a card-sorting task. *Child Development, 77*(6), 1589–1607.

Yochim, B. P., Baldo, J. V., Kane, K. D., & Delis, D. C. (2009). D-KEFS Tower Test performance in patients with lateral prefrontal cortex lesions: The importance of error monitoring. *Journal of Clinical and Experimental Neuropsychology, 31*, 658–663.

Yochim, B. P., Baldo, J. V., Nelson, A., & Delis, D. C. (2007). D-KEFS Trail Making Test performance in patients with lateral prefrontal cortex lesions. *Journal of the International Neuropsychological Society, 13*, 704–709.

Zahr, N. M., & Sullivan, E. (2008) Translational studies of alcoholism bridging the gap. *Alcohol Research & Health, 31*(3), p. 215 [Public domain], via Wikimedia Commons Retrieved 10/15/2013 from http://commons.wikimedia.org/wiki/File:Prefrontal_cortex.png

5   Understanding and Assessing Memory

Diane was fourteen and a freshman in a local private high school. She was born full term and her developmental milestones were within normal limits. She developed diabetes at the age of twelve, and the diagnostic process was quite protracted and the ambiguity and uncertainty involved was very traumatic for her. While she had been a somewhat anxious and disorganized child, who began having separation issues at four years, once she had finally gotten a clear diagnosis in respect to her diabetes, she actually became more organized, more confident and more social, somehow rallying and becoming more independent around the demands involved in managing her disease. At the time of testing, she was performing well in school regarding math, science and Spanish but was having difficulty with history and English due to difficulties with comprehension.

Diane had requested that she be evaluated. She sought to understand why she was struggling with specific aspects of her learning and why she was feeling so badly about her performance in school. Throughout testing, she was extremely engaging and talkative and was able to very clearly articulate the emotional impact the confusion and uncertainty around the diagnosis of her diabetes had on her. While she explained how she was feeling bad about school, she also proudly reported on her perseverance and ability to manage her diabetes.

On the *Wechsler Intelligence Scale for Children–Fourth Edition* (WISC-IV, 2003), Diane's verbal abilities fell in the Average range (VCI = one hundred and eight; seventieth percentile). Her perceptual organizational abilities also fell in the Average range (PRI = one hundred and four; sixty-first percentile). Her working memory was in the Very Superior range (WMI = one hundred and thirty-two; ninety-eighth percentile) while her processing speed was in the Average range (PSI = one hundred and six; sixty-sixth percentile). Although her verbal abilities were average, she demonstrated a significant relative vulnerability in abstract reasoning. Similarly, though her perceptual reasoning skills were average, she also had a vulnerability in the processing of complex, abstract visual information. Her performance on tests measuring processing speed was average but was supported considerably by her ability to memorize the number/symbol relationships on the Coding subtest. Most remarkable, however, was her very superior performance on the Digit Span Backwards and the Letter-Number Sequencing subtests of the WISC-IV.

Diane's memory functioning was a very significant relative strength. She scored in the Superior range on the California Verbal Learning Test— Children's Version (CVLT-C, Delis et al., 1994), a test of learning and recall that required she memorize a "shopping list" of items presented over five trials and which also included an interference list, a delayed recall trial as well as a recognition trial. On the *Woodcock-Johnson III Tests of Achievement* (WJ III, 2001) battery, she received a Standard Score of one hundred and eighteen (High Average) on the Story Recall subtest and a one hundred and thirty (Superior) on the Understanding Directions subtest, both tests requiring that she access different aspects of memory. On the Passage Comprehension subtest, however, she received a Standard Score of ninety-nine. On tests of emotional functioning, results indicated that she was more a doer than a thinker, relative abilities that were reflected in her underlying neurological strengths and vulnerabilities, the former including her very strong memory and organizational skills, while the latter included her relative vulnerabilities with abstract reasoning. Under conditions of uncertainty or ambiguity, she tended to simplify complexity so as to avoid having to process more information than she could manage through her strong organizational and memory abilities, particularly when that information was more abstract in nature and required a significant degree of integration.

Thus, Diane was relying, to an inordinate degree, on her extremely strong executive functioning, working memory and memory skills to manage the academic environment. When required to reason abstractly and integrate material that she had memorized, she was overwhelmed and unable to function at a level commensurate with her strengths. The information provided through testing allowed her to appreciate her considerable abilities in organization and recall and relieved her of the emotional burden she was carrying regarding her vulnerabilities.

Memory

Until the twentieth century, the understanding of memory was largely philosophical, anecdotal or gleaned from descriptions in literature. Research in the latter half of the twentieth century, however, began to explore what we now understand about the many different facets of memory (see Squire, 2004). For example, Brenda Milner (1962/1965) described the profound deficits or amnesia for anterograde (recent) memory formation in the famous patient "HM," who had undergone bilateral resection of his temporal lobes in an attempt to treat his debilitating epilepsy. While his past memories were intact, he could no longer learn new information or recall ongoing events. However, he could learn new motor skills and other procedures that did not rely on conscious recall. Thus, a distinction was made between declarative (explicit) and procedural (implicit) memory.

More recent studies have provided further insights into both declarative and procedural memory. It is now understood that declarative memory, the type of memory that allows us to retain, recall or recognize previous experiences, requires a certain level of awareness and intention (Lezak, 2012). Research has also broken down **declarative or explicit** memory into different stages:

Registration or sensory memory involves the selection and recording of perceptions as an entry into memory systems. It is a form of encoding.

Immediate memory is the first stage of short term memory storage and it temporarily holds on to data from the registration stage.

Rehearsal is the process of repeating data to extend the length of a memory trace.

Long-term memory is related to learning and the ability to store information and retain it over long periods of time.

Procedural or nondeclarative memory is "dispositional and is expressed through performance rather than recollection. Nondeclarative forms of memory occur as modifications within specialized performance systems. The memories are revealed through reactivation of the systems within which the learning originally occurred" (Squire, 2004, pp. 173–174). Procedural memory is what allows one to carry on the activities of daily life such as talking, eating, walking, etc., even in individuals who suffer amnesia for current events.

Research has demonstrated that each of these types of memory has a distinctly different neuroanatomical substrate. For example, the medial temporal lobe includes a system of anatomically related structures that are essential for declarative memory (conscious memory for facts and events). The system consists of the hippocampal region (CA fields, dentate gyrus and subicular complex) and the adjacent perirhinal, entorhinal and parahippocampal cortices. While this network is primarily concerned with memory, it also functions in coordination with the neocortex to establish and maintain long-term memory and becomes independent of long-term memory through a process of consolidation (Squire, Stark, & Clark, 2004).

Neuroimaging studies of a form of procedural or implicit learning (sequence learning) indicate the involvement of frontal/striatal-cerebellar networks (Doyon, 2008). However, implicit learning of spatial contextual information depends on a network involving the medial temporal lobes (Chun & Jiang, 1998). Neuroimaging studies of spatial contextual learning reveal activation in entorhinal and perirhinal cortex (Preston & Gabrieli, 2008).

Development of Memory

Recall memory has been studied over the course of development. Nine-month-old infants demonstrate recall of events one month later, but not three months later, whereas ten-month-olds can recall events after three months. By twenty months of age, infants can recall an event that occurred twelve months ago. There has been considerable speculation about the contributions of different mechanisms regarding retrieval and storage as well as the development of the neural substrates involved in each. For example, developmental changes in temporal lobe structures involved in memory storage, such as the hippocampus, as well as prefrontal structures, have been correlated with different aspects of memory storage and retrieval (see Bauer, 2005). In a longitudinal study of children between five-and-a-half and six-and-a-half years of age, evidence suggested that declarative and procedural memory followed different developmental trajectories (Lum, 2010).

Imitation has been a principal construct in studies examining the development of learning and memory. Newborns are able to imitate actions immediately following a model and, over the course of development, are increasingly able to defer, from minutes to days, the imitation of simple, object-based actions demonstrated by a human model (Kolling, Goertz, Frahsek, & Knopf, 2010). Experimental and clinical work indicates that deferred imitation relies on declarative memory skills (Mandler, 2004) and, based on longitudinal studies, improves with age (Kolling, Goertz, Frahsek, & Knopf, 2009). In a longitudinal deferred imitation study, Kolling et al. (2010) were also able to identify two developmental groups that demonstrated different growth and stability patterns in declarative memory related to language and self-development or body awareness skills. Tulving (2002) has linked the development of a conceptual self that occurs around two years of age with the ability to demonstrate episodic remembering (the conscious memory for events and facts specific to an individual's experience) of deferred imitation actions.

Maturation of memory skills over development also has been useful in predicting development in other functional domains. In one longitudinal study, for example, visual recognition memory at six months, deferred imitation at nine months and turn-taking skills at fourteen months predicted the emergence of language skills in fourteen-month-olds (Heimann et al., 2006). Furthermore, joint attention and deferred imitation predicted cognitive abilities at four years of age (Strid, Tjus, Smith, Meltzoff, & Heimann, 2006).

Interestingly, Barnes (2010) found that implicit sequence learning, a cognitive process mediated by frontal/striatal/cerebellar circuitry, was atypical in children diagnosed with ADHD compared to healthy controls. In an fMRI study of adults who were born very preterm (Kalpakidou et al., 2012), increased neonatal brain injury was correlated with decreased activation in the right parietal region of the brain on a paired associates memory test. Differential activation between preterm adults and controls was most evident in the right middle frontal gyrus during encoding and in the right posterior cingulate gyrus during recall. These latter findings suggest that premature birth can affect the developmental sequelae of memory and its neural substrate.

Memory Types

We rely on various types of memory for daily functioning. As with other neuropsychological domains, it is the integration of the various types of memory that enables us to manage the demands of everyday life. The interplay between long-term memory, short-term memory and working memory lead to the acquisition of skills and knowledge. Each memory type is required for the encoding, consolidation and retrieval of information and impacts behavior.

Memory types can be categorized by three subsets of memory: long-term, short-term and working memory. All three subsets are required for learning skills such as those needed to read. The following sections define the three subsets of memory and briefly discuss assessment tools. In assessing memory, stand-alone tests and batteries have been developed and subtests of neuropsychological batteries, such as the WISC-IV, assess memory functions.

The distinction between long-term, short-term and working memory has been made for all of the human sensory modalities, including the visual (Velichkovskii, 1978), verbal (Dupont, Samson, Le, & Baulac, 2002), motor (Krakauer & Shadmehr, 2006), kinesthetic (Marteniuk, 1976), gustatory (Miranda, Ferreira, Ramirez-Lugo, & Bermúdez-Rattoni, 2003), olfactory (White, 1998) and tactile (Gallace & Spence, 2009) senses. A neuropsychological assessment will typically include an evaluation of different aspects of verbal and visual memory. At times, an individual's performance on certain tasks, such as the *Rey-Osterrieth Complex Figure Test* (Meyers & Meyers, 1995), suggests that he is recalling information using a motor memory. Often this is observed because he will complete the recall portions using the same motor sequence used in the copy. While this is certainly not a formal assessment of motor memory, it is an interesting observation that warrants remark. Assessment of other sensory modalities such as taste, smell, kinesthesia and touch are beyond the purview of neuropsychological evaluations.

Long-Term Memory

Early in the school year, the classroom group always reviewed how to write street addresses and reviewed their personal home address. Chloe was a sweet, nine-year-old kid with profoundly delayed language skills. Her treatment for the last several years focused primarily on receptive and expressive language, making sure she understood language and how to formulate verbal responses. She had made enough progress that it was now possible to discriminate and atone for learning difficulties. Was she learning slowly primarily because her language difficulties were so great, or were there other neurological issues contributing to her slow academic progress? During the lesson on addresses, Chloe sat attentively in her chair and happily drew a picture of her house while the other children carried on a lively conversation about their houses and hometowns. Each kid was asked what their address was, and if they didn't know, was given a piece of paper containing their address clearly printed. Chloe didn't know hers. She was given her address and asked to copy it onto her drawing. She continued to display difficulties remembering her address, so it became part of her daily routine. She would say it, write it, draw it, but even after a month, she could not recite her home address without prompting and support. Chloe was having difficulty with long-term memory.

Long-term memories are the events, habits, facts and images that you remember over long periods of time, even years. These types of memories can be verbal, visual and even sensory. This ability requires consolidation and storage of information, which can then be accessed and retrieved in the future (Baron, 2004).

Figure 5.1 Children who struggle with long term-memory difficulties benefit from visual cues within the environment.

Explicit/Declarative Memory

As described previously, declarative or explicit memory is the conscious recalling of a life event or learned knowledge (Schacter, 1992; Squire, 1982). Childhood memories and stories, ingredients to a recipe, facts memorized in history class are all memories that can be categorized as explicit. Two memory subtypes, episodic and semantic, rely on conscious awareness.

Episodic memory is the conscious memory for events and facts specific to an individual's experience (Tulving, 1972, 1983). This is an individual's life story. The loss of this memory is associated with typical adult aging as well as clinical syndromes of Alzheimer's disease and other dementias. Helpful assessment tools for episodic memory include list-learning, story-learning and design-learning tests (Baron, 2004).

The ability to recall facts, rely on base knowledge, remember concepts and word meaning and give meaning to sensory experiences relies on *semantic memory* (Squire, 1982). While both episodic and semantic memory can be impacted by Alzheimer's disease (Baron, 2004), injury and lesion studies indicate that these memory subtypes rely on different neural substrates. For example, an individual with damage to the medial/temporal/lobe–ventral/frontal/lobe system may experience difficulty recalling episodic memories but can still utilize the semantic system and report on the history of the Civil War (Kolb & Whishaw, 2009). Semantic memory can be assessed using word fluency and category fluency, vocabulary, naming and free association tests. Semantic information can also prove to be useful in supporting the development of strategies to aid recall. For example, the ability to categorize information into groups, called "semantic clustering," can enhance the amount of information and fluidity of recall.

Implicit/Procedural

Implicit or procedural memory is another memory system that relies on long-term storage information, but here the information is unconscious or unintentional (Cermak, 1996). Rote activities, such as riding a bike, the use of native language or playing a sport utilize implicit memory. This infers that prior exposure is required to establish these unconscious memories, and that there is no conscious recalling of the acquisition event (Roediger, 1990). This type of memory relies on different neural substrates rather than explicit memories. Processing of data is "bottom-up" and sensory driven (Kolb & Whishaw, 2009). Thus, implicit memory utilizes different neural substrates rather than explicit memory and can be assessed across numerous modalities, including verbal, non-verbal, and visual motor functioning (Baron, 2004).

Emotional Memory

Emotional experience, both pleasant and unpleasant, has an impact on memory functioning. These memories can be explicit or implicit. Events that evoke emotions are more memorable then events that lack emotional relevance, impacting both visual and verbal memory. The heightened salience of emotional stimuli for the formation of explicit memories has been an adaptive evolutionary development in humans (Barrett & Barr, 2009). Neuroimaging, neuropsychological, drug and neural stimulation studies indicate that emotional arousal influences encoding and modulation of memory consolidation (Hamann, 2001). Likewise, items or objects associated with emotions are more memorable (Sakaki, Niki, & Mather, 2011). Emotional memory utilizes a different neural circuit than does other long-term memory systems. The amygdala along with the hypothalamus play a crucial role in emotional memories as well as the visceral responses, such as heart rate and blood pressure. Close connections with the medial temporocortical structures as well as the periaqueductal gray matter in the brain stem may account for conscious aspects of emotional memory, and connections with the basal ganglia may influence the development of implicit emotional memories (Kolb & Whishaw, 2009). Amygdalar modulation of hippocampus, caudate nucleus, insula, entorhinal cortex, and prefrontal regions has also been found to be a critical component in the formation of emotional memories (McGaugh, McIntyre, & Power, 2002). Studies examining the influence of genes on emotional memory suggest that specific neuromodulatory systems that alter the amygdala's sensitivity to salient stimuli vary as a result of genetic makeup (Todd, Palombo, Levine, & Anderson, 2011). This enhancement of emotional memory has been associated with a specific deletion variant that may influence encoding and consolidation of emotional memory (de Quervain et al., 2007).

Thus, these findings suggest that the encoding of information into memory can be highly influenced by the emotional valence of the memory as well as by an individual's capacity to modulate the significance of the emotional experience associated with that memory—a capacity to modulate that may be based in that individual's genetic constitution. Consequently, a child's ability to take in information, store it and retrieve it on demand can vary significantly depending on that child's previous as well as current emotional experience.

For example, a child with an undiagnosed reading disability and who had a genetic variant that made it difficult for her to regulate her emotional reactivity may have had the repeated experience of failure when required to read within a school setting. Perhaps her new teacher, who experienced her as very capable verbally, did not understand the child's underlying shame and resultant refusal to read, along with her dysregulated reaction and attributed it to oppositional behavior. Perhaps, then, the teacher implemented a behavioral system that embarrassed and angered the child further, resulting in more general opposition to any rules and limitations. Perhaps the child's escalated behavior was met with a concomitant escalation of a behavioral program that further worsened the situation. Then the initial reason for the child's resistance, an underlying reading disability, was lost because of the emotional and behavioral overlay, and the child was increasingly traumatized by the reaction of her environment. Any of the child's subsequent attempts to read, either in school or at home, then carried with it an emotional memory that made reading too painful.

Far too often, scenarios like this have been played out in school settings, resulting in a form of a posttraumatic stress disorder (PTSD) that has negatively impacted a child's capacity to learn within an academic environment. While this is perhaps a mild form of PTSD, consider children who have been far more severely traumatized. Their capacity to attend to and encode into memory academic information that has far less emotional significance for them would be significantly compromised.

Nineteen-year-old Frankie was born in Florida when his mother was fourteen. His father lived with the family for a time while they were in Florida, but he had extensive court involvement over the course of Frankie's life and was eventually incarcerated for bank robbery. Earlier reports did not indicate any delays in developmental milestones for Frankie. However, according to previous reports, there was an early history of neglect and both sexual and physical abuse. Frankie, his mother and sisters moved to Boston in 2001, where Frankie was enrolled in third grade.

In middle school, Frankie began having more difficulty both at home and school, and a probation officer and the Department of Social Services became involved. In 2006, he was briefly placed in foster care and then moved to residential care for forty-five days. He eventually returned to his mother's home for a brief period but, due to continued conflict, he was removed again. He returned to foster care for a few days and was again placed in a forty-five day residential program. He once again returned to foster care during the summer of 2006, ran away for four days but continued to live there through the winter of 2008. He had begun a mentor relationship with new foster parents who were then appointed as his legal educational advocates when Frankie began living with them in December 2008. Frankie had attended a local high school but was expelled in tenth grade because of incidents of verbal and physical aggression. He then transferred to another Boston high school in February 2009. While there, he was diagnosed with a dissociative identity disorder and a dependent personality disorder as well as ADHD, PTSD and a mood disorder/not otherwise specified by his outside therapists.

Frankie's new foster parents were very concerned about his continued academic delays, his lack of social boundaries, his difficulty responding to limits and authority, his racial and sexual identity issues and his misuse of fantasy. Frankie was not learning because he could barely pay attention to the demands of the academic environment. Testing on the WISC-IV placed him in the borderline range for working memory and perceptual organization and the low average range for verbal comprehension and processing speed with a significant vulnerability in executive functions. In respect to memory processing, he had significant difficulty learning and consolidating verbal information. This process was impacted by his variable attention and his failure to actively organize information in a manner that facilitated consolidation and retrieval. Both his auditory and visual memory skills were below average, but he did somewhat better on a task providing more context from which he could draw some details, albeit in a disorganized fashion.

Frankie's underlying neurological issues related to impaired executive functioning, visual spatial organization, memory and phonological processing had been further exacerbated by his very significant emotional difficulties. These included his difficulty managing intrusive ideation, dysregulation of affect with irritability and angry outbursts, difficulty concentrating and emotional detachment. He also met criteria for an affective disorder characterized by a significant depression and instances, in which he became emotionally labile in a manner that impaired not only his ability to reason logically and coherently but also his ability to accurately perceive and test his reality. This tendency was compounded further by an emotional immaturity that underlay his choice to exert less control over his feelings than one would expect of a young man his age. Furthermore, his maladaptive self-consciousness made focusing on his struggles difficult and was symptomatic of his poor self-esteem and lack of confidence. He also displayed a significant negative attitude towards himself and his body as well as a hypervigilant stance towards relationships as a means to protect himself from harm. Frankie could neither attend to nor recall the information that he was supposed to be learning in school. He was focused on trying to survive.

Measures of Long-Term Memory

Various assessment tools have been developed to measure different aspects of long term memory. Table 5.1 provides a list of assessments for visual and verbal long term memory.

Table 5.1 Tests of long-term memory.

Assessment	Description	Age
Verbal Long-Term Memory		
Children's Memory Scales (CMS): Stories Delayed Recall and Recognition	Retell a story after a delayed period of time. Next, the individual is asked questions about story details in a true or false format.	5–16
CMS: Word Pairs Learning, Delayed Recall and Delayed Recognition	The individual learns a list of word pairs. Next, the individual is presented with one word from the list, and asked to supply the word associated with it. Following three learning trials, the individual is asked to recall as many of the word pairs as possible without cueing. After a delay, the individual is asked to recall the word pairs without cues. Lastly the individual is asked to identify previously learned word pairs from a list of learned and new pairs.	5–16
CMS: Word Lists Learning, Delayed Recall, Delayed Recognition	After learning a list of unrelated words, the individual is asked to recall the list both immediately and after a delay. Next, the examiner states a word and the individual identifies it as off or on the original list.	5–16
NEPSY II: List Memory Delayed	25–35 minutes after learning a list of unrelated words that are nouns, the child is asked to recall the words.	7–12
NEPSY II: Narrative Memory—Free and cued recall.	After hearing a story, the child is asked to repeat the story. They are also asked questions to elicit missing details.	3–12
Woodcock Johnson III-Cognitive Abilities (WJ III-COG): Retrieval Fluency	The individual is asked to name as many examples from a given category (things to eat or drink, animals and first names of people) within a one minute time period.	2–80+
Test of Memory and Learning and Memory (TOMAL2): Memory for Stories—Delayed Recall	The individual listens to a story and is asked to remember the story after a delay.	5–19.11
TOMAL2: Word Selective Reminding—Delayed Recall	The individual learns a list of words and, after a delay, is asked to repeat it and is informed when a mistake is made.	5–19.11
CVLT-C: List A Short and Long Delay Free Recall, Short and Long Delay Cued Recall	The child is asked to recall as many items as possible from a grocery list after each of five trials. An interference list is read once and they are asked to recall the original list. They then recall the original list given category cues. After a delay of twenty minutes they recall the original list and then are given cues. The child is also assessed for semantic clustering skills.	5–16
Wide Range Assessment of Memory and Learning—2 (WRAML2): Story Memory—Delayed Recall, Retention and Recognition	After hearing a story, the individual is given three tasks: recall the story, recognize details using multiple choice answers and finally recall elements of the story after a 15 minute delay.	5–90

(Continued)

Table 5.1 (Continued)

Assessment	Description	Age
WRAML2: Verbal Learning—Delayed Recall and Recognition	The individual learns a list of words over four trials. After a delay, the individual is asked to recall the list. They are also asked to recognize words as either off or on the list.	5–90

Visual Long-Term Memory

Assessment	Description	Age
NEPSY II: Memory for Faces—Delayed Recall	The child looks at a series of faces and after a delay in time, is then presented with a series of three photographs and asked which faces were previously viewed.	5–16
CMS: Dot Locations Long Delay	After a delay, the individual is asked to recall a visual array of dots by placing chips in a grid in the same positions as the visual model.	5–16
CMS: Face Delayed	After a delay, the individual is asked to indicate whether a series of photographs of faces are or are not one of those they had been asked to remember during an exposure trial.	5–16
TOMAL2: Facial Memory—Delayed Recall	Assesses recognition and identification of faces after a delayed period of time.	5–19.11
TOMAL2: Visual Selective Reminding—Delayed Recall	Requires recall of the sequence of a series of meaningless geometric designs after a delayed period of time.	5–19.11
WRAML2: Design Memory Recognition	After a delay, recognize if a shape was one of an original array of geometric shapes.	5–90
WRAML2: Picture Memory Recognition	While viewing a picture, the child is asked to recognize elements that have been added, changed or moved from a previously seen and nearly identical picture.	5–90

Verbal-Visual Associated Delayed Memory

Assessment	Description	Age
WRAML2: Sound/Symbol Delayed Recall and Retention	This is a paired associated learning task for children in which the child is taught a sound and symbol relationship and is asked to retain and recall it later.	5–8
KABC II: Atlantis Delayed	The individual learns nonsense names for pictured animals and plants, then demonstrates learning by pointing at the correct picture from an array, after a time delay.	3–18
KABC II: Rebus Delayed	The individual learns the meanings of a simple pictograph of words (♥ = love), then learns the meaning of a rebus (I ♥ New York). After a period of time, they are asked to recall the meaning.	4–18
NEPSY II: Memory for Names—Delayed Recall	The individual learns the name for a pictured child and is asked to recall the name after a time delay.	5–12
WJ III-COG: Visual-Auditory Learning, Delayed	The individual learns the meanings of simple word-rebus associations. After a period of time, he is asked to recall the meaning by constructing sentences using the rebuses.	2–80+

Table 5.2 briefly outlines tests of semantic memory

Table 5.2 Measures of long-term memory.

Assessment	Description	Age
CMS: Sequences	Assesses the ability to manipulate and sequence previously learned verbal information as quickly as possible.	5–16
K-ABC II: Riddles	The child points or names a concept described by the examiner.	3–7
K-ABC II: Verbal Knowledge	The child selects from an array of 6 pictures the image that describes a vocabulary word or the answer to a question.	7–18
K-ABC II: Expressive Vocabulary	The child names a pictured object.	3–18
Stanford-Binet Scales of Intelligence, Fifth Edition (SB5): Procedural Knowledge (nonverbal)	The individual is asked to complete common activities and use common objects.	2–85+
SB5: Picture Absurdities (nonverbal)	The individual is asked to identify absurd or missing details in an image.	2–85+
SB5: Vocabulary (Verbal)	The individual is asked to display knowledge regarding body parts, toys and actions in images and is asked to define real words verbally.	2–85+
WISC-IV: Comprehension	See Chapter 3	6–16.11
WISC-IV: Information	See Chapter 3	6–16.11
WISC-IV: Vocabulary	See Chapter 3	6–16.11
WISC-IV Integrated: Comprehension Multiple Choice	The child is asked questions that grow increasingly complex and abstract, then chooses an answer from multiple choice options.	6–16.11
WISC-IV Integrated: Information Multiple Choice	The child is asked questions related to quantitative and calendar facts, science, history and general factual knowledge. He or she then selects an answer from multiple choice options.	6–16.11
WISC-IV Integrated: Vocabulary Multiple Choice	Young children view a picture and are asked to name the object. Older children hear and read printed words, then select the best definition for the word.	6–16.11
WISC-IV Integrated: Picture Vocabulary Multiple Choice	The examiner shows the child an array of four pictures, and the child points at the image that best matches a vocabulary word.	6–16.11
WJ III-COG: Verbal Comprehension	Comprised of four subtests, the individual is asked to 1) identify familiar and unfamiliar objects using a picture, 2) hear a word and provide a synonym, 3) hear a word and provide an antonym and 4) complete an analogy.	2–80+
WJ III-COG: General Information	Composed of two subtests, the individual is asked 1) Where would you find (an object)? and 2) What would you do with (an object)? Items become increasingly difficult and unusual.	2–80+

Short-Term Memory

Short-term memory refers to the ability to hold information for a short period of time in consciousness, then encode it. This process is a bit like a buffer or filter, holding information in the immediate time for use (registration), but then either letting it go or moving the information into the consolidation process (encoding; Baron, 2004). For example, remembering a seven-digit phone number for use, then either forgetting it seconds after dialing, or moving the phone number into long-term storage for use in the future. To do so, individuals may rely on the rehearsing of the seven digits, repeating them consciously in the mind, until the call has been made. Like other types of memory, short-term memory is multimodal, involving visual, verbal, motor and sensory stimuli (Kolb & Whishaw, 2009). Clinical measures of immediate memory recall include Digit Span Forward Tests and Block Span Forward Tests (Baron, 2004).

Measures of Short-Term Memory

Table 5.3 further outlines tests of short term memory.

Table 5.3 Measures of short-term memory.

Assessment	Description	Age
Verbal Immediate Memory		
CVLT-C: List A Trial 1	The child is asked to recall as many items as possible from a grocery list after each of 5 trials. They are then provided with category cues to determine if they aid recall.	5–16
CMS: Stories—Immediate Recall	Listen to a story and immediately recall meaningful and semantically related verbal material.	5–16
CMS: Word Pairs—Total Score and Supplemental Word Pairs—Immediate Recall	Learn a list of word pairs over 3 trials.	5–16
K-ABC II: Number Recall	The child is asked to repeat a series of numbers stated by the examiner.	3–18
K-ABC II: Word Order (without color interference)	The child is asked to touch a series of silhouettes of common objects in the same order as the examiner states.	3–18
NEPSY II: Sentence Repetition	The child hears sentences of increasing complexity and is asked to immediately recall the sentence.	3–12
TOMAL2: Memory for Stories	The child is asked to recall a short story read by the examiner.	5–19.11
TOMAL2: Word Selective Reminding	The child learns a list of words, then repeats it and is reminded of words left out.	5–19.11
TOMAL2: Object Recall	Over four trials, the child is asked to recall names associated with pictures.	5–19.11

Assessment	Description	Age
TOMAL2: Digits Forward	The child is asked to recall a series of digits.	5–19.11
TOMAL2: Paired Recall	A verbal immediate recall of learning word pairings. After a learning period, the examiner states the first word, and the child states the paired word.	5–19.11
WISC-IV Integrated: Digit Span—Forward	The examiner reads a series of numbers and the child is asked to repeat them in the same order.	6–16.11
WISC-IV Integrated: Letter Span—Forward	The examiner reads two lists of letters, one rhyming the other non-rhyming, and the child repeats the series in the same order.	6–16.11
WC JIII-COG: Memory for Words	The individual is asked to recall a list of unrelated words in the correct sequence.	2–80+
WRAML2: Story Memory	The individual is asked to recall a short story read by the examiner.	5–90
WRAML2: Verbal Learning	The individual is asked to learn a list of words over four trials.	5–90
WRAML2: Sentence Memory	The individual is asked to repeat sentences of increasing semantic and syntactic complexity read to them by the examiner.	5–90
Visual Immediate Memory		
CMS: Faces—Immediate Recall	The child is asked to remember and recognize a series of faces.	5–16
CMS: Dot Location—Total Score	The individual is asked to learn the spatial location of dots over three learning trials.	5–16
CMS Supplemental: Family Pictures—Immediate Recall	The individual is asked to recall scenes of family members during various activities.	5–16
K-ABC II: Face Recognition	The child is asked to recall a series of faces from memory.	3–18
K-ABC II: Hand Movements	The individual is asked to repeat a series of taps performed by the examiner on the table.	3–18
NEPSY II: Memory for Faces: Immediate Recall	The child views a series of faces, and is then presented with three photographs at a time and asked to identify any previously viewed faces.	5–16
TOMAL2: Face Memory	The child recalls pictures of faces.	5–19.11
TOMAL2: Visual Selective Reminding	The child is asked to point at specified dots on a card and is reminded when incorrect.	5–19.11
TOMAL2: Abstract Visual Memory	The child views abstract meaningless images without the importance of order.	5–19.11
TOMAL2: Visual Sequential Memory	Requires the child recall the sequence of a series of meaningless geometric shapes.	5–19.11
TOMAL2: Memory for Location	The child is presented with a set of dots on a page and is asked to recall the position of the dots after a short delay.	5–19.11

(*Continued*)

Table 5.3 (Continued)

Assessment	Description	Age
TOMAL2: Nonverbal supplemental Tests: Manual Imitation	The child is asked to repeat a series of hand movements modeled by the examiner in the same sequence.	5–19.11
WISC-IV Integrated: Visual Digit Span—Forward	The child is asked to repeat a series of numbers in the same order as they were presented.	6–16.11
WISC-IV Integrated: Spatial Span—Forward	The child repeats a sequence of blocks in the same order as demonstrated by the examiner.	6–16.11
WJ III-COG: Picture Recognition	The individual is asked to recognize a subset of previously presented pictures within a field of distracting pictures.	2–80+
Universal Nonverbal Intelligence Test (UNIT): Spatial Memory (non-symbolic)	After viewing a random pattern of green, black and green/black dots on a grid for 5 seconds, the child is asked to recreate that pattern by placing chips on the grid.	5–17
UNIT: Symbolic Memory (symbolic)	Using the universal symbol for boy, girl, man and woman, the child views an image of these symbols in random orders and is asked to recreate the sequence using cards.	5–17
UNIT: Object Memory (symbolic)	The child views a random pictorial array of common objects for 5 seconds. A second array is present containing the same objects with new objects. The child is asked to cover familiar objects with a chip.	5–17
WRAML2: Design Memory	After viewing a grid with geometric forms for 5 seconds, the individual is asked to replicate the forms in a grid by drawing them.	5–90
WRAML2: Picture Memory	The individual is asked to identify all the elements that have been changed, moved or added in a picture they have previously viewed for a 10-second interval.	5–90

Working Memory

Working memory, considered an important element of executive functions, is the ability to temporarily store and manipulate information (Fougnie & Morois, 2011). Information used during this process may originate from short-term memory, stores of long-term memory, sensory memory/information or novel stimuli. As mentioned in Chapter 4, Baddeley and colleagues proposed that working memory can be divided into a three-part system with an overarching *central executive* and two subsystems, the *visuospatial sketchpad* and *phonological loop* (1992). The central executive system coordinates the other subsystems, relaying information. The visuospatial sketchpad is thought to be responsible for retaining and manipulating visual information, while the phonological system does so for auditory information. For a review on working memory, see Chapter 4.

Measures of Working Memory

For an outline of tests of working memory, see Chapter 4.

Memory and Learning

Throughout this chapter, the role of memory during functioning in daily life has been noted. As with other functional domains, it is possible to tease various elements apart, differentiating functioning and neuroanatomy. While individual elements of memory are important, the integration of all memory types is essential for the acquisition, maintenance and usage of skills, both simple and complex. One example of the role played by multiple memory types during the process of learning is the development of reading skills. Keep in mind, reading is a complex function, involving many other cognitive and motor skills aside from memory, but here, memory is the focus.

In 1985, British psychologist Uta Frith developed a reading acquisition model that can be used to provide a framework for the role of memory in learning to read (Frith, 1985). This three-stage process begins around the age of five or six. First, during the "pictorial" stage, the child has not yet grasped the logic of writing. Instead, the visual system attempts to recognize words, based on physical features (straight lines, curves, etc.). The child may recognize the name or the brand name of food or toys. The emotional importance of these visual representations earmark spoken words and visual representations, assisting in the development of explicit recall and implicit recognition (Khairudin, Valipour, Nasir, & Zainah, 2012). Visual long-term memory is employed, and meaning develops from symbols.

During the second stage, the "phonological" stage, the emphasis is on recognizing individual letters and associating sound with image. The child learns individual speech sounds and the associated letter groups ("ch", "ai" ...). This phonological awareness is used to build words out of letters. Here, verbal/visual associated memory plays a role in the development of phonological awareness and students with deficits in this area struggle. Phonological short-term memory allows individuals to access multiple sounds at one time upon viewing letters (Polychroni, Economou, Printezi, & Koutlidi, 2011). Evidence suggests working memory also plays a role in phonological processing (Baddeley, Gathercole, & Papagno, 1998; Loosli, Buschkuehl, Perrig, & Jaeggi, 2012). Other theories suggest that phonological memory represents the ability to encode, discriminate and retrieve sound associations into and from a long-term store that can become available for working memory functioning (Garthercole, 2006). And yet, another theory suggests that short-term *semantic* memory, categorizing sound/symbol relationships, plays an important role in phonological development, sometimes referred to as semantic clustering (Haarmann, Davelaar, & Usher, 2003). As a result, this complicated process consumes the first few years of reading instruction, leading to the explicit representation of speech sounds (Dehaene, 2009).

Finally, during the third "orthographic" stage, the child no longer needs to slowly decode each word but can rely on a vast lexicon of visual units. Reading rate is no longer determined by how quickly a child phonologically decodes words but is increasingly influenced by how often the child has encountered the word. High-frequency words are read quickly whereas longer or unfamiliar words are read slowly. Here, reading moves from an explicit process to a more implicit skill. Reading can now occur without consciously relying on phonological awareness and decoding. A second reading pathway develops, parallel to the phonological pathway, increasing rate and fluency. It has been shown that working memory contributes to the rate of reading (de Jong & de Jong, 1996). Comprehension evolves, and learning to read becomes reading to learn. Working memory and short-term memory continues to be important during comprehension, and long-term memory is employed for encoding, retention and retrieval.

References

Baddeley, A. (1992). Working memory. *Science, 255,* 556–559.

Baddeley, A., Gathercole, S., & Papagno, C. (1998). The phonological loop as a language learning device. *Psychological Review, 105*(1), 158–173.

Barnes, K. J. (2010). Two forms of implicit learning in childhood ADHD. *Developmental Neuropsychology, 35*(5), 494–505.

Baron, I. S. (2004). *Neuropsychological evaluation of the child.* New York, NY: Oxford University Press.

Barrett, L. F., & Bar, M. (2009). See it with feeling: Affective predictions during object perception. *Philosophical Transactions of the Royal Society of London: B Biological Sciences, 364,* 1325–1334.

Bauer, P. J. (2005). Developments in declarative memory. *Psychological Science, 16*(1), 41–47.

Bracken, B. A., & McCallum, R. S. (1998). *Universal Nonverbal Intelligence Test.* Itasca, IL: Riverside Publishing.

Cermak, L. S. (1996). *Current issues in the neuropsychology of memory disorders: Handout.* International Neuropsychological Society Continuing Education Course, Honolulu, HI.

Chun, M., & Jiang, Y. (1998). Contextual cueing: Implicit learning and memory of visual context guides spatial attention. *Cognitive Psychology, 36,* 28–71.

Dehaene, S. (2009). *Reading in the brain.* New York, NY: Penguin Group.

de Jong, P., & de Jong, P. F. (1996). Working memory, intelligence and reading ability in children. *Personality and Individual Differences, 21*(6), 1007–1020.

Delis, D. C., Kramer, J. H., Kaplan, E., & Ober, B. A. (1994). *California Verbal Learning Test—Children's version.* San Antonio, TX: Psychological Corporation.

de Quervain, D. J., Kolassa, I. T., Ertl, V., Onyut, P. L., Neuner, F., Elbert, T., et al. (2007). A deletion variant of the alpha2b-adrenoceptor is related to emotional memory in Europeans and Africans. *Nature Neuroscience, 10,* 1137–1139.

Doyon, J. (2008). Motor sequence learning and movement disorders. *Current Opinion in Neurology, 21,* 478–483.

Dupont, S., Samson, Y., Le, B. D., & Baulac, M. (2002). Anatomy of verbal memory: A functional MRI study. *Surgical and Radiologic Anatomy, 24,* 57–63.

Fougnie, D., & Marois, R. (2011). What limits working memory capacity? Evidence for modality-specific sources to the simultaneous storage of visual and auditory arrays. *Journal of Experimental Psychology: Learning, Memory & Cognition, 37*(6), 1329–1341.

Frith, U. (1985). Beneath the surface of developmental dyslexia. In K. E. Patterson, J. C. Marshall, & M. Coltheart (Eds.), *Surface dyslexia: Cognitive and neuropsychological studies of phonological reading* (pp. 301–330). Hillsdale, NJ: Erlbaum.

Gallace, A., & Spence, C. (2009). The cognitive and neural correlates of tactile memory. *Psychological Bulletin, 135*(3), 380–406.

Garthercole, S. E. (2006). Nonword repetition and word learning: The nature of the relationship. *Applied Psycholinguistics, 27,* 513–543.

Haarmann, H. J., Davelaar, E. J., & Usher, M. (2003). Individual differences in semantic short-term memory capacity and reading comprehension. *Journal of Memory and Language, 48,* 320–345.

Hamann, S. B. (2001). Cognitive and neural mechanisms of emotional memory. *Trends in Cognitive Science, 5,* 394–400.

Heimann, M., Strid, K., Smith, L., Tjus, T., Ulvund, S. E., & Meltzoff, A. N. (2006). Exploring the relation between memory, gestural communication, and the emergence of language in infancy: A longitudinal study. *Infant and Child Development, 15,* 233–249.

Kalpakidou, A. K., Allin, M. P., Walshe, M., Giampietro, V., Nam, K. W., McGuire, P., . . . Nosarti, C. (2012). Neonatal brain injury and neuroanatomy of memory processing following very preterm birth in adulthood: An fMRI study. *Plos One, 7*(4), 1–9.

Khairudin, R., Valipour, G. M., Nasir, R., & Zainah, A. Z. (2012). Emotion intermediaries for implicit memory retrieval processing evidence using word and picture stimuli. *Asian Social Science, 8*(10), 58–67.

Kolb, B., & Whishaw, I. Q. (2009). *Fundamentals of human neuropsychology* (6th ed.). New York, NY: Worth.

Kolling, T., Goertz, C., Frahsek, S., & Knopf, M. (2009). Stability of deferred imitation in 12- to 18-month-old-infants: A closer look into developmental dynamics. *European Journal of Developmental Psychology, 6,* 615–640.

Kolling, T., Goertz, C., Frahsek, S., & Knopf, M. (2010). Memory development throughout the second year: Overall developmental pattern, individual differences, and developmental trajectories, *Infant Behavior and Development, 33,* 159–167.

Krakauer, J. W., & Shadmehr, R. (2006). Consolidation of motor memory. *Trends in Neurosciences, 29,* 58–64.

Lezak, M. D., Howieson, D. B., Bigler, E. D., & Tranel, D. (2012). *Neuropsychological assessment* (5th ed.). New York, NY: Oxford University Press.

Loosli, S. V., Buschkuehl, M., Perrig, W. J., & Jaeggi, S. M. (2012). Working memory training improves reading processes in typically developing children. *Child Neuropsychology, 18*(1), 62–78

Lum, J. (2010). Longitudinal study of declarative and procedural memory in primary school-aged children. *Australian Journal of Psychology, 62*(3), 139–148.

Mandler, J. M. (2004). A synopsis of the foundations of mind: Origins of conceptual thought. *Developmental Science, 7,* 499–505.

Marteniuk, R. G. (1976). Cognitive information processes in motor short-term memory and motor production. In G. E. Stelmach (Ed.), *Motor control: Issues and trends.* New York, NY: Academic Press.

McGaugh, J. L., McIntyre, C. K., & Power, A. E. (2002). Amygdala modulation of memory consolidation: Interaction with other brain systems. *Neurobiology of Learning and Memory, 78,* 539–552.

Meyers, J. E., & Meyers, K. R. (1995). *Rey Complex Figure Test and Recognition Trial: Professional manual.* Lutz, FL: Psychological Assessment Resources, Inc.

Milner, B. (1965). *The problems with memory following bilateral hippocampal lesions.* Princeton, NJ: Van Nostrand, (pp. 97–111).

Miranda, I., Ferreira, G., Ramirez-Lugo, L., & Bermúdez-Rattoni, F. (2003). Role of cholinergic system on the construction of memories: Taste memory encoding. *Neurobiology of Learning and Memory, 80,* 211–222.

Polychroni, F., Economou, A., Printezi, A., & Koutlidi, I. (2011). Verbal memory and semantic organization of children with learning disabilities. *Learning Disabilities: A Contemporary Journal, 9*(2), 27–44.

Preston, A. R., & Gabrieli, J. D. (2008). Dissociation between explicit memory and configural memory in the human temporal lobe. *Cerebral Cortex, 18,* 192–207.

Roediger, H. L. (1990). Implicit memory: Retention without remembering. *American Psychologist, 45,* 1043–1056.

Roid, G. H. (2003). *Stanford-Binet intelligence scales* (5th ed.). Austin, TX: PRO-ED.

Sakaki, M., Niki, K., & Mather, M. (2011). Updating existing emotional memories involved in frontopolar/orbito-frontal cortex in ways that acquiring new emotional memories does not. *Journal of Cognitive Neuroscience, 23*(11), 3498–3514.

Schacter, D. L. (1992). Understanding implicit memory. *American Psychologist, 47*(4), 559.

Squire, L. R. (1982). The neuropsychology of human memory. *Annual Review of Neuroscience, 5,* 241–273.

Squire, L. R. (2004). Memory systems of the brain: A brief history and current perspective. *Neurobiology of Learning and Memory, 82,* 171–177.

Squire, L., Stark, C., & Clark, R. (2004). The medial temporal lobe. *Annual Review of Neuroscience, 27,* 279–306.

Strid, K., Tjus, T., Smith, L., Meltzoff, A. N., & Heimann, M. (2006). Infant recall memory and communication predicts later cognitive development. *Infant Behavior & Development, 29,* 545–553.

Todd, R. M., Palombo, D. J., Levine, B., & Anderson, A. K. (2011). Genetic differences in emotionally enhanced memory. *Neuropsychologia, 49,* 734–744.

Tulving, E. (1972). Episodic and semantic memory. In E. Tulving & W. Donaldson (Eds.), *Organization of memory* (pp. 381–403). New York, NY: Academic Press.

Tulving, E. (1983). *Elements of episodic memory.* New York, NY: Oxford University Press.

Tulving, E. (2002). Episodic memory and common sense: How far apart? In A. Baddeley, J. P. Aggleton, & M. A. Conway (Eds.), *Episodic memory: New directions in research* (pp. 269–287). New York, NY: Oxford University Press.

Velichkovskii, B. M. (1978). Visual memory and models of human information-processing. *Journal of Russian and Eastern European Psychology, 16*(4), 68–89.

Wechsler, D. (2003). *Wechsler intelligence scale for children* (4th ed.). San Antonio, TX: The Psychological Corporation.

White, T. L. (1998, January 1). Olfactory memory: The long and short of it. *Chemical Senses, 23,* 433–41.

Woodcock, R. W., McGrew, K. S., & Mather, N. (2001). *Woodcock-Johnson III Tests of Achievement.* Itasca, IL: Riverside Publishing.

6 Understanding and Assessing Visual Motor Functioning

The ability to use various sensory modalities to scan one's environment and organize an appropriate motor response is crucial to one's survival. In the context of a neuropsychological evaluation, tests of visuoconstructive abilities are typically used as a measure of one's ability to combine perception with some organized response. Necessarily, visuoconstructive ability involves a visuospatial element. Human figure drawings are often used as part of a battery assessing visuoconstructive abilities over the course of a child's development.

Figure 6.1 An example of early visuoconstructive skills in drawing a human figure.

Figure 6.2 An example of a more advanced segmentation of the human form.

Development of Visuoconstructive Skills

Visuoconstructive skills can be understood in the context of two major areas of functioning—drawing and assembling, with drawing tasks being further separated into copying and free-drawing categories (Lezak, Howieson, Bigler, & Tranel, 2012). In respect to drawing, ability in this area follows a developmental sequence in children, moving from simple geometric shapes to three-dimensional shapes to segmented human figures and on to complete human figures (Barrett & Eames, 1998). A child's ability to copy geometric forms was examined extensively by Beery (1967), who, based on his findings, described a sequence that children followed in the development of their visual motor skills and, using this data, developed the *Beery-Buktenica Developmental Test of Visual-Motor Integration* (Beery VMI; Beery, Buktenica, & Beery, 2010), a developmental test of visual motor integration. Essentially, when beginning to use paper and pencil to draw, children tend to be able to negotiate vertical, then horizontal and then circular lines (Beery et al., 2010).

Assembly tasks examine sensorimotor functioning, particularly in respect to the integration of visuospatial and motor skills, in both two and three dimensional space (Lezak et al., 2012). Studies of a child's ability to construct spatial relations have described a developmental sequence. Before twelve months of age, there is very little systematic organization of objects. Stacking begins at twelve months and side by side relations arise at eighteen months. Between three and four years, children are able to build both vertical and horizontal elements in a single construction. As they age, children are able to incorporate more complex spatial patterns, a skill that depends on the interaction of both the features of the spatial array as well as the development of particular strategies a child employs to define the structure of the pattern (Stiles & Stern, 2001).

Neuroanatomy of Visuoconstructive Skills

As discussed in Chapter 3, visuospatial and visuoconstructive skills are largely mediated by the right hemisphere. Patients with right-hemisphere lesions take a part-oriented approach to constructional tasks, often reproducing small details without appreciating how they fit into the whole, thus missing the forest for the trees. Patients with a left-hemisphere dysfunction may get the big picture but fail to include important details, missing the trees for the forest (Lezak et al., 2012). Performance on a design-fluency task can also be impaired by right-hemisphere premotor lesions (Jones-Gotman and Milner, 1977; Ruff, Allen, Farrow, Niemann, & Wylie, 1994). While nonspecific effects of the dementing process in patients with multi infarct and alcohol-related dementias contributed to impaired design-fluency production, visuoconstructive deficits, in particular, impaired design fluency, with a difficulty generating novel designs and a tendency to perseverate, in patients with dementia of the Alzheimer's type (Bigler, 1995).

Visuoconstructive skills have also been studied in relation to visually guided interactions with three-dimensional objects. In a fMRI study, Shikata et al. (2003) found that the human anterior intraparietal area (AIP) was activated by the surface orientation and spatial adjustment of finger position towards an object during a visually guided hand movement. In contrast, the caudal intraparietal area (CIP) was activated by the surface orientation but not by spatial adjustment of finger position, suggesting that the function of the CIP is more involved in coding 3-D features of the objects, whereas the AIP is more involved in visually guided hand movements. Another fMRI study monitoring hand shaping (Begliomini, Nelini, Caria, Grodd, & Castiello, 2008) found significant activation in the right dorsal premotor cortex, right cerebellum and the AIP bilaterally and suggested that there is specific grasping-related neural activity that is dependent on handedness.

Visuoconstruction, Achievement and Emotional Development

Visuoconstructive abilities have been studied in children in relation to other functional domains. For example, in a study of children's performance on the *Bender Visual-Motor Gestalt Test–Second Edition* (Bender-Gestalt-II, Brannigan & Decker, 2003), Decker, Englund, Carboni, and Brooks (2011) concluded that nonverbal reasoning and visuospatial attention are important contributing factors to visual motor integration and that Nonverbal Fluid Reasoning, Quantitative Reasoning, and Nonverbal Visual–Spatial abilities subtests were significantly related to Bender-Gestalt-II performance. Furthermore, visual motor skills have been found to be correlated with school adjustment, school readiness, and social/emotional functioning. For example, a study in kindergartners found that verbal and visual motor readiness skills were significantly related to aptitude scores, passing proficiency tests, and end-of-year academic performance (Kurdek & Sinclair, 2000). Bart, Hajami, and Bar-Haim (2007) found that an aggregate measure of a child's ability in various motor domains was a strong predictor of scholastic achievement and disruptive behavior. Piek, Bradbury, Elsley, and Tate (2008) found a significant correlation between motor ability and anxiety/depression in school-age children, while Yair and Bart (2006) reported that children with low motor abilities, including measures of visual motor integration, demonstrated a lower frequency of social play and a higher

Table 6.1 Fine motor skill development required for visuoconstruction skills (from Carter, 2009; Broderick & Blewitt, 2010).

Age	Developing Skill
0–4 Months	Hands most often closed, grasp reflex, opens and closes hands, reaches inaccurately for objects and clasps hands.
4–10 Months	Begins accurate reaching, holds small objects, develops accurate forward and side reach, scoops up small objects using whole hand, picks up objects using finger and thumb.
10–18 Months	Pokes and points with index finger, holds a crayon with hand.
18 Months–3 Years	Independently uses a spoon, draws and copies a vertical and horizontal line, snips paper with scissors.
3–4 Years	Can build a tower using 9 blocks or more, can place small pegs into holes.
4–5 Years	Uses scissors to cut straight and curved lines, can draw and copy a cross, folds paper to make matching edges.
5–6 Years	Cuts simple shapes with scissors, ties shoelaces, draws and copies diagonal lines, develops tripod grasp on writing utensils, able to copy a sequence of letters and numbers.

frequency of social reticence compared to children with average or high motor abilities. Visuospatial and fine motor skill deficits were also predictive of poor long-term outcome in individuals who had been diagnosed with obsessive/compulsive disorder as children (Bloch et al., 2011). In a study of two groups of children, one with traumatic brain injury and the other with ADHD, scores on the Beery VMI were sensitive to the visuoconstructional and motor deficits in both groups (Sutton et al., 2011). In order to assess motor skill functioning, basic knowledge of significant developmental milestones is important. Table 6.1 lists some useful examples of these milestones.

Sensorimotor Subdomains and Assessment

As with other functional domains, sensorimotor functioning can be assessed by focusing on specific isolated abilities that can then be reintegrated to describe overall functioning in a particular domain. The following section considers skills, abilities and functioning relevant to sensorimotor functioning and related assessment tools.

Lateral Dominance: Handedness

In previous chapters, we discussed different functional and neuroanatomical dimensions of the right and left hemispheres. While most verbal skills tend to correlate with specific regions of the left hemisphere, and the neural substrata for perceptual skills are found in the right hemisphere, there are substantial connections integrating the two. Although this is an oversimplification of anatomy, functioning and integration, it is a general principal that describes how each hemisphere is specialized and yet works together to support overall functioning. Cerebral asymmetry is well documented and develops out of genetic and environmental influences (Kolb & Whishaw, 2009).

Lateral dominance is the tendency to use or rely on one hemisphere over the other. Handedness is an expression of and venue into an understanding of an individual's hemispheric preference. Right-handed individuals, who represent a majority in the human population, tend to utilize their left hemisphere to carry out most lateralized motor functions while left-handed individuals employ the right hemisphere. This observation reflects the fact that most sensory systems perceive information from one side of the body and, as information travels from an extremity to the brain (and vice versa) it crosses the body in the spinal cord or brainstem to the opposite side of the brain. The motor system is organized in this manner as well with, for example, the left hemisphere organizing motor output on the contralateral side of the body. Many theories account for hand preference, including environmental, anatomical, hormonal and genetic influences (Kolb & Whishaw, 2009).

As there is some evidence that cognitive functioning in left-handed individuals is more bilaterally organized than in right-handed individuals, it is not always safe to make assumptions regarding handedness and hemispheric dominance. For example, if the dominant hemisphere is injured at an early age, the young brain can move handedness skills from the naturally occurring dominant hemisphere to the less dominant. However, damage on one side of the brain not only effects functioning on the contralateral side but can compromise functioning on both sides. For example, Bumin and Kavak (2010) found that right-handed, left-hemiplegic children with cerebral palsy were significantly less skilled at handwriting than their right-handed, healthy peers. The impairment in proprioception seen in the nonhemiplegic side in the children with cerebral palsy as well as the impairment in bilateral coordination, speed and dexterity of the upper extremities, visuospatial perception, visual motor organization, and tactile-sensory impairments negatively affected their handwriting skills.

Motor Planning and Sequencing

A group of children were playing basketball during recess. They had attempted to scrimmage, but after several minutes of arguing, teachers convinced the group to play P-I-G, an elimination game that required kids to take individual shots at the hoop. Henry was happy to be included. He was eight, of medium height and possessed an endearing smile. At his turn, he held the ball with both hands on either side. He raised his arms in the air and jumped, landing with the ball still in his outstretched arms. Then he flicked his wrists, sending the ball in a straight line. The ball ricocheted off the pole, he smiled awkwardly, shrugged and said, "I'll try again next time." While Henry had good muscle tone and posture, he struggles with timing the sequence of movements to shoot a basketball. A teacher pulled him aside, and while he waited for his next turn, they practiced the movements several times. While Henry's timing improved slightly, he was still awkward and unable to connect the jump and release smoothly.

Movement requires the use of multiple muscles at one time, in coordination with sensory input, to complete a motor task. This process integrates feedback from sensory, motor and cognitive systems. As a result, actions require planning and sequencing for fluidity and the attainment of motor goals. For example, the simple act of picking up a glass of water requires movement of the arm and hands, depth perception and spatial awareness, muscle tone and strength as well as tactile and proprioceptive feedback. While some movement patterns are learned, most individuals utilize prewired movement lexicons from the motor cortex. These lexicons represent movement patterns commonly used by humans, such as the pincer grasp (using the thumb and point finger to hold small objects: Kolb & Whishaw, 2009). While some of these movement lexicons are hardwired, they require practice to perfect. Other movement patterns, especially small, complex movements, such as those utilized by musicians, become a series of movements. The musician does not think about the movement required to make individual notes, but rather the chain of small movements are coordinated by the neocortex of the frontal lobes.

Muscles are the vessels used to carry out motor operations. Both novel and well-rehearsed motor activities rely on the integration of sensorimotor communication but also muscle tone and strength. Hypotonia is a condition in which individuals have decreased or absent muscle tone. Other difficulties occur during the sequence of neuronal events required to achieve motor planning and sequencing, resulting in various motor planning conditions. Apraxia is the inability to plan and execute learned voluntary movements smoothly, not due to muscle weakness or failure to understand directions. Individuals with difficulty coordinating movement due to disease of sensory or cerebellar pathways experience ataxia. Tics are another form of motor planning difficulty. These sudden, rapid, repetitive motor movements or vocalizations disrupt functioning on various levels. The most common tics include eye blinking, repeated throat clearing or coughing, arm thrusting, kicking, shrugging or jumping. These conditions are assessed and diagnosed by neurologists but are observable during neuropsychological testing. Children who have difficulty with motor planning and sequencing may have a hard time following directions in a classroom setting and may struggle with interpreting nonverbal social cues and generating an appropriate response (Greenspan, 2001).

Motor Speed

During a group music time, children between the ages of four and twelve sat in a large circle singing and smiling. Sally sat quietly, slowly clapping. The song instructed children wearing particular items of clothing to stand up then sit down. Each time a clothing item or color that Sally wore was called out, she would carefully, slowly stand up. She had good balance and muscle tone, but she moved at a different rate then the rest of the children. By the time she got to her feet, other children were already sitting back down.

Along with assessing planning and sequencing of motor movements, motor speed and timing are often considered. Individuals are asked to use fingers to tap a sequence as quickly as they can. This may reveal a lack of fluidity of movement but also assess the rate at which the task is performed. The timing of the tapping is also considered (Baron, 2004). Kaspar and Sokolec (1980) found the children with neurological impairments performed motor tasks at a slower rate than those who were unimpaired, especially with the nonpreferred hand. Timing of motor output is hypothesized to consist of two components: a central time-keeping operation and a motor delay component. Together, these components produce movements that are specific and accurate. This function is predominantly mediated by the cerebellum and the basal ganglia and their reciprocal connections with the cerebral cortex (Rommelse et al., 2008).

Processing Speed

During reading instruction, seven-year-old Victoria was finishing a "Frog and Toad" book with her teacher and a peer. She slowly verbally responded to who, what, when, where and why questions, demonstrating that she remembered the characters, the plot and setting. The teacher put a graphic organizer in front of Victoria, and the two carefully considered the tool. Now, Victoria was asked to write her brief responses to the comprehension questions. Because she struggled with short-term and working memory, the teacher wrote her responses on a separate piece of paper in careful, clear handwriting. Victoria began to carefully, slowly copy the words onto the graphic organizer. Writing single-sentence responses to the questions took Victoria fifteen minutes. Once completed, she held the paper overhead, triumphantly smiled and said, "Look! I did it!"

As a measure of cognitive efficiency, processing speed refers to the ability to fluently execute easy or automatic, unconscious tasks. Evidence indicates that visual processing speed predicts reading speed in children (Lobier, Dubois, & Valdois, 2013) and that teacher-reported measures of hypoactivity (slow, sluggish, low energy, difficulty starting a task) in children were correlated with low Processing Speed scores on the WISC-III (Lundervold et al., 2011). Over the course of development, children process information more rapidly. Both verbal and nonverbal processing follow this developmental trajectory, suggesting that there is a general increase in global processing speed across childhood and adolescence that matures in adults (Kail & Miller, 2006; Miller & Vernon, 1997). Presumably, both environmental and genetic factors can influence the speed of information processing. For example, Bosco (1972) reported that disadvantaged children required more time to process visual information than did middle-class children in lower elementary school grades, while Weiner (1975) found that reflective children were significantly faster than impulsive children at processing information, a finding that appeared to be related to efficient use of processing strategies.

In respect to neuropsychological testing, processing speed is most frequently measured using tasks that assess the speed and accuracy of an individual's ability to rapidly scan visual information and organize a fine motor response. However, the integrity of a number of functional domains is required for efficient performance on these tasks. For example, the Coding subtest of the WISC-IV, the fourth Index of the WISC-IV that has been discussed, involves speed and accuracy of visual-motor coordination, speed of mental operation (processing speed), attentional skills, visual acuity, visual scanning and tracking (repeated visual scanning between the code key and answer spaces), short term memory for learning (paired associate learning of an unfamiliar code), cognitive flexibility (in shifting rapidly from one pair to another), handwriting speed, and, possibly, motivation (Sattler, 2008).

Table 6.2 identifies and describes the most commonly used measures of processing speed employed during a neuropsychological assessment.

Table 6.2 Tests of processing speed.

Assessment	Description	Age
WISC-IV—Coding	The child copies symbols paired with other symbols. For six to eight year olds a specific mark is associated with each of five shapes while for eight to sixteen year olds, boxes divided into two parts contain the numbers one to nine in the top and nine different symbols paired with each in the bottom. The child is timed to see how many symbols they can complete in a specified time.	6:0–16:11
WISC-IV—Symbol Search	The child looks at one (6 to 8 year olds) or two (8 to 16 year olds) target symbol(s) on the left column and decides whether or not the target symbol(s) appear(s) in an array of symbols on the right. The child is timed to determine how many discriminations they can complete in a specified time.	6:0–16:11
WISC-IV—Cancellation	The child is required to scan both random and structured arrays of colored items and cross out any animals within a forty five second period.	6:0–16:11
WPPSI-IV—Bug Search	Similar to the Coding subtest of the WISC-IV, the target symbol is a bug in the left column and the child discriminates the target symbol from an array of bugs on the right. A dauber is used to mitigate any fine motor confounds.	4:0–7:7
WPPSI-IV—Cancellation	Similar to the Cancellation subtest on the WISC-IV. The random and structured arrays are less complex and the child finds articles of clothing they mark with a dauber.	4:0–7:7
WPPSI-IV—Animal Coding (optional)	Working within a specified time limit and using a key, the child marks shapes that correspond to pictured animals.	4:0–7:7
Woodcock Johnson-III—Cognitive—Visual Matching	The child rapidly locates and circles identical numbers from a defined set of numbers.	2:0–90
WJ-III—Cog. Decision Speed	The individual locates and circles two pictures most similar conceptually in a row. A measure of semantic processing speed.	2:0–90
WJ-III—Cog. Cross Out	The individual rapidly locates and marks identical pictures from a defined set of pictures. A measure of pictorial processing speed.	2:0–90

Fine Motor Skills

The classroom was in the midst of a math project, using paper and scissors to create visual fractions. The bright paper was marked clearly, with straight, black lines indicating how to cut different shapes. Richie was seven, possessed a mathematical mind and enjoyed projects using manipulatives. As he picked up the scissors, he awkwardly placed his thumb and fingers through the holes. Considering his hand, he watched himself slowly open and close the scissors in the air before inserting the paper between the blades. He focused intently on cutting, but all the effort resulted in ragged cuts that wavered off of the black lines. Richie let out a howl of despair, dropping the scissors and paper on the table. He grasped his head, and between sobs said, "I'm trying but I just can't do it!" A teacher approached Richie, comforted him, and offered to help. Once calm, the teacher used a hand-over-hand technique to help Richie cut out the shapes. His vulnerabilities with fine motor skills left Richie feeling sensitive and perfectionistic.

Fine motor skills involve the coordination of small muscles, usually in the hands. Generally, this occurs in tandem with the processing of visual information but can include other senses (e.g., tactile, proprioceptive). Fine motor tests typically include multiple tasks with visual, cognitive and manual dexterity demands as well as spatial organization. This includes activities such as drawing with a pencil, building with blocks, tying shoe laces or holding cards while playing *Uno*. Development of fine motor skills is an important and time consuming element of the school day (McHale & Cermak, 1992). Given this emphasis, it is no surprise that skills such as the ability to match motor movement with an external visual stimulus, such as copying a design, can be a predictor of handwriting development and domains related to literacy development (Bart et al., 2007; Cameron et al., 2012). These skills tend to be a greater predictor of children's achievement than other motor skills (Bart et al., 2007). Fine motor skill development has also shown to predict development of math skills (Grissmer, Grimm, Aiyer, Murrah, & Steele, 2010).

Graphomotor Skills

Graphomotor skills are a particular subset of fine motors skills that, in conjunction with cognitive and perceptual abilities, allow an individual to develop handwriting skills and express thoughts through writing. Handwriting is the integration of linguistic, psychomotor, biomechanical, maturational and developmental processes that involves learning (Accardo et al., 2007). Difficulty with graphomotor skills may impact legibility of handwriting, speed of writing, spacing between words and letters, conceptual fluency and error control. This can lead to frustration, especially if the individual can think quickly but cannot produce writing quickly. Children with learning disabilities may also struggle with graphomotor output, independent of language demands (Marcotte & Stern, 1997).

Gross Motor Skills

While fine motor skills involve the coordination of small muscle groups, gross motor skills involve the usage and coordination of larger muscle groups throughout the body. The ability to walk, sit in a chair, ascend a staircase, play basketball all rely on gross motor movement. Successful gross motor movement requires adequate muscle strength, tone and feedback from neurological systems. Development in infancy begins with strengthening muscles, controlling limb movements and coordinating muscle systems required for sitting and maintaining posture. In tandem, neurological development supports communication between the brain and sensory systems. Proprioception, awareness of relative placement of neighboring body parts, utilizes sensory neurons in joints and muscles to help coordinate body parts required for large movements. Sensory neurons within the inner ear provide information for balance and orientation. Teamwork between proprioception, strength and muscle tone, and balance eventually allows for locomotion through space.

Research suggests that gross motor development and cognitive development are linked. Specifically, executive functions and gross motor movement interact to carry out daily functioning. Neurobiological and neuroimaging studies reveal a relationship between the cerebellum, prefrontal cortex and both the primary and secondary motor cortex during gross motor activities (Hartman, Houwen, Scherder, & Visscher, 2010). Gross motor ability also impacts children with emotional and behavioral disabilities (Emck, Bosscher, Beek, & Doreleijers, 2009). A relationship between emotional dysregulation, balance and coordination has been noted, which leads to poor self-perception of motor competence for these children. As a result, these children may restrict participation in games and play, leading to greater psychosocial complications. To assess gross motor development, awareness of significant developmental milestones is important. Some examples of significant milestones are provided in Table 6.3.

Table 6.3 Gross motor skill development by age (from Carter, 2009; Broderick & Blewitt, 2010).

Age	Developing Skill
0–6 Months	Rolls over from front to back, sit with support, then independently
6–12 Months	Crawls forward on belly, transitions to several seated and crawling positions
12–18 Months	Pulls self to stand, 2-3 unsupported steps
18 Months–2 Years	Sits, crawl, walks, runs awkwardly
2–3 Years	Smooth walking and running, pulls toys, walks up and down stairs with support, climbs up and down furniture
3–4 Years	Imitates simple bilateral movement, climbs jungle gyms, pedals tricycle, alternates feet up and down stairs
4–5 Years	Hops on one leg, unsupported on stairs, catches bounced ball and throws over hand
5–6 Years	Skips forward after demonstration, walks up and down stairs holding objects

Measures of Sensorimotor Integration

Table 6.4 outlines assessment tools useful for measuring sensorimotor development and abilities.

Table 6.4 Tests of sensorimotor development.

Assessment	Description	Age
Beery-Buktenica Developmental Test of Visual-Motor Integration, 6th Ed (Beery VMI)	A developmental sequence of 30 geometric forms that are copied with paper and pencil. Two optional standardized tests, the Beery VMI Visual Perception and the Beery VMI Motor Coordination tests evaluate relatively pure visual and motor performance.	2.0–99.11
Bender Visual-Motor Gestalt, 2nd Ed (Bender-Gestalt II)	A series of 13 (ages 4 to 8) or 12 (ages 8 and above) geometric designs that are copied with paper and pencil. Visual and Motor supplementary tests are also available.	4–85+
Dean-Woodcock Sensory-Motor Battery	Comprised of 8 sensory tests and ten tests of motor functions, subtests can be selected for individual use or the entire battery can be used.	4–80+
Full Range Test of Visual-Motor Integration	By asking individuals to copy designs that become increasingly complex, their ability to relate visual stimuli to motor responses is assessed.	5–74
Neitz Test of Color Vision	A screener for color vision deficiencies, primarily for blue-yellow and green-red. The individual is asked to identify the color of shapes within an array of green dots.	All Ages
NEPSY II: Design Copying	The child copies two dimensional geometric figures using paper and pencil to assess motor and visuoperceptual skills.	3–16
NEPSY II: Fingertip Tapping	A timed test with 2 parts in which the child copies a series of finger motions demonstrated by the examiner. Part 1 assesses a child's finger dexterity and motor speed while part 2 assesses rapid motor programming.	5–16
NEPSY-II: Imitating Hand Positions	The child imitates various hand positions demonstrated by the examiner as a means to assess the child's ability to copy hand and finger positions.	3–12
NEPSY II: Manual Motor Sequences	The child repeats a series of hand movements demonstrated by the examiner to assess his/her ability to imitate rhythmic movement sequences.	3–12
NEPSY II: Visuomotor Precision	The child uses his or her preferred hand to draw lines inside of tracks as quickly as possible. This timed test assesses graphomotor speed and accuracy.	3–12
Quick Neuropsychological Screening	Taking only 20 minutes, this assessment detects soft neurological signs that may coexist with learning difficulties. It assesses manual dexterity, visual tracking, spatial orientation, tactile perception abilities and fine and gross motor movements.	5–18

(*Continued*)

Table 6.4 (Continued)

Assessment	Description	Age
Test of Visual-Motor Skills-Revised and the Test of Visual Motor Skills Revised Alternate Scoring Method	The child is asked to copy up to 23 geometric designs. Original scoring is based on: closure, angles, line intersections, size, rotation, line length under/over presentation and design modification.	3–13
Visual Motor Assessments	The individual is asked to reproduce 6 Gestalt designs. Scoring is based on the degree of rotation, number of separations, and number of distortions.	6–Adult
Wide Range Assessment of Visual Motor Abilities	Consisting of three subtests, visual motor abilities are assessed. The Drawing Test assesses visual motor integration and graphomotor production. The Matching Test measures visuospatial processing. During the Pegboard Test, the child is asked to sequentially insert pegs into grooved slots, first with his or her dominant hand, then with the nondominant hand.	3–17
Rey-Osterrieth Complex Figure Test	A complex, geometric figure is presented to the child and he/she is asked to copy it on a separate sheet of paper. In the absence of the original model, the Immediate Recall portion is assessed once the Copy portion is completed and the Delayed Recall portion is then assessed 20–30 minutes later. For further explanation, see Chapter 3.	5–89
Grooved Pegboard Test	The child places pegs in an array of grooves, first with the preferred hand, then the other hand and then both at the same time under timed conditions.	5–60

Let's take a look, once again, at eleven-year-old Charles and his performance on tasks of visuoconstruction. As you may recall from Chapter 3, his Perceptual Reasoning Index on the WISC-IV was one hundred and seventeen with a scaled score of fifteen on Block Design.

On the Block Design subtest, Charles assembled the blocks in a logical, stepwise and sequential fashion but tended to proceed from the right to the left, usually using only his right hand. In addition, he tended to assemble the blocks in pairs and then place them within the larger design, appearing to integrate the parts into the whole. Lastly, he made a few mistakes, but then corrected himself before the time was up. For example, at one point he was distracted by an internal, salient detail that caused him to lose set, but he eventually reorganized and corrected the design, retaining the appropriate configuration.

Charles took an unusual approach in processing complex visual and spatial information on the *Rey-Osterrieth Complex Figure Test*. On this task, he was required to copy a complex geometric figure followed by immediate and delayed reproductions from memory. On the copy portion, Charles took a part-oriented approach and proceeded to draw the figure from right to left, starting with components of the internal structure. As he had on the Block Design subtest of the WISC-IV, he tended to organize his reproduction in chunks that he then integrated into the whole design. He did so successfully, scoring strongly for organization. On the immediate recall portion, he again took a part oriented approach and proceeded from right to left. He was able to reconstruct the external configuration but had difficulty integrating the internal underlying organizational structure and tended to perseverate on an internal detail, performing at the low end of the average range. He did somewhat better on his delayed recall reproduction by more accurately consolidating and reproducing the configuration in spite of his part-oriented, right to left approach. He again had difficulty with the internal underlying organizational structure but appeared to benefit from a motor memory consolidated from his previous attempts. Nonetheless, relative to his copy, he had some difficulty integrating and recalling complex visual information.

Charles's visual motor abilities, as measured by an untimed paper-and-pencil task of visual motor integration (i.e., copying progressively more complex designs), were in the Average range (VMI Raw Score = twenty-three/thirty; Scaled Score = nine; thirty-fourth percentile; Age Equivalent = nine years, eight months). His performance on the separate visual component of the VMI was significantly better and in the Superior range (Raw Score = twenty-nine/thirty; Scaled Score = fourteen; ninety-second percentile; Age Equivalent = sixteen years, zero months) while the Motor Coordination portion was significantly weaker than the visual but again in the Average range (Raw Score = twenty-five/thirty; Scaled Score = nine; forty-second percentile; Age Equivalent = ten years, one month). On the VMI and motor portions, when copying the most difficult figures, Charles tended to increase the pressure he exerted on the pencil and rotated the paper, a sign of increased effort. He lost points for lack of motor precision and difficulty managing angles and spatial relationships.

Thus, together, results from tests of visuospatial organization and motor functioning indicated that Charles demonstrated above-average skills in the processing of visuospatial information. He was able to integrate part to whole relationships when he could break down visual complexity into more manageable parts but had relative difficulty consolidating and recalling the underlying organizational structure of complex visual details. He also demonstrated a relative vulnerability in fine motor functioning that impacted his graphomotor skills.

References

Accardo, A., Chiap, A., Borean, M., Bravar, L., Zoia, S., Carrozzi, M., & Scabar, A. (2007). A device for quantitative kinematic analysis of children's handwriting movements. In T. Jarm, P. Kramar, & A. Zupanic, (Eds.), *11th Mediterranean Conference on Medical and Biomedical Engineering and Computing*, IFMBE. New York, NY: Springer Science and Business Media LLC.

Adams, W., & Sheslow, D. (1995). *Wide Range Assessment of Visual Motor Abilities*. Odessa, FL: Psychological Assessment Resources.

Baron, I. S. (2004). *Neuropsychological evaluation of the child*. New York, NY: Oxford University Press.

Barrett, M., & Eames, K. (1998). Sequential developments in children's human figure drawing. *British Journal of Developmental Psychology, 14*, 219–236.

Bart, O., Hajami, D., & Bar-Haim, Y. (2007). Predicting school adjustment from motor abilities in kindergarten. *Infant and Child Development, 16*, 597–615.

Beery, K. E. (1967). *Visual motor integration*. Chicago, IL: Follet.

Beery, K. E., Buktenica, N. A., & Beery, N. (2010). *The Beery-Buktenica developmental test of visual-motor integration* (6th ed.). San Antonio, TX: Pearson.

Begliomini, C., Nelini, C., Caria, A., Grodd, W., & Castiello, U. (2008). Cortical activations in humans grasp-related areas depend on hand used and handedness. *Plos ONE, 3*(10), 1–9.

Bigler, E. D. (1995). Design fluency in dementia of Alzheimer's type, multi-infarct dementia and dementia associated with alcoholism. *Applied Neuropsychology, 2*(1), 7.

Bloch, M. H., Sukhodolsky, D. G., Dombrowski, P. A., Panza, K. E., Craiglow, B. G., Landeros-Weisenberger, A., . . . Schultz, R. T. (2011). Poor fine-motor and visuospatial skills predict persistence of pediatric-onset obsessive-compulsive disorder into adulthood. *Journal of Child Psychology & Psychiatry*, (9), 974–983.

Bosco, J. (1972). The visual information processing speed of lower and middle-class children. *Child Development, 43*(4), 1418–1422.

Brannigan, G. G., & Decker, S. L. (2003). *Bender Visual Motor Gestalt Test* (2nd ed.). Itasca, IL: Riverside Publishing.

Broderick, P. C., & Blewitt, P. (2010). *The life span: Human development for helping professionals*. Upper Saddle River, NJ: Pearson Education.

Bumin, G., & Kavak, S. (2010). An investigation of the factors affecting handwriting skill in children with hemiplegic cerebral palsy. *Disability & Rehabilitation, 32*(8), 692–703.

Cameron, C. E., Brock, L. L., Murrah, W. M., Bell, L. H., Worzalla, S. L., Grissmer, D., & Morrison, F. J. (2012). Motor skills and executive function both contribute to kindergarten achievement. *Child Development, 83*(4), 1229–1244.

Carter, R. (2009). *The human brain book*. New York, NY: DK Publishing.

Dean, R. S., & Woodcock, R. W. (2003). *Dean-Woodcock Neuropsychological Battery*. Itasca, IL: Riverside Publishing.

Decker, S. L., Englund, J. A., Carboni, J. A., & Brooks, J. H. (2011). Cognitive and developmental influences in visual-motor integration skills in young children. Psychological Assessment, *23*(4), 1010–1016.

Emck, C., Bosscher, R., Beek, P., & Doreleijers, T. (2009). Gross motor performance and self-perceived motor competence in children with emotional, behavioural and pervasive developmental disorders: A review. *Developmental Medicine and Child Neurology, 51*(7), 501–517.

Fuller, G. (2006). *Visual motor assessments*. North Tonawanda, NY: Multi-Health Systems, Inc.

Gardner, M. F. (1995). *Test of Visual Motor Skills—Revised*. Novato, CA: Academic Therapy Publications.

Greenspan, S. I. (2001). Working with children who have motor difficulties. *Early Childhood Today, 15*(4), 20–22.

Grissmer, D., Grimm, K. J., Aiyer, S. M., Murrah, W. M., & Steele, J. S. (2010). Fine motor skills and early comprehension of the world: Two new school readiness indicators. *Developmental Psychology, 46,* 1008–1017.

Hammill, D. D., Pearson, N. A., Voress, J. K., & Reynolds, C. R. (2006). *Full Range Test of Visual Motor Integration.* Austin, TX: Pro-Ed.

Hartman, E., Houwen, S., Scherder, E., & Visscher, C. (2010). On the relationship between motor performance and executive functioning in children with intellectual disabilities. *Journal of Intellectual Disability Research, 54*(5), 468–477.

Jones-Gotman, M., & Milner, B. (1977). Design fluency: The invention of nonsense drawings after focal cortical lesions. *Neuropsychologia, 15,* 653–674.

Kail, R. V., & Miller, C. A. (2006). Developmental change in processing speed: Domain specificity and stability during childhood and adolescence. *Journal Of Cognition & Development, 7*(1), 119–137.

Kaspar, J. C., & Sokolec, J. (1980). Relationship between neurological dysfunction and the test of speed of motor performance. *Journal of Clinical Neuropsychology,* 13–21.

Klove, H. (1963) Clinical neuropsychology. In F. M. Foster (Ed.) *The medical clinics of North America.* New York: Saunders.

Kolb, B., & Whishaw, I. Q. (2009). *Fundamentals of human neuropsychology* (6th ed.). New York, NY: Worth.

Kurdek, L. A., & Sinclair, R. J. (2000). Psychological, family, and peer predictors of academic outcomes in first- through fifth-grade children. *Journal of Educational Psychology, 92,* 449–457.

Lezak, M. D., Howieson, D., Bigler, E., & Tranel, D. (2012). *Neuropsychological assessment* (5th ed.). New York, NY: Oxford University Press.

Lobier, M., Dubois, M., & Valdois, S. (2013). The role of visual processing speed in reading speed development. *Plos ONE, 8*(4), 1–10.

Lundervold, A. J., Posserud, M., Ullebø, A., Sørensen, L., & Gillberg, C. (2011). Teacher reports of hypoactivity symptoms reflect slow cognitive processing speed in primary school children. *European Child & Adolescent Psychiatry, 20*(3), 121–126.

Marcotte, A. C., & Stern, C. (1997). Qualitative analysis of graphomotor output in children with attentional disorders. *Child Neuropsychology, 3,* 147–153.

McHale, K., & Cermak, S. (1992). Fine motor activities in elementary school: Preliminary findings and provisional implications for children with fine motor problems. *American Journal of Occupational Therapy, 46,* 898–903.

Meyers, J. E., & Meyers, K. R. (1995). *Rey Complex Figure Test and Recognition Trial: Professional manual.* Lutz, FL: Psychological Assessment Resources, Inc.

Miller, L. T., & Vernon, P. A. (1997). Developmental changes in speed of information processing in young children. *Developmental Psychology, 33*(3), 549.

Mutti, M. C., Sterling, H. M., Martin, N. A., & Spalding, N. V. (1998). *Quick Neurological Screening Test—II.* Odessa, FL: Psychological Assessment Resources, Inc.

Neitz, J., Summerfelt, P., & Neitz, M. (2001). *Neitz Test of Color Vision.* Los Angeles: Western Psychological Services.

Piek, J. P., Bradbury, G. S., Elsley, S. C., & Tate, L. (2008). Motor coordination and social-emotional behaviour in preschool-aged children. *International Journal Of Disability, Development & Education, 55*(2), 143–151.

Reitan, R. (1969). *Manual for administration of neuropsychological test batteries for adults and children.* Unpublished manuscript, Indianapolis University Medical Center.

Rommelse, N. N. J., Altink, M. E., Oosterlann, J., Beem, L., Buschgens, C. J. M., Buitelaar, J., & Sergean, J. A. (2008). Speed, variability and timing of motor output in ADHD: Which measures are useful for endophenotypic research. *Behavioral Genetics, 38,* 121–132.

Ruff, R., Allen, C., Farrow, C., Niemann, H., & Wylie, T. (1994). Figural fluency: Differential impairment in patients with left versus right frontal lobe lesions. *Clinical Neuropsychology, 9*, 41–55.

Sattler, J. (2008). Assessment of children: *Cognitive Foundations* (5th ed.). San Diego, CA: Jerome M. Sattler.

Shikata, E., Hamzei, F., Glauche, V., Koch, M., Weiller, C., Binkofski, F., & Büchel, C. (2003). Functional properties and interaction of the anterior and posterior intraparietal areas in humans. *European Journal Of Neuroscience, 17*(5), 1105–1110.

Stiles, J., & Stern, C. (2001). Developmental change in spatial cognitive processing: Complexity effects and block construction performance in preschool children. *Journal Of Cognition & Development, 2*(2), 157–187.

Sutton, G. P., Barchard, K. A., Bello, D. T., Thaler, N. S., Ringdahl, E., Mayfield, J., & Allen, D. N. (2011). Beery-Buktenica developmental test of visual-motor integration performance in children with traumatic brain injury and attention-deficit/hyperactivity disorder. *Psychological Assessment, 23*(3), 805–809.

Weiner, A. S. (1975). Visual information-processing speed in reflective and impulsive children. *Child Development, 46*(4), 998–1000.

Yair, B., & Bart, O. (2006). Motor function and social participation in kindergarten children. *Social Development, 15*(2), 296–310.

7 Understanding and Assessing Academic Skills

Throughout this book, numerous vignettes have demonstrated that a child can have relatively high scores on intelligence indices and yet struggle in the school setting. Sometimes, disparities within the constellation of cognitive abilities lead to emotional and behavioral dysregulation, making the child unavailable for instruction. Other children are able to display appropriate student behavior but struggle to learn specific academic skills due to pockets of cognitive vulnerabilities. While the whole neuropsychological evaluation considers various cognitive domains and develops a full scale IQ score, it also assesses academic readiness and achievement. This functions as a measure of academic skill attainment. While distinct cognitive domains appear hardwired into functioning, certain academic skills only emerge through instruction and practice. Reading, for example, is a specific skill set that without exposure, instruction and practice is unlikely to develop. Assessment of academic achievement screens for specific learning disabilities, as well as strengths. In this chapter, three major academic skill sets are discussed in terms relevant to the process of administering a complete neuropsychological evaluation. Reading, writing and arithmetic are at the core of many school curricula. Each of these academic skills are discussed in terms of underlying processes required for skill attainment as well as assessment tools.

Reading

At the age of ten, Craig was shutting down. He was increasingly expressing negativity about school and feelings that he was "not normal," was stressed doing his work and was reporting that writing was "torture." While his early language milestones were within normal limits, he was described as having an unusual way of expressing himself. At seven years of age, he was diagnosed with expressive language delays and in third grade was diagnosed with dyslexia, a diagnosis that had been given to another member of his family. On the *Wechsler Intelligence Scale for Children–Fourth Edition* (WISC-IV) (Wechsler, 2003), Craig's verbal abilities fell in the High Average range while his perceptual organizational abilities fell at the low end of the Superior range. His working memory scored at the lower end of the Average range while his processing speed fell at the upper end of the High Average range. On the *Comprehensive Test of Phonological Processing, Second Edition* (CTOPP-2; Wagner, Torgesen, Rashotte, & Pearson, 2013), Craig scored below average for Phonological Awareness and Phonological Memory and at the low end of the Average range for Rapid Naming. He had difficulty both blending individual phonemes to make a word as well as separating out individual sounds from words. His ability to code phonological information into short-term memory was also compromised, as was his ability to rapidly retrieve phonologically based lexical information from memory. On the Wechsler Individual Achievement Test, Third Edition (WIAT-III; Pearson, 2009), his Word Reading standard score was low average. On the *Gray Oral Reading Test, Fifth Edition* (GORT-5; Wiederholt & Bryant, 2012), the score for rate was at the low end of the Average range, the score for accuracy was in the Poor range and the fluency score was in the Below Average range. His accuracy was impacted by his difficulty decoding individual words and his mistakes, consistent with the observations on the WIAT-III, related to his tendency to substitute words that began with the same letter or sound or that were somewhat similar in appearance. He also tended to skip words, add words that were not in the text or failed to decode word endings or added additional suffixes. Craig's reading disability was contributing to a level of anxiety and depression about his abilities, and his self-image was suffering. This compounded some already evident social difficulties by making it difficult for him to confidently engage in relationships. He was becoming increasingly withdrawn and was preferring to play video games, identifying with fantasy figures that overcame difficulties in an unrealistic manner—a strategy that was just as unrealistic.

Reading is an incredibly complex process that has become part of the human repertoire only very recently in our evolutionary history. Because there was no neurologically based preexisting reading network, for one to read, a number of separate structures and functions in the human brain had to be brought together and reorganized. Over the last few thousand years, we humans have drawn on our extraordinary ability to adapt and use our experience to exploit the brain's capacity to change. This genetic and environmental dance has enabled the reconfiguration of a network of structures that makes reading possible.

To read, one must coordinate a number of neural systems that have carried on separate functions over the course of evolution. Perhaps the most obvious is the visual system. However, we also draw on auditory, attentional, memory, linguistic and executive processes as well. In order to read, all of these neural systems must be integrated, not only to decode a string of words but to give those words meaning.

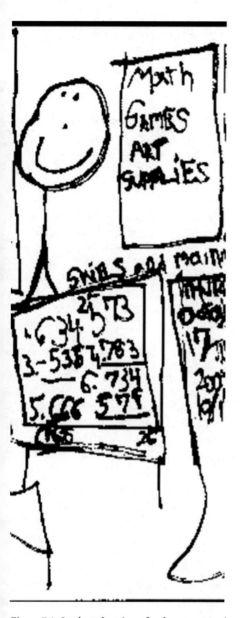

Figure 7.1 Student drawing of a classroom environment.

Decoding

Decoding is the process of linking symbols with sounds. It requires phonologic and orthographic processes that combine to interpret a symbol. The word, *phonological* comes from the Greek root *phon,* meaning "sound or voice." "Phonological processing refers to the use of phonological information, especially the sound structure of one's oral language, in processing written language (i.e., reading, writing) and oral language (i.e., listening, speaking; Wagner, Torgeson & Rashotte, 1999, p. 4).

There are three levels of phonological representation: the level of the sound wave (phones), the phonetic level (the strings of phones), and the phonological level (related phones combined into families called phonemes). There are also three levels of phono-logical processing: phonological awareness (an individual's awareness of the phonologi-cal structure of words in one's language), phonological memory (coding phonological information for temporary storage in working or short-term memory) and rapid nam-ing (rapid naming of objects, colors, digits or letters that requires the efficient retrieval of phonological information from long-term or permanent memory; Torgesen, Wagner & Rashotte, 1994).

Orthographic processing refers to the individual's understanding that the written word represents oral language. It is based on "the formation of visual long-term mem-ory representation of letters, letter patterns, and sequences of letters that serve to map spatially the temporal sequence of phonemes within words" (O'Brien, Wolf, Miller, Lovett, & Morris, 2011, p. 112). Phonologic and orthographic processing must be integrated in order to decode the written word and, as such, form the foundation for reading.

Phonological Processing

Two of the three levels of phonological processing, phonological awareness and phono-logical memory are closely related to what is considered the first steps on the pathway of reading development (Nithart et al., 2011; Wagner & Torgesen, 1987). Developmen-tal studies suggest that these foundational skills are so closely linked they are regarded as a single phonological ability in young children, and with age they become more distinct, especially between kindergarten and the first grades of primary school (Wag-ner et al., 1999).

Phonological awareness is an umbrella term used to describe a variety of tasks, such as blending and segmenting phonemes, detecting syllables in a word, and rhyme detec-tion tasks (Soltani & Roslan, 2013). An individual's ability to distinguish individual sounds in spoken word (awareness of phonemes while listening) lays a foundation for developing the association between the image of a letter and its relationship to sound (grapheme). This process is referred to as mastering the alphabetic code (Pugh et al., 2013). Several theorists and researchers have postulated that lower level audi-tory temporal processing and visual temporal processing may be involved in the development of phonological awareness, but current research is inconclusive (Geor-giou, Papadopoulos, Zarouna, & Parrila, 2012). Evidence suggests that phonologi-cal awareness abilities are a strong predictor of later reading development and that reading instruction further improves phonological abilities (Pugh et al., 2013). They have also been shown to predict later math and science outcomes (Savage, Carless, & Ferraro, 2007).

Phonological memory utilizes short-term, long-term and working memory abili-ties. Phonological short-term memory involves storing distinct phonological features for a short period of time (Soltani & Roslan, 2013). The result enables the reader to blend isolated phonemes together, building word sounds (Wagner & Torgesen, 1987). The process of holding phonological information in a memory buffer, then using it to blend phonemes requires the use of phonological working memory. In turn, then matching the sound to phonological lexical representations, giving the sound meaning, depends on long-term memory stores (Gathercole, 1995; Tree, Longmore, Majerus, & Evans, 2011). Current phonological memory assessment is usually completed through immediate serial recall tasks for objects using both visual and auditory stimuli together or separate. Assessment is complicated by the overlay of short-term memory, long-term phonological knowledge and memory for serial order (Nithart et al., 2011). Reference Box 7.1 provides definitions for common linguistic terms.

Reference Box 7.1 Linguistic Terms

- Phonemes—The smallest unit of sound capable of meaning. Example: /s/, /k/, /a/
- Grapheme—Visual representation of a letter or letters combined to make a distinct sound. Example: /k/, /ch/, /ea/, /igh/
- Morpheme—The smallest grammatical unit in a language. Example: Unbreak-able is composed of three morphemes: *un-, break* and *-able.*
- Lexicon—A language's systematic set of vocabulary and word meanings. Also called the semantic system.

Rapid automatized naming (RAN) is the third element of phonological process-ing. This final element draws upon long-term memory stores for the rapid retrieval of phonological information. Assessment of RAN usually involves naming a series of familiar visual stimuli (numbers, colors, letters, etc.) as quickly as possible. The speed at which children can name these items strongly predicts that rate at which they acquire word-reading skills in later grades (Denckla & Cutting, 1999; Torgesen & Wagner 1994). While the tasks often involve alphanumeric (letters and digits) stimuli, there is evidence that color and object stimuli can also be good predictors of reading skills (Denckla & Cutting, 1999). Early RAN task abilities are predictive of later flu-ency skills, although its specific role is unknown (Jones, Ashby, & Branigan, 2012). While initially related to phonological awareness, it has been suggested that RAN skills become increasingly independent of phonological awareness as reading skills develop. This implies that while working together to develop reading skills, phonological aware-ness and RAN may have separate but connected underlying neurological correlates that can be accessed while teaching children with dyslexia (Araujo, Pacheco, Faisca, Petersson, & Reis, 2010). While RAN has been repeatedly proven to predict later read-ing skills development, the underlying mechanism for its role in reading development remains unclear.

To summarize, phonological processing is considered to be the mechanism typically utilized by developing readers to become increasingly accurate in word-reading ability

(Lyon & Moats, 1997). Historically, the purview of most research and methodological development in reading has focused on this process as well as the development of word-reading accuracy and its subsequent role in comprehension.

Fluency

Phonological processing abilities are widely recognized as predictors of reading ability, but their role in the development of fluency remains unknown (Ashby, Dix, Bontrager, Dey, & Archer, 2013). Fluency, the ability to read words and sentences accurately and at the rate of speech with appropriate intonation and comprehension, is increasingly scrutinized in both fields of research and teaching methodology. Fluency includes specific skills, such as letter naming, whole-word identification, reading rate, accuracy and comprehension at the passage level (Katzir et al., 2006). Reading fluency occurs at three levels: letter, word and connected text.

Development of fluency requires text exposure, spending more time with words and sentences and the consistent application of the alphabetic principle. This increases word-recognition speed. With practice, less time is spent slowly decoding words, and readers begin to apply conversational sound, or prosody, as they read longer sentences and passages (Ashby, Dix, Bontrager, Dey, & Archer, 2013). Fluency skills are thought to provide the bridge between word recognition and comprehension through the development of automaticity and prosody (Raskinski, 2012).

Another important aspect of fluency development relates to the contributions made by the visual processing system. Automaticity depends upon the apparently simple way our eyes move across letters and pages (Wolf, 2007). As reading skills develop, the eyes are trained to move in the direction dictated by the language. Reading English requires that the eyes move left to right, and exposure and practice lead to the training of these precise eye movements (oculomotor training; Medland, Walter, & Woodhouse, 2010). Some studies suggest that difficulty with eye movements can lead to difficulty with reading. The rate at which individuals process information also plays a role in reading development. It also influences the left-to-right scanning strategy and is a predictor of literacy acquisition (Ferretti, Mazzotti, & Brizzolara, 2008). Furthermore, research reveals that the seemingly smooth eye movements are actually complex (Jones et al., 2012; Rayner, 1998). As the eyes move, they make continual small movements, called saccades. During brief moments, called fixations, the eyes pause, during which time the eyes almost stop and gather information. During this fixation time, the foveal region of the eye focuses on visual information, such as a few letters, and transforms the letters into conscious awareness. The parafovea, the region of the eye alongside the fovea, is busy processing neighboring information—priming the brain for conscious awareness. These two streams of information, foveal and parafoveal, have been demonstrated to be different in respect to acuity and conscious awareness and are therefore considered separate information processing streams. Thus, the reader must integrate information on a visual level while also processing information on a linguistic level. Foveal processing has been shown to play an important role in serial naming, object naming and silent reading (Jones et al., 2012).

Comprehension

Avery was a slender, willowy, nine-year-old girl. She enjoyed routine and faithfully attended all academic activities. During reading instruction, she preferred short exercises in single-word vocabulary building or spelling. She was a fluent reader, able to read grade-level material aloud. However, she would read in a toneless clipped style, inflecting no emotion or meaning. When given a three-paragraph essay on a well-known topic, she could not locate the main idea of any paragraph or answer who, what, when, where and why questions. During a unit on simile and metaphor, Avery stiffly stood up and walked out of the room, asking for the bathroom, and didn't return for ten minutes. While Avery typically displayed excellent student behavior and decoding skills, she had a limited ability to make meaning out of written text.

Reading-readiness skills, such as phonologic and orthographic processing, are crucial in the early stages of literacy formation. In order to comprehend written language, however, the ability to decode a word is not sufficient. Several steps beyond decoding must occur, and these involve semantic, syntactic and morphological awareness.

Semantic awareness refers to an individual's ability to understand the meaning of a word. This is done through exposure to language and culture and enables one to more efficiently and quickly recognize words. **Syntactic awareness** relates to one's ability to understand the grammatical forms and structure of sentences. An understanding of syntax is necessary for one to make sense of the way words are used in sentences, in paragraphs and in written narratives. **Morphological awareness** enables one to understand the underlying relationships between a word's root and variations of that root to form more complex words (e.g., integrate, integra*ting*, integra*tion*, *dis*integrate, etc.). The understanding of the semantic, syntactic and morphological structure of written language not only enables one to more effectively decode words but also facilitates the ready comprehension of what one reads (see Wolf, 2007).

As individuals learn to decode and attach meaning to a single word, reading development continues from understanding single words to understanding simple sentences, grammatical information, entire paragraphs to entire books. Doing so, individuals utilize long-term memory stores to draw from prior knowledge to integrate contextual information. Executive functions play a role in prediction, anticipation and planning. Working memory is employed to "hold" relevant information in mind as more information is integrated from new words, phrases and concepts. In addition to these processes, individual life experiences also influence meaning derived from text and continues to evolve as an individual does. Comprehension is not a static skill attained during reading instruction but a dynamic process weaving together several cognitive processes and experiences of an individual, rendering comprehension itself an evolving process (Wolf, 2007).

The following two sections further describe two elements of comprehension that are assessed during tests of academic achievement; first, vocabulary, important as decoding skills pave the way for more semantic understanding and, second, the ability to increasingly understand abstract concepts.

Vocabulary

As children continue to develop decoding skills and fluency, their knowledge of semantic meaning is also developing. When decoding, fluency is enhanced if the child has awareness of the meaning of the word (Wolf, 2007). Vocabulary can be thought of as the stock of word meanings used by or known to a group of people, otherwise referred to as the semantic representations in the mental lexicon. Just as vocabulary size promotes the development of fluency skills, there is as strong evidence that vocabulary size contributes to variance in reading comprehension (Poulsen & Elbro, 2013). For some toddlers, problems with vocabulary acquisition can be an indication of persisting language difficulties that are associated with behavioral problems, social competence, attention-deficit/ hyperactivity disorder, cognitive delays and reading problems (Henrichs et al., 2011).

Spoken-word vocabulary growth directly relates to reading-skills acquisition. Children who experience "word rich" environments, meaning exposure to various words and meanings, develop reading skills at a faster rate than children in "word poor" environments (Wolf, 2007). Vocabulary growth refers to two processes (Metsala, 1999): first, the number of recognizable words, acquired due to frequency of exposure and use, and, second, phonological patterns and similarities that relate to a developing mental lexicon, referred to as a lexical neighborhood. In other words, phonological segments can take on a meaning, and differences in one phoneme substitution, deletion or addition allow the individual to derive meaning from an otherwise familiar word.

An influential theory of vocabulary development proposed by Baddeley, Gathercole and Papagno (1998) claims that short-term memory plays an important role in constructing meaning from and for phonological forms. Other research suggests that vocabulary learning cannot be accounted for by a single cognitive mechanism but by a cognitive system involving short-term memory, working memory and a subset of long-term memory interacting with phonological skills and attentional resources (Morra & Camba, 2009). The underlying processes utilized during vocabulary acquisition can be assessed using nonword repetition tasks as well as tests of phonological short-term memory (Metsala, 1999). Also, recall that the WISC-IV directly tests vocabulary abilities by asking the individual to define the meaning of words arranged in order of increasing difficulty, and this ability correlates highly with overall intelligence (Sattler, 2008).

Abstract Concepts

As semantic word knowledge expands, the type of words used in spoken and written language becomes more complex and abstract. Most forms of communication require the use of both concrete and abstract words and concepts. Concrete words often refer to a sensory experience while abstract words refer to indirect, intangible concepts or affective states (Crutch & Warrington, 2007). Not only does word meaning become increasingly complex, but concepts become more complex and abstract. As a result, the reader learns to understand figurative language (metaphor, personification, etc.), make inferences, relate complex concepts, integrate details with the main idea and understand irony and multiple points of view (Wolf, 2007). Neuropsychological assessments and academic achievement assessments often include subtests that measure vocabulary and use of metaphor and analogical reasoning as they relate to overall comprehension of a passage. To illustrate, the following considers the role of inference and the understanding of figurative language.

While reading text, information can be stated explicitly, or information can be implied. At this level of reading, an individual must be able to make inferences, recall prior knowledge, understand context and integrate new information in order to make connections and fully understand the text. Two types of inferences have been identified: bridging and elaborative (Calvo, 2001). Bridging inferences are required for sentences and texts to be coherent. Elaborative inferences refine and extend information, making text more meaningful and relatable but are not necessary for full comprehension. The inferential process is influenced by experiences of the individual reader (Wolf, 2007). As the reader accesses their store of prior knowledge, accomplished through the use of long-term memory, personal experience influences comprehension. Perhaps certain concepts are made more important or a character's actions are more relatable.

Integrating new information from text and bringing it to the reader's awareness employs several neurocognitive processes and correlated substrates. Working memory plays a crucial role in holding new information on line while integrating prior knowledge, although the exact mechanism is unknown (Calvo, 2001). Combining old and new information seems to activate an entire language system in the right hemisphere. Researchers have found that while individuals are generating inferences based on text, bihemispheric frontal systems around Broca's area are activated. When the words are semantically and syntactically complex, this frontal area interacts with not only other linguistic centers, such as Wernicke's area, but also with the cerebellum and some parietal areas (Wolf, 2007).

Abstract concepts within reading texts rely on inference to make connections between the concrete and abstract as well as the literal and figurative. Figurative language, such as the use of metaphor, occurs during daily communication (Coney & Lange, 2006; Runbald & Annaz, 2010). Figurative language comprehension is clinically relevant in development disorders and neuropsychiatry (Runbald & Annaz, 2010). As a result, an individual's ability to understand abstract concepts and reasoning is often assessed through comprehension of metaphor or analogical reasoning. Both involve comparing two dissimilar concepts, selecting relevant features of each and making a connection to determine meaning (Prat, Mason, & Just, 2012). Researchers have attempted to identify which cognitive processes underlie the comprehension of metaphor and analogical reasoning, and if they are distinctly different from those involved in literal language (Coney & Lange, 2006). What is clear is that these two forms of abstract thinking rely on lateral prefrontal regions.

The Development of Reading

Word learning requires that infants have established the neural memory structures for word forms and meaning as well as the ability to make associations between the new memories (Friedrich & Friederici, 2011). Infants at six months of age are able to associate the words *mama* and *papa* with the faces of their mother and father (Tincoff & Jusczyk, 1999), and at approximately eight to ten months are able to comprehend their first words (Bates, Thal, & Janowsky, 1992). While six-month-olds can quickly encode connections between objects and words, in contrast to fourteen-month-olds, they cannot sufficiently consolidate this relationship into long-term memory. Up until one year of age, an infant must have frequent exposure to a word and its referent to establish memories of phonological and semantic representations and the association between them. At one year, however, this becomes a much quicker process, requiring less frequent exposure, and this process accounts for the much more rapid buildup of vocabulary that occurs at about eighteen months (Friedrich & Friederici, 2011).

Oral-language proficiency (vocabulary and listening comprehension) as well as phonological skills impact reading development (Nation & Snowling, 2004). Direct assessment of early speech/language functions has been positively correlated with later reading competence. At the preschool age, larger vocabulary and better grammatical abilities predicted advanced reading abilities in adolescence (Bartl-Pokorny et al., 2013). A one-year longitudinal study of children over the first year of reading instruction found that reading skills were primarily predicted by phonological awareness in kindergarten and then, later, by phonological memory. Short-term memory for serial-order information supported decoding skills while phonological knowledge stored in long-term memory impacted word recognition (Nithart et al., 2011). Semantic variables and interest in books at the age of three and the phonological variables at the age of six predicted reading development significantly at the age of sixteen (Frost et al., 2005).

Reading is a skill that develops over a protracted period and is significantly influenced by a child's early experience. The rate at which a child develops reading skills in the preschool year is much faster in those children who enter preschool with well-developed antecedent skills (Leppänen, Niemi, Aunola, & Nurmi, 2004). Parental literacy habits and reading beliefs have been connected to parent/child literacy and language activities at home which, in turn, were positively associated with children's print knowledge and interest in reading (Weigel, Martin, & Bennett, 2006). Thus, the more exposure a child has to the experience of being read to and the availability of material within the home, the more likely that child is to be prepared to begin reading once instruction starts.

As Wolf (2007) has described, reading development can be considered to proceed in stages. The **emerging prereader** benefits from the amount of language, concepts, stories, availability of print materials and literacy that they are exposed to in their environment. The **novice reader** understands the concept that letters connect to the sounds in language. They can hear, segment and blend the larger phonemic units while associating these sounds with orthographic patterns that, in English, proceed from left to right. Novice readers also are acquiring a semantic knowledge base or vocabulary that enables them to more quickly decode words. The **decoding reader** is able to more smoothly decode words and is semifluent. He or she is consolidating an understanding of phonologic and orthographic rules and developing the ability to see letter/pattern and vowel/pair "chunks" that constitute sight words. Vocabulary and grammar are expanding as is an understanding of the morphological foundations of words related to roots, stems, prefixes and suffixes. The decoding reader is on the edge of becoming fluent but does not necessarily comprehend what he or she is reading. The **fluent, comprehending reader** is building up categories of knowledge and demonstrates an increased capacity to understand word usage in respect to more abstract concepts, such as irony, metaphor, voice and point of view. In this stage, children integrate their knowledge base, make predictions and inferences and become aware of what they do and do not know. Development in this stage depends on higher level instruction and a child's desire to read. It is a period of greater independence and more fluent comprehension. Lastly, the **expert reader** is instantly and simultaneously integrating cognitive, linguistic and affective experiences to fluidly decode and comprehend what he or she is reading.

The Neuroanatomy of Reading

Visual word identification primarily involves a left-hemisphere posterior-cortical reading system with ventral, dorsal and anterior components. The dorsal region maps visual percepts of the printed word onto the phonological and semantic aspects of language and includes the angular gyrus and supramarginal gyrus in the inferior parietal lobe and the posterior part of the superior temporal gyrus, also known as Wernicke's area. As an individual first learns to decode print, the dorsal system predominates, and evidence suggests that it is involved in learning the relationship between phonologic and orthographic forms and connecting them to semantic information.

The anterior system is located in the posterior part of the inferior frontal gyrus and is involved in phonological memory and syntactic processing. The anterior aspect of the inferior frontal gyrus is involved in the retrieval of semantic information. It appears that the anterior system may work together with the temporoparietal system in decoding new words during the development of reading.

The ventral system is later developing and plays a role in fluent reading. It includes the left hemisphere occipitotemporal/fusiform area and extends anteriorly to the middle and inferior temporal gyri. More anterior aspects of this system support semantic analysis. When moving along the more anterior dimensions of this system, subregions respond to increasingly abstract lexical information. Pugh et al. (2005) have argued that while a beginning reader uses a more widely distributed cortical system, including regions of the right hemisphere, as reading skill increases, the left hemisphere ventral system becomes the crucial nexus for fluent recognition of the printed word. However, fMRI studies have implicated the dorsolateral prefrontal cortex and right hemisphere language areas in the generation and integration processes of inferential reasoning (Mason & Just, 2004). Nevertheless, skilled readers are more efficient and use this system on an "as needed" basis. Consequently, they activate the right hemisphere homologues to the left hemisphere language network to a lesser degree than do unskilled readers (Prat et al., 2011).

Reading Disorders

Numerous theories attempting to explain why some individuals have difficulty reading have been explored for nearly a hundred and fifty years and have attributed reading disorders to problems processing either visual or auditory information. More recently, explanations have moved from primary sensory-processing deficits to theories related to higher order cognitive systems, including the phonological theory, the rapid auditory processing theory, the cerebellar theory and the magnocellular theory (see Shaywitz, Lyon, & Shaywitz, 2006).

It is now believed that individuals with a reading disorder or developmental dyslexia have a fundamental disorder of the phonological processing component of the language system. They employ neural circuits different from those of a typical, nonimpaired reader. Because of an impairment in left hemisphere posterior neural systems, individuals with dyslexia employ more right hemisphere than left hemisphere networks. These include visual association and occipitotemporal regions and extend through the right angular gyrus, supramarginal gyrus and temporal areas. Furthermore, they demonstrate delayed activation in the frontal regions of both hemispheres. Thus, individuals with a "dyslexic brain" appear to be both processing information more slowly and using a different and less efficient right hemisphere dominant method of decoding and comprehending the written word (Shaywitz & Shaywitz, 2006).

In a fMRI study of children six to nine years of age, employing a reading intervention strategy that utilized a specific, systematic and explicit phonologically based system, results correlated improved reading accuracy, fluency and comprehension with increased activation in left hemisphere regions, including the inferior frontal gyrus and the posterior region of the middle temporal gyrus. A year after the intervention ended, the improved group demonstrated increased activation in bilateral inferior frontal gyri, left superior temporal sulcus, the occipitotemporal region and the anterior aspect of the middle occipital gyrus, the inferior occipital gyrus and the lingual gyrus. These findings demonstrated that a phonologically based reading system facilitated the development of fast-paced neural systems that are critical for skilled reading (Shaywitz et al., 2006).

Assessing Reading Skills

The following tables list assessment tools that measure Reading Accuracy (Table 7.1), Reading Comprehension (Table 7.2) and Reading Fluency (7.3).

Table 7.1 Measures of reading accuracy.

Assessment	Description	Age
Kaufman Test of Educational Achievement—2nd Edition (K-TEA II): Letter and Word Identification	The student identifies letters and pronounces words of gradually increasing difficulty. Most words are irregular to ensure that the subtest measures word recognition rather than decoding ability.	4.6–25.11
K-TEA II: Nonsense Word Decoding	The student applies phonics and structural analysis skills to decode invented words of increasing difficulty.	Grade 1– Age 25.11
K-TEA II: Phonological Awareness	The student responds orally to items that require manipulation of sounds. Tasks include rhyming, matching sounds, blending sounds, segmenting sounds and deleting sounds.	Grade 1–6
WIAT-III: Word Reading	The individual is asked to read a list of words aloud and is scored for accuracy and speed.	4.0–19.11

Assessment	Description	Age
WIAT-III: Pseudoword Decoding	The individual is asked to read aloud from a list of single nonwords, assessing decoding skills, accuracy and speed.	4.0–19.11
WIAT-III: Early Reading Skills	Items present auditory, visual, or auditory/visual stimuli and require oral and pointing responses.	4.0–19.11
Woodcock-Johnson III Tests of Achievement (WJ III-ACH): Letter-Word Identification	Initially asks individual to identify letters in large type then pronounce words correctly. Does not require knowledge of meaning.	2–95+
WJ III-ACH: Word Attack	Asks individuals to produce sounds for individual letters, then using letter combinations that are phonically consistent, regular or patterns in English, read nonsense words of increasing difficulty.	2–95+
Gray Oral Reading Tests— 5th Edition (GORT5)	The individual reads up to 16 passages at grade level or reading ability and is scored on rate and accuracy.	6.0–23.11
Comprehensive Test of Phonological Processing (CTOPP): Elision	The individual listens to words and is asked to drop a sound within the word to make a new word.	5–24
CTOPP: Blending Words	The individual listens to audiocassette-recorded separate sounds and is then asked to put the sounds together to make a word.	5–24
CTOPP: Sound Matching	While the examiner says a words and points at a corresponding image, the individual listens, then repeats the words. For the last test items, the examiner asks, "Which words starts with the same sound as __?" And the individual must point at the appropriate picture and say the word.	5–6
CTOPP: Nonword Repetition	The individual listens to an audiocassette-recording of made-up words and is asked to repeat it exactly as he or she heard it.	5–24
CTOPP: Blending Nonwords	The individual listens to a series of audiocassette-recorded speech sounds and is asked which made-up nonsense word they create.	7–24
CTOPP: Segmenting Words	The individual is told to repeat a word, then say it one sound at a time.	7–24
CTOPP: Segmenting Nonwords	The individual listens to an audiocassette-recorded series of nonwords, repeats each and is then asked to say the nonword one sound at a time.	7–24
CTOPP: Phoneme Reversal	The individual listens to an audiocassette-recorded series of nonwords, then is asked to say the nonword backwards to form a real word.	7–24

Table 7.2 Measures of reading comprehension.

Assessment	Description	Age
K-TEA II: Reading Comprehension	The individual is first asked to read words and point at corresponding pictures, then read simple command statements and complete the required action. Then the student reads a passage and answers literal and inferential questions.	Grade 1– Age 25.11
WIAT-III: Reading Comprehension	The individual is asked to read a passage, either silently or aloud, then asked a series of comprehension questions while referring to the text. Both literal and inferential comprehension is assessed.	4.0–19.11
WJ III-ACH: Passage Comprehension	Initially, the individual is asked to match a rebus with an actual picture of the object. They are then asked to read a phrase, and point at a picture of the object described. Finally, individuals are asked to read a short passage and supply a missing word that is meaningful in the context of the passage.	2–95+
WJ III-ACH: Reading Vocabulary	Three subtests: Synonyms asks the individual to read a word and supply a synonym. Antonyms asks the individual to read a word and supply an antonym. Analogies requires the individual to read three words, and supply a fourth to complete the analogy.	2–95+
GORT5	The individual reads up to 16 passages and answers oral comprehension questions without referring to the text. Answers to questions are scored on a measure of comprehension.	6.0–23.11

Table 7.3 Measures of reading fluency.

Assessment	Description	Age
CTOPP: Rapid Naming Composite: Rapid Color Naming and Rapid Object Naming	In separate subtests, the individual views 6 high frequency objects and colors that are organized in rows, that randomly repeat. They are asked to name them as quickly as possible and are measured for time and accuracy. Each subtest contains 72 items.	5–6
CTOPP Rapid Naming Composite: Rapid digit naming and rapid letter naming	In separate subtests, the individual views five high-frequency numbers and letters in rows that randomly repeat. They are asked to name them as quickly as possible and measured for time and accuracy. Each subtest contains 72 items.	7–24
K-TEA II: Word Reading Fluency	The student reads isolated words as quickly as they can for 1 minute.	Grade 3– Age 25.11
K-TEA II: Decoding Fluency	The student applies decoding skills to pronounce as many nonsense words as they can in 1 minute.	Grade 3– Age 25.11
K-TEA II: Associational Fluency	The student says as many words as possible in 30 seconds that belong to a semantic category or have a specified beginning sound.	Ages 4.6– 25.11

Assessment	Description	Age
K-TEA II: Naming Facility	The student names objects, colors, and letters as quickly as possible.	Ages 4.6– 25.11
Rapid Automatized Naming and Rapid Alternating Stimulus Test (RAN/RAS): Objects, Colors, Numbers, Letters	In separate subtests, the individual views 5 high-frequency objects, colors, numbers and letters that randomly repeat 10 times, are asked to name them as quickly as possible and are measured for time.	5.0–18.11
RAN/RAS: 2–Set and 3–Set	The individual views a series of numbers and letters that are familiar and randomized, and asked to name them. The individual then views a series of letters, numbers and colors in a random pattern and is asked to name them. Scored for speed and accuracy.	5.0–18.11
WC JIII-ACH: Reading Fluency	The individual is asked to read simple sentences and circle yes or no if the statement is true. In 3 minutes, the individual must see how many sentences he or she can complete.	2–95+
WIAT-III: Oral Reading Fluency	The individual reads grade-level expository and narrative passages. This test yields separate scores for accuracy, rate and fluency.	4.0–19.11
GORT5	The individual reads up to 16 passages and is scored on his or her reading fluency.	6.0–23.11

Written Expression

Like reading, writing is a complex process that involves a number of separate skills that must be integrated in order to create a product. The act of writing brings together inter-related cognitive, executive, linguistic and orthographic components. A difficulty in any one of these areas can potentially cause an individual to avoid or resist this form of communication.

Written language can be understood as the "comprehension and expression of thoughts through the use of characters, letters, or words that are etched, traced, or formed on the surface of some material. Written language is one of the two principal manifestations of language, the other being spoken language" (Hammill & Larsen, 2009, p. 1). Written language, like oral language, has two components, both receptive and expressive. While reading constitutes the receptive aspect of written language, writing embodies the expressive.

One line of research suggests that both reading and writing develop in tandem and that there are shared knowledge and cognitive processes involved in their development. This belief is based on the view that "reading and writing are constellations of cognitive processes that depend on knowledge representations at various linguistic levels (phonemic, orthographic, semantic, syntactic, pragmatic). Reading and writing are connected, according to such views, because they depend on identical or similar knowledge representations, cognitive processes, and contexts and contextual constraints. Therefore, we

Figure 7.2 Student drawing of a writing activity.

should expect reading and writing to be quite similar, their developments should parallel each other closely" (Fitzgerald & Shanahan, 2000, p. 40).

While reading and writing are very closely interrelated, there is another line of research that suggests that they can be seen as separate functions. For example, studies of patients with brain injuries have identified those who can read but not write or who could write but not read what they wrote (Kemmerer, Tranel, & Manzel, 2005; Stotsky, 1983). Studies have also identified students who could either read well and write poorly or read poorly but write well (Stotsky, 1983).

Development of Writing Skills

While there is considerable literature on the development of reading, relatively little has been studied regarding the development of written expression. In examining the relationship between reading and writing, however, Fitzgerald and Shanahan (2000) have proposed a model in which writing parallels the development of reading ability. They suggest that there are six stages involved:

Stage 1: Literacy roots—This is the emergent literacy period during which different forms of knowledge (meta, content, text attribute and procedural knowledge) as well as phonological awareness develop.

Stage 2: Initial literacy—Letters and sounds are connected and an understanding of semantics and syntax as well as text attributes is crucial. In respect to writing, there are further stages regarding the development of spelling during this period.

Precommunication stage—Children make markings, thinking it is writing.

Semiphonetic stage—Children recognize that letters stand for sounds.

Phonetic stage—Writers can represent sounds phonetically.

Transitional stage—Writers realize that words have particular morphological structures.

Conventional stage—Greater knowledge of orthographic system.

Stage 3: Confirmation, fluency, ungluing from print—Consolidation of previous learning, automaticity. Increased internalization of graphophonics, orthographic patterns of more complex words.

Stage 4: Writing for learning the new—Meaning becomes the focus. An increase in more abstract content, new ideas and new vocabulary and more complex syntactical structure.

Stage 5: Multiple viewpoints—Metaknowledge and self-monitoring allow for deeper understanding of meaning and the ability to take other perspectives and analyze text. Critical thinking develops, enabling revision or alternative ways of writing to better match content and style with the writer's audience.

Stage 6: Construction and Reconstruction—Individuals move from knowledge as factual to an understanding of knowledge as more subjective.

Neuroanatomy of Written Expression

The ability to write involves a complex network of structures both on the right and left sides of the brain. The particular network involved depends on the level of written expression one is considering.

The most common neurologically based forms of agraphias (partial or complete impairment in written language skills) have been described based on observations of patients with brain lesions. Pure agraphia describes a condition in which agraphia is evident in the absence of any disturbance in language processing. This form of agraphia is most often associated with focal lesions, including the second frontal convolution, superior parietal lobule, posterior perisylvian region and the left caudate and internal capsule and other subcortical structures. Aphasic agraphia is associated with various forms of aphasia (disturbance in language due to brain damage), and lesions associated with this form of agraphia are not usually different from left-sided lesions that typically cause the aphasic disorder. Agraphia with alexia (inability to see words or read) usually occurs in patients with lesions of the parietal cortex. These individuals make poorly formed graphemes when writing and have difficulty spelling, though they can accurately spell aloud. Apraxic Agraphia is a disturbance in the ability to form graphemes when writing spontaneously or in response to dictation, and lesions in these patients usually are in the parietal lobe opposite the dominant hand. Lastly, patients with spatial agraphia have difficulty writing in a horizontal line, write on just the right side of the paper, and have spaces between graphemes. This form of agraphia is usually associated with a neglect syndrome and may be a result of lesions in the nondominant parietal lobe (Roeltgen, 1993).

More recent studies have generally concluded that partial or complete impairments in writing can be associated with linguistic disturbances (aphasia) as well as disturbances unrelated to language, such as motor, spatial and conceptual problems. The most common form of agraphia is a result of lesions on the left side, often in the posterior association cortical area (Roeltgen & Ullrich, 2011).

In respect to higher level disturbances in written expression, Ardila and Surloff (2006) reported that complex components of writing, including planning, narrative coherence and maintained attention, were significantly compromised in patients with prefrontal lesions and impairments in executive functions. They proposed the term *dysexecutive agraphia* to describe this disorder of writing.

Developmental dysgraphia is a form of agraphia that refers specifically to a disorder in which otherwise functioning individuals do not make progress in written expression over the course of development. The term *dysgraphia* has also been used to describe an impairment in written expression due to a difficulty managing the mechanics of writing. For example, a five-year longitudinal study of second graders found that children with dysgraphic handwriting had lower fine motor ability and, in the higher grades, showed less preference for a personal style. Their structural performance also was poorer than that of the other writers (Hamstra-Bletz & Blote, 1993).

Thus, the ability to use writing as an effective form of communication can be impacted by variables on a wide-ranging level of cognitive and motor functioning. For example, it is not unusual for a child with very superior language skills to struggle with writing because their processing speed is significantly below average or, in some instances, even just average. In such cases, the rate at which he or she can formulate a thought and organize a sentence mentally is quite disparate from the rate with which he or she can organize the fine motor act necessary to write it down. This disconnect between formulation and written expression could be because of deficits in motor planning, graphomotor precision, difficulty holding the thought in mind due to deficits in working memory, etc. As such, any one of these factors can determine whether or not a child finds the act of writing rewarding or frustrating, fatiguing and, ultimately, not worth the effort. Understanding the origins of writing difficulty allows for integrated intervention. Two important elements of the writing process frequently assessed during academic assessment, encoding and composition, are discussed in the following sections as they relate to a complete neuropsychological evaluation.

Encoding

If decoding resembles the ability to break words apart to generate individual sounds in an effort to identify a word and apply meaning, encoding is the process of building a word, otherwise known as spelling. Efficient written communication demands that the writer retrieve spellings from memory, and thus this skill represents an important academic achievement (Kwong & Varnhagen, 2005). As with other literacy skills, the language spoken by the individual has an important influence in the process of learning how to spell (Nassaji, 2007). For the purpose of this discussion, we focus on the development of spelling skills in English.

While distinctly different from decoding, encoding relies on some of the very same underlying processes as decoding, namely, phonological awareness, phonological memory, the alphabetic principle, concepts of print, orthographic and morphological awareness and the development of fluency. Some researchers suggest that spelling development follows along the same lines as reading development; an individual moves through a series of stages that rely on cognitive development, starting with simple activities and moving to more complex activities (Gentry, 1982, 1984). The progression begins with the knowledge that random symbols represent words, then the awareness that sounds are represented by a word, followed by awareness of orthographic patterns, the awareness of morphemes and syllables and application of derivational/meaning knowledge, eventually resulting in accurate, fluid spelling skills and long-term storage of spelling rules (Young, 2007). Another proposed process, the overlapping waves theory, proposes that spelling strategy development is not so regular and sequential but that children may apply more and less sophisticated spelling strategies at various times (Kwong & Varnhagen, 2005). "Sounding out" words as they match letters to sounds is a familiar strategy based in phonological processing. Applying orthographic and morphological knowledge (spelling rules such as doubling a final consonant before adding the morpheme -*ing* to a word, such as *running*) is another strategy. While a complicated process, some children make analogies to a known word as a device for retrieval. And, finally, a child may engage multiple senses and write the word or spell it out loud to see or hear how it sounds (Kwong & Varnhagen, 2005). While the debate on spelling strategy continues, it is evident that reading and spelling skills are related. Relying on orthographic and phonological representations, spelling requires a more complete and accessible representation for success (Friend, DeFries, Wadsworth, & Olson, 2007). This suggests similar but distinct cognitive and neurological substrates.

Cognitive variables shown to influence novice spelling abilities include working memory, long-term memory, phonological awareness, multisyllable word naming (morphemic awareness) and RAN skills (Strattman & Hodson, 2005). Research regarding neurological substrates are scarce. However, an Austrian study has demonstrated that during an fMRI study of morpheme-based strategy development, German-speaking students displayed increased activation in the left temporal, parahippocampal and hippocampal regions. Right posterior regions, including the lateral occipital cortex, gyrus angularis and gyrus supramarginalis, also show increased activity, which implies that there is a cognitive compensatory mechanism for poor spellers (Gebauer, Fink, Kargl, Reishofer, & Koschutnig, 2012).

Organizing and Sequencing

As mentioned previously, the developmental process of learning to write is rooted in skills related to phonological processes but also to linguistic rules related to syntax. In writing longer compositions, the individual relies on a complex set of skills, such as the ability to consider the aim, readers, rhetorical elements, outlines, detail, the end result and overall coherence (Rodriguez et al., 2011). This requires significant cognitive effort and attention as the individual retrieves words from memory, considers the written representation of a topic, is aware of the perspective of the audience and exercises self-regulation (García & Fidalgo, 2006, 2008; Graham & Perin, 2007). High cognitive effort is required during the deployment of these skills (Torrance, Fidalgo, & García, 2007). Younger, less experienced writers, or those with a learning disability, may experience cognitive overload as they attempt the delicate balancing act that is writing composition.

Many theoretical models of composition have been developed, beginning with Hayes and Flower's (1980), which proposed that written compositions have three subprocesses: generating/planning, translating, and reviewing. While their model has been refined and adapted since its inception, these three processes remain constant. An important element of this model is that these processes can occur in stages but are more likely intertwined as the writer manages internal and external constraints. For example, during planning, the individual must consider what to say and how to say it while retrieving information from long-term memory and integrating new information and managing other regulatory processes. Translation involves shaping preverbal ideas into words and creating text, all the while managing the rules dictated by the language. Reviewing is an ongoing process in which ideas and text are evaluated and considered (Myhill, 2009). During this nonlinear process, working memory, fluency and self-feedback contribute to the already heavy cognitive load, spearheaded by long-term memory and attention. As a result, the writing process is the art of combining phonological processes with executive functions, toward the end goal of a written composition (Ardila & Surloff, 2006).

Assessments of Written Expression

The following tables list assessment tools that measure written language (Table 7.4) and writing fluency (Table 7.5).

Mathematics

Mathematical abilities, like reading and writing, rely on a complex constellation of skills that evolve over the course of development. As proposed by Geary (2003), current understanding of particular skills sets needed for math proficiency include the following:

Procedural skills—The ability to use counting procedures to solve simple arithmetic problems. Necessary for skill in this area are intact working memory abilities and an adequate foundation in conceptual knowledge.

Semantic memory skills—Facilitate the storage and retrieval of math facts from long-term memory.

Visuospatial skills—Theoretically necessary for performance in mathematical domains such as geometry and solving complex word problems.

Table 7.4 Measures of written language.

Assessment	Description	Age
K-TEA II: Written Expression	Kindergarten and prekindergarten students trace and copy letters and write letters from dictation. At grade 1 and higher the student completes age-appropriate tasks in the context of a storybook. Tasks include: writing sentences from dictation, adding punctuation and capitalization, filling in missing words, completing sentences, combining sentences, writing compound and complex sentences and an essay based on the story.	Ages 4.6–25.11
K-TEA II: Spelling	Early items require the student to write single letters that represent sounds. Remaining items require the student to write dictated words both orthographically regular and irregular words of increasing complexity.	Grade 1–Age 25.11
WIAT-III: Sentence Composition	Two subtests: During Sentence Combining, the individual listens to and reads 2 or 3 sentences, then rewrites them as one, without excluding important information. In Sentence Building, the individual is given a target word, then writes a sentence correctly with appropriate context.	4.0–19.11
WIAT-III: Spelling	The individual listens to a dictated word, then listens to the word in a sentence, then writes the word.	4.0–19.11
WIAT-III: Essay Composition	The individual is given instructions for writing an essay using a prompt. He or she has 10 minutes to plan, write and finalize the composition.	Grade 3–Grade 12
WJ III-ACH: Writing Samples	The individual must write a sentence in response to a demand and is evaluated on quality of expression. Item difficulty increases in length, vocabulary, grammatical complexity and concept abstraction. Not assessed on spelling or punctuation.	2–95+
WJ III-ACH: Editing	Identify and correct errors in spelling, word usage, punctuation and capitalization. Increases in difficulty.	2–95+
WJ III-ACH: Punctuation and Capitalization	The individual is asked to punctuate and capitalize items correctly.	2–95+
WJ III-ACH: Spelling	Initial items measure prewriting skills, such as drawing lines, tracing letters and using upper- and lowercase letters. Then the individual is orally dictated a word to write and spell correctly.	2–95+
WJ III-ACH: Spelling of Sounds	Initial items ask the individual to write single letter sounds. Then listen to an audio recording of letter/sound patterns common in English, and use letters to write the sounds.	2–95+
WJ III-ACH: Writing Evaluation Scale (WES)	Assess writing skills by informal, analytic evaluation of longer, more complex passages.	2–95+
Test of Written Language 4th Edition (TOWL4): Vocabulary	The individual views a list of words, then writes a sentence using each word, scoring for proper usage and meaning of the word.	9.0–17.11

(Continued)

Table 7.4 (Continued)

Assessment	Description	Age
TOWL4: Spelling and Punctuation	The individual listens to a dictated sentence, then writes the sentence. T Scored separately for accurate spelling and proper use of capitalization and punctuation.	9.0–17.11
TOWL4: Logical Sentences	The individual views a series of sentences, then makes corrections for grammar, punctuation and meaning.	9.0–17.11
TOWL4: Sentence Combining	The individual views two or more sentences and is asked to combine them, making one proper sentence that captures important elements of the original sentences.	9.0–17.11
TOWL4: Contextual Conventions and Story Composition	The individual writes an essay in response to a visual cue. Orthographic and grammatic conventions are assessed as well as the quality of the composition.	9.0–17.11

Table 7.5 Measures of writing fluency.

Assessment	Description	Age
WJ III-ACH: Writing Fluency	Individuals are given a stimulus picture and are required to write a sentence that includes a set of 3 given words.	2–95+
WIAT-III: Alphabet Writing Fluency	During a 30-second time limit, the individual is asked to write letters in an order of their choice, without repeating letters.	PreK–Grade 3

Development of Math Skills

Human infants possess a basic sense of quantity and, even in the first week of life, are able to mentally represent quantities of up to four. Five-month-old infants are aware of the consequences of adding and subtracting on the number of objects in their environment for quantities of one and two. Around eighteen months of age, infants begin to understand ordinal relationships, knowing three things are more than two. In the preschool years, a child's use of language becomes important in their ability to represent numerical information and relationships. Between the ages of two and eight years, children develop basic number skills and memorize number words, understand that each word represents a different quantity and develop counting skills. In this process, they learn ordinal and cardinal meanings for increasingly larger sets and are able to apply that knowledge to measurement and arithmetic. By seven or eight years, children come to understand that numbers reflect the groupings of smaller sets of numbers, and they are able to use number knowledge to make quantitative decisions rather than relying on concrete information, such as length or density (Geary, 1994).

While infants and children have an implicit understanding of limited quantities, it is unclear whether this knowledge gradually increases with age or is related to language development. Nevertheless, this implicit knowledge lays the foundation for later development of arithmetical skills, development that is dependent on environmental factors related to culture, parenting and education. Research in respect to the latter suggests that development takes place in phases and includes changes in strategy, from the use of manipulatives to verbal counting and lastly to retrieval-based strategies. All of which transpire as the child's conceptual understanding of numbers and arithmetic also changes, particularly in respect to problem-solving strategies, memory representations and abstract schema-based knowledge, which, in turn, prepare the way for solving more complex word problems involving arithmetic and algebra. These latter skills are dependent on factors such as reading comprehension, the ability to translate text into equations and metacognitive skills (Geary, 1994).

Attempts to understand individual differences in mathematical-skill development have taken a number of perspectives, and each distinguishes between numerical facility (arithmetic) and mathematical reasoning (mathematical problem solving). The psychometric and behavioral genetic views hold that an intuitive understanding of arithmetic may be inherent. From the cognitive perspective, development of arithmetic skills is correlated with differences in working memory, in conceptual understanding of arithmetic and related domains, such as counting, in the ability to use effective, alternate problem-solving strategies and in the speed with which basic arithmetical operations can be carried out. Behavioral genetics studies find that about half of individual differences in arithmetical abilities are inherited (Geary, 1994).

In respect to mathematical reasoning, psychometric studies suggest that a separate set of math problem-solving skills emerges for most people during the high school years and are a learned rather than an inherent ability. People skilled in this area are also likely skilled in quickly and efficiently performing basic arithmetical operations, are able to use working memory to simultaneously manipulate a number of mathematical operations and have well-developed conceptual templates that allow them to represent, translate and solve complex problems. In the realm of behavioral genetics, evidence suggests that while for most people reasoning skills are learned, some individuals may possess a particular facility for understanding quantitative relationships before being taught complex mathematics (Geary, 1994; Geary, Hoard, Nugent, & Bailey, 2012).

Mathematical Disabilities and Their Neuroanatomical Correlates

Developmental dyscalculia is a learning disability that impacts the normal acquisition of arithmetic abilities. It affects five to six percent of children in school and genetic, neurobiological and epidemiological evidence indicates that it is a neurological disorder (Shalev, 2004). Disabilities in arithmetical skills have been described in relation to three major domains of mathematical ability: procedural, semantic memory and visuospatial (Geary, 2003).

Procedural deficits relate to a child's difficulties using counting procedures to solve simple arithmetic problems. When attempting to do so, children with an arithmetic disability (AD) make more errors and use less mature problem-solving strategies. They make more miscounting errors, tend to use fingers and, on multistep problems, make errors of misalignment and carrying. Deficits in working memory are likely the reason AD children use their fingers, miscount and have difficulty monitoring and coordinating the sequencing of more complex problem-solving steps. In addition, poor conceptual knowledge of procedures can delay a child's use of more mature strategies and prevent them from detecting errors (Geary, 2003).

Semantic memory deficits occur in AD children when they fail to make the shift from procedural-based problem solving to memory-based problem solving, suggesting that AD children are having difficulty storing or retrieving arithmetic facts in or from long-term memory. Even when they are able to recall facts, they commit more errors and demonstrate different reaction time patterns that are characteristic of children with damage to left hemisphere and subcortical structures. Furthermore, some studies suggest that retrieval of basic math facts can be compromised by difficulties filtering out irrelevant information that then enter working memory and interfere with problem solving (Geary, 2003).

Lastly, visuospatial deficits in AD children can make it difficult for them to represent numerical information in the spatial domain (Geary, 2003). Examples of spatial dyscalculia include misaligning numbers in long division or multistep multiplication, misplacement of numbers relative to each other, confusion of columns or rows of numbers or neglect of one or more numbers (Lezak et al., 2012).

Generally, procedural deficits have been associated with damage to the right parietal and right frontal cortical regions, the latter likely related to difficulty with executive functions related to sequencing and monitoring (Geary, 2003). A significant increase in glucose metabolism in the left hemisphere and a small increase in right frontal areas were observed in adults while they were taking the Arithmetic subtest of the WAIS-III, while greater oxygenation in parietal and posterior frontal regions was observed in children performing calculations (Lezak et al., 2012). Acalculia (another term for dyscalculia) has been correlated with lesions in the left inferior parietal lobule and generally is most common and severe with lesions in the left posterior cortex (Lezak et al., 2012).

Deficits in semantic memory have been associated with damage to neural networks typically related to phonetic and semantic memory systems, including left parieto/occipito/temporal regions, as well as left basal ganglia, either due to damage to or developmental anomalies in these regions (Dehaene & Cohen, 1997). Retrieval deficits associated with disorders of working memory are likely due to damage or disrupted development of prefrontal areas that mediate inhibitory processes (Bull, Johnston, & Roy, 1999).

Less is known about the contribution of visuospatial skills to mathematics. However, some data suggest that processes such as quantity manipulation, estimation and approximation of magnitudes depend on bilateral regions of the parietal lobes that are involved in visuospatial processing (Dehaene, Spelke, Pinel, Stanescu, & Tsivkin, 1999)

Math Calculation

Difficulties with mathematics, despite adequate learning opportunities, affects approximately six percent to fourteen percent of school-aged children, even though age-appropriate achievement in other educational domains is obtained (Barbaresi, Katusic, Collagin, Weaver, & Jacobsen, 2005). This indicates that a certain subset of children require specific mathematical interventions in order to progress academically. Two lines of research attempt to address concerns related to the unfolding of mathematical disabilities (Mazzocco, Feigenson, & Halberda, 2011). The domain-specific approach posits that dyscalculia is, in part, the result of numerical processing difficulties or, in other words, deficient "number sense" (Dehaene, Piazza, Pinel, & Cohen, 2003). The second line of research, the domain-general approach, suggests that difficulties arise out of complications in other cognitive systems, such as phonological skills, working memory, long-term memory or visuospatial processing (Geary, 1993). Ongoing research continues to ascertain the impact of both domain-specific and domain-general concerns related to dyscalculia, with the likelihood that both overlap functionally as predictors of future math abilities (Passolunghi & Lanfranchi, 2011). Beyond these foundational skills, the use of abstract reasoning, as it relates to mathematical problem solving, is also relevant. In the following section, both approaches are discussed as they relate to achievement assessment.

Dyscalculia and Calculation

Number sense is a child's ability to understand what numbers mean, to flexibly employ number concepts and use them to perform mental mathematical operations and make comparisons (Gersten & Chard, 1999). This skill relies on the ability to understand that numbers represent or symbolize real-world concepts, much like letters represent sounds. Number sense allows individuals to count, estimate, utilize number patterns and so on. Elements of number sense seem to be innate, natural to development, while other aspects are a more complicated skills set that is more likely to develop with instruction and experience (Jordan & Levine, 2009). The ability to perform more advanced abstract math appears to rely on a strong foundation in number sense.

Research continues to attempt to clarify the development and role of number sense in mathematical calculations. Several contributing factors to this basic underlying skill set include ordinality (Rubinsten & Sury, 2011), estimation and the approximate number system (ANS) (Feigenson, Dehaene, & Spelke, 2004). The ANS allows an individual to approximate number representations during both nonsymbolic approximations (judging quantity of items without counting) and symbolic number tasks (assessing if a series of digits is increasing or decreasing). This system is activated during mathematical operations but also during everyday tasks, such as choosing which grocery store checkout line is the shortest and fastest. This system appears in early development, is universally shared among humans and emerges without explicit instruction. A subset of children with mathematical difficulties display impairment in this system (Mazzocco et al., 2011). Difficulty in mathematical judgment and approximation may lead to difficulty with developing accurate number sense skills.

Related is the ability to perform basic calculation. This is the ability to add and subtract numbers with sums less than twenty. This ability has consistently proven to covary with overall math achievement. While evidence suggests a strong connection between basic calculation and the ability to perform higher level mathematical computations, research is unable explain the relationship (Cowan et al., 2011). Typically, progress within basic calculation relies on three phases (Baroody, 2006). First, children solve basic calculation problems by counting fingers or using manipulatives, an activity rooted in concrete thinking and processing. Next, they develop knowledge regarding mathematic principles, such as inverse operations (recognizing that the answer for 10 – 5 is the inverse of 5 + 5). Finally, basic mathematical calculations are stored in long-term memory for ready retrieval and manipulation (Reyes, Suydam, Lindquist, & Smith, 1998). The development of these abilities ensures that the child can employ multiple computational strategies for completing various types of mathematical problems (Cowan et al., 2011).

Dyscalculia and Executive Functions

While the domain specific approach to understanding mathematical abilities focuses on number sense, the domain general approach encompasses other cognitive abilities employed during math performance. The domain general approach suggests that working memory (both verbal and visuospatial), short-term memory, processing speed and general intelligence play a role mathematical abilities. It has also been suggested that phonological awareness and verbal counting are also contributing factors (Passalunghi & Lanfranchi, 2012). In an effort to further understand underpinning cognitive factors of mathematical performance, researchers are investigating the role played by executive functions.

Various elements of executive functions may have an impact on mathematical performance, particularly working memory, inhibition and shifting sets (Toll, Van der Ven, Kroesbergen, & Va Luit, 2011). The act of mathematical problem solving requires individuals to hold information in working memory, shift their attention to various elements of the problem, inhibit the tendency to respond to extraneous information and self-regulate (Blair & Razza, 2007). Problems with working memory, set shifting abilities and inhibition have all been implicated as predictors of future mathematical difficulties, with working memory as the most reliable and shifting set as the least reliable. Important to note is that subsets of executive functions develop at different rates. Therefore, these skills may be employed more or less, depending on the age and rate of development of each child. Regarding neuropsychological testing, the Stroop test of inhibition has not been shown to be a reliable predictor of mathematical abilities (Stroop, 1935), but tests of inhibition containing numerical contents do (Bull & Scerif, 2001).

Mathematical Reasoning

Similar to the mastery of reading skills, mathematical proficiency is built upon underlying cognitive skills and basic mechanics but also abstract thinking. A distinction can be made between calculation abilities and reasoning skills (Nunes, Bryan, Barros, & Sylva, 2012). For example, individuals can be taught the steps of long division, but if their basic understanding of place value is not solid, they will have more difficulty applying this skill when appropriate or manipulating the function in later, higher level math. The ability to conceptualize a task, make inferences, develop patterns and draw connections between mathematical information (analogical reasoning) allows individuals to make decisions regarding task completion.

Reasoning, as it applies to math, has not been clearly defined by researchers or educators (Boesen, Lithner, & Palm, 2010). Lithner (2008) proposed a framework for mathematical reasoning that includes various subtypes. He stated that reasoning is the line of thought adopted to produce assertions and reach conclusions. Furthermore, argumentation is the ability to display the line of thought used to reach the conclusion. In doing so, differences between intrinsic properties of math and surface properties arise. Intrinsic properties relate to underlying mathematical concepts, such as fractions, and surface properties are the expression thereof. For example, when trying to determine which fraction is the largest between 99/120 and 3/2, an individual focused on surface properties would choose 99/120, because the numbers are bigger. An individual utilizing intrinsic properties would understand that 3/2 actually represents a larger fraction (Lithner, 2000, 2003).

At the root of mathematical reasoning is the ability to build relationships or correspondences between some physical or symbolic entity and the abstract concept it is intended to represent (such as money or time; Hudson, 1983 ; Resnick, 1991). Researchers White, Alexander and Daugherty (1998) contend that these abilities develop in children at a much younger age than proposed by some developmental theorists. They proposed that analogical reasoning in math is predicated by a child's ability to perceive basic attributes of an object or symbol, relate it to a concept using inferences and recognize or detect patterns, similar to what a child might do using words (White, Alexander, & Daugherty, 1998). This ability can be observed in children as young as the age of two while engaged in symbolic play (Clements & Sarama, 2004). Through play, abstract mathematical reasoning skills develop, such as one-to-one correspondence and the cardinal rule (the last number stated while counting represents a group, not an individual object), as well as an understanding that objects can be counted in any order and the number will stay the same. Furthermore, a child comes to comprehend that any object can be gathered and counted, including actions, and that number symbols represent quantity. The use of a shape (2-D or 3-D to represent a real-world object), ability to recognize the part to whole relationship of individual shapes and groups of shapes and the development of map skills (using symbols to represent actual objects and navigate a 3-D space) also develop through play.

Assessment of Mathematical Skills

The following tables list assessments that are used to measure mathematical reasoning and calculation (Table 7.6) and mathematical fluency (Table 7.7).

Table 7.6 Measures of mathematical reasoning and calculation.

Assessment	Description	Age
K-TEA II: Math Concepts and Applications	The student responds orally to test items that focus on the application of mathematical principles to real-life situations. Skill categories include number concepts, operation concepts, rational numbers, measurement, shape and space, data investigations and higher math concepts.	4.6–25.11
K-TEA II: Math Computation	The student computes solutions to math problems printed in a response booklet. Skills assessed include addition, subtraction, multiplication and division operations, fractions and decimals, square roots, exponents, signed numbers and algebra.	Grade K– Age 25.11

(Continued)

Table 7.6 (Continued)

Assessment	Description	Age
WIAT-III: Math Problem Solving	The individual listens as the examiner reads a math problem and views corresponding visual stimuli, then provides oral or pointing responses. Not timed.	4.0–19.11
WIAT-III: Numerical Operations	The individual completes written mathematical operations without being timed.	4.0–19.11
WJ III-ACH: Applied Problems	The individual listens to a math problem, must recognize the procedure to follow and perform relatively simple calculations. Items include extraneous information.	2–95+
WJ III-ACH: Quantitative Concepts	Assess math concepts, symbols and vocabulary through two subtests. In Concepts, the individual must identify shapes, numbers and sequences. In the second, Number Series, they view a series of numbers, determine a pattern, and supply missing numbers.	2–95+

Table 7.7 Measures of mathematical fluency.

Assessment	Description	Age
WIAT-III: Math Fluency	The individual completes timed additions, subtraction and multiplication problems. Performance is scored for speed and accuracy.	4.0–19.11

Charles

The reader may recall that Charles was eleven years and two months at the time of testing and that parents were reporting that he was having increasing difficulty with academics at home, particularly around the introduction of new topics, writing and accepting corrections. His increasing resistance to the academic materials taught by his mother was preventing him from making adequate educational progress.

Tests of Achievement

Charles was administered a set of tests from the *Woodcock-Johnson III Tests of Achievement* (Woodcock et al., 2001). These tests measured various aspects of scholastic achievement. Comparisons were made among his achievement scores, and such comparisons can help determine if any significant intra-achievement discrepancies exist. Interpretation is referenced to his age and includes level of development, degree of mastery and peer comparison scores.

Skill Areas

Broad Reading—The Broad Reading cluster provides a comprehensive measure of reading achievement, including reading decoding, reading speed and the ability to comprehend connected discourse while reading. It is a combination of Letter-Word Identification, Passage Comprehension and Reading Fluency. On this measure of reading ability, Charles scored at an age equivalent of fourteen years, ten months with a Standard Score of one hundred and twenty-one and a grade equivalent of 9.3.

Broad Math—The Broad Math cluster provides a comprehensive measure of math achievement including problem solving, number facility, automaticity and reasoning. This cluster includes Calculation, Math Fluency and Applied Problems. On this measure of math ability, Charles scored at an age equivalent of fourteen years, nine months with a standard score of one hundred and twenty and a grade equivalent of 9.3.

Broad Written Language—The Broad Written Language cluster provides a comprehensive measure of written language achievement, including spelling of single-word responses, fluency of production and quality of expression. Tests included in this cluster are Spelling, Writing Fluency and Writing Samples. On this measure of written language, Charles scored at an age equivalent of thirteen years, eight months with a standard score of one hundred and fifteen and a grade equivalent of 8.2.

Math Calculation—The Math Calculation Skills cluster is an aggregate measure of computational skills and automaticity with basic math facts and provides a measure of basic mathematical skills. It is composed of the Calculation and Math Fluency tests. On this measure of basic math skills, Charles scored at an age equivalent of thirteen years, six months with a standard score of one hundred and sixteen and a grade equivalent of 8.1.

Written Expression—The Written Expression cluster is an aggregate measure of meaningful written expression and fluency providing a measure of written expression skills. This cluster is a combination of Writing Fluency and Writing Samples. On this measure of written expression, Charles scored at the age equivalent of twelve years, nine months with a standard score of one hundred and ten and a grade equivalent of 7.4.

Academic Skills—The Academic Skills cluster is a combined measure of reading decoding, math calculation and spelling of single-word responses providing an overall score of basic achievement skills. It is a combination of Letter-Word Identification, Calculation and Spelling. On this overall measure of achievement, Charles scored at an age equivalent of fifteen years, five months with a standard score of one hundred and twenty-six and a grade equivalent of 9.9.

Academic Fluency—The Academic Fluency cluster is a combination of Reading Fluency, Math Fluency and Writing Fluency and provides an overall index of academic fluency. On this timed measure of proficiency,

Charles scored at the age equivalent of thirteen years, seven months with a standard score of one hundred and fifteen and a grade equivalent of 8.2.

Academic Applications—The Academic Applications cluster is a combination of Applied Problems, Passage Comprehension and Writing Samples. These three tests require the application of academic skills to academic problems. On this measure, Charles scored at an age equivalent of fourteen years, three months with a standard score of one hundred and thirteen and a grade equivalent of 8.8.

Individual Achievement Tests

Letter-Word Identification—This test measures an individual's word identification skills and requires the correct pronunciation of increasingly difficult words. On this measure, Charles scored at an age equivalent of fifteen years, zero months with a standard score of one hundred and nineteen and a grade equivalent of 9.5.

Reading Fluency—This test measures an individual's reading speed and rate and requires the ability to quickly read simple sentences, decide if the statement is true and then circle yes or no. The difficulty of the sentences gradually increases. On this measure, Charles scored at an age equivalent of fifteen years, six months with a standard score of one hundred and nineteen and a grade equivalent of 10.0.

Calculation—This test measures the ability to perform mathematical computations and requires an individual to perform a variety of calculations ranging from simple addition to calculus. On this measure, Charles scored at an age equivalent of sixteen years, six months with a standard score of one hundred and twenty-three and a grade equivalent of 11.0.

Math Fluency—This test is a measure of math achievement and number facility requiring the individual to rapidly and accurately solve simple addition, subtraction and multiplication problems. On this measure, Charles scored at an age equivalent of eleven years, zero months with a standard score of ninety-nine and a grade equivalent of 5.6.

Spelling—This test measures knowledge of spelling and requires the individual to produce words in response to oral prompts. On this measure, Charles scored at an age equivalent of fifteen years, eight months with a standard score of one hundred and seventeen and a grade equivalent of 10.2.

Writing Fluency—This test measures the individual's ability to write rapidly with ease (automaticity) and requires the production of legible, simple sentences with acceptable English syntax. It is impacted by an individual's fine motor control, response style, ability to sustain attention and reading or spelling skills. On this measure, Charles scored at an age equivalent of thirteen years, seven months with a standard score of one hundred and fourteen and a grade equivalent of 8.2.

Passage Comprehension—This test is a measure of reading comprehension and lexical knowledge and requires the ability to use syntactic and semantic cues. On this measure, Charles scored at an age of thirteen years, four months with a standard score of one hundred and nine and a grade equivalent of 7.9.

Applied Problems—This test is a measure of quantitative reasoning, math achievement and math knowledge, requiring the individual to analyze and solve math problems. It also measures an aspect of fluid reasoning. On this measure, Charles scored at an age equivalent of sixteen years, eleven months with a standard score of one hundred and eighteen and a grade equivalent of 11.4.

Writing Samples—This test measures the ability to convey ideas in writing and requires the production of meaningful written sentences in response to a variety of task criteria. On this measure, Charles scored at an age equivalent of eleven years, seven months with a standard score of one hundred and two and a grade equivalent of 6.2.

Based on the findings in both Skill Areas and Individual Achievement tests, Charles's academic skills were superior while his fluency with academic tasks and his ability to apply academic skills were high average. His broad reading skills were superior while his broad mathematics, math calculation and broad written language skills were high average. His written expression skills were average.

References

Araujo, S., Pacheco, A., Faisca, L., Petersson, K.M., & Reis, A. (2010). Visual rapid naming and phonological abilities: Different subtypes in dyslexic children. *International Journal of Psychology, 45*(6), 443–452.

Ardila, A., & Surloff, C. (2006). Dysexecutive agraphia: A major executive dysfunction sign. *International Journal of Neuroscience, 116*(5), 653–663.

Ashby, J., Dix, H., Bontrager, M., Dey, R., & Archer, A. (2013). Phonemic awareness contributes to text reading fluency: Evidence from eye movements. *Psychology Review, 42*(2), 157–170.

Baddeley, A., Gathercole, S., & Papagno, C. (1998). The phonological loop as a language learning device. *Psychological Review, 105,* 173–258.

Barbaresi, W.J., Katusic, S.K., Collagin, R.C., Weaver, A.L., & Jacobsen, S.J. (2005). Math learning disorder: Incidence in a population-based birth cohort, 1976–82, Rochester, Minn. *Ambulatory Pediatrics, 5,* 281–289. doi:10.1007/s10803-008-0645-8

Baroody, A.J. (2006). Why children have difficulty mastering the basic number combinations and how to help them. *Teaching Children Mathematics, 13,* 22–31.

Bartl-Pokorny, K.D., Marschik, P.B., Sachse, S., Green, V.A., Zhang, D., Van Der Meer, L., . . . Einspieler, C. (2013). Tracking development from early speech-language acquisition to reading skills at age 13. *Developmental Neurorehabilitation, 16*(3), 188–195.

Bates, E., Thal, D., & Janowsky, J. S. (1992). Early language development and its neural correlates. In I. Rapin & S. Segalowitz (Eds.), *Handbook of neuropsychology, child neurology* (Vol. 6, pp. 69–110). Amsterdam, Netherlands: Elsevier.

Blair, C., & Razza, R.P. (2007). Relating effortful control, executive function, and false belief understanding to emerging math and literacy ability in kindergarten. *Child Development, 78*(2), 647–663.

Boesen, J., Lithner, J., & Palm, T. (2010). The relation between assessment tasks and mathematical reasoning. *Educational Studies in Mathematics, 75*, 89–105.

Bull, R., Johnston, R., & Roy, J. (1999). Exploring the roles of the visual-spatial sketchpad and central executive in children's arithmetical skills: Views from cognition and developmental neuropsychology. *Developmental Neuropsychology, 15*, 421–442.

Bull, R., & Scerif, G. (2001). Executive functioning as a predictor of children's mathematics ability: Inhibition, switching, and working memory. *Developmental Neuropsychology, 19*, 273–293.

Calvo, M.G. (2001). Working memory and inferences: Evidence from eye fixations during reading. *Memory, 9*, 365–381.

Clements, D.H., & Sarama, J. (2004). Building abstract thinking through math. *Early Childhood Today, 18*(5), 34–40.

Coney, J., & Lange, A. (2006). Automatic and attentional process in the comprehension of unfamiliar metaphors. *Current Psychology: Developmental, Learning, Personality, Social, 25*(2) 93–119.

Cowan, R., Donlan, C., Sheperd, D., Cole-Fletcher, R., Saxton, M., & Hurry, J. (2011). Calculation proficiency and mathematics achievement in elementary school children. *Journal of Educational Psychology, 103*(4), 786–803.

Crutch, S.J., & Warrington. E.K. (2007). Semantic priming in deep-phonological dyslexia: Contrasting effects of association and similarity upon abstract and concrete word reading. *Cognitive Neuropsychology, 24*(6), 583–602.

Dehaene, S., & Cohen, L. (1997). Cerebral pathways for calculation: Double dissociation between rote verbal and quantitative knowledge of arithmetic. *Cortex, 33*, 219–250.

Dehaene, S., Piazza, M., Pinel, P., & Cohen, L. (2003). Three parietal circuits for number processing. *Cognitive Neuropsychology, 20*, 487–506. doi:10.1080/ 02643290244000239

Dehaene, S., Spelke, E., Pinel, P., Stanescu, R., & Tsivkin, S. (1999). Sources of mathematical thinking: Behavioral and brain imaging evidence. *Science, 284*, 970–974.

Denckla, M.B., & Cutting, L.E. (1999). History and significance of rapid automatized naming. *Annals of Dyslexia, 49*, 29–42.

Feigenson, L., Dehaene, S., & Spelke, E.S. (2004). Core systems of number. *Trends in Cognitive Sciences, 8*, 307–314. doi:10.1016/j.tics.2004.05.002

Ferretti, G., Mazzotti, S., & Brizzolara, D. (2008). Visual scanning and reading ability in normal and dyslexic children. *Behavioral Neurology, 19*, 87–92.

Fitzgerald, J., & Shanahan, T. (2000). Reading and writing relations and their development. *Educational Psychologist, 35*(1), 39–50.

Friedrich, M., & Friederici, A. D. (2011). Word learning in 6-month-olds: Fast encoding—Weak retention. *Journal of Cognitive Neuroscience, 23*(11), 3228–3240.

Friend, A., DeFries, J.C., Wadsworth, S.J., & Olson, R.K. (2007). Genetic and environmental influences on word recognition and spelling deficits as a function of age. *Behavioral Genetics, 37*, 477–486.

Frost, S. J., Mencl, W. E., Sandak, R., Moore, D. L., Rueckl, J., Katz, L., . . . Pugh, K. R. (2005). An fMRI study of the trade-off between semantics and phonology in reading aloud. *Neuroreport, 16*, 621–624.

García, J.N., & Fidalgo, R. (2006). Effects of two types of self-regulatory instruction programs on students with learning disabilities in writing products, processes, and self-efficacy. *Learning Disability Quarterly, 29*, 181–211.

García, J. N., & Fidalgo, R. (2008). Orchestration of writing processes and writing products: A comparison of sixth grade students with and without learning disabilities. *Learning Disabilities: A Contemporary Journal, 6*(2), 77–98.

Garthercole, S.E. (1995). Is nonword repetition a test of phonological memory or long-term knowledge? It all depends on the nonwords. *Memory and Cognition, 23*(1), 83–94.

Geary, D.C. (1993). Mathematical disabilities: Cognitive, neuropsychological, and genetic components. *Psychological Bulletin, 114,* 345–362. doi:10.1037/0033-2909.114.2.345

Geary, D.C. (1994). *Children's mathematical development: Research and practical applications.* Washington, DC: American Psychological Association.

Geary, D.C. (2003). Learning disabilities in arithmetic: Problem solving differences and cognitive deficits. In H.L. Swanson, K. Harris, & S. Graham (Eds.), *Handbook of learning Disabilities* (pp. 199–212). New York, NY: Guilford Press.

Geary, D.C., Hoard, M.K., Nugent, L., & Bailey, D.H. (2012). Mathematical cognition deficits in children with learning disabilities and persistent low achievement: A five-year prospective study. *Journal of Educational Psychology, 104*(1), 206–223.

Gebauer, D., Fink, A., Kargl, R., Reishofer, G., Koschutnig, K., et al. (2012). Differences in brain function and changes with intervention in children with poor spelling and reading abilities. *PLoS ONE, 7*(5), e38201. doi:10.1371/journal.pone.0038201

Gentry, J.R. (1981). Learning to spell developmentally. *The Reading Teacher, 34*(4), 378–381.

Gentry, J.R. (1984). Developmental aspects of learning to spell. *Academic Therapy, 20*(1), 11–19.

Georgiou, G., Papadopoulos, T.C., Zarouna, E., & Parrila, R. (2012). Are auditory and visual processing deficits related to developmental dyslexia? *Dyslexia, 18,* 110–129.

Gersten, R., & Chard, D. (1999). Number sense: Rethinking arithmetic instruction for students with mathematical disabilities. *The Journal of Special Education, 33*(1), 18–28.

Graham, S., & Perin, D. (2007). A meta-analysis of writing instruction for adolescent students. *Journal of Educational Psychology, 99*(3), 445–476.

Hammill, D.D., & Larsen, S.C. (2009). *Test of written language* (4th ed.). Austin: TX: Pro-Ed.

Hamstra-Bletz, L., & Blote, A.W. (1993). A longitudinal study on dysgraphic handwriting in primary school. *Journal of Learning Disabilities, 26*(10), 689.

Hayes, J., & Flower, L. (1980). Identifying the organisation of writing process. In L. Gregg & E. Steinberg (Eds.), *Cognitive processes in writing.* Hillsdale, NJ: Erlbaum.

Henrichs, J., Rescorla, L., Schenk, J.J., Schmidt, H.G., Jaddoe, V.W.V., Hofman, A., . . . Tiemeier, H. (2011). Examining continuity of early expressive vocabulary development: The generation R study. *Journal of Speech, Language and Hearing Research, 54,* 854–869.

Hudson, T. (1983). Correspondences and numerical differences between disjoint sets. *Child Development, 54,* 84–90.

Jones, M., Ashby, J., & Branigan, H.P. (2012). Dyslexia and fluency: Parafoveal and foveal influences on rapid automatized naming. *Journal of Experimental Psychology: Human Perception and Performance, 39*(2), 554–567.

Jordan, N.C., & Levine, S.C. (2009). Socioeconomic variation, number competence, and mathematics learning difficulties in young children. *Developmental Disabilities Research Review, 15,* 60–68.

Katzir, T., Kim, Y., Wolf, M., O-Brien, B., Kennedy, B., Lovett, M., & Morris, R. (2006). Reading fluency: The whole is more than the parts. *Annals of Dyslexia, 56*(1), 51–82.

Kaufman, A.S., & Kaufman, N.L. (2005). *Kaufman Test of Educational Achievement* (2nd ed.). Circle Pines, MN: American Guidance Service Publishing.

Kemmerer, D., Tranel, D., & Manzel, K. (2005). An exaggerated effect for proper nouns in a case of superior written over spoken word production. *Cognitive Neuropsychology, 22,* 3–27.

Kwong, T.E., & Varnhagen, C.K. (2005). Strategy development and learning to spell new words: Generalization of a process. *Developmental Psychology, 41*(1), 148–159.

Leppänen, U., Niemi, P., Aunola, K., & Nurmi, J. (2004). Development of reading skills among preschool and primary school pupils. *Reading Research Quarterly, 39*(1), 72–93.

Lithner, J. (2000). Mathematical reasoning in school tasks. *Educational Studies in Mathematics, 41*(2), 165–190.

Lithner, J. (2003). Students' mathematical reasoning in university textbook exercises. *Educational Studies in Mathematics, 52*(1), 29–55.

Lithner, J. (2008). A research framework for creative and imitative reasoning. *Educational Studies in Mathematics, 67,* 255–276.

Lezak, M., Howieson, D., Bigler, E., & Tranel, D. (2012). Neuropsychological assessment (5th ed.). New York, NY: Oxford University Press.

Lyon, G. R., & Moats, L. C. (1997). Critical conceptual methodological considerations in reading intervention research. *Journal of Learning Disabilities, 30*(6), 578–588.

Mason, R. A., & Just, M. (2004). How the brain processes causal inferences in text: A theoretical account of generation and integration component processes utilizing both cerebral hemispheres. *Psychological Science, 15*(1), 1–7.

Mazzocco, M. M. M., Feigenson, L., & Halberda, J. (2011). Impaired acuity of the approximate number system underlies mathematical learning disability (dyscalculia). *Child Development, 82*(4), 1224–1237.

Medland, C., Walter, H., & Woodhouse, J. M. (2010). Eye movements and poor reading: Does the developmental eye movement test measure cause or effect? *Opthalmic and Physiological Optics, 20,* 740–747.

Metsala, J. L. (1999). Phonological awareness and nonword repetition as a function of vocabulary development. *Journal of Educational Psychology, 91*(3), 3–19.

Morra, S., & Camba, R. (2009). Vocabulary learning in primary school children: Working memory long-term memory components. *Journal of Experimental Child Psychology, 104,* 156–178.

Myhill, D. (2009). Children's patterns of composition and their reflections on their composing process. *British Educational Research Journal, 35*(1), 47–64.

Nassaji, H. (2007). The development of spelling and orthographic knowledge in English as an L2: A longitudinal case study. *Canadian Journal of Applied Linguistics, 10*(1), 77–98.

Nation, K., & Snowling, M. J. (2004). Beyond phonological skills: Broader language skills contribute to the development of reading. *Journal of Research in Reading, 27*(4), 342–356.

Nithart, C., Demont, E., Metz-Lutz, M., Majerus, S., Poncelet, M., & Leybaert, J. (2011). Early contribution of phonological awareness and later influence of phonological memory throughout reading acquisition. *Journal of Research in Reading, 34*(3), 346–363.

Nunes, T., Bryan, P., Barros, R., & Sylva, K. (2012). The relative importance of two different mathematical abilities to mathematical achievement. *British Journal of Educational Psychology, 82,* 136–156.

O'Brien, B. A., Wolf, M., Miller, L. T., Lovett, M. W., & Morris, R. (2011). Orthographic processing efficiency in developmental dyslexia: An investigation of age and treatment factors at the sublexical level. *Annals of Dyslexia, 61*(1), 111–135.

Passolunghi, M. C., & Lanfranchi, S. (2011). Domain-specific and domain-general precursors of mathematical achievement: A longitudinal study from kindergarten to first grade. *British Journal of Educational Psychology, 82,* 42–62.

Pearson. (2009). *Wechsler Individual Achievement Test* (3rd ed.). San Antonio, TX: Author.

Prat, C. S., Mason, R. A., & Just, M. (2011). Individual differences in the neural basis of causal inferencing. *Brain and Language, 116*(1), 1–13.

Prat, C. S., Mason, R. A., & Just, M. A. (2012). An fMRI investigation of analogical mapping in metaphor comprehension: The influence of context and individual cognitive capacities on processing demands. *Journal of Experimental Psychology: Learning, Memory and Cognition, 38*(2), 282–294.

Poulsen, M., & Elbro, C. (2013). What's in a name depends on the type of name: The relationship between semantic and phonological access, reading fluency and reading comprehension. *Scientific Studies of Reading, 17,* 303–314.

Pugh, K.R., Landi, N., Preston, J.N., Mencl, W.E., Austin, A.C., Sibley, D., Fulbright, R.K., . . . Frost, S.J. (2013). The relationship between phonological and auditory processing and brain organization in beginning readers. *Brain & Language, 125,* 173–183.

Pugh, K.R., Sandak, R., Frost, S.J., Moore, D., & Mencl, W. (2005). Examining reading development and reading disability in English language learners: Potential contributions from functional neuroimaging. *Learning Disabilities Research & Practice, 20*(1), 24–30.

Raskinski, T. V. (2012). Why fluency should be hot! *The Reading Teacher, 65*(8), 516–522.

Rayner, K. (1998). Eye movements in reading and information processing: 20 years of research. *Psychological Bulletin, 124*(3), 372–422.

Resnick, L. B. (1991). *From protoquantitites to operators: Building mathematical competence on a foundation of everyday knowledge.* Pittsburgh, PA: University of Pittsburgh, Learning Research and Development Center.

Reyes, R.E., Suydam, M.N., Lindquist, M.M., & Smith, N.L. (1998). *Helping children learn mathematics* (5th ed.). Boston, MA: Allyn & Bacon.

Rodriguez, J.N., Garcia, J.N., Gonzalez-Castro, P., Alvarez, D., Cerezo, R., & Bernardo, A. (2011). Written composition process, evaluation difficulties and modalities: An experimental study. *Learning Disabilities: A Contemporary Journal, 9*(2), 45–63.

Roeltgen, D. (1993). Agraphia. In K. M. Heilman & E. Valenstein (Eds.), *Clinical neuropsychology* (3rd ed.). New York, NY: Oxford University Press.

Roeltgen, D., & Ullrich, L. (2011). Agraphia. In K. M. Heilman & E. Valenstein (Eds.), *Clinical Neuropsychology* (5th ed., pp. 130–151). New York, NY: Oxford University Press.

Rubinsten, O., & Sury, D. (2011). Processing ordinality and quantity: The case of developmental dyscalculia. PLoS ONE, 6(9), 1–12.

Runbald, G., & Annaz, D. (2010). Development of metaphor and metonymy comprehension: Receptive vocabulary and conceptual knowledge. *British Journal of Developmental Psychology, 28,* 547–563.

Sattler, J. (2008). *Assessment of children: Cognitive foundations* (5th ed.). San Diego, CA: Jerome M. Sattler.

Savage, R., Carless, S., & Ferraro, V. (2007). Predicting curriculum and test performance at age 1 year from pupil background, baseline skills and phonological awareness at age 5 years. *Journal of Child Psychology and Psychiatry, and Allied Disciplines, 48*(7), 732–739.

Shalev, R.S. (2004). Developmental dyscalculia. *Journal of Child Neurology, 19*(10), 765–771.

Shaywitz, B.A., Lyon, G., & Shaywitz, S.E. (2006). The role of functional magnetic resonance imaging in understanding reading and dyslexia. *Developmental Neuropsychology, 30*(1), 613–632.

Shaywitz, B. A., & Shaywitz, S. E. (2006). Neurobiological indices of dyslexia. In H. Swanson, K. Harris, & S. Graham (Eds.) *Handbook of learning disabilities* (pp. 514–531). New York, NY: Guilford Press.

Soltani, A., & Roslan, S. (2013). Contributions of phonological awareness, phonological short-term memory and automated naming, toward decoding ability in students with mild intellectual disability. *Research in Developmental Disabilities, 34,* 1090–1099.

Stotsky, S. (1983). Research on reading/writing relationships: A synthesis and suggested directions. *Language Arts, 60,* 627–643.

Strattman, K., & Hodson, B.W. (2005). Variables that influence decoding and spelling in beginning readers. *Child Language Teaching and Therapy, 21*(2), 165–190.

Stroop, J.R. (1935). Studies of interference in serial verbal reactions. *Journal of Experimental Psychology, 18,* 643–662.

Tincoff, R., & Jusczyk, P. W. (1999). Some beginning of word comprehension in 6-month-olds. *Psychological Science, 10,* 172–175.

Toll, S.W.M., Van der Ven, S.H.G., Kroesbergen, E.H., & Van Luit, J.E.H. (2011). Executive functions as predictors of math learning disabilities. *Journal of Learning Disabilities, 44*(6), 521–532.

Torgesen, J. K., & Wagner, R. K. (1994). Longitudinal studies of phonological processing and reading. *Journal of Learning Disabilities, 27*(5), 276.

Torrance, M., Fidalgo, R., & García, J. N. (2007). The teachability and effectiveness of strategies for cognitive self-regulation in sixth grade writers. *Learning and Instruction, 17,* 265–285.

Tree, J. J., Longmore, C., Majerus, S., & Evans, N. (2011). SKOOL vs. ZOOL: Effects of orthographic and phonological long-term memory on nonword immediate serial recall. *Memory, 19*(5), 487–500.

Wagner, R. K., & Torgesen, J. K. (1987). The nature of phonological processing and its causal role in the acquisition of reading skills. *Psychological Bulletin, 101,* 192–212.

Wagner, R. K., Torgesen, J. K., & Rashotte, C. A. (1999). *Comprehensive test of phonological processing.* Austin, TX: Pro-Ed.

Wechsler, D. (2003). *Wechsler Intelligence Scale for Children* (4th ed.). San Antonio, TX: The Psychological Corporation.

Weigel, D. J., Martin, S. S., & Bennett, K. K. (2006). Contributions of the home literacy environment to preschool-aged children's emergent literacy and language skills. *Early Child Development and Care, 176,* 357–378.

White, C. S., Alexander, P. A., & Daugherty, M. (1998). The relationship between young children's analogical reasoning and mathematical learning. *Mathematical Cognition, 4*(2), 103–123.

Wiederholt, J. L., & Bryant, B. R. (2012). *Gray Oral Reading Tests* (5th ed). Austin, TX: Pro-Ed.

Wolf, M. (2007). *Proust and the Squid: The story and science of the reading brain.* New York, NY: HarperCollins.

Wolf, M., & Denckla, M. B. (2005). *The Rapid Automatized Naming and Rapid Alternating Stimulus Tests, Examiner's manual.* Austin, TX: Pro-Ed.

Woodcock, R. W., McGrew, K. S., & Mather, N. (2001). *Woodcock-Johnson III Tests of Achievement.* Itasca, IL: Riverside Publishing.

Young, K. (2007). Developmental stage theory of spelling: Analysis of consistency across four spelling activities. *Australian Journal of Language and Literacy, 30*(3), 203–220.

8 Understanding and Assessing Emotional Functioning

The *Report of the Surgeon General's Conference on Children's Mental Health* (U.S. Public Health Service, 2000) revealed that sixteen to twenty-two percent of children and adolescents have emotional or behavioral difficulties that are significant enough to justify a diagnosis of a mental health problem. Between twelve and twenty-seven percent of children may have behavioral problems, depression and anxiety, but only one sixth to one third of these children receive treatment. While it is more difficult to identify children with internalizing problems such as depression, anxiety or suicidal ideation, the nationwide Youth Risk Behavior Survey of 2003 (Grunbaum et al., 2004) found that in the one-year period preceding the survey, nearly seventeen percent of high school students either considered suicide or had made a plan to commit suicide, while nearly nine percent had attempted suicide (Weist et al., 2007). Increasingly, schools are being asked to screen for and identify mental health issues for which they are not necessarily equipped.

As we have contended throughout this book, a thorough evaluation of emotional functioning is essential to the process of understanding the whole person when conducting a neuropsychological evaluation. While screening in school is important, it does not necessarily provide a comprehensive evaluation of neurological and emotional issues that can place a child at significant risk. For example, Michael was a child who demonstrated a number of underlying neurological issues—including a nonverbal learning disability, slow processing and deficits in executive functions—that were continuing to make his attempts to progress academically and socially rather challenging. However, even more challenging were his emotional dysregulation and resultant risky behaviors that were consistent with posttraumatic stress disorder, including both anxiety and depression, and which threatened to destroy his life. By constructing a narrative that integrated both his cognitive strengths and vulnerabilities with their impact on his social, behavioral and emotional functioning and vice versa, Michael and his therapist were able to make use of the resulting document to address those issues and help Michael develop the capacity to self-reflect and better understand his academic, social and emotional experience and behavior.

Behavioral and Emotional Functioning

The predominance of research on behavior and emotional functioning has distinguished between externalizing and internalizing problems.

Externalizing problems largely refer to externalizing behaviors, behaviors that, according to a meta-analytic study by Frick et al. (1993) can be understood as falling into four categories:

- Aggression (fights, bullies)
- Oppositionality (temper, stubborn)
- Property violations (lies, cruel to animals)
- Status violations (substance use, runaway).

While most children with moderate or high levels of externalizing behavior problems early in development exhibit decreases in behavioral problems after the preschool years, about five to seven percent of antisocial children do not (Fanti & Henrich, 2010). Using the previous categories, in a twenty-four year longitudinal study, Reef, Diamantopoulou, Meurs, Verhulst, & Ende (2011) found that all of the more extreme externalizing behavior types that were identified in children between the ages of four and eighteen years demonstrated "significant associations with disruptive disorder in adulthood." (p. 233) Children and adolescents who had property and status violation behaviors showed the strongest predictive outcome. Studies have also found that externalizing behaviors over the course of development are influenced by both genetic and shared environmental factors (see Marceau et al., 2012) as well as factors related to cognition and temperament (Miner & Clark-Stewart, 2008) and sociodemographic risk factors (Ackerman, D'Eramo, Umylny, Schultz, & Izard, 2001).

Internalizing problems have been described as including features of withdrawal, anxiety, fearfulness and depression (Achenbach, 1992). While the incidence of externalizing behaviors in the general population of children (e.g., toddlers who were solving problems using aggression and destructive behavior) tends to decrease over time, a preponderance of research indicates that internalizing problems generally increase from infancy to early childhood in normal (Gilliom & Shaw, 2004) and clinical (Achenbach, Howell, Quay, & Conners, 1991) populations of children. Children exhibiting pure internalizing problems over time were at higher risk for being asocial with peers as early adolescents (Fanti & Henrich, 2010). Sociodemographic risk factors such as maternal depression and lack of control over their children (Coyne & Thompson, 2011) and factors, similar to those impacting externalizing problems, related to cognition and temperament (Booth-LaForce & Oxford, 2008; Bub, McCartney, & Willett, 2007) all contribute to this trend.

Additional research has attempted to determine the extent to which both externalizing and internalizing factors are co-occurring over development. A number of studies indicate that externalizing and internalizing behaviors begin to co-occur at an early age. As discussed above, sociodemographics, temperament, home environment, maternal depression, and cognitive factors are correlated with both internalizing and externalizing problems, and children with co-occurring problems are at higher risk for the development of negative relationships with peers, delinquent acts, and of being associated with deviant peers (see Fanti & Henrich, 2010). In their longitudinal study of over twelve hundred children between the ages of two and twelve, Fanti and Henrich (2010) found that children exhibiting continuous externalizing or continuous co-occurring internalizing and externalizing problems had a higher incidence of risky behaviors, association with deviant peers, rejection by peers and greater likelihood to be asocial with peers in early adolescence. They also found that "additive effects of individual and environmental early childhood risk factors influenced the development of chronic externalizing problems, although pure internalizing problems were uniquely influenced by maternal depression" (p. 1159). Reef et al. (2011) found that childhood externalizing behaviors also correlated with adult internalizing problems such as anxiety and mood disorders.

Neuroanatomy of Emotional Functioning

Speculation about the brain's involvement in the processing of human emotion extends back to the nineteenth century with William James's (1884) proposal that bodily sensations create our experience of emotion. The James-Lange theory of emotion was countered by Cannon (1927) who claimed the hypothalamus mediated emotional responsiveness. Other theories involving specific neural structures included the Papez circuit (Papez, 1937), the limbic system (MacLean, 1949), the amygdala (Meunier, Bachevalier, Murray, Malkova, & Mishkin, 1996) and the prefrontal cortex (e.g., Phineas Gage's prefrontal lesion from a tamping rod). More recently, the James-Lange theory of emotion has received some support from PET studies linking cortical areas and upper brainstem nuclei involved in the mapping and regulation of internal states, underscoring the relationship between emotion and homeostasis (Damasio et al., 2000).

Most recent research suggests that there are multiple discreet and overlapping neural systems that process specific emotions. A meta-analysis of PET and fMRI studies by Berthoz, Blair, Le Clec'h and Martinot (2002) found that individuals processing facial expressions of emotion activated separate neural circuits that were dependent upon the category of facial expression. Fearful expressions fairly consistently activated the amygdala while sad and happy expressions did so only sometimes. Disgust was most frequently associated with activation in the anterior insula and putamen. Anger was primarily associated with anterior cingular and orbitofrontal cortical activity. The authors reported that the anterior cingulate cortex played "a specific role in representing subjective emotional response" (p. 193).

A separate meta-analytic review of PET and fMRI studies by Phan, Wager, Taylor and Liberzon (2002) looked at activation in response to specific emotions (positive, negative, happiness, fear, anger, sadness, disgust) to different induction methods (visual, auditory, recall/imagery), and in emotional tasks with and without cognitive demand. They found that the medial prefrontal cortex had a general role in emotional processing. Fear specifically engaged the amygdala. Sadness was associated with activity in the subcallosal cingulate. Emotional induction by visual stimuli activated the occipital cortex and the amygdala, while induction by emotional recall/imagery recruited the anterior cingulate and insula. Lastly, emotional tasks with cognitive demand also involved the anterior cingulate and insula.

A third meta-analysis of PET and fMRI studies by Murphy, Nimmo-Smith and Lawrence (2003) found greater left-hemisphere activity for approach emotions while negative/withdrawal emotions activation was more symmetrical. Furthermore, they reported neuroanatomical distinctions between emotions such as fear (amygdala), disgust (insula and globus pallidus) and anger (lateral orbitofrontal cortex).

Lesion studies lend some support to hemispheric specialization, with the right hemisphere managing the multidimensional and alogical stimuli conveying emotion such as facial expression as well as prosody, while the left hemisphere tends to process the words of emotion. However, medial prefrontal cortical structures on both sides appear to mediate self-referential processing. Furthermore, lesion studies also support the role of the amygdala in processing fear responses as well as anxiety, delusions and mood. The amygdala also appears to provide an emotional valence to memory traces in the hippocampus (Lezak, 2012).

Thus, neural substrates of emotional experience have been identified for a range of emotions. While some fraction of overall emotional experiences may generally share some common pathways, for the most part, separate neural networks appear to be involved that allow for highly individualized processing of separate emotions. Future research will, no doubt, further identify those networks as they relate to more subtle forms of emotional functioning.

Psychological Assessment of Emotional Functioning

We have argued that when conducting a complete neuropsychological evaluation, a thorough battery of psychological tests should be employed in order to assess emotional functioning and integrate those findings with results from the traditional neuropsychological battery. As research discussed previously has demonstrated, an understanding of the interrelationships between neurology, emotion and achievement is essential to an appreciation of the cascading effect of any one on the others. A disturbance in any one can have profound consequences for a child and determine a successful or troubled outcome for him or her as an adult.

When conducting tests of emotional functioning, however, one must be cognizant of some important caveats and differences between, on one hand, tests of cognitive functioning that assess domains such as intellect, executive functions, memory, etc. and tests designed to assess emotion. While the former lend themselves to quantification and more rigorous statistical analysis, the latter frequently do not do so to the same extent or, in some cases, at all. Although attempts have been made to standardize a number of the latter tests, critics of these types of psychological instruments abound.

For example, in the early 1970s, John Exner began developing the Comprehensive System for the Rorschach (Exner, 2003) in an attempt to standardize administration, improve interscorer reliability and base interpretation on normative data that would withstand measures of validation. However, the system has been criticized in respect to interscorer findings and validation data (Wood, Nezworski, & Stejkal, 1996), while it was also criticized for overdiagnosing pathology in nonpatient populations (Wood, Nezworski, Garb, & Lilienfeld, 2001). However, a number of meta-analytic studies have supported the validity of the Rorschach (Hiller, Rosenthal, Bornstein, Berry, & Brunell-Neulieb, 1999; Meyer & Archer, 2001) and Viglione and Hilsenroth (2001) have made the case that many of the criticisms of the Rorschach are based on a misunderstanding of the test.

The controversy around the Rorschach underscores the different perspectives about psychological assessment and the difference between nomothetic and idiographic approaches. This is an important distinction. Nevertheless, as Handler and Meyer (1998) contend, there is an important difference between psychological testing and psychological assessment. While testing involves the administration of a specific instrument to derive a particular score based on norms and nomothetic data, assessment involves results from testing, but focuses on:

> taking a variety of test-derived pieces of information, obtained from multiple methods of assessment, and placing these data in the context of historical information, referral information, and behavioral observations in order to generate a cohesive and comprehensive understanding of the person being evaluated. These activities are far from simple; they require a high degree of skill and sophistication to be implemented properly.
>
> (pp. 4–5)

Psychological assessment of emotional functioning must rely on nomothetic and idiographic sets of data to begin to construct a picture of the whole child. It cannot rely solely on either type of information because, in doing so, one would fail to include essential details without which the picture or narrative of the child would be distorted or lacking. Furthermore, relying on observation and rating scales alone pose significant limitations on the picture one can construct, leaving analysis at the level of behavior or dependent on the perspective of the rater. While these are important sources of information, they do not focus sufficiently on the underlying psychological and emotional processes that drive behavior (Exner, 2003). As Smith and Handler (2007) have argued, assessment must proceed from a "multimethod-multirater-multidomain perspective" (p. 12). And, as we have proposed in this book, that perspective should include instruments that provide a thorough assessment of emotional functioning, taken from a developmental history, observation, multiple rating scales, clinical interview and a battery of evaluator administered instruments that include projective tests. It is only then that this information can be weighed and integrated to derive an interpretation of the data and a narrative that describes a child in all of his or her complexity and idiosyncrasies. In some cases, findings may fit fairly neatly into a particular diagnostic category. In other cases, however, a diagnosis will not do justice to that particular child's range of strengths and vulnerabilities. It is then imperative that the evaluator respect the complexity and unique features of the child and do his or her best to convey that to the parents, teachers and other professionals involved in the child's care. As such, assessment of this sort is a combination of science and art, with the latter being just as important as the former.

Assessments

Several types of assessments have been developed with the goal of obtaining information related to emotional functioning. The following section briefly describes various assessments developed to achieve this goal.

The Rorschach

The Rorschach was developed by Hermann Rorschach and introduced in 1921 through his monograph *Psychodiagnostik* (1921/1942). Over the ensuing, nearly one hundred years, it has been in use as a psychodiagnostic tool and has generated a large body of research. While a number of systems of application, scoring and interpretation were employed over the first fifty years of its existence, it was in the early nineteen-seventies that John Exner began developing the Comprehensive System in an effort to integrate the different systems and standardize administration, scoring and interpretation. As discussed previously, this has met with considerable success and is used widely throughout the world (Exner, 2003). While Exner's system remains open to criticism (Wood et al., 1996, 2001), a recent meta-analytic study (Mihura, Meyer, Dumitrascu, & Bombel, 2013) identified a large number of Comprehensive System variables that had a significant level of validity. The authors conclude that the Rorschach is a valuable diagnostic tool if used appropriately.

All Rorschach systems in current use employ the same set of the ten inkblot stimuli originally developed by Hermann Rorschach (1921/1942). Examinees scan each inkblot and say what it might be. Five of the inkblots are shades of black and gray while two inkblots are black and red. The remaining three inkblots have varied colors. The ink on each blot is somewhat blotchy or uneven, giving rise to responses that may include descriptions of shading, texture or depth. Other features of the responses that are considered in the Comprehensive System include location, shape, movement, use of color, content, pairs and any bizarre qualities associated with the response. Examinees can give one or several responses per inkblot stimulus. The Comprehensive System requires that the examinee give at least one response per blot and at least fourteen responses across the entire set of ten inkblots in order to provide a sufficient data base to compare to norms. On average, a protocol will contain about twenty responses. Each response is recorded verbatim by the examiner. Following the initial set of responses, an inquiry phase is undertaken during which the examiner reads back each response and asks the examinee to identify where on the card they saw what they saw, and what it was that made it look like that to them. This is done, as the examiner explains, to be sure the examiner sees the things the examinee reported like the examinee saw them. The responses are again recorded. At some later time, the examiner scores the protocol according to the guidelines developed by the Comprehensive System and uses the codes derived to interpret the data (Exner, 2003).

One of the controversies surrounding the Rorschach is its perception as a projective rather than objective test. It should be noted, however, that unlike the *Thematic Apperception Test* (TAT; Murray, 1943), for example, the Rorschach is not considered to be a projective test alone but rather has both objective and projective elements. As Exner (2003) has contended,

> the nature of the Rorschach task provokes a complicated process, that includes processing, classification, conceptualization, decision making, and lays open the psychological door for projection to occur. When the reasonably simple standard procedures for administering the test are faithfully employed, this process yields substantial information about habits, traits and styles, the presence of states, and about many other variables that can be listed under the broad rubric encompassed by the term personality.

(p. 185)

In addition, a model linking the Rorschach with cognitive neuropsychology has been proposed that articulates the underlying cognitive processes involved in the information processing and response process during the response and inquiry phases of the test (Ack-lin & Wu-Holt, 1996).

Both Exner (2003) and Weiner (2000) have argued that it is important to use constructs of personality to conceptually relate the empirically based information derived from the Comprehensive System to clinical inferences. The Rorschach also allows one to take a developmental perspective, assessing how an individual moves through the demands of childhood and adolescence (Erdberg, 2007). For example, young, nonpathological children pass through the stages of perseveration, confabu-lation and confabulatory combination before about seven years when they are then able to respond with a balance of internal and external input that represents mature responding. There are also a number of domains of functioning that can be assessed in children:

- Coping strategies—The developmental shift in a younger child's problem-solving style from a more interpersonal perspective to a more internal focus can be mea-sured while also assessing the psychological resources they bring to problem solving.
- Affect—As well as the child's capacity for impulse control, openness to affective material and self-regulation.
- Interpersonal functioning—The Rorschach can provide information about their interpersonal competence as well as their expectations about interpersonal relation-ships.
- Self-concept—Measures the balance between the child's importance placed on self versus the importance placed on others.
- Information processing—Determining how much energy and complexity the child brings to processing tasks.

These domain-related variables shift with the age of the child, and failure to do so provides important information about a child's developmental course (Erdberg, 2007).

In her discussion of the use of the Rorschach with neurologically impaired patients, Lezak (2012) has described two approaches in the use of the Rorschach. While the first relies on clinical interpretation, the second relates to a sign system that is constructed out of quantifiable aberrant responses that occur with significant frequency, nearly always only in brain damaged patients. As Lezak noted,

> nonetheless, the Rorschach . . . may yield useful observations, and clinicians may take good advantage of these in their clinical practice; it just has to be kept in mind that adequate normative and other statistical studies are not available for neuro-logically impaired groups. This is not surprising as it is so difficult to cast many of the data on which clinical inferences are based, or the inferences themselves, into a form suitable for statistical analysis. For clinical purposes, however, the integration of inferences drawn from both the sign and clinical interpretation is apt to yield the most information, with each kind of interpretation serving as a check on the appropriateness of conclusions drawn from the other. By this means, symptomatic cognitive and behavioral aberrations can be viewed in interaction with personality

predispositions so that the broader social and personal implications of the patient's brain injury may be illuminated.

(p. 827)

This approach, recommended for neurologically impaired patients, in which one relies on a combination of quantifiable data and clinical interpretation is reflected in the approach one can take in using the Rorschach for neuropsychological assessments of children. Often, because of the misperception about the Rorschach as a projective test alone, its use in a comprehensive neuropsychological battery is relatively rare as is the use of most projective tests. As part of a neuropsychological battery, however, use of the Rorschach, as well as projective tests, provide information about an individual's emotional functioning and its impact on other domains, and vice versa. The neuropsychologist should only draw conclusions about results from tests of emotional functioning, however, when considered within the context of the entire battery. Salient threads of information from a variety of instruments that consider a question from a number of perspectives must be weighed and woven together to construct a narrative that describes the whole child.

The Hand Test

Like the Rorschach, the *Hand Test* (Wagner, 1983) utilizes visual stimuli to elicit information related to emotional and behavioral functioning. During the administration process, the child or adolescent is shown ten cards total, one at a time. Nine cards display line-drawn hands in various positions, with varying degrees of ambiguity. The individual is asked to, say what it looks like the hands might be doing. The tenth card is blank, and the examinee is asked to imagine a hand and say what it might be doing (Wagner, 1983). Responses are recorded verbatim. Hands are an important component in daily functioning, both interpersonally and as they act on the environment. Given their familiarity and functionality the use of hands as visual stimuli may "pull" for expectations and impressions of self and others as well as efficacy and action possibilities (Clemence, 2007). The game-like nature of the assessment makes for a relaxed atmosphere in which rapport can be developed easily.

The *Hand Test* is useful in the assessment of behavioral tendencies of children, adolescents and adults. It can be used to distinguish handicapped and emotionally disturbed children and adolescents from control groups. Perhaps most useful, the *Hand Test* can distinguish between children and adolescents with aggressive and nonaggressive tendencies. The ambiguous nature of the *Hand Test* makes it difficult for examinees to fabricate responses designed to make themselves appear more or less mentally healthy (Clemence, 2007).

Thematic Apperception Test

The TAT, a storytelling task, utilizes a format for assessment that is appealing for individuals across ages and cultures. Storytelling strategies have been useful and popular as applied to clinical assessment for a variety of reasons. During the process of generating a story, elements of the individual are revealed that might not be otherwise. The stories can be evaluated for thoughts, behaviors, emotions, perceptions of self, relationships with others and coping and problem solving skills (Cashel, Killilea, & Dollinger, 2007).

The TAT was originally developed by Henry Murray, in collaboration with Christiana Morgan, in 1943, for use with children, adolescents and adults (Morgan & Murray, 1935; Murray, 1943). The TAT, and other storytelling techniques, were developed based on the theory of projection. This construct suggests that individuals perceive and interpret events in their life based upon their memories and past interpretation of past events. As applied to the TAT, projection is renamed as "apperception," and considered to be the process through which individuals make sense of or understand what they see, hear and experience (Cashel et al., 2007). In creating a story, the individual may identify with a particular character and their needs, wishes and conflicts. In turn, this may directly or symbolically reflect the needs, wishes and conflicts of the individual (Lindzey, 1952).

The TAT is comprised of thirty-one black and white images that are emotionally evocative but ambiguous in content. For example, a boy gazing despondently at a violin, hands propping up his chin, or a girl seated on a couch, limply holding a doll while an adult leans over her shoulder. Instructions are, "This is a story telling test. I have some pictures here that I am going to show you, and for each picture I want you to make up a story. Tell what has happened before and what is happening now. Say what the people are feeling and thinking and how it will come out. You can make up any kind of story you please." This could be repeated or restated for clarification as many times as necessary (Murray, 1943, p. 4). Once the individual has completed the first story, the administrator asks any questions about missing elements within the story, encouraging development and details. In following stories, the administrator might not ask as many questions but will try to capture all main components of the tale. Most clinicians administer ten or fewer TAT cards, and specific cards have been recommended for children and adolescents (Obrzut & Boliek, 1986). Story content that adheres strictly to the images on the picture card will yield less interesting and useful results. Themes that are repeated over many images are most likely to provide meaningful information. Stories generated by individuals are influenced by their life events, so consideration of sociocultural, recent situational events and ethnic ties are important to consider in the context of additional information.

The Children's Apperception Test and Children's Apperception Test–Human Figures

As the TAT became increasingly popular for assessing adult individuals, its application to children and adolescents was hindered in that it only contained two images of children. As a result, several similar measures were developed specifically for assessing children, including the *Children's Apperception Test* (C.A.T.; Bellack & Bellack, 1949) and the *Children's Apperception Test–Human Figures* (C.A.T.H.; Bellack & Bellack, 1965). In the C.A.T., visual stimulus cards use imagery of animals rather than people, with the hope of elucidating a child's intrapsychic needs, drives and relationships. It was developed with the intended use for children between the ages of three and ten. Subsequent research suggested that when comparing animal images versus human forms, narratives derived from images of people were more useful, while some studies found no differences (Armstrong, 1954; Biersdorf & Marcuse, 1953; Budoff, 1960). As a result, Bellack and Bellack developed the C.A.T.H. (1965).

The Roberts Apperception Test

The *Roberts Apperception Test for Children*, which is now in its second edition (Roberts-2), was developed as another storytelling task used for assessing interpersonal skills in children (McArthur & Roberts, 1982; Roberts & Gruber, 2005). Similar to the TAT, the Roberts-2 uses images of everyday life that are emotionally evocative, yet ambiguous. After viewing an image, the child is asked to develop a story. The Roberts-2 is composed of twenty-seven stimulus cards, with realistic illustrations emphasizing daily interpersonal events as experienced by children or adults in a variety of social situations. This assessment is appropriate for individuals six to eighteen years of age and has an emphasis on assessing social cognition and interpersonal problem-solving skills. As such, the authors indicate that the Roberts-2 is not a projective test but an assessment of children's expressive language skills as an index of their cognitive social skills (Roberts & Gruber, 2005). Unlike the TAT, the Roberts-2 requires the use of at least sixteen stimulus cards, presented in a specific order. Requests for elaboration through questioning is restricted to the first two cards. The child's lack of response to the questions is considered clinically significant while scoring the profile.

Drawing Assessments

The use of drawing assessments with children has a long history, with a variety of strengths and weaknesses related to the acquisition of clinical information. In general, the examiner gives a directive, asking the individual to make a drawing with a certain set of criteria, while watching and discussing the drawing. Several specific drawing assessments have been developed, including the *House-Tree-Person* (H-T-P; Buck, 1948), *Draw A Person* (DAP; Naglieri, 1988), and the *Kinetic Family Drawing* (KFD; Burns & Kaufman, 1970), which are discussed further in more detail. Outside this brief list, other drawing assessments have been developed, such as The *Diagnostic Drawing Series* (Cohen, 1983) and the *Silver Drawing Test* (Silver, 2002).

The use of the drawing assessment technique broadens the range of clinical information gathered during an assessment battery, as it transcends language limitations and is thought to circumvent cultural barriers. These types of assessments are developmentally appropriate, take little time to administer and are generally enjoyable for the child. However, when interpreting drawings of this nature, one must keep in mind any fine motor or graphomotor difficulties or delays. Historically, they have been used to assess intelligence, personality characteristics and family dynamics. While drawing assessments have been used for decades, there are persistent concerns about validity and scoring systems. As such, they are an important clinical tool and should not be used as stand-alone assessments but as part of an assessment battery as means of formulating a hypothesis regarding emotional functioning (Matto, 2007).

Developed from the *Goodenough-Harris Draw-A-Man* test (Harris, 1963), Naglieri's *Draw A Person: Screening Procedure for Emotional Disturbance* (DAP:SPED; Naglieri,

McNeish, & Bardos, 1991) requires the child to draw three human figures, a man, a woman and the self. Some research has indicated that the DAP:SPED is better at detecting internalizing behaviors than externalizing behaviors within a clinical population (Matto, 2002). It also demonstrates predictive abilities for internalization of behavioral disturbances beyond that of standard paper/pencil assessments. Furthermore, the DAP:SPED has demonstrated validity in identifying youths with emotional/behavioral disorders, such as distinguishing between individuals with conduct/oppositional defiance disorder and a control group as well as identifying children experiencing emotional difficulties within a group of regular-education students (Naglieri & Pfeiffer, 1992). The drawn images are scored according to fifty-five item indicators. These indicators examine structure and content dimensions such as figure omissions, presence of objects, placement on page and the size of the figures. The standardization sample consisted of two thousand three hundred and fifty-five individuals, ages six to seventeen, who were representative of the U.S. population for age, gender, geographic region, race ethnicity and socioeconomic status.

The KFD was originally developed by Burns and Kaufman in 1970. The child is asked to draw a picture of everyone in his or her family, including him- or herself, doing an activity. Prior to the KFD, drawing assessments did not include asking the individual to represent action in the drawing, figures were static and unengaged in an activity. Interestingly, the request for action provides different information regarding family dynamics and interpersonal interactions as well as the emotional relationships among family members (Burns & Kaufman, 1970). In response to criticism regarding imprecise interpretations of drawing variables, Burns developed a new scoring method in 1982 that included four major categories relevant to the scoring procedure: 1) actions; 2) distances, barriers and positions; 3) physical characteristics and 4) styles (Handler & Habenicht, 1994). While other systems for scoring have been developed and proven more reliable and valid, these categories may be noteworthy and may provide points of discussion or the development of questions to ask the child artist.

Figure 8.1 Kinetic family drawing.

In 1990, Tharinger and Stark developed and tested an integrative holistic scoring system that can be applied to both the DAP and the KFD. Under this system, raters are able to offer a general impression of a child's drawing, which is then placed on an overall scale of pathology ranging from 1 (no psychopathology present) to 5 (severe psychopathology). The dimensions used by raters include 1) inhumanness of human figure drawing; 2) lack of agency/ineffectual human figure; 3) indication of lack of well-being; and 4) presence of hollow, vacant or stilted person in the drawing. Using this same method, clinical impressions can be developed from the KFD using the following dimensions: 1) inaccessibility of family members to each other, 2) degree of member engagement/involvement, 3) inappropriate family structure (e.g. roles, boundaries) and 4) inhumanness of family figures.

The *House-Tree-Person*, originally developed in 1948 by Buck, assesses an individual's orientation to self and to family life (Matto 2007). From a psychodynamic perspective, the house represents the home life of the child and his or her family experiences, and the tree represents the unconscious world and perspective on reality testing and ego strength, the propensity towards growth and the nature of the child's support network.

Minnesota Multiphasic Personality Inventory–Adolescent

The *Minnesota Multiphasic Personality Inventory–Adolescent* (MMPI-A) is a widely utilized self-report inventory developed to capture elements of an individual's developing personality and emotional/behavioral functioning. Relatively few self-report personality measures are available for the use with adolescents and children, in part because of the constraints of reading and writing, comprehension ability, cognitive/affective developmental status and motivational level inherently required by this technique (Archer, Krishnamurthy, & Stredny, 2007). Responding to a self-report personality inventory requires that the individual can engage in self-reflection and abstract thinking. Developmentally, many adolescents are capable of these processes, allowing for accurate responses on a self-report personality inventory (Archer, 2005). The MMPI-A was developed after concerns that the widely used adult inventory, the *Minnesota Multiphasic Personality Inventory* (MMPI) and its successor, the MMPI-2, which were being used with adolescents, did not account for developmental concerns, such as reading ability and content validity for this age group (Archer et al., 2007). To address these concerns, the MMPI-A was developed as an appropriate assessment tool for this population (Butcher et al., 1992).

The MMPI-A consists of 478 true/false items taking approximately sixty minutes to administer in its full form. At the discretion of the administrator, the clinical scales and three of the validity scales can be scored from the first three-hundred and fifty items, saving administration time. The test was normed for individuals between the ages of 14 to 18 but can be administered to adolescents as young as 12 or 13, depending on the individual's reading ability. While the minimum reading level required is Grade 4.9, it is suggested that the individual display a seventh-grade reading level for the best comprehension of test items. If reading deficits exist, but cognitive ability is sufficient to understand test items, it can be administered via audiotape (Archer et al., 2007). The MMPI-A can be administered as a paper-and-pencil task, or by using a computer with the appropriate software, or by online administration. The normative sample consists of 805 adolescent boys and 815 adolescent girls.

Extensive research confirms the validity and reliability of the MMPI-A (Archer et al., 2007). The MMPI-A generates a wealth of information, including multiple scales including validity indicators, clinical scales, subclinical scales, content scales, content component scales and supplementary scales. Once the MMPI-A has been scored, the administrator should verify validity, then the basic clinical scales should be examined. The higher a basic scale, the more likely the individual is to display the symptoms or characteristics associated with the code type. Supplementary scales can then be examined to support and refine basic scale interpretation. The intent is to inform diagnosis and treatment, as profile patterns are not directly associated with specific psychological disorders. For example, adolescents with eating disorders may show elevations on a number of internalizing scales, but this is not enough information to assign a diagnosis.

The Millon Pre-Adolescent Clinical Inventory and the Millon Adolescent Clinical Inventory

Like the MMPI-A the *Millon Pre-Adolescent Clinical Inventory* (M-PACI) and the *Millon Adolescent Clinical Inventory* (MACI) are self-report questionnaires developed to assess adolescents when the adult version proved inadequate for this population. Along with the adult version, these two assessments are based in Millon's theory of personality (Tringone, Millon, & Kamp, 2007). The theory postulated that 1) there are three polarities that combine, resulting in observable disorders, 2) eight clinical domains form a classification system, with all personality disorders exhibiting prototypal features and 3) perpetuating processes, including behaviors, thought patterns or affective expressions exhibited by an individual, create interactions with the outer world and reinforce underlying perceptions, beliefs and experiences (Millon, 1981, Millon & Davis, 1996).

The application of Millon's personality theory is mediated by the construct of temperament (Tringone et al., 2007). Recall that temperament is thought to have three core features: 1) it is typically seen as an inherited or biologically based process, 2) it is evident early in life and 3) the expression of temperament is relatively stable over time (Frick, 2004). When infants arrive in the world, they express a disposition towards positive or negative affect and behavior. As they grow, interactions with caregivers and the environment develop a feedback loop, either reinforcing the temperament style or modifying it. With repeated reinforcement, the child develops a repertoire of behaviors that begin to form his or her personality, which can then characterize the child's "style" of interacting with other people and within an environment (Millon, 1981). During this process, three polarities of personality emerge that can further characterize an individual's style. The self/other polarity represents the source to which the individual turns to enhance his or her life, gain satisfaction or to avoid pain and discomfort. Some individuals turn to themselves (termed *independent*), while some turn to others (termed *dependent*). Those who are unsure if they should look to themselves or others are termed *conflicted*. The second polarity, active/passive, describes behaviors employed to maximize rewards and minimize pain. Active personalities typically take the initiative to interact with the environment to achieve gratification and avoid distress. Passive personalities tend to be more reserved, maintaining a more accommodating stance and response to their environment. Finally, the pleasure/pain polarity represents the nature of the response elicited from others (Millon, 1969, 1981, 1990). Returning to the concept of temperament, the emerging personality style can be mediated by understanding the interactions of the individual's style with the environment and generating a "good fit" between the environment and the emerging personality style. Certain characteristics, such as adaptability or vulnerability, are involved in the development of coping mechanisms; the ability to withstand stress and development of effective responses. Whether looking at temperament, or the more complex emerging personality style, it is generally recognized that certain characteristics may enhance or mediate the development of a disorder (Compas, Connor-Smith, & Jaser, 2004). Some evidence suggests that personalities in late adolescence demonstrate a higher level of stability than previously believed, which in turn, may contribute to significant problems in adulthood (Chanen et al., 2004). Preadolescents tend to have more flexible personality styles and may be more reactive or responsive to influences from their environment. Thus, assessment during both preadolescence and adolescence are important tools for guiding intervention.

The M-PACI's multidimensional self-report inventory is used with nine- to twelve-year-olds seen in clinical settings. It is composed of ninety-seven true and false items. Answers correlate with fourteen *profile scales* grouped into two sets: Emerging Personality Patterns and Current Clinical Signs. Scores on these scales are reported as base rate scores, scaled to reflect the relative prevalence of the characteristics they measure. High scores on these scales indicate a higher level of difficulty with personality patterns or the degree of clinical concern. It includes measures of clinical symptoms that are most prevalent among preadolescents (Tringone et al., 2007).

The MACI is a one hundred and sixty item self-report inventory developed in 1993 for individuals ages 13 to 18 (Millon, 1993). For successful administration, the individual must display a sixth-grade reading level. As with the M-PACI, it is geared to be completed independently, requiring approximately twenty minutes. MACI materials consist of two paper-and-pencil forms, one for hand scoring and the other for computer scoring. Audiocassette recordings of the MACI are available in both English and Spanish. It has thirty-one scales that are divided into four sections: 1) twelve Personality Pattern scales, 2) eight Expressed Concerns scales 3) seven Clinical Syndrome scales and 4) one Reliability scale and three Modifying indices. Notice that the MACI Personality Patterns contains twelve scales, whereas the M-PACI only contains seven. This reflects the development and stabilization of the emerging personality in older individuals. The Personality Patterns scale utilized the theory from which it was derived, by integrating the three personality polarities. For example, of the twelve Personality Patterns, three are detached styles: Detached Inhibited, Detached Introversive and Detached Doleful. This allows the observable behavior and underlying contribution of the personality style to both be described in the assessment results. The MACI test manual provides considerable detail regarding assessment reliability, internal structural validity and external criterion validity (Tringone et al., 2007). While the MACI provides valuable information regarding personality development, coping skills and areas for clinical concern, it does not provide a Diagnostic and Statistical Manual of Mental Disorders—Fourth Edition, Text Revision (DSM-IV-TR, American Psychiatric Association, 2000) diagnosis but is relevant for this process.

Behavior Assessment System for Children, Second Edition

Like the MMPI-A, the MACI and the M-PACI, the *Behavior Assessment System for Children, Second Edition* (BASC-2), is an inventory tool used to collect information on the individual's functioning. The BASC-2 uses a multidimensional approach to assessment, not intended to categorize individuals but to understand the "severity" of subsyndromal pathology and normal variations. The BASC-2 measures multiple dimensions (as enumerated in Reference Box 8.1), or traits, including personality and behavioral problems, emotional disturbances and positive traits such as adaptability. The authors intended its use in an integrative approach to assessment; that information obtained through the BASC-2 should be integrated with data from others assessments, to corroborate hypotheses and support conclusions. As such, information gathered can be used to assist in differential diagnoses both in emotional/behavioral and educational arenas. The BASC-2 is a sensitive instrument, able to ascertain if symptoms are subthreshold, not severe enough for a clinical diagnosis, but severe enough to impact functioning (Kamphaus, VanDeventer, Brueggemann, & Berry, 2007).

Reference Box 8.1 BASC-2 PRS and TRS Scaled Score Categories

Clinical Scales

- Hyperactivity
- Aggression
- Conduct Problems
- Anxiety
- Depression
- Somatization
- Atypicality
- Withdrawal
- Attention Problem

Adaptive Scales

- Adaptability
- Social Skills
- Leadership
- Activities of Daily Living
- Functional Communication

Composites

- Externalizing Problems
- Internalizing Problems
- Behavioral Symptoms
- School Problems

The BASC-2 is considered a multimethod instrument because of the inclusion of five separate components that allow clinicians to obtain information in a number of ways from multiple sources and settings. Components include the following:

- Parent rating scale (PRS) that gathers descriptions of the child's observable behavior from the parent's perspective.
- Teacher rating scale (TRS) that gathers descriptions of the child's observable behavior from the teacher's perspective.
- A self-report scale on which the child or young adult can indicate his or her emotions and self-perceptions.
- A structured developmental history form that allows the clinician to gather information on the child's background history.
- A student observation system for recording and classifying directly observed classroom behavior.

The parent and teacher rating forms are available in three forms for different developmental age groups: a preschool form for ages two to five, a child form for ages six to eleven and an adolescent form for ages twelve to twenty-one. The TRS is a measure of adaptive and problem behaviors in the school, whereas, the PRS captures the same information regarding functioning in the community and home environment. Both forms utilize a four-point rating scale, ranging from Never to Almost Always. The TRS contributes five composites for children and adolescents including Adaptive Skills, Behavioral Symptoms Index, Externalizing Problems, Internalizing Problems and School Problems. Interpretation of the PRS and TRS generate information for three scaled scores. First, high scores on the clinical scales represent difficulty within the assessed emotional/ behavioral domain. *T* scores ranging from sixty to sixty-nine are considered At Risk. Scores of seventy or higher indicate a Clinically Significant range of difficulty. Adaptive scales measure positive adjustment and low scores on these scales represent possible areas of difficulty. *T* scores ranging from thirty to thirty-nine are considered At Risk and scores below thirty are considered Clinically Significant. In addition to the clinical scales and the adaptive scales, composite scores are generated, allowing the clinician to make more general or global interpretations of how an individual is perceived by a teacher or parent (Reynolds & Kamphaus, 2004).

Reference Box 8.2 BASC-2 Self-Report Scaled Scores

Clinical Scales

- Attitude to School
- Attitude to Teachers
- Atypicality
- Locus of Control
- Social Stress

- Anxiety
- Depression
- Sense of Inadequacy
- Attention Problems
- Hyperactivity

Adaptive Scales

- Relations with parents
- Interpersonal Relations
- Self-esteem
- Self-reliance

Composite Scores

- School Problems
- Internalizing Problems
- Inattention/Hyperactivity
- Emotional Symptoms Index
- Personal Adjustment

The self-report form is also available in a developmentally appropriate format. Children ages six to seven participate in an interview, then three separate forms are available for children ages eight to eleven, twelve to twenty-one and college aged eighteen to twenty-five. The self-report form has items that require a true/false response, whereas other items ask for a rating response on a four-point scale of frequency, ranging from Never to Almost Always. Interpretation of the self-report generates information on the clinical scale scores and high scores on these scales represent difficulty within the assessed emotional/behavioral domain. *T* scores ranging from sixty to sixty-nine are considered At Risk. Scores of seventy or higher indicate a Clinically Significant range of difficulty. The adaptive scales measure positive adjustment (see Box 8.2). Low scores indicate possible areas of difficulty. T scores ranging from thirty to thirty-nine are considered At Risk and scores below thirty are considered Clinically Significant. As with the TRS and PRS, the self-report includes a composite score intended for a more general interpretation of the respondents self-perception and emotions (Reynolds & Kamphaus, 2004).

The BASC-2 can be particularly helpful when a child or adolescent is displaying different types of behavior in different settings. It is not uncommon for a child to do so, especially if one setting is supporting their unique needs while the other is not. It can also clarify if stress related to interpersonal relationships or the development of coping mechanisms happens in a particular context, be it relational or environmental.

Achenbach System of Empirically Based Assessment

The *Achenbach System of Empirically Based Assessment* (ASEBA) is composed of a variety of checklists intended to assess a broad spectrum of problems and adaptive functioning in individual's ages 1 1/2 to 90+ (Achenbach, 2007). Like the BASC-2, the ASEBA utilizes checklists in order to gather information from various environments and the individual being assessed, through the involvement of multiple informants, including teachers, parents and the children. Often, different sources provide slightly different information, meaning no one form or subject is better than the other, but that they all contribute to the overall collection of clinical information. The inclusion of various components, informants and checklists are tailored to be developmentally appropriate for different age groups.

As the focus of this chapter is on children and adolescents, the focus will remain on forms used to assess children, specifically children six to eighteen year olds (see Reference Box 8.3). However, making oneself familiar with the adult forms can be useful for a variety of reasons. While assessing children and adolescents, it may be relevant for parents to complete adult forms as a means of elucidating family dynamics related to the child's functioning (Achenbach, 2007).

Achenbach System of Empirically Based Assessment

Reference Box 8.3 Achenbach Syndrome Scales for 6- to 18-Year-Olds

- Anxious/depressed
- Withdrawn/depressed
- Somatic complaints
- Social problems
- Thought problems
- Attention problems
- Rule-breaking behavior
- Aggressive behavior
- Anxious
- Language/motor problems
- Self-control problems

Data forms can be completed within ten to twenty minutes and are composed of structured items that are scored quantitatively and open-ended items that elicit clinically useful information in the respondents' own words. If the individual cannot complete the self-report form independently, items can be read by a nonclinician who acts as a scribe. On checklists used by teachers and parents, assessment items asks teachers or parents to rank observable behavior between 0 = *not true* and 2 = *very true* or *often true*. Results from the Complete Behavior Checklist, Teacher's Report Form, Youth Self-Report Form and the Semistructured Clinical Interview are compiled. During the development of the ASEBA, it became clear that while interpreting information, patterns emerged. These patterns were used to develop *syndrome scales*. Scores are compiled from the various forms and are compared to normative sample responses for eight different syndrome scales. High scores on the syndrome scales indicated clinically significant difficulties

Along with the syndrome scales, competence scales were developed with the intention of describing patterns of behavior related to social relationships, school functioning, participation in activities and overall competence. Low scores on the competence scales indicate clinically significant difficulty (Achenbach, 2007).

Sentence Completion Tests

Sentence completion tests (SCT) are a popular choice among clinicians as an easy means to gather information regarding an individual's personality and self-perceptions in an indirect and informal manner (Holaday, Smith, & Sherry, 2000). A variety of SCTs are available, with differences in purpose and scoring systems as well as intended use with a specific population. These tests present a sentence fragment that the respondent completes with his or her own words and ideas (Dykens, Schwenk, Maxwell, & Myatt, 2007). For example, "I wish that I . . . " or "People think that I . . . " and so forth. Generally, this open-ended format is nonthreatening and engaging, yielding helpful clinical information. In a survey completed by Holaday et al. (2000), practitioners report that they use SCTs to obtain information to corroborate diagnoses and to generate quotable statements to support their diagnostic framework and treatment plan.

A complete list of sentence completion tests frequently used by clinicians to assess children and adolescents can be found in Holaday et al., 2000.

Clinical Interview (Parents and Child)

Behavioral observations and the mental status exam were discussed in Chapter 2 as part of the overall outline for a complete neuropsychological evaluation. Observations made throughout the assessment period further inform the clinician regarding the child's level of cognitive and emotional functioning, interpersonal style, self-perception and coping skills. In addition to ongoing observations, the parent(s) or guardian(s) interview is essential as part of an intake session, prior to the child's evaluation. Likewise, it is also important to conduct a clinical interview with the child or adolescent, receiving their perspective on current functioning and circumstances.

The mental status exam (MSE) provides a framework for collecting information relevant to making clinical decisions. Originally developed by Karl Jaspers (1997), he believed that insight into the individual's functioning is best understood through his or her own words and subjective experience. Originally, it was intended to provide a framework for empathic observations. In more recent years, the MSE has become increasingly based on objective descriptions of the individual rather than on his or her subjective experience. Regardless, it provides a framework for observation and interviews that allow for increased consistency. Information gathered from the MSE can be combined to inform diagnosis, identify individual strengths and struggles and develop a treatment plan.

The MSE is divided into the following domains: appearance, attitude, behavior, mood and affect, speech, thought process, thought content, perception, cognition and judgment. Elements of the MSE have been discussed throughout this book.

Domain Overlap and Integration

Throughout the entire neuropsychological assessment, it is important to note areas of overlap between different domains of functioning, including emotional functioning. The following segments describe ways in which emotional functioning overlaps with other domains and parallels the outline of a complete neuropsychological evaluation. To demonstrate the overlap outside the testing situation, vignettes describe instances in which domains assessed during an evaluation of neuropsychological and emotional functioning come to life in a classroom setting.

Cognition and Emotion

Annette was an intelligent, precocious eleven-year-old girl. During a recent cognitive assessment, she achieved very superior scores on both Verbal IQ (156) and Performance IQ (146), deriving a Full Scale IQ of 159, the 99.9 percent for her age group. During an academic assessment, her scores were consistent with the cognitive assessment, correlating with Grade 12.9 for both math and reading skills. And yet, in a highly therapeutic classroom, she struggled to complete teacher-assigned tasks, even those designed to meet her exceptional abilities. Annette was a voracious reader, consuming print at a rapid pace. When the teachers approached her about tailoring a literature unit to her needs, they proposed books of advanced content relative to her peers, providing several options. With one suggestion, *Tuck Everlasting*, by Natalie Babbitt, a sixth-grade-level book, Annette grew visibly anxious. She sat, back straight, hands clasped, eyes wide, and asked, "Isn't that about a boy that lives forever?" The teachers confirmed, yes, and she began to shake. "I don't know," her voice trembled. "It would be sad to read about a boy who watches everyone he cares about die." Her eyes welled up with tears. "I don't think I could do that." The rate of her speech accelerated and soon, she was rapidly monologuing about immortality, appearing emotionally overwhelmed. The teachers assured her there were other choices and asked her what she needed to help calm herself down. Annette took a break in a quiet space in the room for twenty minutes, and only then was she able to return to academic instruction.

The efficient processing of emotion relies on neural mechanisms supporting the detection, identification and processing of stimuli essential for survival. The evolution of these mechanisms is recapitulated over development. Emotions can influence cognition by either facilitating or interfering with cognitive processing, an impact that can occur at various levels of cognition, from sensorimotor levels to higher levels of memory and executive functions (Dolcos, Iordan, & Dolcos, 2011). For example, an event with positive emotional valence can improve memory for that event, while excitement about a project can focus one and enable one to make and carry out a plan to complete it

Negative emotions can also prevent one from efficiently processing information, as is the case when one is anxious about taking a test and cannot overcome the anxiety in order to cognitively process the questions. Conversely, emotional processing is influenced by cognitive factors. This enables one to regulate emotional reactivity or distractibility as well as cope with more chronic emotional experiences. Strategies for modulating emotional functioning evolve over the course of development, and one's success or failure in developing these strategies can determine one's ability to successfully manage the demands of life. Thus, this reciprocal interaction between emotion and cognition is fundamental to our human experience (Dolcos et al., 2011).

One line of research examining the relationship between cognition and emotion has focused on the question of whether or not the processing of emotion is automatic or depends on some level of conscious, attentional processes. The argument for automaticity contends that fast, unintentional and unconscious processing of emotional stimuli was necessary for survival and therefore not under conscious control. The amygdala has been implicated in this process, and brain imaging findings suggest that that it can process emotionally loaded facial expressions without the individual's awareness (Whalen et al., 1998) and that this involves subcortical pathways connecting with the amygdala, independent of cortical systems (Vuilleumier, 2005).

The competing view, that processing of emotion depends on attentional resources, was supported in a study by Pessoa, McKenna, Gutierrez and Ungerleider (2002) that demonstrated a role for conscious, attentional processes when the individual is required to process information at a higher level. It is likely that both positions have merit, and a review of the literature suggests that, depending on circumstances, emotional information can be processed automatically but also profits from the engagement of available attentional resources (Dolcos et al., 2011).

Cognition's impact on emotional processing has been examined in respect to the idea of emotional regulation, an important evolutionary strategy that matures over the course of an individual's development (Orgeta, 2009). Most research has focused on the conscious forms of regulation, such as instructed reappraisal (altering one's thoughts about a target event to control the initial emotional response), suppression (attempting to conceal one's emotions after the initial response has occurred) and cognitive distraction (coping with task irrelevant emotional distractions), all of which involve regions of the prefrontal cortex (Dolcos et al., 2011).

Executive Functions

Executive functions have been found to play a central role in the regulation of emotion. These are goal directed behaviors used to modulate certain features of emotion, such as the intensity and temporal extent of behavioral, experiential and physiological reactions (Thompson & Gross, 2007). Various lines of research, including lesion and neuroimaging studies, have documented the role of the frontal lobes in emotional regulation (Goldin, McRae, Ramel, & Gross, 2008; Stuss & Levine, 2002). For example, it has been suggested that by holding on to information for a certain amount of time, working memory may play a role in enhancing the effects of emotion on long-term memory. Dorsal, or "top-down," executive systems, including regions associated with working memory, and ventral "bottom-up" affective systems appear to be interrelated and influence one another. Thus, bottom-up emotional distractors could negatively impact the processing of top-down, goal-directed information by diverting processing resources. However, cognitive, executive control regions can be engaged to regulate emotional reactivity and distractibility (Dolcos et al., 2011). In addition, the executive process of decision making has been demonstrated to be influenced by somatically based influences that have emotional and motivational import and which involve ventromedial prefrontal areas (Damasio, 1996). Gyurak, Goodkind, Kramer, Miller and Levenson (2012) found that higher scores on a measure of verbal fluency correlated with a greater ability to regulate emotion in both down-regulation and up-regulation conditions, suggesting that verbal/fluency performance best captured the more complicated sequence of planning, activation and monitoring necessary for successful emotion regulation.

Memory

Eight-year-old Jessica had long, blonde hair and bright, blue eyes and a very quiet disposition. She enjoyed playing with stuffed animals with the other girls in the classroom and, despite her silence, was often smiling and laughing. Every Monday morning, the classroom group would talk about their weekend activities. Jessica frequently had nothing to say. Testing had indicated that she struggled with word retrieval and long-term memory. On this particular weekend, her parents had mentioned the family would go boating. The teachers prompted Jessica, asking her where they had boated or what they had seen, but Jessica lowered her big eyes, shrugging. On the table, the teachers placed handmade drawings displaying a range of emotions made by Jessica. They asked if she remembered how she felt on the boat. Jessica indicated happy and scared. They asked, "What made you feel scared, Jessica?" Her eyes glanced up, "My brother yelled at me because I sat where he wanted to sit on the boat." The teachers thanked her for sharing, and then asked what made her happy. She smiled, eyes alight, "We stopped and had french fries. We ate them on the boat!" The teachers praised Jessica for sharing her memories with the group, as Jessica shyly smiled.

Emotion has long-term effects that ultimately support the consolidation of memory for certain events, a process that appears to be related to emotional intensity rather than meaning alone, and which is mediated by the enhancing influence of the amygdala or the medial temporal lobe neural circuits associated with memory formation (Dolcos, Kragel, Wang, & McCarthy, 2006). Furthermore, in neuroimaging studies, successful retrieval of emotional memories has been correlated with the medial temporal lobe memory systems similar to those involved in the encoding of emotional memories (Dolcos, LaBar, & Cabeza, 2004). The prefrontal cortex has also been found to be involved in the encoding of emotional memory, particularly in respect to semantic and working memory processing (Dolcos et al., 2011). Thus, evidence suggests that emotion enhances long-term memory through its influence on both the medial temporal lobe memory system in respect to encoding, consolidation, storage and retrieval and the prefrontal cortical system in respect to semantic, strategic and working memory processes (Dolcos et al., 2011).

Sensory Motor Integration

Research examining the relationship between sensory processing and emotion has primarily focused on the relationship between ease of visual processing and its effect on affective responses (Winkielman & Cacioppo, 2001). Cannon, Hayes and Tipper (2010), however, examined the role of sensorimotor fluency on emotion and found that the ease with which individuals could integrate visual stimuli with grasp was correlated with affective response. They suggest that this finding supports a hedonic model of fluency in which fluent processing elicits a direct affective experience. The authors also note that changes in cognitive processes as a result of positive emotional feedback can guide efficient patterns of behavior. A study examining fluent sensorimotor coupling (coupling sensory and motor processes while engaged with music) found that the degree of pleasure experienced as ease, or "groove," was inversely related to the experienced difficulty of bimanual sensorimotor coupling while tapping. Furthermore, in a study evaluating motor fluency on affect, Beilock and Holt (2007) reported that ease of typing, whether executed or simulated, was correlated with a more positive emotional experience.

Behavioral and Emotional Functioning and Achievement

Prior to arriving at a small therapeutic school, Kim had been out of control. Although she was only eight, she was well coordinated, strong and very angry. She had injured herself and staff at the public school during protracted unsafe episodes that usually ended when a parent arrived at school to take her home. When not upset, she was bright, creative, charismatic and possessed excellent verbal skills. During a destructive rampage, she was unrelenting, but afterwards, she felt guilty and would try to atone for her misdeeds. In her new school, the staff afforded her time and space to develop relationships, learn the routines and make friends. Slowly, academic demands moved from learning games and play to paper-and-pencil activities. Her reluctance to participate was palpable throughout the classroom. With time, she became more willing, and with the help of medication, her powerful reactive emotions and behavior subsided. She was better able to tolerate more academic work. It became clear that Kim had serious gaps in basic skills and knowledge, which she could hide under her strong verbal and social skills. Eventually, during an academic period, she said, "I'm just not good at this school stuff," and then blew out a breath of air in a self-defeated sigh. After that day, she would gloss over her mistakes, assert that she was always correct and took on a "know-it-all" attitude, despite the fact that she clearly did not. Her peers grew increasingly annoyed with her bossy behavior. During an annual academic assessment, it became clear that underneath the reactive behaviors, there were discrete learning vulnerabilities that had previously been overshadowed. As she turned nine, her willingness to participate in academic activities ebbed and waned daily as she struggled to come to terms with accepting help for her vulnerabilities or to mask them, pretending she was doing just fine and that it was the "stupid school" that blocked her success. Kim's perception of herself as a student had formed around her unsafe behaviors, missed learning opportunities and fear of appearing weak.

In addition to the risk factors discussed above, academic achievement has been found to have a significant impact on the development of both externalizing and internalizing symptoms and vice versa. There have, however, been few longitudinal studies linking domains of competence with problems of both types. As Masten et al. (2005) argued, there are three reasons why achievement and pathology may be related;

• Symptoms undermine adaptive functioning (behavior interferes with learning)
• Failures in adaptive functioning contribute to symptoms (failure to learn impacts self-perception or judgments of others)
• Some other cause contributes to both competence and symptoms (an unmeasured variable).

They go on to describe how previous studies linking externalizing, internalizing and academic behavior have suggested that "there may be developmental cascades by which functioning in one domain of adaptive behavior spills over to influence functioning in other domains in a lasting way" (p. 735). In a twenty-year longitudinal study (Masten et al., 2005) conducted on several hundred children, beginning when they were between eight and twelve years old, the authors concluded that a developmental cascade model accounts for the way in which functioning in one domain of behavior impacts other domains from childhood into adulthood. Externalizing problems in childhood predicted problems, progressing from externalizing, to academic, to internalizing areas of functioning by young adulthood. The authors contend that, "mental health professionals have underestimated or neglected the centrality of academic success and failure in the progression of mental health symptoms, because it falls under the purview of school professionals" (p. 743). They concluded that developmental cascades and tasks of development are integrally connected, and behavioral symptoms associated with psychopathology should be understood within the context of the "waxing and waning of developmental tasks" (p. 744).

In a more recent study, Obradović, Burt and Masten (2010) found that there was a cascading effect of social competence in childhood on adolescent internalizing problems. In emerging adults, there was a dual cascading effect of both social and academic competence on internalizing problems in young adults. These findings suggest that both academic success and social relationships in the transition from emerging to young adulthood play an important role in social and mental health. Herman, Lambert, Reinke, and Lalongo (2008) reported that academic competence in first grade predicted the incidence of depressive symptoms in seventh grade, and that a measure of perceived control (as a reflection of others' perception of the individual as academically incompetent) in grade six mediated the relationship between academic competence and depressive symptoms. Failure feedback within the school setting resulted in increased feelings of helplessness and led to greater levels of depression (Rudolph, Kurlakowsky, & Conley, 2001). Autocratic and chaotic classroom environments were found to disrupt a child's developing sense of mastery and contribute to his or her sense of helplessness and disinvestment in academic tasks (Eccles et al., 1991). While individual differences in children's measured intelligence was related to variations in classroom performance as well as cognitive functioning, anxiety/depression and withdrawal contributed to the prediction of classroom performance and cognitive functioning over and above the effects of intelligence (Rapport et al., 2001).

The role of neurologically based influences on academic performance and psychiatric symptoms has also been investigated. For example, Aronen, Vuontela, Steenari, Salmi and Carlson (2005) found that children with deficits in working memory, particularly audiospatial memory, had more academic difficulties and teacher-reported behavioral problems and anxiety/depressive symptoms. Other studies have documented the relationship between inattention, poor academic performance and subsequent depression (Herman, Lambert, Ialongo, & Ostrander, 2007; Herman & Ostrander, 2007).

In summary, research has demonstrated a strong relationship between behavioral, social, and emotional functioning and academic performance, a relationship that proceeds in both directions and results in developmental cascades that resonate through adulthood.

Charles

In this section, we return to eleven-year-old Charles and consider the results from a battery of assessments that included the *Rorschach Inkblot Test,* the *Roberts Apperception Test,* the *Conger Sentence Completion Test, House-Tree-Person, Kinetic Family Drawing* (KFD), *Clinical Interview* (parents and child), *Behavior Assessment System for Children, Second Edition* (self-report, parent and teacher rating scales), review of school records and previous evaluations.

On the BASC-2, significant concerns were raised regarding Charles's anxiety, depression, somatization, withdrawal and adaptability. In addition, his mother reported that within the context of his academic functioning, additional concerns were related to his anger control, emotional self-control, negative emotionality and resiliency. Charles, himself, reported that he was within the average range on all measures, excluding his rating of his relationship with his parents, which was scored as At Risk. This was a surprising finding, given his reported level of anxiety and inability to function at school, but consistent with his own report that "I don't think about that stuff," suggesting that he was actively avoiding an awareness of the extent to which his functioning had been compromised.

Regarding evaluator administered tests of emotional functioning, Charles presented as a very bright young boy who demonstrated good reality testing abilities but who was experiencing a chronic degree of overload in the form of emotional stress and anxiety for which he had inadequate psychological resources to cope. Much of this affective overload was based on his reaction to his experiences within his family and, particularly, in relation to his father's ongoing medical issues. In addition, he demonstrated a constellation of learning vulnerabilities that, over the years, increasingly began to impinge on his image of himself as extremely competent. He appeared to be actively avoiding an awareness of his affective dysfunction and learning vulnerabilities and was, instead, attempting to exert control over his environment by narrowing his experience and using his family to buffer the demands of the outside world, thereby maintaining his facade of competence.

Based on the battery of tests, results indicated that Charles lacked the psychological resources required for him to adequately meet the emotional and academic demands being placed on him. He demonstrated an aversion to the processing of complex information, particularly when doing so elicited some affective response. This avoidant style therefore required that Charles simplify complex, affectively charged situations or attempt to ignore ambiguity or uncertainty; the latter approach also being operational when faced with novelty in respect to social or academic challenges. In addition, when his attempts to avoid certain affectively stimulating situations were unsuccessful, he tended to misperceive events and impose arbitrary or circumstantial reasoning that could lead to confusion and further uncertainty, thereby creating a situation in which he felt he needed to exert even more control. This approach to managing himself was exacerbated by a level of cognitive inflexibility that appeared to be both neurologically and emotionally based. Furthermore, it could worsen his additional vulnerabilities in executive functioning skills, making learning much more challenging than it need be by lowering his frustration tolerance threshold and contributing to a much greater degree of irritability and anxiety. This could further lead to emotional outbursts, an even greater need for control over his environment, withdrawal and depression.

In spite of his intelligence and capacity for insight, Charles was actively avoiding any degree of self-reflection as a means to preserve his self-image. He had been faced with a rather unique set of challenges and circumstances, given his father's cancer and ongoing medical issues, that had, at times, been life threatening and to which Charles had reacted very strongly. In addition, being the twin of a brother who was succeeding in school both socially and academically provided a mirror, of sorts, that was a constant reminder of his own failures. As a result, in order to maintain the image of himself as extremely competent, he not only had to avoid thinking "about that stuff" but also had to take a perfectionistic approach to learning. This "all or nothing" stance was difficult to sustain and could succeed only by even more actively avoiding situations in which either approach would not work. Thus, his experience was becoming even more restricted and was creating greater anxiety, particularly in situations when an avoidant approach might be challenged. Despite his inability to acknowledge it, however, Charles's self-image was suffering greatly. His responses on projective testing contained many references to a desire to be "cute" and an aversion to being "ugly" or "old" that would result in one being "alone." On the *House-Tree-Person,* he drew an extremely small boy at the bottom of the paper and created a story about the boy becoming "lost" in his attempts to find a "treasure" (see Figure 8.2). In addition, on the Roberts, he told stories about a boy being "kicked out" of scouts, a girl who was "an outsider," and a boy who was put up for adoption by his family because he didn't "look like them."

Figure 8.2 Charles self-portrait.

While Charles was actively seeking the protection and comfort of his family by narrowing his exposure to the rest of the world, this attempt to manage his experience was fraught with difficulty. Although he clearly felt safer at home, his relationships with his parents also tended to be a great source of anxiety and uncertainty. Charles, himself, identified his relationship with his parents as "At Risk" on the BASC-2. His stories on the Roberts were replete with images of loss and death. In fact, twelve out of sixteen of the stories focused on those topics, with three directly involving the death of a father. In another story, the rest of the family died and visited the father in heaven. In Charles's family drawing, he depicted a tiny drawing of his family in a rectangle and, in his story about his family, referred to the treasure sought by the boy in his drawing on the H-T-P mentioned previously: "We're very gullible. We're sitting in a box and we're trapped. The treasure did it, it's very mean. We're trapped forever and we'll die as a family" (see Figure 8.3). Nevertheless, on the *Conger Sentence Completion Test,* when asked who his best friend was, he replied "my family." Thus, while Charles was actively seeking the solace his family provided from the complexity of the outside world, it was a solace that was rife with his perception that his family was "trapped" by a quest for a "treasure" that was doomed.

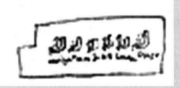

Figure 8.3 Charles's kinetic family drawing.

References

Achenbach, T. M. (1992). *Manual for the child behavior checklist–2–3 and 1992 profile.* Burlington: University of Vermont, Department of Psychiatry.

Achenbach, T. M. (2007). Application of the Achenbach System of Empirically Based Assessment to children, adolescents, and their parents. In S. R. Smith & L. Handler (Eds.), *The clinical assessment of children and adolescents: A practitioner's handbook* (pp. 327–344). New York, NY: Psychology Press, Taylor and Francis Group.

Achenbach, T. M., Howell, C. T., Quay, H. C., & Conners, C. K. (1991). National survey of problems and competencies among 4- to 16-year-olds: Parents' reports for normative and clinical samples. *Monographs of the Society for Research in Child Development, 56,* 1–131.

Ackerman, B. P., D'Eramo, K. S., Umylny, L., Schultz, D., & Izard, C. E. (2001). Family structure and externalizing behavior of children from economically disadvantaged families. *Journal of Family Psychology, 15,* 288–300.

Acklin, M. W., & Wu-Holt, P. (1996). Contributions of cognitive science to the Rorschach technique: Cognitive and neuropsychological correlates of the response process. *Journal of Personality Assessment, 67*(1), 169.

American Psychiatric Association. (2012). *Diagnostic and statistical manual of mental disorders* (4th rev. ed.). Arlington, VA: APA.

Archer, R. P. (2005). *MMPI-A assessing adolescent psychopathology* (3rd ed.). Mahwah, NJ: Erlbaum.

Archer, R. P., Krishnamurthy, R., & Stredny, R. V. (2007). Minnesota multiphasic personality inventory–Adolescent. In S. R. Smith & L. Handler (Eds.). *The clinical assessment of children and adolescents: A practitioner's handbook* (pp. 237–266). New York, NY: Psychology Press, Taylor and Francis Group.

Armstrong, M. (1954). Children's responses to animal and human figures in thematic pictures. *Journal of Consulting Psychology, 18,* 67–70.

Aronen, E. T., Vuontela, V., Steenari, M.-R., Salmi, J., & Carlson, S. (2005). Working memory, psychiatric symptoms, and academic performance at school. *Neurobiology of Learning and Memory, 83,* 33–42.

Beilock, S. L., & Holt, L. E. (2007). Embodied preference judgments: Can likeability be driven by the motor system? *Psychological Science, 18,* 51–57.

Bellak, L., & Bellak, S. (1949). *The children's apperception test.* Larchmont, NY: CPS.

Bellak, L., & Bellak, S. (1965). *The C.A.T.-H.—A human modification.* Larchmont, NY: CPS.

Berthoz, S. S., Blair, R. R., Le Clec'h, G. G., & Martinot, J. L. (2002). Emotions: From neuropsychology to functional imaging. *International Journal of Psychology, 37*(4), 193–203.

Biersdorf, K. R., & Marcuse, F. L. (1953). Responses of children to human and animal pictures. *Journal of Projective Techniques, 17,* 455–459.

Booth-LaForce, C., & Oxford, M. L. (2008). Trajectories of social withdrawal from grades 1 to 6: Prediction from early parenting, attachment, and temperament. *Developmental Psychology, 44,* 1298–1313.

Bub, K. L., McCartney, K., & Willett, J. B. (2007). Behavior problem trajectories and first-grade cognitive ability and achievement skills: A latent growth curve analysis. *Journal of Educational Psychology, 99,* 653–670.

Buck, J. N. (1948). The H-T-P technique: A qualitative and quantitative scoring manual. *Journal of Clinical Psychology, 4,* 317–396.

Budoff, M. (1960). The relative utility of animal and human figures in a picture story test for young children. *Journal of Projective Techniques, 42,* 347–352.

Burns, R. C. (1982). *Self-growth in families: Kinetic Family Drawings (K-F-D) research and application.* New York, NY: Brunner/Mazel.

Burns, R. C., & Kaufman, S. H. (1970). *Kinetic family drawing* (K-F-D). New York, NY: Brunner/Mazel.

Butcher, J. N., William, C. L., Graham, J. R., Archer, R. P., Tellegen, A., Ben-Porath, Y. S., et al. (1992). *Minnesota multiphasic personality inventory–Adolescent* (MMPI-A): *Manual for administration, scoring and interpretation.* Minneapolis: University of Minnesota Press.

Cannon, P. R., Hayes, A. E., & Tipper, S. P. (2010). Sensorimotor fluency influences affect: Evidence from electromyography. *Cognition & Emotion, 24*(4), 681–691.

Cannon, W. B. (1927). The James–Lange theory of emotions: A critical examination and an alternative theory. *American Journal of Psychology, 39,* 106–124.

Cashel, M. L., Killilea, B., & Dollinger, S. J. (2007). Interpretation of storytelling in the clinical assessment of children and adolescents. In S. R. Smith & L. Handler (Eds.), *The clinical assessment of children and adolescents: A practitioner's handbook* (pp. 185–205). New York, NY: Psychology Press, Taylor and Francis Group.

Chanen, A. M., Jackson, H. J., McGorry, P. D., Allot, K. A., Clarkson, V., & Yuen, H. P. (2004). Two-year stability of personality disorder in older adolescent outpatients. *Journal of Personality Disorders, 18,* 526–541.

Clemence, A. J. (2007). Use of the hand test with children and adolescents. In S. R. Smith & L. Handler (Eds.). *The clinical assessment of children and adolescents: A practitioner's handbook* (pp. 223–235). New York, NY: Psychology Press, Taylor and Francis Group.

Coyne, L., & Thompson, A. (2011). Maternal depression, locus of control, and emotion regulatory strategy as predictors of preschoolers' internalizing problems. *Journal of Child & Family Studies, 20*(6), 873–883.

Cohen, B.M. (Ed.). (1983). *The diagnostic drawing series handbook.* Available from Barry M. Cohen, P.O. Box 9853, Alexandria, VA 22304.

Compas, B.E., Connor-Smith, J., & Jaser, S.S. (2004). Temperament, stress reactivity and coping: Implications for depression in childhood and adolescence. *Journal of Clinical Child and Adolescent Psychology, 33*, 21–31.

Damasio, A.R. (1996). The somatic marker hypothesis and the possible functions of the prefrontal cortex. *Philosophical Transactions of the Royal Society of London: Biological Sciences, 351B,* 1413–1420.

Damasio, A.R., Grabowski, T.J., Bechara, A., Damasio, H., Ponto, L.B., Parvizi, J., & Hichwa, R.D. (2000). Subcortical and cortical brain activity during the feeling of self-generated emotions. *Nature Neuroscience, 3*(10), 1049.

Dolcos, F., Jordan, A.D., & Dolcos, S. (2011). Neural correlates of emotion–cognition interactions: A review of evidence from brain imaging investigations. *Journal of Cognitive Psychology, 23*(6), 669–694.

Dolcos, F., Kragel, P., Wang, L., & McCarthy, G. (2006). Role of the inferior frontal cortex in coping with distracting emotions. *Neuroreport, 17,* 1591–1594.

Dolcos, F., LaBar, K., & Cabeza, R. (2004). Interaction between the amygdala and the medial temporal lobe memory system predicts better memory for emotional events. *Neuron, 42,* 855–863.

Dykens, E., Schwenk, K., Maxwell, M., & Myatt, B. (2007). The Sentence Completion and Three Wishes task: Window into the inner lives of people with intellectual disabilities. *Journal of Intellectual Disability Research, 51*(8), 588–597.

Eccles, J.S., Buchanan, C., Flanagan, C., Fuligni, A., Midgley, C., & Yee, D. (1991). Control versus autonomy during early adolescence. *Journal of Social Issues, 47*(4), 53–68.

Erdberg, P. (2007). Using the Rorschach with children. In S. Smith & L. Handler (Eds.), *The clinical assessment of children and adolescents* (pp. 139–147). New York, NY: Psychology Press.

Exner, J.E. (2003). *The Rorschach: A comprehensive system* (4th ed.). Hoboken, NJ: John Wiley & Sons.

Fanti, K.A., & Henrich, C.C. (2010). Trajectories of pure and co-occurring internalizing and externalizing problems from age 2 to age 12: Findings from the national institute of child health and human development study of early child care. *Developmental Psychology, 46*(5), 1159–1175.

Frick, P.J. (2004). Integrating research on temperament and psychopathology: Its pitfalls and promise. *Journal of Clinical Child and Adolescent Psychology, 33*, 2–7.

Frick, P., Lahey, B., Loeber, R., Tannenbaum, L., Van Horn, Y., Christ, M., Hart, E., & Hanson, K (1993). Oppositional defiant disorder and conduct disorder: A meta-analytic review of factor analyses and cross-validation in a clinic sample. *Clinical Psychology Review, 13,* 319–340.

Gilliom, M., & Shaw, D.S. (2004). Codevelopment of externalizing and internalizing problems in early childhood. *Development and Psychopathology, 16,* 313–333.

Goldin, P., McRae, K., Ramel, W., & Gross, J. (2008). The neural bases of emotion regulation: Reappraisal and suppression of negative emotion. *Biological Psychiatry, 63,* 577–586.

Grunbaum, J.A., Kann, L., Kinchen, S., et al. (2004).Youth risk behavior surveillance—United States, 2003. *MMWR Morbidity and Mortality Weekly Report, 53,* 1–95.

Gyurak, A., Goodkind, M.S., Kramer, J.H., Miller, B.L., & Levenson, R.W. (2012). Executive functions and the down-regulation and up-regulation of emotion. *Cognition & Emotion, 26*(1) 103–118.

Handler, L., & Habenicht, D. (1994). The Kinetic Family Drawing technique: A review of the literature. *Journal of Personality Assessment, 63*(3), 440–464.

Handler, L., & Meyer, G. (1998). The importance of teaching and learning personality assessment. In L. Handler & M. J. Hilsenroth (Eds.), *Teaching and learning personality assessment* (pp. 3–30). Mahwah, NJ: Erlbaum.

Harris, D. B. (1963). *Children's drawings as measures of intellectual maturity.* New York, NY: Harcourt, Brace, & World.

Herman, K. C., & Ostrander, R. O. (2007). The effects of attention problems on depression: Developmental, cognitive, and academic pathways. *School Psychology Quarterly, 22,* 483–510.

Herman, K. C., Lambert, S., Ialongo, N., & Ostrander, R. O. (2007). Academic pathways between attention problems and depressive symptoms among urban African American children. *Journal of Abnormal Child Psychology, 35,* 265–274.

Herman, K. C., Lambert, S. F., Reinke, W. M., & Lalongo, N. S. (2008). Low academic competence in first grade as a risk factor for depressive cognitions and symptoms in middle school. *Journal of Counseling Psychology, 55*(3), 400–410.

Hiller, J., Rosenthal, R., Bornstein, R., Berry, D., & Brunell-Neulieb, S. (1999). A comparative meta-analysis of Rorschach and MMPI validity. *Psychological Assessment, 11,* 278–296.

Holaday, M., Smith, D. A., & Sherry, A. (2000). Sentence completion tests: A review of the literature and results of a survey of members of the Society for Personality Assessment. *Journal of Personality Assessment, 74*(3), 371–383.

James, W. (1884). What is an emotion? *Mind, 9,* 188–205.

Jaspers, K. (1997). *General psychopathology* (Vols. 1–2, J. Hoenig & M. W. Hamilton, Trans.). Baltimore, MD: Johns Hopkins University Press.

Kamphaus, R. W., VanDeventer, M. C., Brueggemann, A., & Barry, M. (2007). Behavior Assessment System for Children–Second Edition. In S. R. Smith & L. Handler (Eds.), *The clinical assessment of children and adolescents: A practitioner's handbook* (pp. 311–326). New York, NY: Psychology Press, Taylor and Francis Group.

Lezak, M. D., Howieson, D. B., Bigler, E. D., & Tranel, D. (2012). *Neuropsychological assessment* (5th ed.). New York, NY: Oxford University Press.

Lindzey, G. (1952). Thematic apperception test: Interpretive assumptions and empirical evidence. *Psychological Bulletin, 49,* 1–25.

Loevinger, J. (1987). *Paradigms of personality.* New York, NY: Freeman.

Loevinger, J. (Ed.). (1998). *Technical foundations for measuring ego development: The Washington University Sentence Completion Test.* Mahwah, NJ: Erlbaum.

Loevinger, J., & Wessler, R. (1970). *Measuring ego development* (Vol. 1). San Diego, CA: Jossey-Bass.

Loevinger, J., Wessler, R., & Redmore, C. (1970). *Measuring ego development* (Vol. 2). San Diego, CA: Jossey-Bass.

MacLean, P. D. (1949). Psychosomatic disease and the "visceral brain": Recent developments bearing on the Papez theory of emotion. *Psychosomatic Medicine, 11,* 338–353.

Marceau, K., Humbad, M., Burt, S. S., Klump, K., Leve, L., & Neiderhiser, J. (2012). Observed externalizing behavior: A developmental comparison of genetic and environmental influences across three samples. *Behavior Genetics, 42*(1), 30–39.

Masten, A. S., Roisman, G. I., Long, J. D., Burt, K. B., Obradović, J., Riley, J. R., ... Tellegen, A. (2005). Developmental cascades: Linking academic achievement and externalizing and internalizing symptoms over 20 years. *Developmental Psychology, 41*(5), 733–746.

Matto, H. C. (2002) Investigating the validity of the Draw A Person: Screening procedure for emotional disturbance: A measurement validity study with high-risk youth. *Psychological Assessment, 14,* 221–225.

Matto, H. C. (2007). Drawings in clinical assessment of children and adolescents. In S. R. Smith & L. Handler (Eds.), *The clinical assessment of children and adolescents: A practitioner's handbook* (pp. 207–221). New York, NY: Psychology Press, Taylor and Francis Group.

McArthur, D. S., & Roberts, G. E. (1982). *Roberts apperception test for children manual.* Los Angeles, CA: Western Psychological Services.

Meunier, M., Bachevalier, J., Murray, E. A., Malkova, L., & Mishkin, M. (1996). Effects of aspiration vs. neurotoxic lesions of the amygdala on emotional reactivity in rhesus monkeys. *Society for Neuroscience Abstracts, 13,* 5418–5432.

Meyer, G., & Archer, R. (2001). The hard science of Rorschach research: What do we know and where do we go? *Psychological Assessment, 13,* 486–502.

Mihura, J. L., Meyer, G. J., Dumitrascu, N., & Bombel, G. (2013). The validity of individual Rorschach variables: Systematic reviews and meta-analyses of the comprehensive system. *Psychological Bulletin, 139*(3), 548–605.

Millon, T. (1969). *Modern psychopathology: A biosocial approach to maladaptive learning and functioning.* Philadelphia, PA: Saunders.

Millon, T. (1981). *Disorders of personality: DSM-III: Axis II.* New York, NY: Wiley.

Millon, T. (1990). *Toward a new personology: An evolutionary model.* New York, NY: Wiley.

Millon, T. (1993). *Millon Adolescent Clinical Inventory (MACI) manual.* Minneapolis, MN: National Computer Systems.

Millon, T., & Davis, R. D. (1996). *Disorders of personality: DSM-IV and beyond* (2nd ed.). New York: Wiley.

Miner, J. L., & Clarke-Stewart, K. (2008). Trajectories of externalizing behavior from age 2 to age 9: Relations with gender, temperament, ethnicity, parenting, and rater. *Developmental Psychology, 44*(3), 771–786.

Morgan, C. D., & Murray, H. M. (1935). A method for investigating fantasies: The Thematic Apperception Test. *Archives of Neurology and Psychiatry, 34,* 289–306.

Murphy, F. C., Nimmo-Smith, I., & Lawrence, A. D. (2003). Functional neuroanatomy of emotions: A meta-analysis. *Cognitive, Affective and Behavioral Neuroscience, 3,* 207–233.

Murray, H. A. (1943). *Thematic apperception test manual.* Cambridge, MA: Harvard University Press.

Naglieri, J. A. (1988). *Draw-A-Person: A quantitative scoring system.* San Antonio, TX: Psychological Corporation.

Naglieri, J. A., McNeish, T. J., & Bardos, A. N. (1991). *Draw A Person: Screening procedure for emotional disturbance.* Austin, TX: Pro-Ed.

Naglieri, J. A., & Pfeiffer, S. I. (1992). Validity of the Draw A Person: Screening procedure for emotional disturbance with a socially-emotionally disturbed sample. *Psychological Assessment, 4,* 156–159.

Obradović, J., Burt, K. B., & Masten, A. S. (2010). Testing a dual cascade model linking competence and symptoms over 20 years from childhood to adulthood. *Journal of Clinical Child & Adolescent Psychology, 39*(1), 90–102.

Obrzut, J. E., & Boliek, C. A. (1986). Thematic approaches to personality assessment with children and adolescents. In H. M. Knoff (Ed.), *The assessment of child and adolescent personality* (pp. 183–98). New York, NY: Guilford Press.

Orgeta, V. (2009). Specificity of age differences in emotion regulation. *Aging & Mental Health 13*(6), 818–826.

Papez, J. W. (1937). A proposed mechanism of emotion. *Archives of Neurology and Psychiatry, 38,* 725–743.

Pessoa, L., McKenna, M., Gutierrez, E., & Ungerleider, L. (2002). Neural processing of emotional face requires attention. *Proceedings of the National Academy of Sciences of the USA, 99,* 11458–11463.

Phan K. L., Wager, T., Taylor, S. F., & Liberzon, I. (2002). Functional neuroanatomy of emotion: A meta-analysis of emotion activation studies in PET and fMRI. *Neuroimage, 16,* 331–348.

Rapport, M. D., Denney, C. B., Chung, K., & Hustace, K. (2001). Internalizing behavior problems and scholastic achievement in children: Cognitive and behavioral pathways as mediators of outcome. *Journal of Child Psychology, 30,* 536–551.

Reef, J., Diamantopoulou, S., Meurs, I., Verhulst, F., & Ende, J. (2011). Developmental trajectories of child to adolescent externalizing behavior and adult DSM-IV disorder: Results of a 24-year longitudinal study. *Social Psychiatry & Psychiatric Epidemiology, 46*(12), 1233–1241.

Reynolds, C. R., & Kamphaus, R. W. (2004). *The behavioral assessment system for children* (2nd ed.). Circle Pines, MN: AGS.

Roberts, G. E., & Gruber, C. (2005). *Roberts-2.* Los Angeles, CA: Western Psychological Services.

Rorschach, H. (1942). *Psychodiagnostik* [Psychodiagnostics]. Bern, Switzerland: Bircher. (Original work published 1921).

Rotter, J. B., & Willerman, B. (1947). The Incomplete Sentences Test as a method of studying personality. *Journal of Consulting Psychology, 11,* 43–48.

Rudolph, K. D., Kurlakowsky, K. D., & Conley, C. S. (2001). Developmental and social–contextual origins of depressive control-related beliefs and behavior. *Cognitive Therapy & Research, 25*(4), 447–475.

Silver, R. (2002). *Three art assessments: Silver drawing test of cognition and emotion, draw a story, screening for depression and stimulus drawings and techniques.* New York, NY: Brunner-Routledge.

Smith, S., & Handler, L. (2007). The clinical practice of child and adolescent assessment. In S. Smith & L. Handler (Eds.), *The clinical assessment of children and adolescents* (pp. 1–15). New York, NY: Psychology Press.

Stuss, D., & Levine, B. (2002). Adult clinical neuropsychology: Lessons from studies of the frontal lobes. *Annual Review of Psychology, 53,* 401–433.

Tharinger, D. J., & Stark, K. (1990). A qualitative versus quantitative approach to evaluating the Draw-A-Person and Kinetic Family Drawing: A study of mood and anxiety disorder children. *Journal of Consulting and Clinical Psychology, 2*(4), 365–375.

Thompson, R., & Gross, J. (2007). Emotion regulation. In J. Gross (Ed.), *Handbook of emotion regulation* (pp. 3–24). New York, NY: Guilford Press.

Tringone, R., Millon, T., & Kamp, J. (2007). Clinical utility of two child-oriented inventories: The Millon Pre-Adolescent Clinical Inventory and the Millon Adolescent Clinical Inventory. In S. Smith & L. Handler (Eds.), *The clinical assessment of children and adolescents* (pp. 269–287). New York, NY: Psychology Press.

U.S. Public Health Service. (2000). *Report of the Surgeon General's Conference on Children's Mental Health: A National action agenda.* Washington, DC: Department of Health and Human Services.

Viglione, D., & Hilsenroth, M. (2001). The Rorschach: Facts, fictions and future. *Psychological Assessment, 13,* 452–471.

Vuilleumier, P. (2005). How brains beware: Neural mechanisms of emotional attention. *Trends in Cognitive Sciences, 9,* 585–594.

Wagner, E. E. (1983). *The Hand Test manual* (rev. ed.). Los Angeles, CA: Western Psychological Services.

Weiner, I. B. (2000). Making Rorschach interpretation as good as it can be. *Journal of Personality Assessment, 74,* 164–174.

Weist, M. D., Rubin, M., Moore, E., Adelsheim, S., & Wrobel, G. (2007). Mental health screening in schools. *Journal of School Health, 77*(2), 53–58.

Whalen, P., Rauch, S., Etcoff, N., McInerney, S., Lee, M., & Jenike, M. (1998). Masked presentations of emotional facial expression modulate amygdala activity without explicit knowledge. *Journal of Neuroscience, 18,* 411–418.

Winkielman, P., & Cacioppo, J. (2001). Mind at ease puts a smile on the face: Psychophysiological evidence that processing facilitation elicits positive affect. *Journal of Personality and Social Psychology, 81,* 989–1000.

Wood, J., Nezworski, M., Garb, H., & Lilienfeld, S. (2001). The misperception of psychopathology: Problems with the norms of the comprehensive system for the Rorschach. *Clinical Psychology: Science and Practice, 8,* 350–373.

Wood, J., Nezworski, M., & Stejkal, W. (1996). The comprehensive system for the Rorschach: A critical examination. *Psychological Science, 7,* 3–10.

9 Putting It All Together
Feedback and the Report as a Therapeutic Intervention

The feedback to parents and the report represent the most important steps in the entire evaluation process. The child's parents are the critical link between the information gathered about the child and how that information will be used. Unless the parents have an in-depth understanding of the findings and how the results can be applied, they will not be able to function in the most effective manner as their child's advocates. Therefore, the information must be presented in a clear and comprehensible manner that not only informs the parents about their child but also is conducted in a way that the most important information is presented with sensitivity and compassion, so that the parents can receive it. Thus, the feedback, in particular, takes on the role of a therapeutic intervention that will position the parents to understand some of the underlying issues contributing to their child's cognitive, academic, behavioral, social and emotional profile. This is particularly relevant as it relates to the questions posed at the referral and intake, but it is critical in respect to how the parents can use the information to effect any necessary change in the child's world.

Joseph

Joseph was a nine-year-old third grader in public school. He was one of four very active boys in a minority family living in a predominately white community. His parents had been referred by the school's counselor who was strongly recommending that Joseph be evaluated. Despite some apparent academic strengths, Joseph was struggling with a number of executive functions, behavior and social difficulties that were very concerning to his teachers. Repeated efforts on the part of teachers, counselors and the principal to engage parents in a discussion had been rebuffed by Joseph's father. Although his mother shared some of those concerns, her relationship with her husband and his insistence that it was the school's problem and was racially motivated, made her feel that she was in the middle and made it very difficult for her to act. After a number of phone conversations and a meeting with his mother, in which I explained the process and emphasized my independence from the school, she was able to talk to her husband and have him agree to allow Joseph to be tested. Over the course of the evaluation, I was able to reinforce the relationship that I had initially made with his mother. It also helped that Joseph and I made a strong connection that was evident to her.

Joseph's mother attended the feedback session alone. I reviewed the results with her and, as I did so, she was able to reflect on how what I had observed and how the information I shared was consistent with her experience with Joseph. What was further confirming to her was that the profile of the boy I described was also congruent with two of her older children, who shared many of the difficulties that Joseph was encountering. This was particularly relevant because the struggles that both of her older boys were experiencing had not been identified and addressed, and now, in high school, they were engaging in increasingly antisocial behaviors. Just the week before, the oldest had been suspended for the second time in as many months due to his impulsive acting out and aggressive behavior. She was able to reflect at some length on how her concerns about each of her three oldest children were reflected in their similar behaviors and how these behaviors were negatively impacting their academic and social progress. She felt that she had to act but was worried about her husband's reaction. We discussed at length the various options for intervention that included accommodations within the school environment as well as medication options. It was emphasized that medication was only one option and that, independent of issues related to race, it was one that had the potential to aide both Joseph's endeavors and the school's efforts to support him. It also helped that I was able to share personal experiences in helping a wide variety of children whose profile was similar to Joseph's. With this information and sense of trust in the relationship we had established, she felt more confident that she could speak with her husband and present the various options for intervention. I also encouraged her to suggest to her husband that we all meet together.

Joseph's father did not elect to meet with me. However, his mother was able to speak with Joseph's father and present the findings with confidence. He read the report and agreed to begin the accommodations as well as a trial of medication. The relationship between the parents and school improved, and the father became more involved. With the implementation of the recommendations from the report in respect to classroom modifications, as well as beginning some stimulant medication, Joseph was better able to manage his impulsive behaviors and began to feel better in both the classroom and at home.

The Feedback Session

In 2007, Ellen Braaten, a neuropsychologist at Massachusetts General Hospital, wrote a paper about the feedback to parents of psychological test results (Braaten, 2007). At that time, she noted that there were no published studies on how to best provide feedback and a search of the current literature suggests that it is still true today. However, she did cite studies from the medical field of pediatrics that have examined effective communication between professionals and parents as well as parent preferences in how to communicate information. In one study, in which parents were interviewed about their preferences for being given difficult information about their child (Krahn, Hallum, & Kime, 1993), the following themes that they identified also appear to be relevant for the feedback of neuropsychological findings. They noted that information should be given as follows:

- Clearly with detail and certainty, and including positive characteristics of the child
- With specific information on specialty referrals, services, and support
- By individual/professional who is familiar to them and who knows their child
- With compassion and caring
- At a pace they can follow, including opportunity for them to be actively involved (e.g. through asking questions, reviewing child's features)
- In a place that is private, quiet and free from distraction
- As soon as problems are suspected
- When they are together or have other support persons present. (p. 581)

These recommendations were similar to those in a more recent study assessing the delivery of difficult news to neurological patients and their families (Storstein, 2011). Using the information from the Krahn et al. (1993) study as a guideline, Braaten (2007) extrapolated and suggested the following recommendations for providing feedback of personality assessments:

1. Parents should be informed of the results in the context of a clinician-patient relationship that is built on a sense of trust and support and a genuine sense of caring.
2. There are no clear guidelines as to whether it is most important for parents to receive the written report before or after the feedback session, and, thus, clinicians should rely on their clinical judgment in deciding what would be most helpful for a particular family.
3. In a two-parent family, it is ideal to have both parents present for the feedback session. In one-parent households, the parents should be invited to have a supportive adult present if they so choose.
4. Before the feedback session, the professional should identify the most important information that needs to be conveyed. This information should be conveyed early in the session in a manner that is brief, sensitive, and direct. . . . Attention to the parents' cognitive and emotional reactions is important in determining where to go next.
5. The results should acknowledge the child's strengths and positive personal characteristics, as well as limitations, and simple, direct language with as little psychological jargon as possible.
6. The professional should be empathic and supportive of the parents' emotional reactions. . . . Conversely, it is also important to keep the focus of the session on the child.
7. Answer questions directly and do not be afraid to say "I don't know" when there is no clear answer.

8. Parents should be informed of the findings in their own language and should be able to ask questions in their own language. The clinician should attempt to understand the family's cultural views about diagnosis and treatment.

9. Conclude the session with a discussion of plans for the future and recommendations. Make arrangements for further therapeutic and educational services. (p. 82)

In my practice (D. R.), the feedback session nearly always takes place within two weeks of the testing's completion. An hour and a half to two hours is scheduled, usually on the same day of the week that the last tests have been administered. Every effort is made to be sure that, if a child has two or more parents, all can attend. Very often, the child's therapist as well as other significant caretakers are included at the discretion of the parents. In some cases, for older children, the child is included in the feedback with the parents or, if both parents and child prefer, the parents and the child are seen separately. In each case, the presentation of the findings is shaped to the configuration of the participants. I always arrange the feedback prior to sharing the report, as I strongly believe that the information should be shared first within the context of the relationships. Furthermore, I believe that the report should reflect information provided by the parents about the data shared with them in the feedback session. The following section describes the typical feedback provided to one or more parents. It generally follows the outline we have presented in the book, with cognitive, executive functioning, memory, visual motor, academic, behavioral, social and emotional domains discussed.

Relationship

The status of the relationship between me and the parent(s) at the time of the feedback is predicated on our experience together throughout the evaluation process. This has included an appreciation of the relationship both parents and I have with the referral source, conversations between parents and me on the phone, the intake meeting and contact over the course of the two or more testing sessions. One or both parents have had a chance to interact by providing confidential, intimate information, asking questions observing the interaction between me and their child and receiving feedback from their child about his or her experience with me during the evaluation. By the time we meet to discuss the results, hopefully, a relationship has evolved that is based on trust and some level of comfort. Also, hopefully, there is the understanding that our discussion is being conducted with the best interests of the child in mind, both on my part as well as on theirs. In this manner, by the time we sit down together, a "holding environment" (see Chapter 10) has been constructed that is based on the relationship between me and parents that is, an environment in which parents feel held in the relationship we have established and both the child's and parents' interests and needs are being seen and respected by me. This is not necessarily an easy task, as there are times when the interests and needs of the child do not always match those of the parents or, when there is divisiveness between parents who are functioning as a couple or who are separate and have separate perspectives o agendas. In the case of the latter, it is always essential to appeal to their overarching interest in what is best for their child. Nevertheless, it often requires the ability to draw on the resources accrued over my thirty or more years of clinical experience with children and families within a therapeutic context in order to bring parents together to not only process the information presented to them but also develop a plan to best use that information.

Because feedback is such a critical element in the evaluation process, it is imperative that information of a nature this complex and sensitive be delivered with a mixture of genuine compassion and clinical distance. While not every neuropsychologist comes to evaluations of this sort with any significant clinical experience, it is, nonetheless, an important skill that can make a profound difference in the way that parents are able to receive and assimilate the information being shared. Training in therapeutic approaches and family dynamics as well as clinical supervision with an emphasis on self-awareness should be a part of the neuropsychologist's training, and every opportunity to hone these skills should be seized.

Overview and Observations

The feedback session begins by quickly reviewing the presenting questions and the overall arc of the testing process, including the broad areas of cognitive and emotional functioning that were evaluated. The parents are provided with paper and pen if they wish to take notes or, in some cases, have brought along a laptop or electronic notepad to record data. They are encouraged to consider the presentation of the information as a dialogue rather than a monologue and are invited to ask questions or comment as we proceed, particularly in respect to the latter as to whether or not they have observed something similar to what I am describing.

The discussion about specific information related to their child starts with some observations about the child's behavior throughout the testing. This is done to provide a qualitative sense of the child and frame the upcoming quantitative information within the context of some real experience. During this portion, both vulnerabilities and strengths are described. For example, as discussed in Chapter 2, a child's unusual behaviors, enthusiasm or lack of enthusiasm for the overall process or specific areas of testing, as well as their ability to sustain attention, filter distractions, regulate activity, tolerate frustration, etc. are presented. In addition, particular strengths are also described, such as the ability of the child to relate their sense of humor or particular strategies they employed. It is not unusual, during this process, that parents begin to identify characteristics or behaviors that they experience in relation to their child. This, very frequently, reassures parents as well as me that, on some level, I have seen and understood the child that they know. This is particularly poignant when one or both parents emotionally express relief that their perceptions have not been imagined, especially in the far too frequent case that the feedback from school has been such that it has made them feel that they were making things up or were just bad parents. Once again, the blind men and the elephant metaphor is pertinent. Often a child, particularly if they are very socially conscious or, if they require a certain level of structure, can present very differently at school and home. The testing situation provides a unique opportunity to carefully observe a child and his or her response to various demands and, considering reports from both environments, allows the evaluator to see the whole picture and validate and explain the probable reason that both experiences can pertain. This is a perspective that is not necessarily afforded either the parents or teachers.

Cognitive Functioning

What follows then, is a presentation of the quantitative findings, beginning with the results of the tests of cognitive functioning and proceeding in the order we've followed in this book. Throughout this process, each subtest or test is described, and the relevance of the information for the child's experience is explained. Furthermore, when presenting the results from each test, I find it is helpful both to give parents examples of their child's responses and also to invite them to answer some of the questions. For example, I might ask them to take a turn answering some of the problems on the Matrix Reasoning subtest of the *Wechsler Intelligence Scale for Children–Fourth Edition* (WISC-IV; Wechsler, 2003) or describe how they might approach drawing the Copy portion of the *Rey-Osterrieth Complex Figure*. In this manner, parents not only are given a window into what their child experienced but also have the experience of reasoning through a problem them-selves. Quite often this allows them to identify what is easy or difficult for them and relate it to what is easy or difficult for their child. It also often points out differences between each parent. In this manner, parents begin to relate to and empathize with the relative strengths and vulnerabilities their child is experiencing and appreciate the struggle their child may be having. Most often this is done with good humor and, depending on the relationship between the parents, allows each to identify traits in him- or herself and his or her spouse in both a sympathetic and playful manner. Of course, if there is significant tension between parents, then this process has to be modified and some therapy under-taken to keep each parent focused on the child and not to begin to blame each other. But care is taken to distribute evenly the sense of the child's strengths and vulnerabilities between the parents. There are times, however, when, because of factors that have sig-nificantly impaired a child's functioning, there is little in these findings to which a parent can relate. In such cases, of course, one must be much more thoughtful and sensitive to the reactions of the parent, carefully reading their verbal and nonverbal responses and adjusting accordingly. It is also critical that one carefully assess parents' level of compre-hension and learning style so that they are presented with the information in a manner they can understand. For example, visual learners appreciate seeing the two-dimensional pictures on the Block Design subtest when that test is explained or to see how their child failed to cross the midline on one of the figures on the *Beery-Buktenica Developmental Test of Visual-Motor Integration*. By presenting what constitutes a large volume of often very complex information in more of a multisensory format, it also increases the likeli-hood that the data will be rooted in an experiential as well as abstract modality and therefore, better retained.

Behavioral, Social and Emotional Functioning

Upon completion of the discussion of the cognitive functioning domain, the feedback transitions into results from tests of behavioral, social and emotional functioning. There is a brief review of any of the referral questions, and findings from parent and teacher reports are presented. For example, parents are given a copy of the *Behavior Assessment System for Children, Second Edition* (BASC-2; Kamphaus et al., 2007) results in the form of a table that outlines the composites and scales from the parent and teacher report and, when appropriate, the self-report. This is an opportunity to discuss what each composite and scale represents and to consider the similarities or differences between what the parent(s) see(s) at home and what the teacher(s) report(s) from school. It is always interesting when there is significant overlap between the parent and teacher scales reaching significance. This suggests that the child's behavior, social and emotional functioning is consistent across environments. More often, however, there are significant differences and while, at times, the differences are not unexpected, quite often parents are taken aback by disparities between the parent and teacher report. The difference in reports and the response of the parent to this information reflects the efficacy of communication between home and school. As such, it is not only diagnostic but portends something about how results from the evaluation might be received, either on the part of the parent or the school. Furthermore, while there are internal scales on the BASC-2, for example, to discriminate a particular bias on the part of either the parent or teacher, it is always important to be aware of potential bias in either the direction of minimizing or maximizing certain concerns on the part of either parent or teacher that may not be picked up by the instrument.

When examining the results on the self-report scales, parents are given insight into their child's perspective about his or her own functioning. Again, it is always important to compare the child's responses with the results from both the parent and teacher reports. It is not unusual to see a number of scales reaching clinical significance on the latter reports while the child's scales are all average. Findings of this sort suggest that either the child is working hard to cover up some dysfunction and has answered the questionnaire dishonestly or is unconscious of the way his or her behavior is perceived by others due to a lack of self-awareness. Once again, the similarities and differences between child, parent and teacher are considered. The parents are also cautioned that what the child reports, when different from what the parent has reported, may reflect more of what the child is feeling about his or her experience rather than what others may observe and take as objective fact.

At this point, any tests related to social functioning are discussed. These are particularly relevant if there have been questions regarding social pragmatic skills and whether or not a child might be considered to fall somewhere on the autistic spectrum. For example, ruling out a diagnosis of Asperger's (as defined previously in the *Diagnostic and Statistical Manual of Mental Disorders, Fourth Edition, Text Revision* [DSM-IV-TR, American Psychiatric Association, 2000]) might entail not only careful observation of the child's interaction with me, but also results from scales on the BASC-2 as well as a few of the subtests on the *Developmental Neuropsychological Assessment* (NEPSY-II; Korkman et al., 2007) that assess the ability to identify affect or test Theory of Mind. Furthermore, the child's response to the Rorschach and projective tests are factored into this equation.

The results from the battery of tests assessing emotional functioning are then discussed. These results are introduced by first reviewing the results from the previous sections and summarizing the relative strengths and vulnerabilities that were identified from those assessments. The results from the emotional functioning battery are then framed within the context of any underlying neurological issues. The relationship between those underlying issues and the child's behavioral and emotional response to them, as well as the way in which any emotional issues may be impacting the child's neurological functioning, are considered. This includes the child's responses to their varied environments and therefore

Figure 9.1 Family drawing. Sometimes the feedback helps establish better understanding between family members.

takes into account the academic, social and relational milieu of the school environment as well as factors related to the family dynamic. Thus, the cognitive/emotional factors and their interrelationship are described, and examples from the child's responses on the variety of tests are presented as a way to underscore and support the interpretation of the results. This portion of the feedback is usually the most relevant, as it synthesizes all of the findings from the evaluation. In doing so, it creates a narrative that attempts to explain not only the child's strengths and vulnerabilities but also the ways in which the child has either adapted and accommodated the demands of the environment, usually at some significant cost, or has failed to do so and is acting out his or her considerable distress.

Synthesis and Reflection

Throughout this process, parents have been asking questions and offering their observations about the relationship between their experience with their child and the result being presented. The last section, synthesizing all of the findings, is particularly germane and leads to more protracted reflections on the part of the parent. Most often, there is a nearly palpable sense of relief that the narrative describes the child that they know very well but have not had the means to describe in this particular way. Parents frequently explain that there are no real surprises in what has been presented but report more of a sense that their experience has been confirmed and articulated in a manner that is helpful. There are times, however, when certain aspects of the formulation are unexpected and unfamiliar. Some parents greet this information with an open mind while others resist such an interpretation. In the latter case, parents are encouraged to reflect on the information being provided and consider whether or not it might actually describe facets of their child of which they had been unaware and, which, with careful observation or through a more protracted inquiry, might prove to be significant. Parents are also informed that the particular aspect may have been an artifact of the evaluation process. However, drawing any particular conclusion from one aspect of the testing is not done, and any overall conclusion or interpretation comes from the weaving together of a variety of threads taken from the results of a battery of tests and reports. In this manner, one is not left hanging from a thread that does not fit into the overall picture. Therefore, disagreements about the overall interpretation are rare, but the fact that a particular score or response may not accurately reflect a particular child's ability is always a possibility and must be accounted for. In this manner, a parent's feedback is always considered and taken into account.

Recommendations and Referrals

The discussion then turns to a consideration of what the findings mean for the child and his or her family. The recommendations are discussed in the context of what can be done in the school environment and what can be done at home. In addition, it is at this point that any recommendations for further testing or therapies are considered. For example, if there is a finding of some neurological issues, such as a seizure disorder or unaccounted for tremor, a neurological consult is recommended and a referral is made for a possible EEG or MRI. Other recommendations might include consultation with an occupational therapist to evaluate sensory processing issues, a physical therapist to assess functional motor abilities, an audiologist to determine if there is an auditory processing disorder, a speech and language therapist to test receptive and expressive language skills or a technology specialist to focus in on any particular technological supports. Other recommendations might include the suggestion that parents enlist the help of an executive function tutor who can teach the child specific strategies to circumvent, for example, difficulties with organization. There are times when medication might be appropriate and a referral to a psychiatrist or psychopharmacologist is made. Often, given the complexities of the children I tend to evaluate, I will recommend an individual psychotherapy that may be based in a play or narrative therapy or some combination of both, depending on the child's age. This can be done with a psychiatrist, psychologist, social worker, expressive therapist or licensed mental health counselor. The major factor determining the recommendation of one over the other is related to a sense of who would be the best match for that particular child in terms of personality, style and specific therapeutic approach.

The Report

The report is completed and sent off to the parents within a reasonable amount of time. My goal is always to send out the report within four weeks after the completion of testing. The report includes a section on the birth, developmental, medical, extended family and academic histories, as well as a summary of the results of any previous evaluations. It also includes a statement about the referral and a summary of the questions and concerns posed by the parents as well as teachers. A list of the testing instruments that were administered then follows. The format of the report then proceeds along the same line as the one detailed in this book, beginning with results from tests of cognitive, visual motor, executive, memory and academic functioning and continuing through the behavioral, social and emotional domains to arrive at a narrative that integrates all of the findings and provides a picture of the whole child. There then follows a summary section that reiterates the key findings and again synthesizes all of the data in a condensed form. The report includes all of the information covered in the feedback session while considering and taking into account the discussion held with the parents during the feedback. It does not include any new information that was not discussed.

Given the population of children I tend to evaluate, the complexity of their issues does not always lend itself to a clear diagnosis. While I prefer to avoid diagnostic categories and instead provide a detailed description of the complex interplay of various domains, at times it is in the best interest of the child and parents to give a diagnosis. This often supports parental efforts to acquire services for their child and, at times, gives the caretakers a framework in which to organize support. However, it must be said that the DSM categories are not always adequate when attempting to describe a child with complex, neurologically based issues that interrelate with social, behavioral and emotional issues in a very complicated manner.

The Report and the Child

Parents are encouraged to check back in once they have received the report. This provides a venue with which they can request clarification, correction of typos or ask questions about specific recommendations. Often, at this point, a parent will ask me to meet with their child to give him or her a summary of the results, in developmentally appropriate terms. Within the framework of his or her experience of testing, certain vulnerabilities are discussed and placed in the context of the his or her strengths. For example, a child's experience of having difficulty doing math might be acknowledged as an area of vulnerability and explained in respect to their problems organizing number sequences in their head. At the same time, their use of language as a particular strength can be emphasized and the ways that strength can be used to circumvent their math problems can be discussed. Further discussion of how certain challenges make them feel can also be considered. The overall message, however, is one that acknowledges vulnerabilities, strengths and feelings while giving the child a sense that with this understanding, parents and teachers will be able to better support their learning style so that they can feel successful and better about themselves. If appropriate, the child can also be directed toward discussing these issues with his or her therapist so that this topic can be considered over a longer period and within the context of an ongoing, trusting relationship. This is particularly true for older preadolescents and adolescents.

The Report and the School

Once parents are comfortable with the report as a finished document, they are free to do with it whatever they feel is in the best interest of their child. However, in some cases, a parent will request that the report be divided into two sections; one for the school and one for the child's therapist. In the case of the former, given the particular relationship the family has with the school, certain information would not necessarily be appropriate to share with the latter. For example, in a complete neuropsychological evaluation of an adolescent girl with an eating disorder and sexualized behavior, parents requested that details of the psychological evaluation related to those issues not be shared with

Figure 9.2 Student drawing of a school building.

the school, a small setting with a history of poor boundaries and no adequate services that would enable them to implement supports of an emotional nature. In that case, I provided a report to the parents that they then gave to the school that focused on the cognitive issues while the parents shared the complete report with the girl's therapist and medical providers. In some cases, however, such as when the child's well-being or the well-being of others is in question and this has a bearing on school, I will strongly encourage parents to share the entire report, emphasizing the need for services within a broad context. If it is a matter of safety, as a designated reporter, I will notify the proper individuals to ensure the safety of the child or another.

If parents decide to share the report with school administration, the school is then obligated to call a meeting to review the results and determine whether or not any services are appropriate to address the issues raised in the report. Parents will often request that I attend this meeting to discuss the results and recommendations, particularly if they feel that the school administration may not understand the findings or may be resistant to implement interventions that would address the child's challenges. These issues will be explored in the following chapters.

Charles

We return now to eleven-year-old Charles. The feedback session was conducted with Charles' parents and the therapist working with the family. The overall findings came as no surprise, but the parents were very thankful to learn about Charles's very significant strengths as well as the underlying causes of his increasing difficulty and resistance to certain academic tasks. Of particular importance was their ability to appreciate the impact that the family dynamic was having on Charles in respect to his father's ongoing medical issues and his increasingly difficult relationship with his mother within the context of their academic work. The need for Charles to be gradually reintroduced to resources outside of the home was stressed and, with the therapist, a plan was discussed. Both parents received the information with considerable emotion, displaying a mixture of sadness, relief and renewed determination. The presence of the therapist was extremely helpful in that it not only allowed her to ingest and process the information with the parents during the session but also provided a foundation for the work to continue in their subsequent meetings. The following section is taken from his report and summarizes the findings, and lists the recommendations that were felt to pertain to those goals.

Summary and Recommendations

Charles is an eleven-year-old, right-handed boy who recently completed the fifth grade and who is home schooled. Charles has a protracted history of school phobia and anxiety. The current evaluation was sought by

Charles's parents and his public school and at the recommendation of Charles's current therapist to address the concerns they continue to have regarding Charles's severe school phobia, separation and general anxiety and possible learning issues. Parents report that in addition to his fears, Charles has increasingly had difficulty with academics at home. Family history is significant for anxiety, depression and significant medical issues.

Because of his anxiety, testing with Charles was conducted in his home and under very unusual circumstances that necessitated the participation of his older sister. With many accommodations in place, Charles was able to cooperate and made considerable effort, oftentimes taking a perfectionistic approach to materials. He exhibited some motor overflow in the form of leg movements and fidgeting. This increased activity also appeared to be correlated with an increased level of anxiety in response to more challenging materials. Overall, he was engaged with the materials and became more comfortable with my presence. Therefore, the results from the current testing, with the previously mentioned caveats, are felt to be an accurate picture of his cognitive and emotional functioning at this time.

Charles's current level of cognitive functioning was assessed with the WISC-IV. Charles's verbal abilities fell in the Superior range, and his perceptual organizational abilities fell at the upper end of the High Average range. His working memory was in the Average range while his processing speed was at the low end of the Average range. These scores were not significantly different from results obtained on his previous evaluation from second grade. There was no significant difference between the Verbal Comprehension Index and the Perceptual Reasoning Index, suggesting that Charles's verbal and perceptual skills are commensurate. Both his Verbal Comprehension and Perceptual Reasoning Indices were significantly higher than his Working Memory and Processing Speed Indices, however, suggesting that both his verbal and nonverbal skills are strengths relative to both his ability to hold auditory information in his head when required to perform some operation as well as his ability to execute graphomotor tasks and sustain visual attention in a timely manner.

In respect to verbal functioning, Charles displayed a strong ability to reason abstractly when familiar with the material, but when unsure of an answer tended to fall back on a more experientially based and exhaustive approach. When provided with a more structured format, he was able to be both concise and precise. When questions were more open ended, he tended to become more experiential and idiosyncratic in a way that sometimes altered the meaning of the question and reflected the intrusion of emotional material.

Test of visuospatial organization and motor functioning indicated that Charles demonstrates above average skills in the processing of visuospatial information. He is able to integrate part to whole relationships when he can break down visual complexity into more manageable parts but has relative difficulty consolidating and recalling the underlying organizational structure of complex visual details. He also demonstrates a relative vulnerability in fine motor functioning that impacts his graphomotor skills. Furthermore, the discrepancy between his superior verbal skills and below average processing speed may lead to some frustration with extended written assignments.

Regarding attention, working memory and executive functioning, results indicate that Charles has a vulnerability in executive functioning skills related to organizing, planning, filtering distractions, inhibiting responses, switching set and consistently self-monitoring. While he also has difficulty sustaining attention, he does have the ability to rally and deploy his attention more effectively when he is challenged. On tasks of working memory, his ability to hold information on line while performing operations upon it is at least in the average range but is vulnerable to his variable attention.

Results from tests of memory on the *California Verbal Learning Test–Children's Version* (CVLT-C; Delis et al., 1994) and the *Wide Range Assessment of Memory and Learning–Second Edition* (WRAML-2; Adams & Sheslow, 2003)) suggest that Charles demonstrates average to superior recall of verbal information but has difficulty self-monitoring his performance and does best when verbal information is organized into more meaningful contexts. His recall of visual information is relatively weaker when he is required to recall information that is more visually complex and cannot be organized into chunks.

Regarding academic achievement, results from the *Woodcock-Johnson III Tests of Achievement* (WJ III-ACH; Woodcock, McGrew, & Mather, 2001) indicate that Charles's academic skills are superior while his fluency with academic tasks and his ability to apply academic skills are high average. His broad reading skills are superior while his broad mathematics, math calculation and broad written language skills are high average. His written expression skills are average.

Results from the BASC-2 reflect significant parental concerns regarding Charles's anxiety, depression, somatization, withdrawal and adaptability. In addition, his mother, in her role as his teacher, reports that within the context of his academic functioning, additional concerns are related to his anger control, emotional self-control, negative emotionality and resiliency. Charles's responses on the self-report questionnaire suggest that he is actively avoiding an awareness of the extent to which his functioning has been compromised.

Lastly, regarding emotional functioning, Charles demonstrates good reality testing abilities but is experiencing a chronic degree of overload in the form of emotional stress and anxiety, for which he has inadequate psychological resources to cope. Much of this affective overload is based on his reaction to his father's ongoing medical issues. In addition, he demonstrates a constellation of learning vulnerabilities that, over the years, have begun to impinge increasingly on his self-image. At this point, he is actively avoiding an awareness of his affective and learning vulnerabilities and is, instead, attempting to exert control over his environment by narrowing his experience and using his family to buffer the demands of the outside world, thereby maintaining his facade of competence. Nevertheless, his outlook both for himself and his family is extremely negative, and he is quite vulnerable to depression.

In light of these findings, the following recommendations are made:

1 Regarding school programs:

- Parents are encouraged to review the results of this assessment with Charles. It would be helpful for him to appreciate his considerable strengths and to understand his vulnerabilities within the context of these strengths. Being very specific about both his vulnerabilities and strengths would potentially help him develop a more balanced perception of himself and begin to address some of his anxiety about his academic performance.

- Charles eventually will need to transition into a therapeutic school program with a low student-to-teacher ratio and one in which teachers are trained to understand and work with students demonstrating his emotional, behavioral, sensory and learning profile. He should be placed in a small classroom setting with peers at a similar cognitive level and that can accommodate his learning style. A strong therapeutic component will be necessary that includes individual, group and family therapies as a means to deal with his anxiety related to both school and home.

- Until such a placement is possible, Charles would benefit from the provision of a home tutor who can assume the responsibility for his education and relieve his parents of that role. A tutor who is experienced in accommodating curriculum and who is therapeutically trained would have the best chance of establishing and maintaining a productive relationship with Charles. This tutor would need to meet on a weekly basis with a supervisor experienced in both educational and therapeutic approaches.

- The discrepancy between the rate at which Charles can process language and the rate at which he can organize output, as measured by processing speed, is significant. Children with a difference between these areas are often aware of and frustrated with the difficulty they experience getting their thoughts down on paper. Thus, modifications should be in place so that Charles doesn't experience the degree of frustration that he likely has been experiencing. Modifications would include expectations regarding volume of output. Homework modified ahead of time in its amount of written material, clear deadlines and additional time for projects and the use of a computer would all be potentially helpful.

- Charles would benefit from the use of a computer with graphic organizer software to complete written assignments of any length. A program such as Inspiration would enable him to circumvent his graphomotor weakness while also helping him to more easily edit his work. In addition, such a program could provide the scaffolding and organizational support that he needs, enabling him to more easily provide details and interrelate them.
- Additional time to process might help Charles in consolidating and recalling complex visual or inferential information as a means to better integrate part-to-whole relationships. He may require extended time on tests and in-class assignments that demand a significant amount of writing.
- Charles will need support in the development of organizational skills. Particularly, as the demands of school increase regarding independence, he may need explicit strategies to organize his homework and use of time. He may also need support in understanding and maintaining organizational sets, i.e., keeping his eye on the bigger picture and understanding how the details fit into the "big picture." The teaching of these organizational strategies would be done with the goal of Charles becoming an independent learner.
- Specific organizational strategies that would support Charles's progress as an independent learner would include 1) previewing of material, 2) the development of frameworks into which material can be organized to prevent him from losing set or the "big picture," 3) learning to structure new learning and problem solving, 4) learning to rehearse material verbally and 5) learning to develop a summary of expectations of written work.

2 Regarding therapeutic services:

- Charles would benefit from continued individual psychotherapy. He will need ongoing support to better understand his processing style and develop better coping strategies as a means to deal with his anxiety about not knowing. This therapy could also address his self-image to help him gain a better understanding of himself and his relative strengths and vulnerabilities. He will also require considerable support in better understanding his role within his family as well as developing better coping strategies to deal with his anxiety about his father.
- Charles's parents will continue to require consultation to help them in their ongoing efforts to support Charles, both with his learning vulnerabilities as well as his anxiety and more general emotional development.

References

Adams, W., & Sheslow, D. (2003). WRAML2: Wide Range Assessment of Memory and Learning (2nd ed.). Wilmington, DE: Wide Range.

American Psychiatric Association. (2012). *Diagnostic and Statistical Manual of Mental Disorders* (4th rev. ed.). Arlington, VA: APA.

Braaten, E. (2007) Personality assessment feedback with parents. In S. Smith & L. Handler (Eds.), *The clinical assessment of children and adolescents* (pp. 73–83). New York, NY: Psychology Press.

Delis, D. C., Kramer, J. H., Kaplan, E., & Ober, B. A. (1994). *California Verbal Learning Test— Children's Version*. San Antonio, TX: Psychological Corporation.

Kamphaus, R. W., VanDeventer, M. C., Brueggemann, A., & Barry, M. (2007). Behavior Assessment System for Children (2nd Ed.). In S.R. Smith & L. Handler. (2007). *The clinical assessment of children and adolescents: A practitioner's handbook* (pp. 311–326). New York, NY: Psychology Press, Taylor and Francis Group.

Korkman, M., Kirk, U., & Kemp, S. (2007). *NEPSY-II: A developmental neuropsychological assessment*. San Antonio, TX: The Psychological Corporation.

Krahn, G. L., Hallum, A., & Kime, C. (1993). Are there good ways to give "bad news"? *Pediatrics, 91*(3), 578.

Storstein, A. A. (2011). Communication and neurology—Bad news and how to break them. *Acta Neurologica Scandinavica, 191*, 5–11.

Wechsler, D. (2003). *Wechsler Intelligence Scale for Children* (4th Ed.). San Antonio, TX: The Psychological Corporation.

Woodcock, R. W., McGrew, K. S., & Mather, N. (2001). *Woodcock-Johnson III Tests of Achievement*. Itasca, IL: Riverside Publishing.

10 Putting It Into Action

Translating Evaluation Results Into the Classroom and Home

Winnicott (b. 1896, d. 1971), a pediatrician and psychoanalyst, studied development in children beginning in 1923. Over the course of his career, he derived several concepts relevant to the emotional and cognitive development of children. First, he believed in the natural unfolding of the developmental process. That "every human being, given a facilitating environment, intrinsically contains the momentum for growth towards emotional as well as physical maturity, and towards a positive contribution to society" (Davis & Wallbridge, 1981, p. 5). Second, he noted that unfolding occurs in the context of the relationship with a primary caregiver. Winnicott recognized that each infant or child interacts within the environment in unique ways, and that the mother (or primary caregiver) moderates the environment or provides care so the infant or child is able to mature and grow in his or her own process of development. Winnicott noted the tremendous work and self-sacrifice of caring for an infant and raising children. As such, it is impossible for any mother to be perfect, but she can be a "good-enough mother." In other words, the primary caregiver attunes to the unique needs of the developing child, providing environmental support that is "good-enough" to facilitate the natural unfolding of a child (Reinstein, 2006).

The "good-enough mother" and infant exist in a relational space. Within the context of this relationship the infant grows and develops, and a carefully attuned caregiver meets the changing demands of the child's developing systems. This space, in which the child's needs are met by a caregiver who is carefully, although imperfectly, watching, Winnicott called the "holding" environment. At times, meeting the needs of a child requires physical holding, close contact and soothing. At other times, it is the metaphorical holding in mind, remembering what an individual child requires in order to thrive. This includes protecting the child from harm, being aware of sensory needs, participating in the daily routines and ongoing flexibility as the child matures and needs or situations change. As the infant grows, physical, emotional and psychological needs are met through this relationship. Slowly, more space develops between the caregiver and infant as the child learns to crawl, then walk, then travel across a room or playground, then to school and so on. This holding environment becomes internalized within the child as they move into the world, making it possible for them to feel safe, trust in him- or herself, and in essence "hold" themselves (Reinstein, 2006; Winnicott, 1965).

John Bowlby (b. 1907, d. 1990), similarly to Winnicott, focused on the relationship between caregiver and child in his study of the child's emotional development and described this process within the context of attachment (Bowlby, 1988). In 1951, influenced by Konrad Lorenz's (Crain, 2000) work with imprinting, Bowlby conceptualized that human attachment is instinctual and expressed through the behavior of the infant and the response of the primary caregiver. He proposed that certain behaviors—crying, calling, smiling, clinging—were instinctual means to maintain proximity of a caregiver. By doing so, the infants or children ensure that, while they are incapable of coping with stressors of the environment or their own body, a more capable person is available to do so. Through the relationship with a primary caregiver, the child can experience safety and the freedom to develop and explore. Ultimately, the internalization of the relationship ensures that children will be able to participate in other relationships and cope in the world. The caregiver is also rewarded emotionally through the growth of the child, as he or she gains successful independence. Attachment theory has been further developed and researched by Mary Ainsworth, Mary Main and many others (Bowlby, 1988; Reinstein, 2006).

Children impacted by developmental difficulties may have particularly unique styles of attaching and relating to their caregivers. In turn, the caregiver may be confused by their behavior and, unsure of an appropriate response, may feel inadequate, useless or scared. Some parents have prior knowledge regarding development and are able to utilize resources, ask for help and navigate the educational system. Even then, they can experience significant stress. For many, the prospect of caring for and relating to a child with neuropsychological vulnerabilities is overwhelming, uncharted territory and does not align with their expectations of parenting.

In working with children with special needs, it is important to develop a holding environment that encompasses the parents or guardians, providing support and education. A complete neuropsychological evaluation provides a venue for the parents and teachers to learn about the unique attachment behaviors exhibited by these children. In this way, both parents, caregivers and the school setting can work together to construct a "child-world" system (Holmes-Bernstein & Weiler, 2000). In doing so, areas of environmental "match" or "mismatch" between the child's temperament, skill set and demands can be determined and altered. Armed with information provided by the evaluation, parents and educators can make alterations in the environment to promote compensatory strategies or respond to cognitive overload and lessen environmental demands. Under the framework of attachment theory, several types of interventions can be employed, including cognitive, behavioral, play therapy, psychotherapy, expressive therapies, speech and language therapy, occupational therapy and teaching styles.

Integration of the Evaluation Results and Intervention

Upon receiving a complete neuropsychological evaluation, parents and guardians participate in the feedback session. While informative, and discussed with therapeutic intention, the amount of information can be overwhelming, especially when coupled with their own emotional reaction to the information contained within the report. At the end of the report, the recommendation and referrals sections often includes a list of helpful intervention strategies or referral information to further help their child interact with the environment. While reading the evaluation results and participating in a compassionate conversation with the evaluator are excellent first steps to making necessary changes for success, implementing change can feel overwhelming or confusing. Often, ongoing support can be a crucial element for any family undertaking such a task.

Likewise, the final evaluation report is sent to the school (see Chapter 11 for further explanation) and discussed among the staff. While the report is comprehensive, and includes specific suggestions for change, the school may not have the resources (staff, personnel, technology, counseling support) to carry out the recommended changes for the classroom environment or in the delivery of curriculum. Teachers are often over-worked, underappreciated and pressed for time. The opportunity for reading the entirety of the report rarely presents itself.

For both parents and teachers, it is helpful to develop skills for reading the entire evalua-tion as a means for gathering the most relevant information for making integrative changes in the home or school environment. First is developing familiarity with the specific skills and functional domains discussed in the previous chapters of this book. Familiarity with the concepts, language and terms aids in quickly understanding the results of a complete neuropsychological evaluation. Second, developing a framework to extrapolate the most relevant pieces of information quickly clarifies areas of strengths to build upon, and poten-tial weakness that require support. While reading a neuropsychological evaluation, with the intention of using the information within to develop treatment plans, alter curricu-lum or modify the home environment, it can be helpful to take notes. Generating two columns, one to record information related to general cognitive functioning (cognition, processing speed, working memory, executive function, visual motor integration, etc.) and another column related to emotional functioning. In this second column, notes can be made regarding the child's behavioral and emotional reactions that occur while complet-ing specific tasks (see the appendix). The process of developing a framework helps organize information. Of particular note, recording splits in cognitive functioning (high perceptual scores relative to lower verbal scores), the child's strengths and interests, highlights of the history, observations from the Mental Status Exam (MSE) and the level of behavioral con-sistency (or inconsistency) across environments are useful tools. Noting important infor-mation related to all elements of neuropsychological functioning, including emotional and behavioral, will help design interventions.

Once relative strengths and weaknesses have been identified, specific interventions can be developed. The delivery of the intervention can take place under the umbrella of attachment theory, in the context of the relationship developed between the caregivers, teachers and the child or adolescent. It is through the relationship that strengths and struggles are contextualized and the child or adolescent can experience support, under-standing and success. In other words, while they may feel or experience their vulner-abilities are defining characteristics preventing their participation in learning and play through the relationship they can come to terms with accepting their difficulties while developing strategies and ultimately experiencing acceptance.

Developing a Relationship

The first step to intervention is building a relationship. This can be challenging when working with children who have difficulty being in relationships. Both the child and the teachers, therapist or consultant approach each other with their own experience

Figure 10.1 Student drawing of teacher and children.

in relationships, self-concept and awareness of the need for change, which impacts the unfolding of a new relationship. The following list provides suggestions on how to take the first steps in developing a "holding" space within the relationship.

- Carefully attune to the emotional status of the child. Stress, confusion, fear or anger frequently may arise for him or her. Work with the child to problem solve and find a means for deescalation.
- Set clear boundaries and limits. Discuss the boundaries, in developmentally appropriate language, assuring the child that boundaries and limits are intended to be helpful and a sign of caring.
- Carefully pay attention to the child's interests, strengths and desires.
- Play with the child on a developmentally appropriate level. If the child has delayed play skills, meet the child at his or her level rather than attempting to play with them as one would with a typically developing child.
- Be consistent. Follow through on promises and expectations. This involves setting clear boundaries as to what is and is not appropriate in the context of a therapeutic relationship.
- Communicate as clearly as possible. The types of difficulties these children experience, due to processing difficulties, often involve an element of confusion or fear when navigating the environment. Clear language and communication plays a role in alleviating these feelings, creating a safe space.

- Use simplified language in a developmentally appropriate manner and narrate the play or the actions of each other. This begins a dialogue between two people, and assures the child you are paying attention to him or her.
- Play and have fun with the individual. Doing so begins the attunement process and develops reciprocity. Children generally want to please adults that engage in play, which develops a sense of motivation for taking active engagement in the therapeutic process.
- Know yourself well. Understand what behaviors in another individual may be difficult to tolerate or are triggers for frustration. This understanding will allow you to better self-regulate and develop a meaningful understanding of the unfolding relationship.

The Importance of Play and Humor

Heather was an eight-year-old girl, beginning the school year in a new classroom at a small therapeutic school. School refusal had been an increasing issue in her last school. Prior to her first full school day, she visited the classroom, allowing for the opportunity to meet her teachers and peers and ask questions about the classrooms and activities. The teachers and parents intentionally timed the visit to coincide with a quiet play time that occurred daily after lunch. The teacher greeted Heather and her mother at the school entrance and introduced herself. Heather turned towards her mother, and in a playful British accent said, "How long until we go and have tea?" The mother responded, also in an accent, "You will visit for thirty minutes, darling, then it is off to tea time." Heather smiled, but anxiously grasped her mother's hand, and stepped behind her mother's legs. Picking up the accent, the teacher chimed in, "You like tea? Well, we have a lovely tea set in the classroom I would happy to show you." Heather glanced once more at her mother who, dropping the accent said, "Go ahead, you'll be okay. I'll be here waiting for you," and hugged the little girl. The teacher held out her hand, bowing slightly, saying in crisp imitation of the accent, "Come, my dear, the tea set is waiting." Heather smiled shyly, took the teacher's hand and walked through the building. "Tell me, do you enjoy tea and cakes?" asked the teacher. "Oh, they are simply lovely," drawled Heather, with a smile. The pair chatted conversationally until they reached the classroom, where other children played quietly on mats. The teacher reached for a box containing a plastic tea service and wooden food. "Shall we have tea?" As the two arranged the cups on a table, other children approached Heather, introducing themselves. She kindly offered them some tea, and managed well when some declined the offer. After twenty-five minutes, the teacher warned that it would soon be time to clean up. Heather sighed, forgetting her accent and said, "But this is fun. . . . " The teacher followed suit, and using her regular voice assured Heather they would have time to play together and learn together during the next year, telling Heather about both academic and play opportunities. Heather's eyes danced, "Well, then, I shall be a queen," she intoned regally, waving her hand and smiling. Once again resuming the playful tone, the teacher said, "Yes, my dear, and in this kingdom, even queens help clean up." And the two began packing the tea service.

An ultimate tool for developing a relationship and making effective interventions is the use of play. Utilized by every culture and many species, play is a biological process that lies at the core of creativity and innovation. It is highly individualized, experienced differently by each participant, and perhaps the highest form of self-expression (Brown & Vaughan, 2009). Engaging in playful activities can be the means for developing and sustaining a variety of relationships as well as a means for exploring, learning and developing empathy (Elkind, 2007; Szalavitz & Perry, 2011).

Due to the highly individualized nature of play, it can be difficult to define. Understanding the components of play is helpful when employing it to build a relationship or deliver an intervention. John Eberle (as cited in Brown & Vaughan, 2009) proposed that play is a six-step process that does not follow an exact order, involving the following:

- *Anticipation* as the individual develops expectations and curiosity. Perhaps a slight risk will be taken that is not so great it is experienced as overwhelming.
- *Surprise* is experienced as expectations are or are not met. Managing the unexpected or the shifting of an idea can occur.
- *Pleasure* of sharing in a unique experience or unexpected twist.
- *Understanding* emerges as the acquisition of new knowledge or the incorporation of ideas unfolds.
- *Strength* and confidence in the play, interaction or mastery of material develops from the experience.
- *Poise* develops out of contentment and a sense of balance in one's life.

This process can occur several times during a single play session or can be drawn out over a longer period of time (Brown & Vaughan, 2009). Within each stage of this process, there is an opportunity for intervention to take place—perhaps the development of new coping skills if expectations are not met, or the encouragement of flexibility to achieve a goal that was established within the play. This process allows individuals to practice and master skills, especially within the social realm. Play can also contain repetition of themes or behavior as well as rituals. This begets a sense of consistency, allowing the child to feel safe. Play can take place in either the verbal or nonverbal realm, and employ all senses making it accessible to all ages.

Various types of play can be utilized starting at the age of infancy. When caregivers gaze, laugh and giggle with an infant, electrical currents in the brains of both individuals sync, establishing the early stages of emotional regulation and attunement. As the child ages, syncing of experiences has implications for managing stress later in life. With development, he or she engages in play through the movement of limbs and the body. As movement becomes involved in play, it generates thought patterns based in motion, which correlate to linguistic terms (under, over, through, etc.). Young children often engage in parallel play, sitting side by side, using similar toys but not directly interacting. This typically provides a bridge to more social and cooperative play. With the development of language and cognition, imaginative play evolves. The use of objects or concepts as "pretend" helps children make the distinction between what is real and what is not. The engagement in imaginative and fantasy play allows individuals to compare their experiences, which aids in the development of empathy, trust and coping skills. Finally, storytelling and narrative play involves the creation of a storyline, which can be based in real-life events or those experienced by others. This gives life events context, allowing for the opportunity to derive meaning, foster understanding and to rewrite history (Brown & Vaughan, 2009). Structured play, achieved through sports or board games provides the opportunity to engage in play that is less open ended and more containing (Landreth, 2002).

Directly related to neuropsychological intervention is the growing body of evidence that play fosters new connections between neurons and disparate brain centers, which are relevant to developing brain organization. Researcher Jaak Panksepp has found that rough-and-tumble play selectively stimulates brain-derived neurotrophic factor, stimulating nerve growth (DeBenedet & Cohen, 2010; Gordon, Burke, Akil, Watson, & Panksepp, 2003; Panksepp, 2004). It also stimulates the amygdala, the center for processing emotions and the dorsolateral prefrontal area, the seat of executive functions. John Byers (as cited in Brown and Vaughan, 2009), another researcher, found that the time engaged in play directly correlates with brain development in the frontal cortex, a region involved in cognitive functions such as distinguishing relevant from irrelevant information, monitoring and organizing thoughts and feelings, and planning for the future. Likewise, the size of the cerebellum is influenced by play. Once thought to only play a role in the coordination of movements, the cerebellum is more recently implicated in functions such as attention, language process, sensing musical rhythm and more (Brown & Vaughan, 2009).

The amount of time children spend engaged in play is decreasing, and, conversely, time spent in structured activity is increasing (Burdette & Whitaker, 2005). Valuable opportunities to learn through play are increasingly sparse. Play can be encouraged in the school setting as a vehicle for curriculum learning and in providing opportunities for free play in the classroom (Broadhead, 2004; Cattanach, Stagnitti, & Cooper, 2009; Sayeed & Guerin, 2000). In school, it is possible to engage whole classroom groups or small groups in the classroom or on the playground (Bundy et al., 2011; Woolf, 2011). Pull-out specialists can also integrate play into activities, both academic and therapeutic, to enhance learning and motivation. This allows for the development of trusting and consistent relationships with adults outside of the family unit (Woolf, 2011) and provides a venue for socioemotional learning inherent to the act of play (Elkind, 2007).

The potential role of play as an intervention will be discussed in the following sections. Following the format of a complete neuropsychological assessment, interventions that have been developed for vulnerabilities within each functional domain assessed by a complete neuropsychological evaluation will also be discussed. While it is important to develop interventions that target specific needs or utilize strengths, it is the integration of all the tools across functional domains and environments that most benefits individuals. Each functional domain addressed during a neuropsychological evaluation will be discussed.

Cognition

In Chapter 3, language processing and perceptual reasoning were discussed at length. Individuals can experience a relative strength in one or the other, or have deficits in both. The following section outlines possible interventions for these individuals. The presentation of difficulties with verbal or perceptual reasoning can be unique to the individual. As such, intervention should be tailored to their specific needs. Depending on the nature and severity of the disability, they may require different degrees of support. The following strategies are suggested as guidelines that can be modified for an individual's specific needs.

Interventions for Language Processing/Verbal Comprehension

- When verbally giving instructions, use succinct, clear language. If multistep directions are included, use visual cues (written or pictorial) to support understanding and recall.
- Paraphrase complex information using simplified language that is developmentally appropriate. Use simplified sentence structure, slow the rate of presentation and avoid the use of abstract language such as puns, idioms and metaphors.
- Preview new material, including vocabulary and concepts. This applies to both curriculum material, changes in the classroom routine or material for special events.
- Teach concrete concepts before abstract.
- Support acquisition of new vocabulary by using both written and pictorial supports and examples.
- Use visual aids such as graphs, charts, images.
- Use social stories that contain simplified language and images. The stories can be interactive, allowing the individual to fill in blank spaces or participate in writing the story.
- Allow for interactive learning opportunities that engage multiple senses.
- Use graphic organizers.

Interventions for Perceptual Reasoning

- Discuss the environment, pointing out the location of objects and materials. Prepare the individual for changes in the environment by discussing the changes before and after.
- Extend time for completion of written tasks, allowing for use of handwriting aids such as a word processor or scribe.
- Develop narratives for learning concepts.
- Explain gestures and facial expressions as they are happening. Draw the individual's attention to the body posture of self and peers.

- Use multiple choice versus essay questions during test taking.
- Role-play social scenarios, giving the individual the opportunity to practice observing and responding to affect and physical cues.
- Modify worksheets and workbooks to present information and work without extra visual clutter.
- Use graphic organizers or graph paper to organize large amounts of written information.

Environmental Accommodations

- Display the daily schedule, and changes, using both verbal and visual cues. Use calendars when discussing plans for the upcoming week or month.
- Arrange room to appear cheerful, organized and free of unnecessary clutter.

Utilizing a Strength

The approaches outlined previously are designed to accommodate a child's particular vulnerability by taking advantage of his or her relative strengths. For example, a child with a language processing disability will be supported through an emphasis on the provision of visual cues and other sensory modalities that may help him or her better process the information being transmitted. Conversely, a child with difficulties in perceptual organization will rely more heavily on language so that complex visual information can be broken down into parts and labelled and placed in the context of a narrative that will help the child better organize and recall the information. Playing to a child's strengths in this manner more likely will help him or her feel that the learning process is not too arduous, and they will derive considerable satisfaction from the experience of more easily understanding new material that nevertheless may be challenging in other ways. Accommodations of this sort lay the foundation for a learning experience that is embraced by children and, within the context of a relationship, allows them to learn about their particular learning style and, ultimately, learn to advocate for themselves through their strengths.

Executive Functions

For three months, Tucker had been an active member of a fifth-grade classroom. He was generally polite and willing to work hard. However, he rarely completed many tasks, struggling to stay on topic, blurting out answers and daydreaming. Teachers had contacted his parents with concerns regarding incomplete homework. In addition, his locker was a mess. Every morning, Tucker would enter his classroom, excited to share some news with the teacher or friends, and almost always forgot to bring his work folder, a well-established classroom routine. This particular morning, Tucker was excited to show his teacher a new yo-yo as he rushed into the classroom. They discussed the yo-yo for a few minutes, then the teacher kindly asked where his homework folder was. "Oh, no!" cried Tucker and he began to race to the door. The teacher gently asked him to return to the desk, noting that this happened frequently, and that her verbal reminders were not helping much. She suggested they make a sign to put in his locker, reminding him what he needed for the day. "Awe, man!" he cried, "I hate those things!" She suggested that this sign could be different. She opened a folder containing images of yo-yo's and other sleight-of-hand toys, suggesting they use the images to decorate the sign. Tucker enthusiastically responded, "YES!" and gathered the materials, moved to his desk and began to assemble the a visual reminder that would help get his day started.

Children generally develop executive function skills in accordance with their neurological development. Younger children rely on the adults around them to organize, plan and inhibit, in effect, operating as an external set of executive functions. As the frontal lobes develop, the child typically takes on more of these tasks, internalizing the skill set. Children struggling with executive functions require external support in the home and at school. As a result, many interventions support development in two ways: first, by modifying the environment to provide support and, second, by teaching the individual specific skills and strategies. Many of the following suggestions can be found in Dawson and Guare's (2011) book, *Executive Skills in Children and Adolescents: A Practical Guide to Assessment and Intervention*.

Changing the environment can take place on several levels. The physical space of the room can be arranged to decrease distraction and provide organization. Large, open spaces invite fast movement and running. Arranging tables and chairs to provide ease of movement or the provision of several quiet spaces within a room can help to contain impulsive behavior. Changing the nature of the task or demand we place on the individual is also useful. For example, rather than asking the child to generate his or her own sentences containing spelling words, use a fill-in-the-blank method. Providing external cues to prompt the child, either visually or through verbal reminders, externally regulates the child. For example, creating a "thermometer" of feelings, ranging from 1 = *calm and ready to learn* to 5 = *frustrated and in need of a break* provides the child with an opportunity to develop awareness of self-regulation, reminds the child to assess his or her emotional status and advocate for his or her needs prior to emotional or behavior decompensation, all of which promote self-regulation. The adults and caregivers can also alter their interactions with the child to promote the use and development of executive functions.

Environmental Modifications

- Make the task shorter.
- Make the steps of a task clear and explicit.
- Use true or false, fill in the blanks and cloze procedures rather than open-ended tasks.
- Provide choices or options within the task to generate motivation and maintain interest.

- Use verbal or visual prompts intended to help the child remember directions, routines and to stay on task. When implementing the prompt, discuss with the child, giving him or her options for the prompt, using humor.
- Provide classroom schedules or individualized schedules.
- Use lists and checklists for tracking items or steps to follow. Making the list and decorating it with the child increases motivation, understanding and follow-through.
- Offer more adult support, supervision and cuing. For older children, the use of technology and cellular phones can be employed.
- Develop classroom routines, practice and reinforce the routines using games or music.
- Have adults speak aloud as they problem solve, make a plan or organize materials providing a role model to groups and individuals. This also fosters acceptance for different organizational styles and skills.
- Provide praise and positive reinforcement, including a conversation about what happened, what worked and what could be done differently.

Adaptations to the environment, delivery of academic material, and external structure support children struggling with executive functions. Helping the child develop awareness of his or her strengths and struggles and internalizing skills and structure adds another layer of support. This can be achieved by teaching specific skills, in a developmentally appropriate way, and can provide motivation. Often, children struggling with executive functions may appear lazy or oppositional, but in reality, engaging in goal-directed activities requires substantial effort. This can create a vicious cycle of reluctance, perceived or experienced failure, frustration, avoidance, self-deprecation and decreased motivation. In teaching a specific skill, the teacher, parent or therapist must carefully integrate incentives that are relational, intrinsic and extrinsic.

Individual Interventions

The process of developing interventions targeting specific executive functioning skills can be done with the individual, if developmentally appropriate. Integrating their perspective and goals enhances motivation and maintains attunement. First, identify the problem, with honesty, avoiding negative language. With the individual, determine a realistic attainable goal directly related to the problem. This relates to the developmental age of the individual as well as the severity of their executive functioning difficulties. If the goal is not realistic, it is less likely they will accomplish the goal, further entrenching a negative feedback cycle. Next, establish a set of steps or a procedure to attain a goal. Practice the steps and procedures together. As the plan is put in full motion, the child or adolescent may need observation, prompting, support, feedback and praise. After several trials, reevaluate the processes, making changes as needed. If the procedure is working well, gradually decrease the amount of supervision and support.

Throughout this process, integrating specific language or metaphors to describe the problem, the skill being developed and its use in feedback, promotes the internalization of the skill and helps develop self-regulation. Individuals can learn to recognize negative self-talk and self-defeating messages. Replacing this type of thinking with awareness and positivity is part of maintaining motivation. Adults can further support the individual by providing frequent feedback and praise. Praise should occur near the completion of a task, be specific, recognize their hard work and reflect their current emotional state, validating difficulty and acknowledging success.

The development of routines throughout the day provides structure, consistency and support for the individual developing executive functions. While traditionally thought of as an intervention for whole classroom groups, these strategies can be implemented within the home environment as well. Transitions to and from places or activities can be made more manageable with the use of a routine. Emotional issues that may arise around transitions or specific activities can also be addressed. This can include the following broad suggestions, some of which are treated in more detail below:

* Morning routines
* End-of-the-day or nighttime routines
* Homework completion and collection
* Paying attention
* Cleaning backpacks, bedrooms or classroom spaces
* Note taking
* Managing effortful tasks
* Learning to control anxiety, explosive reactions, and impulsive behavior
* Changes in plans or schedules
* Problem solving

In the following section, possible interventions for specific executive function vulnerabilities are presented. Many of these suggestions are tailored for the use in a classroom setting but can be adapted to the home environment as well.

Concept Generation/Formation/Task Initiation

Environmental Modifications

* Provide visual and verbal cues for starting and stopping tasks and activities.

Individual Interventions

* Provide clear options during free play or during academic instruction. For example, if the class is writing fictional narratives, ask the child to choose a main character that is an animal or a person.
* In giving options, use verbal and visual presentations. For visuals, use cue cards, charts or worksheets that the child can either keep for the duration of the project or write on. This generates interest and motivation.
* Avoid open-ended questions during work and conversation. Ask questions that can be answered with yes/no, true/false.
* Provide a variety of examples of the end product. Carefully provide an amount of options that will not be overwhelming to the individual.

- Preview activities, rules and expectations. Some individuals benefit from multiple previewing opportunities, sometimes days in advance. Others need previewing to occur close to the event, task or activity. This accommodates different memory and learning styles.

Plan, Organize, Reason and Problem Solve

Environmental Modifications

- Depending on the developmental stage and abilities, an adult can provide plans and schedules for the child to follow.
- Keep classroom and other environments free of clutter. With the child, organize and plan the environment. This can be done in a game-like fashion.
- Provide checklists for organizing desks and backpacks.
- Provide verbal and visual reminders of routines and schedules.
- Provide binders, folders and individualized space within the classroom or home environment. Encourage the individual to decorate organizational materials.

Individual Interventions

- Develop familiarity with graphic organizers and allow the individual to choose their preference.
- For longer academic tasks, break the task into small, manageable chunks. Use checklists, rubrics, calendars and graphic organizers to track progress of the entire class or individuals as needed.
- Problem solve with the individual, breaking problems into smaller chunks and providing suggestions. Help them develop awareness around their problems solving style and teach strategies.

Shift Set/Perseveration

Environmental Modifications

- Preview changes in the schedule and routines as well as novel events.
- Preview changes in the appearance of the environment, including changes in furniture and the child's preferred place to sit.
- Preview changes in the appearance of adults who care for the child (such as haircut or changes in hair color).
- Preview systematic or gradual exposure to changes in schedule, routines and novel activities.

Individual Interventions

- Provide/teach coping mechanisms for managing stress during changes.
- Utilize social stories, individually tailored to the child.
- Provide step-by-step assistance with positive reinforcement throughout.

- Adapt open-ended tasks to be more closed ended. This will provide expectations and make tasks more concrete.
- Develop awareness around their rigidity. Use developmentally appropriate language, such as, "Sometimes you get stuck. We need to find a way to help you get unstuck."

Inhibition/Distractibility

Environmental Modifications

- Free the environment of clutter and distractions.
- Pay attention to environments that may be overstimulating (noisy, crowded, filled with disorganized toys and materials).
- Post and review classroom rules and behavior expectations.

Individual Interventions

- Increase the amount of supervision. This varies from allowing the child to sit near a teacher/adult, providing a one-to-one aide, or placement in a classroom/school with a high teacher-to-student ratio.
- Name the experience of being impulsive with the individual. Through conversation and visual aids, target impulsive behaviors the child is working on. Practice the skill and try to make the conversation empathic and fun, not during a time of extreme tension or frustration.
- Use established verbal and visual cues in the moment to make the child aware of his or her actions.
- Use positive reinforcement in the moment and throughout the day.
- Avoid reinforcing undesirable actions. Depending on the child, he or she may be seeking a negative reaction as well as a positive interaction. Through the development of the relationship, this pattern may become more clear.

Behavioral and Emotional Regulation

Environmental Modifications

- Break tasks into small, manageable chunks to avoid fatigue and frustration.
- Keep space free of clutter and distracting material. If the child can be explosive or unsafe, keep possible unsafe objects (such a scissors) in a container, accessible only by adults.

Individual Interventions

- Anticipate problem situations/experiences for the child. Discuss possible reactions and provide choices for appropriate expression of his or her feelings and concerns.
- Allow opportunities to teach and practice coping strategies.

- Provide scripts that can be individualized for the child to rely on and to appropriately express him- or herself.
- Provide the opportunity for breaks, and develop language or a cue to initiate the break. Either the teacher or the child can cue for the break, depending on the child's ability to reflect on his or her own emotional and behavioral state.
- Provide encouragement before, during and after tasks.
- Write individualized social stories for the child, reflecting his or her experience, and provide strategies.
- Use a five-point scale, carefully designed and tailored for the individual, to help the child reflect on his or her emotional status. If the child is reaching an unhelpful emotional state, indicate on the scale when a break and the use of coping strategies is warranted.

Use of Feedback/Self-Monitoring

Environmental Modifications

- During classroom routines or academic lessons, ask questions that encourage self-reflection or make comments on the group. For example, "Wow, that was a really smooth transition. Everyone followed directions really well," or, "Good job! How did you solve that problem?"

Individual Interventions

- Ask the individual their opinion on an activity and how well he or she liked or completed it.
- Provide fun formats for giving feedback, such as teaching children a five-star ranking system, similar to those used in restaurants and movies. Provide star-shaped stickers, and give them the opportunity to put stickers on worksheets or projects.
- Use individualized checklists that outline the steps of an activity or project. As the child completes the projects, encourage the child to check off the steps.
- When asking reflective questions, provide sample answers the child can choose from.
- Devise an approach or plan with the child for completing work, and monitor his or her progress.

Working Memory

Environmental Modifications

- Most environmental modifications resemble an external working memory to supplement the child's ability level. These cues can be designed to encourage the child to retrieve information in the moment or at a set time.
- Use calendars, visual schedules and notebooks for to-do lists.
- For multistep instructions, mathematical operations, projects, etc., provide visual cues with both words and images.

- Use electronic devices set with visual, auditory or tactile alarms to remind the child what happens next, or to participate in or complete an activity.

Individual Interventions

- During academic instruction, provide visuals and manipulatives for the performance of various activities. For example, mental math (adding in the mind) can be very difficult for children experiencing difficulties with working memory. Using blocks or number lines or timelines assist in tracking information.
- Use of agreed upon, predetermined and discussed verbal reminders. These can be playful and fun.

Attention

Environmental Modifications

- Provide cues informing the child about the start and stop time of an activity, how many minutes the activity requires, and give ten-, five- and one-minute cues near the end of the activity.
- Use positive reinforcement geared towards the whole group or the individual. This could include earning extra time at recess, the opportunity for a special movement break, a special snack, a certificate of completion, stickers, etc. Gearing an incentive towards the preference of a group or individual is highly motivating. For example, after the completion of a task, offer a dance break using a popular song many of the students appreciate.
- Break tasks into smaller tasks, offering breaks in between.
- Use a visual timer, to help the child monitor the passage of time. These are available in a variety of sizes and formats (digital, visual kitchen timer, sand, etc.).

Individual Interventions

- For difficult or time-consuming activities, choose a time of day when the child is most alert.
- Provide supervision during tasks, at both home and school.
- Build tasks around the child's interests. Individuals work harder and longer on tasks they find interesting, relevant and important.
- Make activities interactive and game-like.
- After a demanding activity, provide the opportunity for the child to do something he or she enjoys.
- Considering developmental level, work with the child, teaching him or her to be aware of his or her attentional capacity, coping strategies, initiation of a break and how to chunk work.
- Gradually transfer responsibility for managing time and activities into the child's hands, using meaningful and rewarding language and activities. This must be done carefully, when the child is ready to take on the challenge.

Memory

A group of seven- and eight-year-old children sat, diligently working on a free-writing activity, at a time where they chose a topic for writing a five-sentence paragraph. The focus of the activity was to generate motivation for writing about their experiences, preferences and opinions. Once the writing work was complete, they would share with a teacher. At the end of each writing session, the teacher would look over the work, hold a brief conversation about the contents of the paragraph, ask questions and elaborate on details. At the end of the conversation, the teacher would point at the wall, wave her finger in the air, making a siren noise. "The cops are coming!" she would say. The children were familiar with this established routine, a reminder to check their work for grammatical and spelling errors. The sign had an image of a police car, with large letters that read, C.O.P.S., an acronym, reminding the students to check for capitalization, organization, punctuation and spelling. Prior to the use of the playful reminder and the mnemonic device, many of the students could not remember how to edit their work.

Along with working memory (discussed previously) long-term and short-term memory have a significant impact on an individual's academic and cognitive performance (Swanson & Saez, 2003), and other areas of functioning. These individuals may appear to be quick learners but are also quick to forget or have difficulty remembering information that was presented visually or verbally. During reading, for example, individuals with dyslexia struggle to rapidly access and retrieve names for visual symbols (Jensen, 2010). While memory is functionally linked to other cognitive skills (attention, self-regulation etc.), it is not a lone factor in determining intelligence, a common misperception of many students (Posner & Rothbart, 2007). This attitude towards memory and intelligence can instigate an unhelpful cycle for an individual that threatens his or her self-image (Autin & Croizet, 2012). Situations in which individuals are pressured to perform their best are, in fact, most likely to have a negative impact on their ability to successfully access memory skills. Without intervention, this cycle may continue to spiral, and the individual may perceive themselves as "stupid," experience external pressure at school or home and fail at a task once again, further reinforcing a negative self-image. As a result accommodations and interventions for individuals struggling with utilizing and accessing memory functions must include instructional and environmental practices to support their learning, but also to support their developing selves as students. The following list of interventions can be individually tailored, modified for use at home or school and support memory functioning.

- During instruction utilize skimming, imagining, drawing, elaborating, paraphrasing, accessing prior knowledge, repetition and frequent review.
- Orient the student(s) toward the critical features of any task or activity and frame the importance of an idea.

- Teach memory aids such as mnemonics, acronyms, rehearsal of information and forming associations.
- Engage multiple senses during activities.
- Narrate and discuss daily activities. If appropriate, ask open-ended, engaging questions.
- Create memorization hooks—make activities multimodal, creating a project using a variety of materials. Photograph the project and display the end result or the photograph, making reference to the product as appropriate throughout the day.
- Use songs to teach new concepts, present new vocabulary or review material—singing, acting out the song and pointing to pictures as the individual sings. Change lyrics of popular songs to match the task content.
- Have students work with a partner to rehearse critical information.
- Give opportunities to review small amounts of material frequently, rather than trying to memorize large amounts of information at once.
- Create vocabulary picture cards.
- Increase motivation for learning tasks.
- Develop awareness of the individual's perspective of intelligence, encouraging the viewpoint that different people learn in different ways, regardless of overall intelligence.
- Chunk information in meaningful ways.

Sensorimotor Functioning

Recall from Chapter 6 that sensorimotor functioning represents a constellation of skills, including visuoconstructive abilities, motor planning and sequencing, motor speed, processing speed, fine and gross motor skills and graphomotor skills. Difficulty within this skill set can impact an individual's ability to navigate the physical environment, take notes during instruction, respond to instruction, integrate sensory information from the environment and develop self-regulation. In addition, individuals with processing difficulties may struggle with understanding, processing and discussing their emotional state (van Middendorp & Geenen, 2008). Working with individuals with these difficulties may require assessment and subsequent intervention/consultation with an occupational therapist. The following accommodations can be used to support an individual struggling with this important functional domain.

- Simplify the presentation of visual information, such as worksheets, charts and graphs.
- Simplify speech, using familiar words, and speak slowly, with careful articulation.
- Allow for extra time to process verbal and visual information.
- Allow extra time to complete projects and assignments.
- Provide access to a sensory diet (fidget toys, cushions for sitting, weighted vests or blankets) with the consultation of an occupational therapist.
- For writing activities, provide paper with larger spaces for writing or darker or raised lines.
- Use "How to Draw" books that use step-by-step instructions for completing an image.

- Use adaptive technology for writing activities.
- Play noncompetitive games that encourage visual processing skills (hunt-and-find games, such as *Where's Waldo* and *I Spy*).
- Take frequent motor breaks, encouraging individuals to move in their chair or around the room.
- Utilize the individual's interests to create highly motivating activities.
- Allow individuals to record lectures or presentations for later review and note taking.

Academic Intervention

Three sixth-grade boys, armed with binders and books, gathered in a small room. All three were bright, able to complete grade-level work, but struggled with processing speed, output and organization. This instructional period was designed to meet their specific needs and teach organizational skills. They were currently working on manipulating fractions and reading *A Wrinkle in Time*. They used the same math text as their peers, but with simplified worksheets, reduced written output demands and less visually overwhelming material. Time was spent organizing material in the binders, highlighting new vocabulary words, spelling words, and graphic organizers for recording key concepts of the book. Prior to participating in this group, all three displayed inappropriate behaviors in the larger group, distracting themselves, and their peers, fueling a negative perception of themselves. Here, time was taken to talk about their day, ask questions about the homework, and just relax for a few minutes. Between math and reading activities they were given a break to chat, get some water and move about the room.

Intervention in the academic setting occurs on a variety of levels through the public school system, depending on the individual needs of the child. Federal law dictates that individuals have access to learning environments that best meet their learning needs without restricting their access or type of environment. For a full discussion regarding legal issues related to educational access, see Chapter 11. Legal matters aside, many special education programs are built on the philosophy of inclusion. Inclusion recognizes that all students benefit from a meaningful and appropriate curriculum that can be delivered within a general education classroom (Idol, 2006). This philosophy promotes fairness rather than sameness, building a diverse community based on acceptance, belonging and community (Bucalos & Lingo, 2005; Sapon-Shevin, 2003). As a result, a continuum of environmental settings has been established, ranging from most broad to increasingly specific (Salend, 2008) (See Reference Box 10.1). As the needs of a child become increasingly specific, it is possible that participation in an inclusive setting, such as a regular education classroom with an aide, is not sufficient to meet his or her individual needs or successfully integrate his or her experience. Consequently, the child may require more specific outplacement. In both public school and outplacement environments, it is critical that full integration of the child's needs occur as a way to accommodate both the child's unique learning style and attune services to his or her social/emotional state. Doing so requires consistent communication between the classroom teacher, specialists, therapists and the family.

Reference Box 10.1 Continuum of Educational Settings

- General education classroom with few or no supportive services
- General education classroom with collaborative teacher's assistance
- General education classroom with itinerant specialist assistance
- General education classroom placement with resource room assistance
- Special education classroom with part-time in general education classroom
- Full-time special education classroom
- Special day school (outplacement)
- Residential school
- Homebound instruction
- Hospital or institution.

In order to accommodate a diverse learning population in any educational setting, differentiated instruction is utilized to blend learning needs with curriculum requirements. Differentiated instruction involves generating various methodologies and strategies to present information in a classroom setting. In doing so, educators differentiate the content, teaching process, generated product, alter the learning environment and have a variety of methods for assessing the impact of a lesson on a child's thinking and feeling (Price & Nelson, 2007; Tomlinson & Eidson, 2003). Effective differentiation requires knowledge of state and federal curriculum requirements and the presentation of material that may appear inappropriate for delayed learners. The more interactive and multimodal the lesson, the more differentiated, allowing for different levels of learning based on sensory and cognitive processing. For example, a unit on measurement can integrate the concept of different measurement units (centimeter, meter, etc.) with written presentation, visual demonstration and physical movement about the classroom. Activities like measuring the distance children can jump, how many strides they make moving across the room and using both centimeters and meters to compare the two units, actively engages the children in a learning activity. Providing the opportunity to complete a more traditional worksheet or a visual art project that includes measurement (such as tracing the child's body on a large sheet of paper, then measuring the length of the body, limbs and head) offers two final products.

In delivering curriculum content to unique learners, instructors must attend to not only their cognitive strengths and vulnerabilities but also to their emotional status. The utilization of differentiated instruction can indeed provide learning opportunities at a variety of levels, but without recognition of the child's baseline emotional status and reaction to concepts and activities, engaging in the learning process and providing the opportunity for the child to experience success is highly restricted. The child's emotional status impacts motivation, attention, behavioral regulation, memory and evolving perception of self as a student.

Within the framework of providing the most optimal learning environment for a student, differentiating curriculum delivery as well as emotional awareness and attunement, a variety of interventions are available for individuals with learning disabilities. The following sections provide examples of interventions that can be applied at both home and school for reading, writing and mathematics.

Reading

Recall from Chapter 7 that reading is a relatively new aspect of human ability, contingent upon various neural systems. These systems, relying upon a variety of structures and functions, were carefully reorganized over time, resulting in this uniquely human skill. Difficulty in developing reading skills can be traced back to deficits in specific systems that point to the need for specific reading interventions. This includes phonological awareness, orthographic processing, decoding, encoding, fluency and automaticity, vocabulary and comprehension. Reading achievement in the first grade is a remarkably strong predictor of high school reading achievement (Cunningham & Stanovich, 1997), fueling the need for early identification and intervention for at risk students.

As with many interventions discussed in this chapter, the support of reading development can occur on many levels. On the environmental level, at both home and school creating a word-rich or literacy-rich environment encourages early development of reading skills, before, during and after a child enters kindergarten. This type of environment supports familiarity, interest and motivation towards literacy activities, enhances vocabulary and provides connections between print and real-world experiences (Johnston, McDonnell, & Hawken, 2008). This can include the following:

- Reading to children at all levels, from infancy and beyond.
- Access to a variety of books at different developmental levels on different topics and story types.
- Literacy-related play areas that contain picture books, props, memo pads, stuffed animals and books that allow children to play with, and act out stories and concept contained in the book.
- Asking children to retell or act out stories using puppets, costumes and props.
- A "Cozy Corner" nook in the classroom or in a home where people can read together or independently. Placing pillows, stuffed animals and blankets fosters the feeling of safety and comfort.
- Placing labels and signs around the room, naming objects and places, developing th connection between print, words and objects or other activities.
- Interactive circle or reading time. Teachers or adults read to the children, but also encourage interaction with the material, asking questions, encouraging discussion of ideas and predicting story outcomes.
- Interactive meal times during which children and adults engage in conversation about their daily activities at home and school.
- Reading and playing out nursery rhymes and rhythm games.
- Playing games that teach letter/word recognition.

While literacy-rich environments support the development of reading skills and inter-est, children with reading disabilities often require more specific intervention directly related to their particular reading vulnerability. Effective reading remediation programs for children with dyslexia must include 1) phonological awareness training, 2) systematic phonics instruction that is linked to spelling and 3) oral reading practices with decodable texts (which include words and sound blends familiar to the child) (Lovett, Barron, & Benson, 2003). Several reading programs have been developed to address the specific learning needs of individuals with dyslexia (see Reference Box 10.2). While extremely helpful, this is another situation in which one program will not be effective with every child. What works for one child may not work for another. Many of these programs require teacher training in strategies and techniques. Within the use of these programs, it remains important to develop a relationship with the individual child to address their emotional state and learning needs, otherwise they may remain unavailable for instruc-tion. Outside of participation in individualized reading programs, teachers, parents and caretakers can continue to support the development of underlying skills required for the development of reading achievement.

Reference Box 10.2 A Few Well Known Reading Programs

- *Orton-Gillingham* (Gillingham & Stillman, 1997)
- *Wilson Reading Program* (Wilson, 1996)
- *Davis Dyslexia Program* (Davis, 2010)
- RAVE-O (*Retrieval, Automaticity, Vocabulary elaboration, Engagement with language and Orthography*) for reading fluency (Wolf et al., 2009)
- Phonological Analysis and Blending/Direct instruction (PHAB/DI) (Engel-mann & Brunner, 1988)

Phonics

- Start with continuous sounds such as /s/, /m/, and /f/ that are easier to pronounce than the stop sounds such as /b/, /k/ and /p/.
- Avoid letter names that can be confused with the letter sound (h,g).
- When discussing a new sound, find objects at home or school that begin with the sound, establishing a real-world connection between the letter, the sound and the environment.
- Relate isolated letter sounds with familiar animals or actions. Such as the buzzing of a bee, *shhhhhhh* for quiet and more. Alliteration can also be used.
- Teach the child to count syllables. Pair this with an action or sound, such as clapping on a syllable, tapping the table, stomping feet or striking a chime.
- Associate sounds with letters using a multisensory approach and games, such as letter/sound bingo.
- Delete or add on sounds to established words, such as adding or removing the *b* from *beat* (from *How the Special Needs Brain Learns,* Sousa, 2007, p. 110).

As children master the ability to read, more demands are placed on their ability to understand what they are reading. Individuals move from learning to read, to reading to learn. Comprehension of reading material plays a role in early reading development, providing curiosity and motivation. When learning to decode, familiar words and topics motivate emerging readers. However, mastery of decoding allows greater access to more material, including unfamiliar content. Sometimes difficulty arises from a lack of fluency or a limited vocabulary (Williams, 2003). Children, adolescents and adults can struggle with making sense of what they have read and require specific support in developing these skills. Many of the strategies for developing reading comprehension emphasize metacognitive skills, developing awareness of these skills during comprehension and their deployment. Another strategy teaches individuals to recognize the structure or format of written material, such as recognizing the main topic of a paragraph or identifying a sequence of events. Depending on the type of text, expository or narrative, the individual is taught to approach the text with a variety of skills (Williams, 2003).

Comprehension

- During reading activities, provide an array of main ideas for the individual to choose from. This circumvents the need to generate the idea independently.
- While reading narrative texts, provide an array of themes, including the prominent and ask the individual to identify the most appropriate theme.
- Teach important story elements, such as setting and characters. This can be done through games or the creation of the child's own setting and characters.
- Conduct a prereading discussion about the purpose of the lesson and the story topic.
- Read the text aloud, inviting children to follow along in their own text copy. Throughout the story, pause, pose questions and ask opinions, and integrate responses into the discussion.
- Discuss important information utilizing a familiar format that has been prelearned (e.g., graphic organizers). Ask questions such as, Who is the main character? What did he or she do? What happened? Or ask the five *Wh*- questions: Who? What? When? Where? and Why?
- Apply the theme of narrative text or topics to real-life situations. Choose reading selections that are relevant and important to the individual(s).
- Utilize story maps and graphic organizer, allowing for a visual representation of story elements, sequence of events and main idea/details.
- Use highlighting to mark and recall salient portions of a text.

Writing

The act of writing, at any level, be it a word, sentence, paragraph or essay, relies on complex constellation of cognitive processes. Basic cognitive components rely on executive functions to sustain attention, self-regulate, monitor progress and feedback and understand, employ working memory and consider the reader's perspective (Graham & Harris, 2003). The act of writing also requires the individual to access knowledge related to grammar, syntax, punctuation and spelling. For some individuals, difficulty with mechanics of writing (such as malformed letters and misspelled words), and attending to punctuation and capitalization, utilize a majority of their cognitive resources, leaving little energy for planning. Difficulty with short-term and working memory can further impact the ability to manage the mechanics of writing, influencing the development of automaticity (Berninger & Amtmann, 2003). Furthermore, the planning process requires the individual to 1) plan what to say and how to say it, 2) translate plans into written text and 3) review written work to improve the existing text (Graham & Harris, 2003). Given the complex nature of this academic skill, intervention can occur on many levels. In an academic setting, underlying difficulties with executive functions, graphomotor skills and memory become evident through instruction and assessment of handwriting skills, spelling ability and in the planning and execution of a composition. Depending on the nature of the individual's writing difficulties, intervention may be specific to each academic skill or target all three. The following sections include a brief discussion on the contribution of handwriting, spelling and organization to the overall writing process, as well as suggestions for intervention.

Handwriting

Handwriting, or the transcription of letters, is more than just a fine motor act. While fine motor skills play an important role, handwriting also integrates orthographic and memory skills to develop representations of letter forms and retrieval of these representations. As a result, children with fine motor difficulties may struggle with handwriting (Berninger & Amtmann, 2003). This functional system is separate from that used during

Figure 10.2 Self-portrait of a student.
In this drawing, a student depicts their perspective of a useful writing environment and activity.

reading and can be thought of as "language by hand" (Berninger & Graham, 1998). Because of this overlay of fine motor and specific cognitive processes, students with high-level thinking skills may struggle with transcription skills, which may be masked by other cognitive skills until higher level demands are place on their writing ability (Berninger & Amtmann, 2003). Interventions may include the following:

- Extensive efforts to make writing activities motivating and fun.
- Practice handwriting in an organized, consistent and meaningful way, allowing for breaks.
- Allow more time to complete written tasks.
- Reduce the amount of work the student may have to copy or produce.
- Implement the use of keyboarding, dictations using a voice recognition system and word prediction programs. While this strategy will bypass handwriting difficulties it does not always ameliorate difficulties with processing language.
- Integrate accommodations that foster self-regulation.
- Consultation with an occupational therapist to understand the nature of the writing difficulty.
- Try cursive rather than print, which is easier for some learners.

Spelling

For children with learning disabilities, spelling is one of the most common difficulties (Bos & Vaughn, 2006). As mentioned in Chapter 7, spelling relies on some of the same foundational skills as reading (phonological processing, phonological memory, concept of print and orthographic and morphological awareness) as well as the ability to retrieve stored information (memory), automaticity and vocabulary knowledge (Berninger, Cartwright, Yates, Swanson, & Abbott, 1994; Hsu, Berninger, Thomson, Wijsman, & Raskind, 2002). Early intervention for individuals at risk for spelling difficulties is more likely to result in improved spelling ability (Berninger & Amtmann, 2003). Several elements have been identified as effective in working with children who struggle with spelling. This includes the instructional delivery method, the use of computer-assisted instruction, multisensory training and explicit study and word practice procedures (Wanzek, Vaughn, Wexler, Swanson, Edmonds, & Kim, 2006). In addition to employing various strategies and techniques during instruction, it is useful to understand what skills or processes the child is currently using during spelling activities, to further individualize instruction (Mercer & Mercer, 2005). The following strategies are helpful in working with children exhibiting difficulties with spelling:

- Teach spelling rules and generalizations based on sound/letter correspondence.
- Teach the child to break words into syllables and apply phonetic rules.
- Integrate multiple senses into spelling lessons, including visual, auditory, kinesthetic and tactile. This can be accomplished as the child watches the teacher write the word, traces it with his or her finger (using a sand tray adds another level of tactile sensation) and says each syllable of the word aloud.
- Pair spelling words with saying words.

- Limit the number of new words. An optimal number of words has not been determined, but research has established three words is a good target number (Bryant, Drabin, & Gettinger, 1981; Gettinger, Bryant, & Fayne, 1982).
- Use technology such as spell checking, word prediction and speech feedback software.
- Integrate technology with traditional spelling instruction.
- Integrate accommodations that foster self-regulation.
- Integrate spelling words into the classroom routine.
- Use spelling games that focus on the spelling words, such as crossword puzzles and word searches. For more spelling game ideas, use *Teaching Students with Learning Problems* by Mercer and Mercer (2005).

Organization/Composition

Writing a composition integrates a number of skills and abilities acquired in earlier stages of writing skill development. Individuals with learning disabilities may struggle with the acquisition of these basic skills, or they may have attained this skill set but struggle using the skills to develop longer compositions. This may be in part due to difficulty with generating, planning and organizing their ideas into a writing plan. Students with learning disabilities may "condense" this process at various stages of the composition process (Graham & Harris, 2003;). They may rely on one step, such as generating ideas and simply write about their current knowledge base, without considering rhetorical goals, whole-text organization, the needs of the reader and constraints imposed by the topic. Two approaches can be used and integrated to foster writing skills in students with learning disabilities (Graham & Harris, 1994, 1997). First, construct an environment that nourishes the development of self-regulation. This includes many of the environmental interventions discussed in the executive functions section of this chapter. In addition, students benefit from the explicit teaching of strategies for organization and integration of monitoring their progress.

Successful planning of a written composition has three ingredients: setting goals, generating ideas and organizing ideas into a writing plan. In addition, many students with learning disabilities also struggle with editing and revising. The following strategies are useful when working with individuals struggling with composition:

- Provide support during the revision process. Utilize rubrics, practice revising work that is not their own, post acronyms (such as COPS: Capitalization, Organization, Punctuation and Spelling) to remind students about editing and revising steps.
- Bring awareness to the different types and styles of writing and literary genres.
- Provide graphic organizers specific to the style of writing and genre. This can be used to encourage development of sequence of events, key elements of a story (setting, character, etc.). For expository texts, graphic organizers can help develop main ideas and supporting sentences and develop an organized flow of writing material.
- Encourage development of self-regulation through environmental modifications.
- Teach children and students to ask themselves questions such as, "Did it say what I really believe?" and "What do I need to do?"

- Completion of a writing project is criterion based, not time based. This allows for extra time to complete the requirements of the project rather than evaluating how quickly a person can meet the criteria.

Mathematics

Mathematics encompasses a wide variety of operations, the successful completion of which are impacted by an individual's relative strengths and weaknesses (Chinn & Ashcroft, 2007). For example, in higher mathematical functions, some individuals prefer geometry over algebra because these tasks rely on separate functions and concepts. Identifying variability in underlying skills can help determine the nature of difficulty and provide clues to methods of instruction. Factors include directional confusion, sequencing problems; visual difficulties; spatial awareness, short-term, long-term and working memory; processing speed; language of mathematics; cognitive/thinking style; conceptual ability; anxiety; stress and self-image. These concepts have been described throughout this book.

Furthermore, research indicates that individuals process mathematics differently (Sousa, 2007). This impacts their learning style as well as what type of instruction best suits their learning preferences. These differences run along a continuum, from a primarily quantitative to a primarily qualitative style. Recognition of these individual differences will help tailor lesson plans and activities. Qualitative learners tend to approach math through the big picture, thinking in terms of quality rather than in separate parts. The propensity toward the big picture can lead to difficulties in precise calculations, algorithms and sequences, resulting in reduced automaticity but also creativity expressed through innovative problem solving, consolidation of procedures and intuitive reasoning. This learning style relies on talking through questions and connections by seeing relationships between concepts and procedures and further drawing associations between familiar and novel concepts. Qualitative learners tend to focus on visuospatial aspects of mathematics. Conversely, quantitative learners tend to be detail oriented, breaking problems into smaller parts, then rebuilding the components to deal with bigger problems. A strong preference for a single approach may develop, as alternative solutions are perceived as distracting. Their approach is systematic, benefiting from a highly structured, continuous presentation. Generally, they have strong deductive reasoning skills and benefit from hands-on materials.

Previous discussion (see Chapter 7) on mathematical development and assessment highlighted calculation skills, the role of executive functions and mathematical reasoning. We return to that format as more specific interventions are considered. But first, a few general accommodations are recommended for use during instruction.

- Create connections between number words, number of objects and number symbols using multiple senses and highly motivating objects and preferred activities.
- Teach functional, not abstract, meaning of math words (*more, less, bigger, longer, twice, before, after,* etc.).
- Ask children to use self-talk during math activities, and talk out loud.
- Keep learning spaces free of clutter and visual distractions.

- Show patience and utilize "teachable moments." If concepts related to mathematics naturally arise out of classroom conversations and activities, highlight the connection in the moment.
- Provide small-group instruction.
- Encourage the student to make his or her own realistic goals to enhance motivation and self-regulation.
- Set a pace that matches the student's rate of learning.

Math Calculation

The ability to employ basic calculation skills provides the foundation for later, higher level mathematical reasoning (Jensen, 2010). Thus, it is important to foster these abilities, maintain motivation and develop confidence.

- Practice recognizing that a small number of objects represents a number, without having to return to counting each item individually (e.g., the number of dots on a domino).
- Practice number patterns (such as skip counting 2s, 5s and 10s) in multiple modalities, visual, tactile and movement.
- Recognize patterns in all operations, such as noticing doubles (4 + 4, or 6 × 6) as special patterns.
- Practice sorting and classifying objects and utilizing objects the child enjoys, such as sorting plastic animals into groups (e.g., live on land vs. live in the water).
- Pair number concepts with games.
- Solidify number facts using multimodal games. For example, write digits 1 through 10 on a ball. Toss the ball back and forth. When individuals catch the ball, they add the numbers closest to their thumbs. This can be done for all mathematical operations.
- Utilize manipulatives (blocks, dice, beads, scales, small candy), visuals (number lines), and real-life examples (money, milk or juice carton, etc.), making the abstract more concrete.
- Teach base 10 concepts with manipulatives such as straws, blocks or coins. Develop a story about 10 individual items, coming together as a group. Be imaginative and involve the child's interests (10 animals live in a cave or tree, 10 robots come together to form one large robot).

Mathematical Reasoning

Students struggling with problem solving generally struggle with basic math calculation skills but also the generalization of knowledge, skills and strategies for novel problems and situations (Fuchs & Fuchs, 2003). This is conceptualized as a *transfer challenge,* which involves three contributing variables. First is the ability to master skills used to find the solution. Second is the development of categories for solving problems that require similar solutions. Third is the awareness that novel problems are related to previous, solved problems (Cooper & Sweller, 1987). This process relies on the ability to conceive and recognize patterns across mathematical concepts, which is based in work-ing memory and abstract thinking.

Mastery of the first variable in this process frees working memory, allowing greater cognitive resources to become available for the second and third variables. Strategies for developing these skills include the following:

- Developing awareness of words and phrases frequently used in problem solving that indicate what operation is required for the solution. For example, phrases such as "all together," "in all," "how many more" and "what is the total" indicate that the solution requires addition.
- Instruct children to highlight key phrases.
- Frequent the practice of similarly worded problems that vary in the cover story and quantities. For example, "Ben has two pieces of chocolate and Sally has three. How many pieces of chocolate do they have all together?" and "Henry has three pencils. Victor also has three pencils. How many pencils do they have in all?"
- Have the students write their own word problems, using a familiar format, and require them to complete each other's problem sets (peer-mediated instruction).

The second and third variable of the transfer challenge can be conceptualized in two distinct forms, low-road and high-road transfer, for making connections between skills and the reasoning process (Solomon & Perkins, 1989). The low-road transfer relies on extensive, varied practice as a means for automatically triggering well-learned, stimulus-controlled behavior in new situations (e.g., teaching math facts to solve multistep com-putation word problems). While this provides structure and consistency, underlying concepts may not be recognized. The high-road transfer involves deliberate abstrac-tion of principles, which can then be generalized across tasks. In essence, patterns are recognized, then utilized in a variety of contexts. In doing so, deliberate awareness of the underlying principle activates metacognitive processes. This can be accomplished through accessing two separate levels of high-road transfers.

1. Forward reaching transfers—Concepts are taught during the initial learning situ-ations. As the learners engage in the task, other situations that the concept applies to are actively discussed or demonstrated.
2. Backwards reaching transfers—As a skill is taught, the learner is encouraged to think back to previous tasks and search for relevant connections.

Drawing connections between mathematical concepts and tasks and recognizing pat-terns can occur during multimodal lessons, engaging the student through a variety of senses, diffusing the cognitive load through a variety of processing systems. Strategies for teaching include the following:

- Over-rehearsal and choral responding.
- Modeling.
- Explicit instruction on both low-road and high-road transfer in small groups.
- Frequent guided feedback and clarification of questions.

- Development of mathematical schemas (Gick & Holyoak, 1983). A generalized description of two or more problems that can be used to sort problem types into groups that require similar solutions.

Emotional/Behavioral

Students managing emotional and behavioral problems display difficulty both academically and behaviorally in our schools (Reid, Gonzalez, Nordness, Trout, & Epstein, 2004). Educational outcomes for these students often include academic underachievement, low grades, grade retention, failure to graduate, dropout, and suspension/expulsion (Wiley, Siperstein, Bountress, Forness &Brigham, 2008). After high school, studies show that only thirty percent of these individuals are employed and fifty-eight percent of them have been arrested (Smith, Katsiyannis, & Ryan, 2011). In effect, we are failing our children and adolescents who are struggling with emotional and behavioral problems.

Behavioral problems are often an indication of underlying emotional difficulties, which may stem from a variety of risk factors that include neuropsychological vulnerabilities, adverse environments at home and school, genetic predisposition, temperament and medical causes or experiences. Often, the focus of intervention is on ameliorating the behavior rather than understanding the root cause. Recall that under the framework of attachment theory, these behaviors can be viewed as a cue, a means for the child to communicate an unmet need. These behaviors can be confusing or unusual attachment behaviors and may be difficult for parents and professionals to interpret and understand. A comprehensive neuropsychological evaluation provides salient information regarding the individual's emotional and cognitive functioning. This information can inform parents and professionals about the root causes of a child's behavior, allowing them to better formulate a response and design appropriate interventions.

Several interventions and accommodations described throughout this chapter can be used as building blocks for the construction of a "child-world system" (Holmes-Bernstein & Weiler, 2000), a system in which the needs of the child are identified and met with interventions that provide a better match between the child's needs and the environmental supports. However, these interventions and accommodations alone are not enough to resolve underlying issues. The method of delivery is crucial. Individuals struggling with emotional and behavioral difficulties may refuse help from teachers, parents and clinicians. Therefore, the provision of interventions within the context of a secure attachment, the development of a "holding" environment and a carefully attuned relationship increases the chance that the accommodations and interventions provided may take root.

First steps involve the creation of an environment that promotes safety, security and consistency. Equally important is the development of a relationship through play and by accessing the individual's strengths. Next, one must undertake the careful observation of the child, noticing patterns of behavior and interpersonal interactions. Often, a child may behave mysteriously, displaying inappropriate behaviors without apparent meaning or reason (Minahan & Rappaport, 2012). Watching and discussing the behavior, free of judgment, full of curiosity, and engaging the individual in the process, may give meaning to these behaviors. Armed with knowledge of developmental milestones and neuropsychological functioning, teachers, clinicians and parents may notice clues to perplexing behavior. In doing so, meaning can be ascribed to the behavior. For example, a child who pushes a peer could have a number of underlying motivations for engaging in unsafe behavior. Perhaps he is seeking attention from either the peer or adults. Maybe it is a strategy to avoid an activity or task the individual finds overwhelming. The child may have had a rigid goal in mind (such as following his own agenda), unable to consider the perspective of the peer. It is possible the child was dysregulated, stemming from difficulties integrating sensory information from the environment. Finally, it may have been a maladaptive response to peer conflict. While the aggressive behavior is untoward, appreciating the underlying motivation can allow for appropriate immediate intervention as well as planning to avoid a similar future circumstance. In making observations to derive meaning, adults must be mindful of their own assumptions and prejudices, careful to avoid ascribing their own agenda or interpretation onto the behavior of the developing individual.

The construction of the "child-world" system may be a time-consuming endeavor. Different accommodations and interventions may be sufficient, alleviating stress and anxiety, or they may prove inadequate. For some individuals, interventions that proved successful one day or week may run their course, proving ineffectual the following day or week. An arsenal of strategies and ideas as well as creativity may be necessary to meet the needs of these children. It is important to draw upon other theoretical frameworks and intervention styles as appropriate for the individual. This includes approaches based in cognitive therapy, behavioral interventions, play therapy, psychotherapy, expressive therapies, speech and language therapy, occupational therapy and varied teaching styles. Depending on the needs of an individual, intervention may include a referral for assessment by other professionals or participation in group or individual therapy.

Throughout the process of implementing, adapting and remodeling interventions discussed throughout this chapter, the relationship remains consistent, providing security, acceptance and safety. In addition, working alongside the child/adolescent and family allows the development of an integrated understanding, for everyone, regarding the connection between the individual's internal and external experience, feelings and behavior.

As described in Chapter 8, the construct of internalizing and externalizing problem has been used to study and explain emotional and behavioral functioning. Internalizing problems represent a cluster of features that include withdrawal, anxiety, fearfulness and depression (Achenbach, 1992). Awareness of developmental concerns related to any cluster of emotional difficulty is important, as manifestation of these symptoms are different in children and adults. For example, children experiencing depression may appear irritable and disruptive rather than withdrawn and tearful. Externalizing problems can be understood as emotional difficulties that manifest through unsafe, destructive or aggressive action, such as fighting and bullying, oppositionality, cruelty to animals and substance use (Frick et al., 1993). Over the course of development, children can exhibit both internalizing and externalizing problems simultaneously (Fanti & Henrich, 2010). The following interventions can be used to address individual instances or any combination of internalizing or externalizing problems:

- Expand the individual's awareness of his/her feelings and triggers for these feelings. This can be accomplished through discussions, games, play, expressive therapies, journaling, etc.

- Set clear boundaries and rules that foster safety and respect. Be consistent and always follow through with consequences and rewards. Both consequences and rewards should match the situation and context, as related to the child's functioning and understanding.
- Identify and acknowledge likable/lovable qualities of the individual. Provide activities that allow the individual to feel successful and build self-esteem.
- Approach the individual openly and honestly, in a genuine manner.
- Develop awareness and acceptance of individual strengths and weaknesses.
- Identify stressors that interfere with daily functioning.
- Verbalize and express that mistakes and imperfections are a natural part of learning and developing. Not one single person is perfect.
- Teach stress management techniques.
- Discuss, practice and implement problem-solving strategies that may be related to a variety of problematic situations, including social interactions, family dynamics and academic difficulties.
- Develop awareness of cause-and-effect thinking and behaving.
- Teach strategies and alternatives for untoward behaviors that are age and context appropriate.
- Identify how stress is manifested in physical symptoms.
- Use self-monitoring charts to record ability to remain calm and relaxed. Use charts to develop awareness of emotional status.
- Allow opportunities for physical movement and exercise.
- Designate a time and place to moderate peer conflict. Identify roadblocks to conflict mediation and acknowledge feelings of those involved.

Family Work

After the evaluation and feedback session, continued contact with the child's parents or guardians is important throughout treatment. Awareness of the need for communication and integration across various environments (school, home, etc.) when working with special needs children and adolescents is expanding (Sheridan et al., 2009). Developing consistent communication ensures that teachers, therapists and parents have the opportunity to share helpful tools and interventions, discussing difficulties as they arise. This feedback loop creates another element of "holding" as the child navigates the environment. Regular communication and parent consultation allows the opportunity to engage the family, offer suggestions and provide support. While families are seeking help, it is important to note that they are the experts on their child. As therapists, teachers and counselors, we have important information to share with parents regarding child development and the manifestation of behavioral symptoms. However, the time spent with their child and the nature of the parent/child relationship gives them expert status on this particular child, offering clinicians and teachers valuable information.

Work with the family of a child with special needs is a dynamic process. The overarching goal is to assist the family and the child to increase functionality at home and school and relieve suffering. Many parents struggle with the experience of raising a special needs child, questioning their own actions and role in the family unit. They are required to learn about development, education and mental health. The reality of life with a child with learning and emotional difficulties can be hard to accept, as can the relinquishment of expectations and dreams for the child. The process of working with family members to develop tools and strategies often involves supporting the process of grieving their expectations of parenting and rearing a child and building hope and resilience to help their child reach their greatest potential. For these and many other reasons, engaging parents and caregivers in the process of constructing a child-world system is crucial.

Here, the "holding environment" continues to provide a theoretical foundation for working with parents and guardians. The establishment of a trusting relationship, authenticity and careful attunement to the feelings and reactions of caregivers is equally as important as careful attunement to their child. Parents and guardians may ask for help learning how to talk about their child's difficulties with other family members and friends. As with the children, a safe environment, clear boundaries and even a playful atmosphere fosters development and understanding. Communication, parent guidance and even therapeutic interventions can be provided through various means. This can include establishing regularly scheduled meetings or phone calls, a communication book or log that is passed between the school and parents, offering or referring for family therapy, group therapy for parents managing special needs children, individual therapy and couples therapy. It is the integration of these services with the school and clinical setting that creates and maintains the "holding environment" beyond interactions with the child or adolescent (see Reinstein, 2006).

It Takes a Village . . .

While numerous interventions are available to address strengths and weaknesses of any individual, humans are complex, and there is no one-stop, quick-fix shop. As an individual grows, multiple factors impact the emergence and maintenance of the self, including neurological development, the impact of the environment, circumstantial changes and gains and losses of relationships. Because of this dynamic process, it is impossible for any individual to be an expert on every element of human functioning. Thus, it often takes more than one professional or intervention to accommodate the complexities of a special needs child.

During the feedback session and included in the report, parents may be referred to other specialists for further assessment and treatment for their child. The list of possible specialist includes the following:

- Neurologist
- Occupational therapist
- Speech and language therapist
- Physical therapist
- Audiologist
- Technology specialist
- Executive functions tutor
- Psychiatrist or psychopharmacologist
- Individual psychotherapy with a psychiatrist, psychologist, social worker, expressive therapist or licensed mental health counselor.

It is important for teachers and parents to work together with these specialists, integrating their recommendations into the classroom and home activities. The more communication and integration among professionals and in treatment planning, the greater the consistency. Developing consistent language, specific to the child, across these treatments and environments generates another venue for "holding" a child, ensuring that all the environments "match" the child's needs and abilities. In doing so, skills gained in one therapy may more easily generalize into another area of the child's life. Sometimes, skills may need to be explicitly taught in each setting. Using the same strategies may alleviate stress and ensure success. Often, the parent falls into the role of coordinating specialists, teachers and physicians. This in itself is a monumental task that is overwhelming.

Of special note, the role of medication in treatment is of utmost importance. First, the use of medication with children is a developing science. The exact mechanism of many psychotropic medications is often unknown, as is the role these medications play on the developing nervous systems and other physiological functions. Secondly, many psychopharmacologists have a heavy caseload. Historically, psychiatrists prescribed medication and also provided psychotherapy. Trends in psychopharmacology have changed, and it is more likely that a prescriber intermittently sees his or her clients. In 2002, a study was released, stating that between the years of 1987 and 1997, as psychotropic medications became more accessible, medication usage increased but the number of visits markedly decreased (Olfson, Marcus, Druss, & Pincus). As such, the daily observation and monitoring of these powerful medications fall on parents and teachers. The role parents and teachers play in the process of prescribing medication is strictly observational but important, as these medications may have significant side effects, deleterious to the child's behavior and health. If a medication trial takes place, parents and teachers should be aware of potential side effects as well as the intention of the medication. The psychopharmacologist should be accessible by phone or meeting for feedback from different environments regarding the impact of the medication.

For further information and additional vignettes, go to www.communitytherapeutic-dayschool.org

Charles

At this point, Charles has completed the evaluation, and his parents have been provided with feedback. They have received the report and have sent it on to the school district.

Over a protracted period, and with the support of the family therapist, Charles was able to accept the help from his in-home tutor, who adapted a teaching style consistent with the results from his evaluation. Meanwhile, the family therapist continued to work with the family in translating the findings from the evaluation and supporting their efforts to understand Charles's emotional difficulties as well as facilitating the separation between Charles and his mother. Both mother and father also had a greater appreciation of Charles's anxiety around his father's illness. Charles, however, continued to be resistant to an individual therapy, as he had been traumatized by some of the interventions carried out by the school counselor, nurse and psychologist at his elementary school.

The following was written by the family therapist:

Once Charles's parents and myself received the results of his testing, the next important step was the implementation of the findings. Although Charles had considerable cognitive abilities, the emotional overlay of receiving instruction from parents was clouding over most of these strengths. Charles and his parents were stuck in a dynamic where most "lessons" ended in frustration, a sense of failure and anxiety about the next time. It became evident to me (and his parents agreed) that Charles needed to start learning from a third party if this pattern was to change.

I was fortunate to work with a special education administrator who had a clinical social work background and was keenly sensitive to the needs of this unique situation. He found a wonderful applicant for the position of "therapeutic tutor"; she had received a degree in therapeutic education and, thus, had a perfect preparation for what was needed.

She and I met alone at first, so that she could get a picture of the complex and fragile state of the entire family. We went through the neuropsychological tests and began brainstorming ways to introduce material and teach him. She had a wonderful disposition and knew that before delving into any academics she would focus solely on forming a relationship with him. She did this steadily and beautifully, and within a few weeks' time they were working on a variety of subjects. Together, we also charted out a slow move out of the house for the lessons—first at the town library and then to empty classrooms in the middle school. Disentangling the learning from the family dynamics and this gradually paced desensitization to school allowed for Charles's reentry to the world outside of his home.

Selene, family therapist

Once the relationship between Charles and his tutor had been established and strengthened, with the assistance and guidance from the family therapist, the tutor began meeting with Charles outside of the home. They began with locations more familiar and comfortable for Charles and gradually moved to less familiar venues, such as the town library. Since Charles had stopped attending school in the fourth grade and had not gone to school for the fifth and sixth grades, he was unfamiliar with the middle school building. Therefore, in the spring of his sixth-grade year, the tutor engaged Charles in running errands to the middle school as a way to familiarize him with and desensitize him to the middle school environment in hopes that he would begin seventh grade there. Their trips included visits to the Learning Center, as it would serve as his therapeutic home base. Over the spring and summer, the family therapist, tutor and Learning Center teacher met frequently to create a support system and familiarize the school personnel with Charles's profile and the recommendations from his evaluation.

References

Achenbach, T. M. (1992). *Manual for the child behavior checklist/2–3 and 1992 profile.* Burlington: University of Vermont, Department of Psychiatry.

Autin, F., & Croizet, J.-C. (2012). Improving working memory efficiency by reframing metacognitive interpretation of task difficulty. *Journal of Experimental Psychology: General, 141*(4), 610–618.

Berninger, V. W., & Amtmann, D. (2003). Preventing written expression disabilities through early and continuing assessment and intervention for handwriting and/or spelling problems: Research into practice. In H. L. Swanson, K. R. Harris, & Graham, S. (Eds.), *Handbook of learning disabilities* (pp. 345–363). New York, NY: Guilford Press.

Berninger, V., Cartwright, A., Yates, C., Swanson, H. L., & Abbott, R. (1994). Developmental skills related to writing and reading acquisition in the intermediate grades: Shared and unique variance. *Reading and Writing: An Interdisciplinary Journal, 6,* 161–196.

Berninger, V., & Graham, S. (1998). Language by hand: A synthesis of a decade of research on handwriting. *Handwriting Review, 12,* 11–25.

Bos, C. S., & Vaughn, S. (2006). *Strategies for teaching students with learning and behavior problems* (6th ed.). Boston, MA: Allyn & Bacon.

Bowlby, J. (1988). *A secure base: Parent-child attachment and healthy human development.* New York, NY: Basic Books.

Broadhead, P. (2004) *Early years play and learning.* London, UK: Routledge.

Brown, S., & Vaughan, C. (2009). Play: How it shapes the brain, opens the imagination and invigorates the soul. New York, NY: Penguin Group.

Bryant, N. D., Drabin, I. R., & Gettinger, M. (1981). Effects of varying unit size on spelling achievement in learning disabled children. *Journal of Learning Disabilities, 14,* 200–203.

Bucalos, A. B., & Lingo, A. S. (2005). What kind of "managers" do adolescents really need? Helping middle and secondary teachers manage classrooms effectively. *Beyond Behavior, 14*(2), 9–14.

Bundy, A. C., Naughton, G., Tranter, P., Wyverd, S., Baur, L., Schiller, W., . . . Brentnall, J. (2011). The Sydney playground project: Popping the bubble wrap—Unleashing the power of play: A cluster randomized controlled trial of a primary school playground-based intervention aiming to increase children's physical activity and social skills. *BMC Public Health, 11,* 680.

Burdette, H. L., & Whitaker, R. C. (2005). Resurrecting free play in young children: Looking beyond fitness and fatness to attention, affiliation, and affect. *Archives of Pediatrics and Adolescent Medicine, 159,* 46–50.

Cattanach, A., Stagnitti, K., & Cooper, R. (2009). *Play as therapy: Assessment and therapeutic interventions.* London, UK: Jessica Kingsley Publishers.

Chinn, S., & Ashcroft, R. (2007). *Mathematics for dyslexics: Including dyscalculia* (3rd ed.). Hoboken, NJ: Wiley.

Cooper, G., & Sweller, J. (1987). Effects of schema acquisition and rule automation on mathematical problems-solving transfer. *Journal of Educational Psychology, 79,* 347–362.

Crain, W. (2000). *Theories of development: Concepts and applications* (4th ed.). Upper Saddle River, NJ: Prentice Hall.

Cunningham, A. E., & Stanovich, K. (1997). Early reading acquisition and its relation to reading experience and ability. *Developmental Psychology, 33,* 934–945.

Davis, M., & Wallbridge, D. (1981). *Boundary and space.* New York, NY: Brunner/Mazel.

Davis, R. D. (2010). *The gift of dyslexia.* New York, NY: Perigree Trade.

Dawson, P., & Guare, R. (2011). *Executive skills in children and adolescents: A practical guide to assessment and intervention.* New York, NY: Guilford Press.

DeBenedet, A., & Cohen, L. (2010). *The art of roughhousing.* Philadelphia, PA: Quirk Books.

Elkind, D. (2007). *The power of play.* Philadelphia, PA: Da Capo Press.

Engelmann, S., & Brunner, E.C. (1988). *Reading mastery I/II fast cycle: Teachers' guide.* Chicago, IL: Science Research Associates, Inc.

Fanti, K.A., & Henrich, C.C. (2010). Trajectories of pure and co-occurring internalizing and externalizing problems from age 2 to age 12: Findings from the National Institute of Child Health and Human Development study of early child care. *Developmental Psychology, 46*(5), 1159–1175.

Frick, P., Lahey, B., Loeber, R., Tannenbaum, L., Van Horn, Y., Christ, M., . . . Hanson, K. (1993). Oppositional defiant disorder and conduct disorder: A meta-analytic review of factor analyses and cross-validation in a clinic sample. *Clinical Psychology Review, 13*, 319–340.

Fuchs, L.S., & Fuchs, D. (2003). Enhancing the mathematical problem solving of students with mathematics disabilities. In H. L. Swanson, K. R. Harris, & S. Graham (Eds.), *Handbook of learning disabilities* (pp. 306–322). New York, NY: Guilford Press.

Idol, L. (2006). Toward inclusion of special education students in general education: A program evaluation of eight schools. *Remedial and Special Education, 27*, 77–94.

Gettinger, M., Bryant, N.D., & Fayne, H.R. (1982). Designing spelling instruction for learning-disabled children: An emphasis on unit size, distributed practice, and training for transfer. *The Journal of Special Education, 16*, 439–448.

Gick, M.L., & Holyoak, K.J. (1983). Analogical problem solving. *Cognitive Psychologist, 12*, 306–355.

Gillingham, A., & Stillman, B. W. (1997). *The Gillingham manual: Remedial training for students with disability in reading, spelling and penmanship.* Cambridge, MA: Educators Publishing Services.

Gordon, N.S., Burke, S., Akil, H., Watson, S.J., & Panksepp, J. (2003). Socially-induced brain "fertilization": Play promotes brain derived neurotrophic factor transcription in the amygdala and dorsolateral frontal cortex in juvenile rats. *Neuroscience Letters, 341*(1), 17–20.

Graham S., & Harris, K.R. (1994). The role and development of self-regulation in the writing process. In D. Schunk & B. Zimmerman (Eds.), *Self-regulation of learning and performance: Issues and educational applications* (pp. 203–228). Hillsdale, NJ: Erlbaum.

Graham S., & Harris, K.R. (1997). Self-regulation and writing: Where do we go from here? *Contemporary Educational Psychology, 22*, 102–114.

Graham S., & Harris, K.R. (2003). Students with learning disabilities and the process of writing: A meta-analysis of SRSD studies. In H. L. Swanson, K. R. Harris, & Graham, S. (Eds.), *Handbook of learning disabilities* (pp. 323–344). New York, NY: Guilford Press.

Holmes-Bernstein, J., & Weiler, M.D. (2000). Pediatric neuropsychological assessment examined. In G. Goldstein & M. Hersen (Eds.), *Handbook of psychological assessment* (3rd ed., pp. 263–300). Kidlington, Oxford, UK: Elsevier Science.

Hsu, L., Berninger, V., Thomson, J., Wijsman, E., & Raskind, W. (2002). Familial aggregation of dyslexia phenotype II: Paired correlated measures. *American Journal of Medical Genetics, 114*(4), 471–478.

Jensen, E.P. (2010). *Different brains different learners: How to reach the hard to reach* (2nd ed.). Thousand Oaks, CA: Corwin.

Johnston, S.S., McDonnell, A.P., & Hawken, L.S. (2008). Enhancing outcomes in early literacy for young children with disabilities: Strategies for success. *Intervention in School and Clinic, 43*(4), 210–217.

Landreth, G.L. (2002). Therapeutic limit setting in the play therapy relationship. *Professional Psychology: Research and Practice, 33*(6), 529–535.

Lovett, M.W., Barron, R.W., & Benson, N.J. (2003). Effective remediation of word identification and decoding difficulties in school-age children with reading disabilities. In H. L. Swanson, K. R. Harris, & S. Graham (Eds.), *Handbook of learning disabilities* (pp. 273–292). New York, NY: Guilford Press.

Mercer, C.D., & Mercer, A.R. (2005). *Teaching students with learning problems* (7th ed.). Upper Saddle River, NJ: Pearson/Prentice Hall.

Minahan, J., & Rappaport, N. (2012). *The behavior code: A practical guide to understanding and teaching the most challenging students.* Cambridge, MA: Harvard Education Press.

Olfson, M., Marcus, S. C., Druss, B., & Pincus, H. A. (2002). National trends in the use of outpatient psychotherapy. *American Journal of Psychiatry, 159,* 1914–1920.

Panksepp, J. (2004). *Affective neuroscience: The foundations of human and animal emotions.* New York, NY: OUP.

Posner, M. I., & Rothbart, M. K. (2007). *Educating the human brain.* Washington, DC: American Psychological Association.

Price, K. M., & Nelson, K. L. (2007). *Planning effective instruction: Diversity responsive methods and management* (3rd ed.). Belmont, CA: Thomson/Wadsworth.

Reid, R., Gonzalez, J. E., Nordness, P. D., Trout, A., & Epstein, M. H. (2004). A meta-analysis of the academic status of students with emotional/behavioral disturbance. *Journal of Special Education, 39*(3), 130–143.

Reinstein, D. K. (2006). *To hold and be held: The therapeutic school as a holding environment.* New York, NY: Routledge.

Salend, S. J. (2008). *Creating inclusive classrooms: Effective and reflective practices* (6th ed.). Upper Saddle River, NJ: Pearson Education.

Sapon-Shevin, M. (2003). Inclusion: A matter of social justice. *Educational Leadership, 61*(2), 25–28.

Sayeed, Z., & Guerin, E. (2000). *Early years play: A happy medium for assessment and intervention.* Abingdon, UK: David Fulton Publishers, Ltd.

Sheridan, S. E., Warnes, E. D., Woods, K. E., Blevins, C. A., Magee, K. L., & Ellis, C. (2009). An exploratory evaluation of conjoint behavioral consultation to promote collaboration among family, school, and pediatric systems: A role for pediatric school psychologists. *Journal of Educational and Psychological Consultation, 19,* 106–129.

Smith, C. R., Katsiyannis, A., & Ryan, J. B. (2011). Challenges of serving students with emotional and behavioral disorders: Legal and policy considerations. *Behavioral Disorders, 36*(3), 185–194.

Solomon, G., & Perkins, D. N. (1989). Rocky roads to transfer: Rethinking mechanisms of a neglected phenomenon. *Educational Psychologist, 24,* 113–142.

Sousa, D. A. (2007). *How the special needs brain learns* (2nd ed.). Thousand Oaks, CA: Sage.

Swanson, H. L., & Saez, L. (2003). Memory difficulties in children and adults with learning disabilities. In H. L., Swanson, K. R. Harris, & S. Graham (Eds.), *Handbook of learning disabilities* (pp. 182–198). New York, NY: Guilford Press.

Szalavitz, M., & Perry, B. (2011). *Born for love.* New York, NY: Harper.

Tomlinson, C. A., & Eidson, C. C. (2003). *Differentiate in practice: A resource guide for differentiating curriculum.* Alexandria, VA: Association for Supervision and Curriculum Development.

van Middendorp, H., & Geenen, R. (2008). Poor cognitive-emotional processing may impede the outcome of emotional disclosure interventions. *British Journal of Healthy Psychology, 13,* 49–52.

Wanzek, J., Vaughn, S., Wexler, J., Swanson, E. A., Edmonds, M., & Kim, A. (2006). A synthesis of spelling and reading interventions and their effects on the spelling outcomes of students with LD. *Journal of Learning Disabilities, 39*(6), 528–543.

Wiley, A. L., Siperstein, G. N., Bountress, K. E., Forness, S. R., & Brigham, F. J. (2008). School context and the academic achievement of students with emotional disturbance. *Behavioral Disorders, 3*(4), 198–210.

Williams, J. P. (2003). Teaching text structure to improve reading comprehension. In H. L. Swanson, K. R. Harris, & S. Graham (Eds.), *Handbook of learning disabilities* (pp. 293–305). New York, NY: Guilford Press.

Wilson, B. A. (1996). *Wilson reading program* [kit] (3rd Ed.). Oxford, MA: Wilson Language Training Corporation.

Winnicott, D.W. (1965). *The maturational process and the facilitating environment.* London, UK: Hogarth Press.

Wolf, M., et al. (2009). The RAVE-O intervention: Connecting neuroscience to the classroom. *Mind, Brain, and Education. 3*(2), 84–93.

Woolf, A. (2011). Everyone play in class: A group play provision for enhancing the emotional well-being of children in school. *British Journal of Special Education, 38*(4), 178–190.

11 Behind the Scenes
Legal Ramifications

Whether or not the results from a child's comprehensive neuropsychological evaluation are considered and the recommendations applied within the school setting is part of a complicated process. As discussed previously, when a private evaluation has been completed and the report has been provided to the parents, they must decide the best way to engage the school system. Once they submit a report to the school, however, this action triggers a process that determines whether or not a child is eligible for support services through a contract known as an Individualized Educational Program (IEP), a process proscribed by federal law but that may differ in details from state to state.

The Individuals With Disabilities Act

Originally passed by the United States government in 1975, the Education of All Handicapped Children Act (EAHCA), later known as the Individuals With Disabilities Act (IDEA), entitled children with disabilities to a "free appropriate public education" (FAPE). In particular, this act related to the provision of specialized instruction and services that were specifically designed for the individual's educational benefit (Herr & Bateman, 2003). In 2004, the Individuals With Disabilities Education Improvement Act (U.S. Department of Education; IDEA, 2004) was passed to address the educational needs of students with disabilities, including early intervention, special education and related services (Lang & Leonard-Zabel, 2010).

As defined in the regulations (see Section 300.1), the purposes for IDEA are to ensure children with disabilities have a free appropriate education, an education provided for at public expense in the least restrictive environment. Furthermore, children with a disability includes those children who demonstrate cognitive, physical, health, specific learning or emotional disabilities.

The following sections summarize IDEA regulations that specifically pertain to the criteria for evaluations and reevaluations, the criteria needed for the determination of a specific learning disability, the guidelines for the development of an IEP, regulations related to the formation of the IEP team, implementation, placement and conflict resolution.

IDEA Regulations for Evaluations and Reevaluations

Either the parent of a child or a public agency can request an initial evaluation to determine whether or not a child has a disability. In some cases, the parent or school will have an independent evaluator complete the assessment. Unless the school agrees, then the outside evaluation will be paid for by the parents. However, according to IDEA regulations, parents have the right to request an independent evaluation at the school's expense. This is the case if the parent disagrees, for example, with the findings from an evaluation conducted by the school. Nevertheless, the school may refuse to pay for an independent evaluation as long as the school can demonstrate, through a hearing, that their assessment was appropriate. Even if a hearing rules in favor of the school, the parent can pursue an independent evaluation at their own expense. In either case, the results from any appropriate independent evaluation conducted by a qualified examiner must be considered by the school in a decision regarding the provision of FAPE to the child (Section 300.502).

If the school is conducting the assessment, once a request has been made and parental consent obtained, the evaluation must be conducted within sixty days and must consist of procedures appropriate to determine if the child has a disability and the extent of his or her educational needs. A screening of a student by a teacher or specialist to assess appropriate learning strategies is not considered an evaluation for special education services. Any reevaluations of a child may not occur more than once a year and must occur at least once every three years.

When an evaluation is conducted, the public agency must use a variety of assessment tools and strategies that enables them to obtain relevant functional, developmental and academic information, including information obtained from the parent, as a means to determine whether the child has a disability and to provide content for the IEP so that the child can make significant progress. Assessment tools cannot discriminate on the basis of race or culture, must be administered in the child's native language, must be used in a manner that is appropriate for that particular tool, and must be administered by trained persons in accordance with instructions for the use of the instrument. The child should be assessed in all of the areas related to the suspected disability, including, if appropriate, health, vision, hearing, social and emotional status, general intelligence, academic performance, communicative status and motor abilities. The evaluation must be comprehensive enough to identify all of the child's special education needs.

As part of the initial evaluation or any reevaluation, the IEP team must review any existing evaluation data, including any evaluations provided by the parent as well as current classroom-based assessments and observations. At that point, it is determined whether or not additional information is required to determine eligibility, to determine the present levels of achievement and developmental needs, the need for special education services and whether or not additional modifications are needed to meet annual goals. An evaluation must be completed to determine that a child no longer needs special education services. Termination must be based on an evaluation, and parents can request additional assessments if they disagree.

Once an assessment has been completed, the team, including professionals and parents, determine whether or not the child has a disability. This determination must be based on information from a variety of sources that includes aptitude and achievement scores, parental input, teacher recommendations and information about the physical, social and behavioral functioning of the child. Once the information is documented and considered, if the child is considered to be eligible for services, an IEP must be developed.

IDEA Regulations for the Identification of Specific Learning Disabilities

Criteria for determination of a specific learning disability cannot require a severe discrepancy between intellectual aptitude and achievement, must allow the utilization of a process based on the child's response to research-based intervention and may allow the use of other research-based procedures. Determination must be made by parents and a team of qualified professionals, including the child's regular teacher and an individual qualified to conduct a diagnostic assessment (school psychologist, reading teacher, etc.). The child may be determined to have a specific learning disability if, in spite of appropriate educational instruction, the child does not achieve adequately in one or more of the areas of oral expression, listening comprehension, written expression, basic reading, reading fluency, reading comprehension, mathematics calculation or mathematics problem solving. In addition, a pattern of strengths and weaknesses in performance or achievement relative to age, grade level standards or intellect based on appropriate assessments may also be used as a basis for determination. Assessments must rule out visual, hearing or motor disabilities, intellectual disability, emotional disturbance, cultural factors, environmental or economic disadvantage or limited English proficiency as the cause for lack of achievement.

The Individualized Education Program

The IEP is a written statement and functions as a legal document for each child who has been determined to have a disability. Eligibility is determined by the team using a decision-tree process that may vary from state to state (see Figure 11.1). It is developed, considered and revised in a team meeting that must be held within thirty days of a determination that the child needs special education and related services. Based on the information obtained from the various evaluations, the IEP states the child's current levels of academic achievement and functional performance. This is done in respect to the impact the disability has on the child's involvement and progress in the general education curriculum. The IEP also must include measurable academic and functional goals that meet the child's specific needs resulting from the disability and describe how those goals will be measured. In addition, a statement of the special education and related services that would be provided to the child must be included as well as the extent to which the child would not participate with nondisabled children in the regular classroom. Any alternate assessments to measure academic achievement must be documented and must be appropriate in respect to the child's disability. The date for the beginning of services must be specified in the IEP as well as the frequency, location and duration of each service, including a list of the modifications and accommodations.

In the course of the IEP's development, the team must consider the child's strengths, parent concerns, evaluation results and the academic, developmental and functional needs

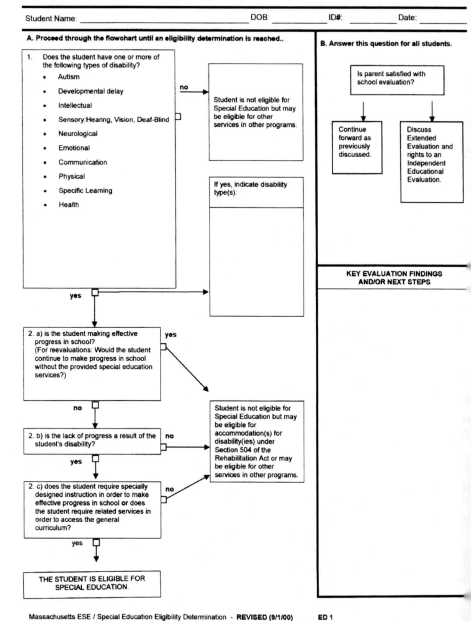

Special Education Eligibility/Initial and Reevaluation Determination

Student Name: _____ DOB: _____ ID#: _____ Date: _____

A. Proceed through the flowchart until an eligibility determination is reached..

1. Does the student have one or more of the following types of disability?
   - Autism
   - Developmental delay
   - Intellectual
   - Sensory:Hearing, Vision, Deaf-Blind
   - Neurological
   - Emotional
   - Communication
   - Physical
   - Specific Learning
   - Health

no → Student is not eligible for Special Education but may be eligible for other services in other programs.

If yes, indicate disability type(s):

yes

2. a) is the student making effective progress in school?
(For reevaluations: Would the student continue to make progress in school without the provided special education services?)

yes

no

2. b) is the lack of progress a result of the student's disability?

no → Student is not eligible for Special Education but may be eligible for accommodation(s) for disability(ies) under Section 504 of the Rehabilitation Act or may be eligible for other services in other programs.

yes

2. c) does the student require specially designed instruction in order to make effective progress in school or does the student require related services in order to access the general curriculum?

no

yes

THE STUDENT IS ELIGIBLE FOR SPECIAL EDUCATION.

B. Answer this question for all students.

Is parent satisfied with school evaluation?

Continue forward as previously discussed.

Discuss Extended Evaluation and rights to an Independent Educational Evaluation.

KEY EVALUATION FINDINGS AND/OR NEXT STEPS

Massachusetts ESE / Special Education Eligibility Determination - **REVISED (9/1/00)**   **ED 1**

Figure 11.1 An example of a decision tree, used to determine eligibility.

of the child. If the child's behavior is preventing their learning or the learning of others, behavioral interventions and supports must be considered. A regular education teacher must be included to determine appropriate behavioral interventions and strategies as well as additional aids and services, program modifications and support for school personnel. Any changes or amendments in the IEP must be made by the team, including parents, and all team members must be informed of any changes. Once a document has been developed, it is submitted to the parents who can either accept the recommendations and plan in full, partially agree with the plan and specify the specific details with which they disagree or reject the plan in full. In the case of the two latter situations, further negotiations, mediation or a hearing may ensue.

The IEP Team

The IEP team is composed of the parents or guardians of the child, at least one regular education teacher of the child (if the child is participating in any aspect of the regular education environment), at least one special education teacher of the child, a qualified representative of the public agency, an individual who can interpret the evaluation results, any other individuals with special expertise regarding the child who attends at the discretion of the parents or public agency and, where appropriate, the child. Every effort on the part of the public agency must be made to ensure that one or both of the child's parents are present at the meeting. A team meeting can be held without the parents' presence only if the agency has not convinced one or both parents to attend. The agency must then document their attempts.

Implementation of the IEP

As soon as possible after the development of the IEP, special education and related services must be made available to the child, as documented in the IEP. At the beginning of each school year, each public agency must have an IEP in effect for each child with a disability. The IEP must be available to each regular education teacher, special education teacher, related services provider or any other service provider responsible for its implementation. Each individual must be informed of his or her specific responsibilities related to the implementation of the IEP, including specific accommodations, modifications and supports.

Placement

Every eligible student is entitled to a placement decision that is determined by the content of the IEP. When the child's education cannot be implemented in a regular classroom to an adequate degree, another setting is permitted. Known as the Continuum of Alternative Placements, according to IDEA regulations, school districts are required to make a range of placement options available to a child with disabilities, including '(instruction in regular classes, special classes, special schools, home instruction and instruction in hospitals and institutions) and make provision for supplementary services such as resource room or itinerant instruction) to be provided in conjunction with regular class placement" (Section 300.115, para. 1–2). In other words, the public school district must pay the cost of outplacement.

Placement of a child with a disability is made according to the principle of the Least Restrictive Environment (LRE), that is, usually the environment that is most similar to a regular education classroom. As Herr and Bateman (2003) have explained, however, this term is used in two very different ways. They note that most legal decisions are made on the basis of the LRE as a particular place on a continuum of placements (i.e. the regular classroom). However, as they contend, more thoughtful decisions include a consideration of:

> whatever placement maximizes options, functioning levels, or possibilities for a given student and allows his or her education to be 'achieved satisfactorily.' Some courts have used the first notion, reflexively and without analysis, to mean placement in the mainstream of public education. More thoughtful courts have used the second and have sometimes acknowledged that the mainstream is not the LRE for a particular student.
>
> (Herr & Bateman, 2003, p. 67)

They go on to argue that "little, if any, consideration is given by some districts to the self-esteem issues raised for students with LD placed all day in mainstream classes" (p. 71).

When Parents and Schools Disagree

It is not unusual, given the economic climate as a result of federal, state and local cutbacks, that a school system is reluctant to provide special education services to children. This is despite or perhaps a correlate to the fact that, according to a study by the Center for Disease Control and Prevention, in collaboration with the Health Resources and Services Administration, the rate of occurrence of developmental disabilities (DDs) has increased significantly between the years of 1997 and 2008 (Boyle et al., 2011). In their study, the prevalence of DDs over that period was 13.87 percent of children between the ages of three and seventeen in the U.S. The prevalence of learning disabilities was 7.66 percent, ADHD was 6.69 percent, developmental delay was 3.65 percent and autism was 0.47 percent. Increasing rates of emotional problems have also been documented, with the incidence of mental health disorders in children and adolescents, estimated by the U.S. Department of Health and Human Services (1999) to be twenty percent. A 2006 review of the literature (Brauner & Stephens) placed the estimate somewhere between five and twenty-six percent.

Given the significantly increased rates of emotional problems and learning disabilities, school systems are struggling to keep up and provide children with public education that is free and appropriate in the least restrictive environment. This often places parents and school systems at odds. When this occurs, parents have the right to appeal recommendations made by the school. Often, parents will engage the support of an educational advocate. An advocate is an individual trained and experienced in the education laws of the state. He or she is familiar with a range of teaching methods and assessments and knows how to interpret the results from evaluations. He or she also is experienced in the development of IEPs and is skilled in teaching parents about the educational needs of their child and negotiating with school systems. Although advocates can be an invaluable resource for parents attempting to resolve a dispute with a school, their ability to negotiate a resolution is limited by the fact that they are not often lawyers. Nevertheless, employing an advocate to help resolve conflicts with schools is often an important step in the negotiation process.

Once all other venues for negotiation have been exhausted, including team meetings, school systems and parents might agree to go to mediation. As it does for all of the steps leading to this decision, IDEA provides guidelines for this process. The regulations stipulate that the mediation process is voluntary on the part of both parties, that it is not used to deny or delay a parent's right to due process and is conducted by a qualified and impartial trained mediator (Section 615(e)). At this point, parents most often are supported by an educational advocate, but some may engage the services of a lawyer. Regardless, the recommendation of the mediator, after hearing the perspectives of each side, is not binding. If an agreement is reached through the mediation process, a written agreement is signed that *is* legally binding. If no resolution is reached, however, the next step is to file a due process complaint. Within fifteen days, a resolution meeting must be held between the school and parent with relevant members of the team (Section 300.510). If no agreement is negotiated, the parties then go to a hearing.

Given that negotiations, mediation and the resolution process have failed, the filing of a due process complaint affords both parties to an impartial due process hearing, with the public agency directly responsible for the education of the child, as determined by State statute. The hearing officer must be impartial and well acquainted with the educational laws of the federal and state governments and be able to conduct the hearing in accordance with appropriate, standard legal practice. Either party has the right to be accompanied and advised by counsel, present evidence, cross examine and compel attendance of witnesses and obtain documentation of the hearing and findings. The decision in a hearing is final. However, either party can appeal that decision, and, after reviewing the records and any additional information, the reviewing official makes a decision that is final and binding. The only other alternative is for either party to bring a civil action suit (Section 300.514).

Charles

Once the evaluation and feedback were completed and parents received the neuropsychological report, they provided a copy to their school district that included the list of recommendations. At a team meeting, it was agreed to provide Charles with an in-home tutor and to continue the therapist's consultation with Charles and his family. Also discussed was the longer term plan to bring Charles back to a public school setting, including the idea that, rather than a therapeutic school, he might be able to function in a therapeutically based classroom within the public school. However, that was not in the very immediate future and, until then, helping Charles accept the support of someone other than his mother was the priority.

References

Boyle, C. A., Boulet, S., Schieve, L., Cohen, R. A., Blumberg, S. J., Yeargin-Allsopp, M., . . . Kogan, M. D. (2011). Trends in the prevalence of developmental disabilities in US children, 1997–2008. *Pediatrics, 127,* 1034–1042.

Brauner, C. B., & Stephens, C. B. (2006). Estimating the prevalence of early childhood serious emotional/behavioral disorders: Challenges and recommendations. *Public Health Report, 121,* 303–310.

Herr, C., & Bateman, B. (2003). Learning disabilities and the law. In H. L. Swanson, K. Harris, & S. Graham (Eds.), *Handbook of learning disabilities* (pp. 57–75). New York, NY: Guilford Press.

Individuals With Disabilities Education Improvement Act of 2004, 20 U.S.C. § 1400 *et seq.* (2004) (reauthorization of IDEA 1990).

Lang, M. J., & Leonard-Zabel, M. T. (2010). Ethical and legal issues related to school neuropsychology. In D. C. Miller (Ed.), *Best practices in school neuropsychology* (pp. 41–60). Hoboken, NJ: John Wiley & Sons.

U.S. Department of Education. *Building the legacy: IDEA 2004.* Retrieved August 13, 2013 from www.idea.ed.gov

U.S. Department of Health and Human Services. (1999). *Mental health: A report of the surgeon general.* Rockville, MD: Author.

12 Overview of the Whole Child and Case Conclusion

Most families must contend with whatever capacity to offer services their particular public school system may have. In the current fiscal environment, schools are underfunded and are hard put to provide extended evaluations that consider the whole child, let alone the services that may be recommended as a result. As a consequence, many school systems are forced to do inadequate testing, insist that screening is sufficient, take a "wait to fail" attitude or rely on a response to intervention (RTI) model. In fact, the new regulations under the 2004 IDEA revision allow for individuals to be identified with specific learning disabilities based on results from RTI alone (300.309 [a][2][i]) and excludes the use of a significant discrepancy between aptitude and achievement to determine a learning disability (300.307[a][i]). It has been convincingly argued, however, that neither RTI nor the aptitude/achievement discrepancy model alone are adequate to both identify a student's learning disability as well as provide an opportunity to learn, particularly if that opportunity is impeded by an underlying and more complex neurological, psychological or emotional profile. Furthermore, use of either alone disregards and distorts the meaning of a specific learning disability (Ofiesh, 2006). Hale, Kaufman, Naglieri and Kavale (2006) have proposed that a multitiered approach must be used, one that starts with RTI methods that, if unsuccessful, leads to a comprehensive evaluation of cognitive processes. We would add, however, that the comprehensive evaluation must include an assessment of emotional functioning as well in order to determine the potential underlying cause of a child's difficulty with learning and provide him or her with an adequate opportunity to learn. As we have discussed, emotional and behavioral difficulties in children and adolescents are a major impediment to learning. Although there is clearly a need for more careful and thoughtful screening for mental health difficulties in schools that includes outreach to families, services in schools and the involvement of community services (Weist, Rubin, Moore, Adelsheim, & Wrobel, 2007), screening alone is likely not sufficient. A multitiered approach to identifying learning difficulties in school that includes comprehensive testing for both cognitive and emotional problems has also been proposed and includes integrating services provided by school psychologists as well as comprehensive neuropsychological and psychological evaluations by consulting clinical neuropsychologists (Cleary & Scott, 2011).

As we have outlined in this book, each child experiencing significant difficulties in school, whether they are related to cognitive, behavioral, social or emotional vulnerabilities, must be assessed in all of those domains to determine the extent to which each needs to be supported. Without considering the whole child and creating an appropriate child-world match, there is a serious risk that the child will not only fail in school but will also never reach his or her potential in life.

Charles

> We return to eleven-year-old Charles, our case study that has been woven throughout the book, for the last time. The conclusion of his story highlights the usefulness of a complete neuropsychological evaluation when assessing the whole child and developing an intervention. At the end of this vignette, Charles's parents and family therapist share their thoughts about this process.
>
> Charles began seventh grade in the Learning Center with his tutor. He was able to attend classes with her support. Accommodations included a modified grading system that was based solely on his attendance. This was gradually adjusted over the year, increasingly to include a percentage that was based on his actual work. By the end of the year, his grades reflected his work alone, and he missed only one or two days of school for the entire year. Charles was very motivated to succeed independently, and over the course of seventh grade came to rely less and less on his tutor. He began eighth grade without the Learning Center and tutor support, and his grading system was no longer modified. He received straight A's, was adjusting well to the middle school and attended school consistently. The family therapy was the only service provided by his IEP. As he began ninth grade, however, the school system could no longer justify an IEP for Charles as he was doing so well. His eighth grade teachers had recommended that he be placed in honors courses for all of his subjects and it was agreed that he would take honors courses for three of the four major areas with the fourth being an Advanced Placement class. He again received straight A's and was described by his teachers as a "model student." He became involved in the back-stage aspect of the school's drama productions at the behest of his friends.

Figure 12.1 Child's group portrait.

The family therapy ended in the middle of his ninth-grade year, with the therapist feeling confident that Charles's parents had a much better understanding of his behavior, his emotional experience and how to approach him. Despite Charles's resistance to individual therapy, the work the therapist had done with his parents and sisters had filtered through to him. Parents saw that he was much more self-aware, able to identify his feelings, was able to express them more directly and was much more emotionally resilient. The language, ability to reflect and strategies the family had developed with the therapist had translated into Charles's behavioral and emotional repertoire. The family had overcome their initial skepticism about this way of working with their child, a skepticism based on generational and cultural bias as well as the negative experience Charles's father had with the mental health field. Nevertheless, they overcame their misgivings, partly out of desperation, but certainly because of the skill of the therapist as well as their unyielding commitment to their son.

The following was written recently by Charles's parents:

As parents, when our children are hurt or need help, we scramble to protect them and to find the appropriate resources for them. Throughout this process with Charles, we found many specialists who were well-meaning but gave us one-size-fits-all solutions. We obediently tried all of them, to no avail—medication, talk therapy, reward and punishment advice and then finally therapeutic school. Until we found Selene, our seventh therapist, we felt that one by one they gave up on our cherished son because he didn't respond according to the textbook. By counseling the parents, Selene taught us to model healing strategies. She also introduced us to Daniel, who was willing to provide untraditional cognitive testing to our son. He had time to feel safe, and he learned that he had control over his own decisions. We credit Selene for why Charles is a healthy and happy child today.

Charles's family therapist contributed the following:

My work with Charles and his family, at the beginning, felt akin to opening up a house that had been shut, airless and dark, for many years. Their "home" had been closed off by the enormous weight of frustration, anxiety and desperation that had built up over many years of misguided attempts, contradictory strategies and fruitless interventions. Just about everything that had been tried had failed and, unfortunately, made things worse.

After an initial phase of building trust and establishing a rapport through compassionate witnessing of their history and current experience, we needed to start deepening our understanding of what was going on inside of Charles—what he could handle intellectually, what skills he had and how he was emotionally perceiving the world. Charles had been so fiercely resistant to anything associated with school or therapy that it was unclear whether he would even agree to participate in the testing, even under the guise of serving his sister. He surpassed all of our expectations by not only completing the two days of testing but also by allowing Dr. Reinstein to administer a significant portion.

Once we had the test results, we were able to chart a course for his gradual reintegration to the outside world (including school) with a clearer understanding of his capacities and areas of fragility. The neuropsychological evaluation and how we were able to use it allowed for many windows of Charles's home to release and open.

As neuropsychologists, psychologists, consultants or teachers, we are in a unique and responsible position. To the best of our ability, we are obligated to consider the whole child. Within the context of the current discussion, this translates into assessing the various domains we have considered. However, we must also realize that our understanding of the particular difficulty a child may be having is limited. Even when, to the best of our ability, we attempt to take the whole child into consideration, there will always be some level of understanding of the problem that we cannot perceive because of a lack of ability to observe that level or because, in the process of observing through testing, we alter what we are observing or are limited to our conclusions because of the instruments we use. Nevertheless, we must continue to attempt to take a comprehensive look with all of the resources at our disposal. In doing so, professionals and parents are better able to create a child-world match that is facilitated by a highly integrated approach and that optimizes success.

From this perspective, an assessment of both neuropsychological and psychological areas of functioning is crucial. It is then, through the application of the findings from a comprehensive assessment, that the real test is conducted. While the RTI models discussed previously may have some utility at the beginning of the questioning about why a child is not making adequate academic progress, the real response to treatment must include questions about how potential perturbations in the other domains of functioning are impacting their overall development. This can only be done by carefully, thoughtfully and scrupulously analyzing the information gathered from a comprehensive evaluation and then testing out the findings by applying the accommodations based on those results. An ongoing process of implementing accommodations and modifications, and evaluating the child's response within the context of an, albeit, limited understanding of the underlying factors, is the crucial next step. All of this must be done with the understanding that we do not have all the answers. As a consequence, any professional who undertakes this process, to varying degrees, must be comfortable with complexity and ambiguity. Nevertheless, despite the uncertainty inherent in this endeavor, it is irresponsible to neglect any aspect of a child that may be impeding his or her growth. Not only an understanding of underlying neurological factors, but an appreciation of emotional factors that are affecting and are affected by a child's neurological profile is crucial.

> Providing for the child is therefore a matter of providing the environment that facilitates individual mental health and emotional development. . . . Emotional development takes place in the individual child if good-enough conditions are provided, and the drive to development comes from within the child. The forces towards living, towards integration of the personality, towards independence, are immensely strong, and with good-enough conditions the child makes progress; when conditions are not good enough these forces are contained within the child, and in one way or another tend to destroy the child.
>
> (Winnicott, 1965, p. 65)

As professionals in the field of child development, we are obligated to examine each part of a child and do our best to integrate each of those parts into a whole picture.

With that, we return to the parable of the Blind Men and the Elephant. Once the blind men have explored the different parts of the elephant and begun their quarreling, the king stops them and explains that they are all correct in their descriptions, but that they have failed to consult with one another to put all of the parts together. The king, having the fortune to see all the parts at once reveals the true nature of the elephant. Although, like the blind men attempting to understand an elephant, our sight as neuropsychologists, psychologists, therapists, teachers and parents is limited, we must take the perspective of the king in the parable and do all we can to see more.

References

Cleary, M., & Scott, A. (2011). Developments in clinical neuropsychology: Implications for school psychological services. *Journal of School Health, 81,* 1–7.

Hale, J., Kaufman, A., Naglieri, J., & Kavale, K. (2006). Implementation of IDEA: Integrating response to intervention and cognitive assessment methods. *Psychology in the Schools, 43,* 753–770.

Ofiesh, N. (2006). Response to intervention and the identification of specific learning disabilities: Why we need comprehensive evaluations as part of the process. *Psychology in the Schools, 43,* 883–888.

Weist, M., Rubin, M., Moore, E., Adelsheim, S., & Wrobel, G. (2007). Mental health screening in schools. *Journal of School Health, 77,* 53–58.

Winnicott, D. W. (1965). *The maturational processes and the facilitating environment.* London, UK: Hogarth Press.

Appendix

Example Graphic Organizer for Neuropsychological Evaluation Information

Neuropsychological Domain	Cognition	Emotion	Possible Intervention
Referral/Background			
MSE/Observation			
General Cognitive			
Verbal Functioning			

Neuropsychological Domain	Cognition	Emotion	Possible Intervention
Perceptual Reasoning			
Executive Functions			
Memory			
Visual/Spatial/ Organization/Motor Functioning			
Achievement			
Emotional/Behavioral Functioning			

Index

Page numbers in italic format indicate figures and tables.